Humanism in Education

C Jebb

BIBLIOLIFE

THE ROMANES LECTURE
1899

Humanism in Education

BY

R. C. JEBB, LITT.D., HON. D.C.L.,

REGIUS PROFESSOR OF GREEK AND FELLOW OF TRINITY COLLEGE
IN THE UNIVERSITY OF CAMBRIDGE,

DELIVERED

IN THE SHELDONIAN THEATRE JUNE 7, 1899.

London
MACMILLAN AND CO., LIMITED
NEW YORK: THE MACMILLAN COMPANY
1899

Price Two Shillings net

THE ROMANES LECTURE 1899

HUMANISM IN EDUCATION

R. C. JEBB

THE ROMANES LECTURE
1899

Humanism in Education

BY

R. C. JEBB, Litt.D., Hon. D.C.L.,

REGIUS PROFESSOR OF GREEK AND FELLOW OF TRINITY COLLEGE
IN THE UNIVERSITY OF CAMBRIDGE,

DELIVERED

IN THE SHELDONIAN THEATRE JUNE 7, 1899.

London
MACMILLAN AND CO., LIMITED
NEW YORK: THE MACMILLAN COMPANY
1899

𝕮𝖆𝖒𝖇𝖗𝖎𝖉𝖌𝖊:

PRINTED BY J. AND C. F. CLAY,
AT THE UNIVERSITY PRESS.

HUMANISM IN EDUCATION.

PETRARCH was born in 1304, when Dante was thirty-nine years old, and died in 1374. That great movement in which he was a pioneer, and which we call the Renaissance, had its central inspiration in the belief that the classical literatures, which were being gradually recovered, were the supreme products of the human mind; that they were the best means of self-culture; that there alone one could see the human reason moving freely, the moral nature clearly expressed, in a word, the dignity of man, as a rational being, fully displayed. All this is implied in humanism, when we speak of humanism as the direction in which the Renaissance chiefly tended. It is larger than the Roman idea of *humanitas*; the scope of which is well illustrated by Cicero when he says in one of his letters that Roman officials ought to treat Greeks with 'humanitas' (gentleness), since it is from Greece that Italy first received 'humanitas,'—i.e., as the context explains, the refining influences of literature and art.

It is difficult adequately to realize now the whole meaning of humanism for the early Renais-

sance, because we cannot quite place ourselves
within the mental horizon of the middle ages. We
know, in a general way, what was the intellectual
background of the Renaissance; the dominance
of the scholastic philosophy in the thirteenth
century; the prominent position held by the studies
of Law and Medicine; the comparative poverty
and inefficiency of the higher literary studies;
for, though portions of the best Latin classics
continued to be read throughout the middle ages,
they were read, as a rule, in a spirit remote from
the classical, or even contrary to it; and the West
had lost Greek altogether. But such facts do
not help us far towards entering into the heart of
the early Renaissance. Perhaps there are two men
who more than any others, assist the effort to
do so; Dante, standing in the borderland between
the darker ages and the revival, when he shows us
a keen intellect and a sublime imagination moving
within the limits, and obedient to the forms, of
medieval thought; and, at the further verge of the
Renaissance, Erasmus, the lifelong antagonist of the
schoolmen, who makes so vivid to us the contrast
between the intellectual atmosphere of scholasticism
and that which the humane letters had created.

Petrarch opens an era, because he was the first
man in medieval Europe, not perhaps who possessed,
but who was able effectively and impressively to
manifest, a strong native affinity with the genius of
the classical Latin writers; the first who succeeded
in making large numbers of people feel that he had

studied those writers with intelligent enthusiasm, and that they were to him living persons. Resembling Goethe in his steadfast pursuit of a complete self-culture, Petrarch proclaimed that the classics supply the best, the unique, instrument for that purpose. He enjoyed in Italy an immense popularity and renown; his Latin epic poem, 'Africa,' though often tame, won scarcely less applause than his Italian lyrics; and his Latin prose-writings were widely read. He was also the first man of great eminence who showed zeal in collecting books, manuscripts, and coins. He did not know Greek; yet, with a sure instinct, he apprehended its significance, and was eager that the knowledge of it should be restored. The age must have been ready for the movement; but it was the powerful and famous personality of Petrarch which gave the initial impulse. His devoted disciple, who died only one year later (in 1375), the gentle and diligent Boccaccio, earliest of Italian Hellenists, propagated and diffused Petrarch's influence; and so, before the close of the fourteenth century, the full tide of the humanistic revival had set in.

Petrarch's ideal of humanism, as a discipline which aims at drawing out all the mental and moral faculties of man, pervades the whole course of the Italian Renaissance. Often, indeed, that ideal was obscured by affectations or puerilities; not seldom it was belied by evil living; but nevertheless it was a real force, which comes out more or less in all the greater and nobler of the humanists. The enthusiasm

Persistence of his ideal.

and the versatile energy which animated the Italian Renaissance for two centuries sprang from a deep and earnest conviction that the recovered literatures were not only models of style, but treasure-houses of wisdom, guides of life, witnesses to a civilisation higher than any which could then be found upon the earth. Even in the early years of the sixteenth century, when the best energies of the movement had in Italy been spent, and when Italian humanism was being narrowed down from the ample scholarship of Politian to the Ciceronian purism of Bembo, this fundamental belief remained unaltered.

One illustration may be cited. In the year 1508, a manuscript containing the first six (or, as then constituted, the first five) books of the Annals of Tacitus, said to have been found in the Westphalian monastery of Corbey, was brought to Rome, and was acquired by Giovanni de' Medici, who, five years later, became Leo X. It is the only manuscript of those books which exists, and is now in the Laurentian Library at Florence. One of Leo's earliest acts, after he became Pope, was to entrust the printing of this codex to a scholar of note, Filippo Beroaldo the younger, whose edition was published at Rome in 1515. As a reward to the editor, Leo conferred upon him a privilege for the sale and reprinting of the work. In the brief which grants this privilege, and which is prefixed to the edition, Leo expresses his estimate of humanistic studies. 'We have been accustomed,' he says, 'even from our early years, to think that nothing more

Leo X. on humanism.

excellent or more useful has been given by the Creator to mankind, if we except only the knowledge and true worship óf··Himself, than these studies, which not only lead to the ornament and guidance of human life, but are applicable and useful to every particular situation ; in adversity consolatory, in prosperity pleasing and honourable ; insomuch, that without them we should be deprived of all the grace of life and all the polish of social intercourse.' He goes on to say that 'the security and extension of these studies' seem to depend chiefly on two things, —'the number of men of learning, and the ample supply of excellent authors.' As to the first, it has always been his earnest desire to encourage men of letters; and as to the acquisition of books, he rejoices when an opportunity is afforded him of thus 'promoting the advantage of mankind.' It would be a mistake to discount such language as conventional. Whatever else in the literary fashions of that time may have been hollow, this feeling, at least, as to the value of the classics, was thoroughly real.

I have insisted on this larger scope of the Renaissance humanism, because we are naturally apt to think of it as having been primarily a cult of style and form, an effort to imitate and reproduce the excellence of the ancient models. And of course this was one of its chief aims,—nay, perhaps, the most characteristic of the special activities which the revival called forth. But we should be in danger of taking this *imitatio veterum* for something less significant than it really was, if we did not

Stylistic side of humanism.

remember the point of view from which the Italian humanists approached it. They regarded the ancient Romans as their forefathers, and Latin as their ancestral speech. During the dark ages, the old civilisation had been effaced, the language had been barbarized: if they could not restore the civilisation, they wished at least to regain the language which attested it. Medieval Italy had many dialects; the literary Tuscan had only a limited currency, while Latin was the universal language. Not long after Dante's death in 1321, the 'Divine Comedy' was translated into Latin. The eminent humanist Francesco Filelfo, who died in 1481 at the age of eighty-three, could still say, 'Tuscan is hardly known to all Italians, while Latin is spread far and wide throughout the whole world.' Thus, in the effort to purify and elevate Latin style, patriotic sentiment and practical convenience conspired with the newborn zeal of scholarship.

Latin prose-writing. During the interval between the middle of the fourteenth century and the earlier part of the sixteenth, a long series of humanists cultivated Latin prose-writing in every branch,—oratory, philosophical discourse, diplomatic or official correspondence, familiar letter-writing. The stress laid on the niceties of the art is shown by the reputation which Lorenzo Valla, best known as the translator of Thucydides, owed to his work called *Elegantiae*, published in 1432—1436. In the generation after his, Politian wrote Latin like a living language. Then the dictatorship passed to Bembo, prince of those Ciceronians whom Erasmus derides. It is easy to make light of such work, but it is better and more important to remember what it was that the humanists achieved in this way. One of our poets has described Dante's immortal poem as 'The first words Italy had said'; and if Dante was the first who found a voice for Italian literature, medieval Latin had altogether failed to preserve the clearness or beauty of classical expression. When Petrarch's contemporaries compared themselves with their Roman predecessors, they felt that they were inarticulate. To write their ancestral tongue with clearness, in the first place, and then with some measure of grace or beauty,—this became to them an object of ardent desire. Gradually, and by painful efforts, they attained it. And thereby they bequeathed to Europe a tradition which the middle ages had lost,—namely, that prose, in whatever language it may be written, should aim at those qualities which the best classical models exhibit. This is the permanently valuable result of the humanistic Latin prose-writing.

As to their copious Latin verse, if there is not much of it which deserves to live, unquestionably it served to cultivate in many men a genuine poetical gift; it was the vehicle of much graceful fancy and much fine perception; and it conduced to a closer study of the best Latin poets. In force and spontaneity, though not in delicacy or finish, Politian is the most remarkable of the Renaissance versifiers. He was only forty when he died

Latin verse.

in 1494, and a still youthful fire breathes in his
impetuous hexameters. When he was lecturing at
Florence, he sometimes began by reciting a Latin
poem of his own, as an introduction to the classical
author. Some of these poems, in hexameter verse,
remain. One of them rapidly surveys the history
of poetry from Homer to Boccaccio; another is a
prelude to the 'Iliad' and 'Odyssey'; a third, to
the bucolic poets, especially Hesiod and Virgil. In
these, as in much other Latin verse of the Renaissance, despite some blemishes which modern
scholarship would have avoided, one can see how
thoroughly the writer was imbued with the style of
diction of his models. A fine ear is a frequent
Italian gift, and some of these Renaissance versifiers
have been singularly successful in catching the
rhythms of the best Latin poets, especially those of
Virgil and of Ovid.

The Italian
humanists'
desire of
fame :

Verse and rhetoric were, indeed, modes of self-
expression irresistibly attractive to men whose
ambition was fired by the example of their Italian
ancestors, and who felt that motive so characteristic
of the Renaissance,—the passionate desire of the
individual to make his own powers stand out,
clear-cut and brilliant, before the world,—the longing for fame in his life-time, and for the praise of
posterity. Italy had no political unity, no common

its national
aspect.

aims in respect to national life. Humanism proposed
what to many men, and coteries, and cities took, in
a way, the place of that,—the dream that the glories
of ancient Rome and Italy were being renewed in

another golden age of letters and art. That vision dawned upon Petrarch in a peaceful time, when, in his poem 'Africa,' he predicted that the new love for the Muses would rival the old; and it continued to cheer students amidst all the foreign invasions and intestine troubles which crowded upon Italy two centuries later. After the sack of Rome in 1527, and when the condition of Italy on every side was deplorable, an accomplished scholar, Marcantonio Flaminio, sent to his patron, Alessandro Farnese, a collection of Latin poems by natives of Lombardy, which was then the region in which letters chiefly flourished. In some verses which accompanied this gift, he cries : ' Happy, too happy, are our days, which have given birth to a Catullus, a Tibullus, a Horace, and a Virgil of their own ! '

The Italian humanists' cult of style was thus connected with a larger aim, that of regaining a lost culture, regarded as ancestral ; and it did a work of lasting value for European literature. But we owe *Their wide* to them much more than that. We owe to them, *range.* for instance, that conception, ever present to the stronger men in their ranks, of classical antiquity as a whole. The outlook of the greater humanists was a wide one. Filelfo, already mentioned, was a typical scholar of the fifteenth century: when he was professor at Florence, about 1428, he lectured in the morning on Cicero, then on Livy, or Homer : in the afternoon, on Terence, followed by Thucydides. Meanwhile, among other private labours, he translated into Latin Aristotle's ' Rhetoric,' some speeches of Lysias, extracts from Xenophon, and some of Plutarch's 'Lives.' Politian edited Catullus in his youth, and the Pandects of Justinian in his riper age: published notes on Ovid and Statius, on Suetonius, the younger Pliny, Quintilian and other Latin authors; made Latin translations from Hippocrates, Plato, Herodian, and Galen. Erasmus became to northern Europe the prophet of this comprehensive humanism in its educational and also in its more popular aspects. Such largeness of range and view, albeit obtained at some sacrifice of other qualities, is, in its own way, an intellectual gain.

To another service of the humanists, one which is more apt to be forgotten, it must suffice to allude in passing,—I mean what they did for erudition, as distinguished from literary scholarship. Their commentaries, their works on antiquities of every kind, have mostly been absorbed or superseded; but in these provinces also the later learning must acknowledge a vast debt. Flavio Biondo, who died in 1463, deserves to be remembered as one of the chief founders of Roman archæology, in virtue of his threefold work, 'Roma Instaurata,' 'Roma Triumphans,' and 'Italia Illustrata.' The study of Latin epigraphy, again, received a notable benefit from Jacopo Mazochi and his collaborator Albertini, who, building partly on earlier collections, published in 1521 their 'Inscriptions of Rome.' It was under the direct influence of humanism that the first Roman Museums of anti-

Their erudite work.

quities and art were formed,—those of the Capitol and of the Vatican.

But Italian humanism has a claim on our gratitude even larger and higher than its work for scholarship and for erudition, great and varied as that work was. Europe owes to humanism the creation of a new atmosphere, the diffusion of a new spirit, the initiation of forces hostile to obscurantism, pedantry and superstition, forces making for intellectual light, for the advance of knowledge in every field, and not merely for freedom, but for something without which freedom itself may be a burden or a curse, the power to comprehend its right limits and to employ it for worthy ends. Take a particular instance. In the fourteenth and fifteenth centuries, the so-called science of Astrology held an exceedingly strong position. Universities endowed it with Chairs; kings and princes consulted the stars in crises of State; a general in the field was not seldom accompanied by his astrologer; cities and citizens had recourse to horoscopes in countless affairs of municipal or private life. But from Petrarch onwards the humanists made open war on this flourishing imposture. Or take another illustration of a somewhat different kind. That vigorous and versatile humanist, Poggio, was at the Council of Constance in 1416, and heard Jerome of Prague recant his recantation. Poggio was then, and had been for many years, a lay secretary in the Papal Chancery. But he does not think of Jerome as of a heretic at

[margin note:] Humanism spread a liberal spirit.

bay. With a detachment which would have been scarcely possible for a medieval spectator of similar antecedents, Poggio is able to contemplate Jerome simply as a man who is evincing heroic fortitude —and thus describes him in a letter to Lionardo Bruni :—' There he stood, undismayed, unfaltering, not merely indifferent to death, but ready to welcome it,—another Cato.'

Humanistic education.

It was impossible that men penetrated by this new spirit, and for whom the new learning was the revelation of a new life, should not soon apply their ideas to the training of the young. Within fifty years after the death of Petrarch, we find a type of education developed which, in contrast with the medieval, may be called the humanistic. It is, in its essentials, a type which satisfied the western world for four hundred years; the generation has not yet passed away which first saw its claims seriously challenged; and its origins must always have for us more than an ordinary measure of historical interest. Among the great teachers of the earlier Renaissance, there is one who has a pre-eminent right to be regarded as the founder of this education, and of him a few words must be said here; I refer to Vittorino da Feltre.

Vittorino da Feltre.

Born in 1378 at Feltre, a small town in Venetia, he went at eighteen to the University of Padua, then second in Italy only to Bologna, and sharing with Pavia the distinction, still rare at that time in Universities, of being comparatively favourable to humanism. He there studied Latin under two

eminent masters in succession, Giovanni da Ra-
venna, and Gasparino Barzizza,—the latter a great
Ciceronian scholar, but exempt from the narrow
purism of a later time. Another Paduan teacher
whose influence Vittorino must have felt was
Vergerius, already celebrated for his essay on
the formation of character ('De Ingenuis Mori-
bus'),—the earliest and most lucid statement of
the principles on which humanistic training rested;
an essay which, amidst the throng of Renaissance
treatises on education, remained a classic for two
centuries, going through some forty editions before
the year 1600. Vittorino, after holding a chair
of Rhetoric at Padua, and then teaching privately
at Venice, was invited by Gian Francesco Gonzaga,
Marquis of Mantua, to undertake the tuition of
his children. A villa was assigned to him at
Mantua, where he was to reside with his pupils.
He settled there in 1425, and remained till his
death in 1446. The villa had been of the most
luxurious kind, and was known as the 'House of
Pleasure' ('La Gioiosa'); Vittorino, by a slight but
meaning change, named it the 'Pleasant House'
('La Giocosa'); banished the luxury which had
environed the young Gonzagas; and turned the
place into a seat of plain living and regular study.
But he was a thorough believer in bright surroundings as conducive to mental and moral health.
The house was cheerful and beautiful; it stood in
large grounds, fringed by a river; there was ample
space and provision for every kind of outdoor

exercise or sport.   Youths were sent from several of the Italian Courts to be educated with the Mantuan princes.   But Vittorino was resolved that the school should be open to any boy who was fitted to profit by it, and maintained at his own cost a large number of poor scholars, for whom lodgings were found near the villa.   The rules of life and study were the same for all.

Vittorino's aim.
Vittorino's aim in education was to develope and train the whole nature of his pupil, intellectual, moral and physical; and to do this, not with a view to any special calling, but so as to form good citizens, useful members of society, men capable of bearing their part with credit in public and private life.   This being his general aim, let us see how his methods differed from those which had prevailed in the middle ages, and in what sense they may be described as humanistic.   In the pre-Renaissance schools for boys, the dominant influence was ecclesiastical.   In teaching grammar and rhetoric, portions of the Latin classics were used; but the method of teaching them was encumbered with fantastic pedantry,—such, for instance, as the doctrine that a passage may have four meanings, literal, metaphorical, allegorical, and mystical,—which went far to annul their value and meaning as literature.   For that value and that meaning an enthusiastic appreciation came in with the humanistic revival; to the humanist, the great writers of antiquity were living men, into whose mind and soul he was striving to penetrate by sympathetic study.   That was the

spirit in which Vittorino took the Latin classics, and made them the basis of intellectual training. Poetry, oratory, history, the ethics of Roman Stoicism, were studied in the best Latin writers. And, if not at first, yet before he had been many years at Mantua, Vittorino introduced some Greek classics also. His own knowledge of that language was chiefly due to his contemporary, the other great schoolmaster of the time, Guarino of Verona. Guarino had studied Greek at Constantinople, and shares with Vittorino the honour of having established Greek as a regular part of liberal education in schools. Vittorino's scholars were constantly practised in Greek and Latin composition, as well as in recitation and reading aloud.

But, while classical literature was thus the basis of Vittorino's system, it was by no means his only subject. Aided by resident tutors, he taught mathematics, including geometry (a subject which the humanists preferred to the schoolmen's logic) and arithmetic, with rudiments of astronomy; also, it seems, some elements of what then passed for Natural Philosophy and Natural History. Music and singing also found a place, though under conditions which Plato and Aristotle would have approved; the standard of attainment aimed at was to be that of the amateur, not of the professional; and the music was to be chosen with regard to its moral effect. Nor was social education neglected: Vittorino inculcated a noble tone of manners, and desired that his pupils should have such accomplishments as would enable them to grace social life.

Physical
training.

As to physical training, he provided instructors in military exercises, in riding, and in swimming, while he encouraged every form of healthy outdoor activity.   In all this he was the typical humanist. The ecclesiastical schoolmaster of the middle ages was not concerned to encourage physical training ; the opinion was rather that the body was something to be despised and' mortified.   The medieval provision for such training was not in schools but in the households of princes or nobles, where riding, tilting, the chase, and other martial or courtly exercises were practised.   On the physical and the social sides of his scheme Vittorino was in some sort continuing this old court training ; many of his pupils, indeed, were nobles destined to the profession

Dominant
idea of
humanistic
education.

of arms.   But the idea which dominated his whole system was the classical, originally Greek, idea of an education in which mind and body should be harmoniously developed.   No antique idea appealed with greater force to the humanists, since none presented a stronger contrast to medieval theory and practice.   When we give the name of humanistic to the type of education established by Vittorino and his contemporaries, it is not simply or chiefly because the intellectual part of it was based on Greek and Latin, but, in a more important sense, because the education was at once intellectual, moral, and physical.

With reference to moral teaching, it should be

said that Vittorino, unlike many of the humanists, was an orthodox, even a devout, Churchman, an earnestly religious man, whose precepts were enforced by his practice. Like almost all the great humanist teachers, he was a layman, engaged in creating a type of education which might be contrasted with the ecclesiastical type that had preceded it: but there was no tinge of paganism in his view of religion or of ethics: he was one of those men who, like Pico della Mirandola, recognised the unity of knowledge,—separated the gold of the new treasure-trove from the dross,—and neither felt nor sought any conflict between the classical and the Christian ideal.

It is interesting for Englishmen to remember that Winchester College was built in Vittorino's boyhood, and that the Mantuan public school was at its zenith when Henry VI. founded Eton. Both those illustrious foundations, since so distinguished as seats of humanistic training, arose before humanism had come to England, and were originally of the ecclesiastical type. Towards the end of the fifteenth century, a few Oxford scholars, who had visited Italy,—William Selling, Grocyn, William Latimer, Thomas Linacre,—brought the taste for humane letters to England, where it was presently quickened by the visits of Erasmus. St Paul's School, founded by the friend of Erasmus, Dean Colet, is the oldest in England which was humanistic from its origin. Its first High Master, William Lily, of Magdalen College, appointed by the

Early humanism in English schools.

founder in 1512, is best remembered as a Latin grammarian, but had also studied Greek at Rhodes and afterwards at Rome. It might almost be said that the relation in which St Paul's School stood to the influence of the earliest Oxford humanists resembled that in which Vittorino's school at Mantua stood to the early humanism of Florence.

'The statutes of St Paul's, dated 1518, prescribe that the High Master shall be 'learned in good and clean Latin, and also in Greek, if such may be gotten.' The proviso is significant. Several great public schools were founded, or re-founded, in or near London, during the century which followed; —Christ's Hospital in 1533, Westminster in 1560, Merchant Taylors' in 1561, Charterhouse in 1611; and in all of these, as in many smaller grammar-schools founded at the same period, the basis was humanistic. But it was probably not much before 1560 that Greek was thoroughly established among English school studies. The statutes of Harrow School, dated 1590, contain directions for the teaching of some Greek orators and historians, and of Hesiod. This seems to be one of the earliest English examples of detailed regulations, as distinguished from merely general prescription, concerning the school study of Greek.

Classical learning since the Renaissance. The resources of humanism as an instrument of education have been expanded and enriched by the manifold development of the higher classical learning in the centuries since the Renaissance. After the age of Petrarch, of Politian, of Erasmus, came

Joseph Scaliger, akin, on the literary side of his work, to the Italian scholars, but more characteristically occupied in the endeavour to frame a critical chronology of the ancient world ; Casaubon, the first who popularized a connected knowledge of ancient life and manners ; Bentley, active primarily in the emendation of texts, but also in the higher criticism of classical history and literature ; then a long series of eminent names, too long to enumerate, which extends from the days of Porson and Elmsley, of Hermann and Lachmann, to those of Mommsen. 'Within the last fifty years, many special branches of classical study have either sprung into existence, or become more methodical ; comparative philology ; epigraphy ; palæography ; archæology in all its departments. In quite recent times, the exploration of ancient sites, stimulated by, and in turn stimulating, archæological research, has yielded results of fascinating interest. All these developments have lent new life and freshness to classical studies generally : they have given a more vivid reality to antiquity. The ideal of humanism has thus been reinforced in a manner which brings back to us something of the spirit which animated the Renaissance when it was largest and most vigorous. For the enthusiasm of the Renaissance was nourished by the monuments of classical art scarcely less than by the masterpieces of literature. Each statue that was disinterred from Italian soil, every stone or coin or gem that could help to illustrate the past, became a source of delight to men whose strenuous aim was to apprehend classical antiquity as a whole.

But the very progress made in recent times has brought us to a point at which the larger educational benefits of humanism become more difficult to harmonise with the new standards of special knowledge. A full comprehension of the Greek and Latin literatures demands at least *some* study of ancient thought, ancient history, archæology, art. But each of the latter subjects is now, in itself, an organized and complex discipline ; to become an expert in any one of them is a work of years. Hence much can be said in favour of a plan by which the University student, who is to devote a course of three or four years to the humane letters, confines himself, during the earlier stage of it, to the languages and literatures ; then turns away from these, viewed in their wider range, and concentrates himself, for the rest of his time, on one or two important aspects of classical antiquity, such as philosophy and history, to the exclusion of the rest.

' The younger student, in the highest form of a school where the classics are taught, has not yet reached the moment at which the need of specializing begins to be felt. We will suppose that he has an aptitude and taste for literary studies ; and the number of such boys is always very considerable— immensely larger, for instance, than the number of those who are fitted to excel in Greek or Latin composition. When he first attains to some appreciation of the best classical poetry and prose, he goes through a little Renaissance of his own; he feels the stimulus of discovery; he perceives, in some measure, a beauty of form unlike anything that he has found elsewhere; there is much in the thoughts of those great writers, much of their charm, much of their music, that fixes itself in his memory, and becomes part of his consciousness. However dimly and imperfectly, there lives before him a world very distinct from that in which he moves, and yet, as he can already feel, by no means wholly alien from it; though perhaps he does not yet understand with any clearness the nature of the links which bind that past to the present. This, as many masters and pupils could testify, is an experience not confined to the school-boy of exceptional temperament or gifts; it is one common to a fairly large proportion of boys who have no more than a good average capacity for literary studies in general. And it is an experience which is not forgotten afterwards. Whatever the man's work may be in after years, if ever he looks back and tries to date epochs in his mental history, he will recur to that early time as a season which made the buds unfold and the leaves grow, which gave him new elements of intellectual life and interest. *Ver illud erat.*

But the conditions under which that early experience was gained are modified when the student passes to the University. It may be that he works under a system which permits him to devote the whole of his academic course to the classical languages and literatures; if so, the humanistic training begun at school is carried to a certain maturity; but it remains exclusively literary. If, on the other hand, he turns, at a certain point, from the general study of the languages and literatures to one or two special subjects, such as ancient philosophy and history, then he is expected to aim at the standards set by modern specialists in those subjects. That through these subjects he can receive an admirable intellectual training, is not disputed. But his range of view is necessarily contracted. The particular educational merits which belong to humanistic studies of a larger scope are different in kind from those which can be claimed for any special department of such studies when isolated from the rest. It may be added that, when specialization has been carried far in any study of literature or art, that study tends to become technical; and then a danger arises lest the pursuit of exact method should obscure the nature of the material with which the study has to deal, namely, productions of human thought and imagination; there is a danger lest analogies drawn from studies conversant with different material should be pushed too far, and what is called the scientific spirit should cease to be duly tempered by æsthetic and literary judgment.

We remember what Gibbon so characteristically said about his early mathematical studies: ' As soon as I understood the principles, I relinquished for ever the pursuit of the mathematics; nor can I lament that I desisted before my mind was hardened by the habit of rigid demonstration, so destructive of the finer feelings of moral evidence.' Might not something analogous be said about some of those ultra-technical aspects which some special departments of classical study occasionally present, when we consider these in relation to the nature and the ends of humane literature? No one will suspect me of underrating the immense services which have been rendered to classical study, in every department, by deeper and more thorough work, by rational and exact methods of research. I only say that the tendency to make those methods too technical is one of the besetting temptations of the higher and more esoteric classical study,—a fashion in which it sometimes appears even to exult, as though it were a warning to the profane to stay outside; and I say that such a tendency is adverse to the appropriate and sympathetic treatment of any subject-matter derived from literature or art. Aristotle observes in the 'Rhetoric' that a speaker unconsciously but inevitably passes out of the province of that art if he begins to reason in the technical terms of a particular science; and one feels that the modern specialist, in certain branches of classical study, may come perilously near to passing out of the province of humanism.

At any rate, I suppose it would be generally agreed that one of the chief problems which we have to face in classical studies at the present day is this:—How are the characteristic and essential

benefits of humanism to be reconciled with the
learned and intellectual demand for specialization?
It would not be my desire, even if the occasion
permitted, to attempt a detailed criticism of any
particular answer to that question which has taken
shape and is now operative in this country. But
one is tempted to ask whether the advance of
knowledge and the subdivision of the field have
really made it impossible to obtain, in the education
of University students, something nearer to that
more comprehensive survey of classical antiquity at
which the earlier humanists aimed. It may be a
dream, but it is an interesting subject of speculation.
Evidently we have to reckon, at the outset, with
a prepossession which the growth of high specializing has strengthened; namely, that the only intel-
lectually valuable knowledge of a subject is such
as is possessed by the specialist, the expert, in
that subject; and that the acquisition of knowledge which is not, in that sense, thorough can be
of little or no worth, either as a discipline or as a
result.

Now, the most general recommendation of all
classical study is the supreme and varied excellence of the classical literatures; these illustrate,
and are illustrated by, all the activities of classical
thought and life. A conceivable ideal of humanistic
study under modern conditions—whether it be prac-
ticable or not, I do not venture to pronounce, though
I am not convinced that it is impracticable—would
be one which took those literatures as the basis

throughout, but also exacted some measure of acquaintance with each of the more important among
the other subjects of classical study. Take, for
example, the subject of classical art, which means
primarily and chiefly Greek art. Even a limited
knowledge of that subject is obviously of the greatest
value to a student of classical literature ; not merely,
of course, as a key to allusions, but often in a far
deeper sense, as throwing light on the spirit which
animates both monuments and books. I repeat,
even a limited knowledge of classical art has that
use,—a knowledge which stops far short of the
equipment requisite for a specialist in the subject.
But, because it is limited, must it therefore be superficial or unsound ? It is difficult to see why it must
be so. The teacher to whom students of the classical
literatures would have recourse in this matter would
be the specialist in classical art. Would he not be
competent to decide what parts of his own subject
are the most essential for such students to know ?
And would he not be competent to secure that, in
those selected parts, and within the limits which he
himself had traced, the knowledge should not be
unsound or superficial ? Like considerations apply
to other special departments.

I must be content to have asked this question,
and leave the judgment upon it to others. I turn
now to the brief consideration of a larger question.
What is the general position of the humane letters
in this country at the present day, and what are
their prospects of retaining that position ? The

most salient feature in the intellectual development of this century has been the progress of science. And this century is the first since the revival of learning in which a serious challenge has been thrown down to the defenders of the humanistic tradition. But I think it will be found that the position of humanism in this country at the close of the century is much stronger than it was at the beginning.

English
humanism
in this
century.

In the earlier part of the century, the classics still held a virtual monopoly, so far as literary studies were concerned, in the public schools and Universities. And they had no cause to be ashamed of their record. The culture which they supplied, while limited in the sphere of its operation, had long been an efficient and vital influence, not only in forming men of letters and learning, but in training men who afterwards gained distinction in public life and in various active careers. There can be no better proof that such a discipline has penetrated the mind, and has been assimilated, than if, in the crises of life, a man recurs to the great thoughts and images of the literature in which he has been trained, and finds there what braces and fortifies him, a comfort, an inspiration, an utterance for his deeper feelings. Robert Wood, in his 'Essay on the Original Genius of Homer' (1769), relates a story which will illustrate what I mean. In 1762, at the end of the Seven Years' War, Wood, being then an Under-Secretary of State, took the preliminary articles of the Treaty of Paris to the

President of the Council, Lord Granville; who was then ill, and had, indeed, but a few days to live. Seeing what his condition was, Wood proposed to withdraw; but the statesman replied that it could not prolong his life to neglect his duty, and then quoted in Greek from the 'Iliad,' the words of Sarpedon to Glaucus:—'Ah, friend, if, once escaped from this battle, we were for ever to be ageless and immortal, I would not myself fight in the foremost ranks, nor would I send thee into the war that giveth men renown; but now,—since ten thousand fates of death beset us every way, and these no mortal may escape or avoid,—*now let us go forward.*' He repeated the last word, ἴομεν, 'let us go forward,' several times, says Wood, 'with a calm and determinate resignation'; and then, after a pause, asked to hear the Treaty read. That is what I meant by a man recurring, in a crisis of life, to the great thoughts of the literature on which he has been nourished. Or, to give one other example: what a forcible testimony to the hold which this discipline could retain on a congenial spirit is afforded by such a man as the Marquis Wellesley, when, at the close of his career, he addresses his old school in those exquisite Latin elegiacs which can be read in the Chapel of Eton College, where he lies buried,—the lines beginning,

> Fortunae rerumque vagis exercitus undis,
> In gremium redeo serus, Etona, tuum.

It was Eton, he says, which had taught him to aim

high, and to approach the bright fountains of the ancient wisdom,—*et purum antiquae lucis adire iubar*; to her he owes whatever he has achieved, and from her he asks a final resting-place.

Yes, to such men the humanities had been a true culture; but the social sphere within which they gave that culture had been, as I have said, limited. And in the earlier years of this century there arose in English letters no popular force tending to spread a recognition of the humanistic ideal. In our imaginative literature the most potent forces, those which exerted the widest influence, were then on the side of the romanticists. The genius of Walter Scott was of course essentially romantic; so, too, was that of Byron, his interest in Greece notwithstanding. Only a very limited audience was in those days commanded by the writers whose genius had a native kinship with the classical, such as Keats and Landor. But a little later came Tennyson, whose influence throughout the English-speaking world has made strongly for an appreciation of the classical spirit, not only directly, through his poems on classical themes, but also generally, by his qualities of form and style. And the influence of Matthew Arnold, both as a poet and as a critic, if less widely popular than Tennyson's, has had a not less penetrating and subtle power in making the Greek spirit, and the distinctive qualities of the best Greek achievement, understood and felt by cultivated readers. Then, in the domain of history, Grote's great work, the work of a man of affairs, has done much, more perhaps than any other one book of the century, to invest his subject with a vivid, an almost modern interest for a world wider than the academic, and has done so all the more effectively just because his own antecedents were not academic. Again, there has been a considerable literature, the growth chiefly of the last forty years, which has sought to popularize the classical literatures in a scholarly sense, and to illustrate them from the modern,—such books as those of the late Mr Symonds and the late Professor Sellar. To these must be added translations of the higher order, such as that by which Professor Jowett has made Plato an English classic.

Further, there has been a most remarkable stimulation of interest in classical topography, archæology, and art. New facilities of travel have enabled thousands to become acquainted with the scenes of Greek and Roman life. The study of classical antiquity has been in many respects revolutionized by a series of striking discoveries in Greece, Asia Minor, and Egypt. The opportunities of exploration for English students have been improved by the establishment in 1883 of a school at Athens, which may probably be followed, ere long, by the opening of a similar school at Rome. The wealth of the British Museum in classical antiquities has received frequent accessions; it was never before so attractive or so well organized as a place of classical study. The Universities have meanwhile done much to improve their resources for the study of classical archæology and art.

In all these ways, the humanistic studies have, during this century, become wider and more real. They have gradually been drawn out of a scholastic isolation, and have been brought more and more into the general current of intellectual and literary interests. So far from losing strength or efficacy by ceasing to hold that more exclusive position which they occupied two or three generations ago, they have acquired a fresh vigour, a larger sphere of genuine activity, and a place in the higher education which is more secure, because the acceptance on which it rests is more intelligent.

The critical moment a generation ago.

There was, indeed, a moment in this century when the attack upon the humanities was somewhat formidable. It was rather more than thirty years ago, towards the end of the period during which the classics had enjoyed a virtual monopoly in literary education. The educational claims of science had been fully developed, and were being powerfully urged by champions of whom Professor Huxley was the most brilliant; but these claims had not yet been effectively recognised by adequate provision for the teaching of science in schools and Universities. Several able men, who had been trained in classical studies and had been successful in them, were discontented with the classical system, were conscious of personal needs which it had not satisfied, and felt a sort of resentment against it. In education, as in other matters, some of these men were advanced and eager reformers, who, by their general habit of mind, apart from their particular complaints against the classics, were unlikely to feel any prejudice in favour of tradition,—were apt to be sceptical, or even scornful, of anything alleged on behalf of the humanities which appeared to them sentimental or conventional,—and were little disposed to conserve any element in education to which they could not assign a definite rational value. As a typical expression of those tendencies, one might mention the volume of 'Essays on a Liberal Education,' published in 1867.

In the sixties, then, considering the strength of the attack both from without and from within, the position of humane studies was certainly more seriously imperilled than it had ever been before. Not, indeed, that even then there was any danger of their being discarded at once. But there was a danger of another kind. Some influential men were saying, 'Keep Latin if you like, but drop Greek, or reserve it for a few boys ; and take care that the classics do not, in any case, trench upon the time which should, in all schools, be given to natural science and to modern studies.' The danger was lest the powerful alliance between insurgent men of science and disaffected humanists, aided by the legions of Philistia, should force on a movement for imposing such restrictions as these in a spirit altogether favourable to the new studies, but unfriendly to the old ;—with the result that classical studies might be so narrowed, so hampered, so maimed, as to lose nearly all their distinctive educational virtue ; and, after languishing for a time, might gradually die out of the schools.

That danger was sensibly increased by a further circumstance. It was the first time in England that classical education had been seriously put upon its defence; and some of its less discreet defenders made some claims on its behalf which were ill-founded or exaggerated. Thus one eminent scholar said, 'If the old classical literature were swept away, the moderns would in many cases become unintelligible, and in all cases lose most of their characteristic charms.' Others averred that no one could write English well who did not know Latin. One distinguished head-master even said, 'It is scarcely possible to speak the English language with accuracy or precision, without a knowledge of Latin or Greek.' Now claims of this kind, all containing some elements of truth, but needing to be carefully limited and defined, struck people in general as preposterous, when stated with crude exaggeration ; and did all the more mischief, because, in the sixties, an apprehension of the true claims of humanism was much less widely diffused, among educated people outside of the academic world, than it is to-day. And when such people, who had no personal knowledge of humanistic study, heard claims made for it which seemed repugnant to experience and common-sense, they not unnaturally suspected that the whole case for the humanities was unsound.

But in the last thirty years the position of the humane letters, relatively to other studies, has been altered in several important respects. The study of the natural sciences is now firmly established in schools and universities; it can no longer be said that a haughty and exclusive humanism keeps them out of the educational field: indeed, there are not a few seats of learning where they hold a clear predominance. Modern languages and literatures have also their recognised place in the higher education; if they do not yet attract as many disciples as they deserve, the reason is not that they are neglected or discouraged by educational authorities, but rather that they are new studies, with methods and aims which are still in some measure tentative, and competing with highly equipped rivals of older standing. This establishment of the modern studies is, so far as I have seen, viewed by humanists generally with cordial satisfaction. The spirit of humanism, indeed, wherever it is not a narrow pedantry, is one which welcomes every accession to the domain of sound knowledge. Meanwhile, the claims of humanism itself, sifted by a period of controversy, and illustrated by the larger views of liberal education which now prevail, are usually stated with more discrimination than formerly, and are more willingly and more widely acknowledged.

Now, what are the true and permanent claims of humanistic studies? They are of two kinds, the intrinsic, and the historical. The intrinsic merits of the classical literatures depend, in the first place, on

Present position of humanism.

Its permanent claims.

their purely literary qualities in respect to form and style.   The creative literature of Greece, from Homer to Demosthenes, had a course of spontaneous and natural growth, throughout which it was in constant touch with life ; and it has left a series of typical standards in prose and poetry.   The excellence of these models is not a scholastic figment or a medieval superstition ; it is a fact which has been recognised, through all the changes of the centuries, by the common feeling and the general consent of civilised mankind.   The Roman literature, though partly imitative, is not only original in some of its types, but original throughout as a manifestation of the Latin genius in the speech which that genius moulded ; and abounds in works of poetry and prose which must always rank as masterpieces.   An unguarded champion of the classics once said of them that 'they utterly condemn all false ornament, all tinsel, all ungraceful and unshapely work.'   That statement, though quite true in a general sense, is not true without exception ; the classics are not perfect, any more than other human productions ; they have their occasional faults or blemishes in style and taste.   But it would argue a strange deficiency in the sense of proportion, a singular want of balance in literary judgment, to affirm that such faults or blemishes detract in any appreciable degree from the intellectual stimulus and the æsthetic pleasure which their great and characteristic qualities afford, or from the admiration due to the artistic harmony of their best work, when viewed as a whole. The utility of the classical languages as subjects of study and as instruments of training depends partly on these qualities of the literatures, but also on the importance of these languages themselves for grammar and comparative philology. They afford, moreover, a discipline in nicety of judgment which is all the better because the questions of idiom and usage which they raise cannot be solved by living authority.

The intrinsic value of the classical literatures depends, further, on their contents. The claim made for them on this score at the present day is much more limited than that which was made by the humanists of the Renaissance ; but, within those limits, it is as valid as ever. The observations and discoveries of the Greeks and Romans in particular sciences, such as Mathematics or Medicine, have been incorporated or transmuted in modern work, and no longer form a practical reason for studying the literatures, though still investing them with a special interest for some students who would not otherwise be drawn to them. But an universal and abiding interest belongs to another and far larger element in their contents. That element is the store of experience and observation accumulated by keen watchers of human nature and conduct through all the centuries from Homer to Justinian. And the utterance of this varied wisdom of life is precisely one of the regions in which the distinctive excellences of classical expression shine most. This is a kind of literary wealth which, as John Stuart

Mill said of it, 'does not well admit of being transferred bodily' into modern books, and 'has been
very imperfectly transferred even piecemeal.'

The historical value of the classical literatures is
that which arises from their relation to the modern.
No one, of course, would now maintain that a
knowledge of Greek or Latin is necessary to success
in writing English; such a statement could be dis-
proved by a cloud of witnesses,—among others, by
Shakespeare, De Foe, Bunyan, Byron, Carlyle,
Cobbett, Charles Lamb. But it is certain that no
one can comprehend the history and development
of English literature, or of any literature of modern
Europe, without a knowledge of the ultimate sources
in ancient Greece and Italy. Without such a knowledge, the process by which the forms of modern
literature have been evolved would be unintelligible.
It has been urged, indeed, that for a student of a
modern literature the important thing is to know the
immediate antecedents of that literature, rather than
the more remote; and that, if the student of English
literature, for instance, studies Early English, it is
needless to trouble him with Greek or Latin. It
may be replied, however, that, in the study of modern
literary history, the light afforded by the nearer past
differs in kind from that which is given by the more
distant past. The nearer past will explain details;
as a study of Chaucer will give the key to some later
forms or usages of the language. But it is necessary
to go further back,—in the case of any European
literature, it is necessary to go back to ancient Greece

and Italy, if you desire to find the points from which the main currents of literary tradition started, and from which the chief types in literature have been derived. An ordinary reader does not require to know the classics in order to appreciate and enjoy modern literature, though such knowledge will enhance his appreciation and enjoyment at many points. But, for any one who aspires to be a scholarly critic of modern literature, the knowledge is indispensable.

Finally, it should not be forgotten that classical literature affords the best, if not a necessary, preparation for the study of classical art; and that Greek art remains, in its own province, the most perfect expression of the artistic spirit.

Such, in outline, are the principal claims that can be made for the humanities. These merits surely entitle them to keep their place in the higher literary education. I do not think that there is any exaggeration in what Mr Froude said thirteen years ago, that, if we ever lose those studies, 'our national taste, and the tone of our national intellect, will suffer a serious decline.' Classical studies help to preserve sound standards of literature. It is not difficult to lose such standards, even for a nation with the highest material civilisation, with abounding mental activity, and with a great literature of its own. It is peculiarly easy to do so in days when the lighter and more ephemeral kinds of writing form for many people the staple of daily reading. The fashions of the hour may start a movement, not in the best direction, which may go on until the path is

Humanism as a safeguard of literary standards.

difficult to retrace. 'The humanities, if they cannot prevent such a movement, can do something to temper and counteract it; because they appeal to permanent things, to the instinct for beauty in human nature, and to the emotions; and in any one who is at all susceptible to their influence they develope a literary conscience.   Nor is this all.   Their power in the higher education will affect the quality of the literary teaching lower down. Every one can see how vitally important it is for us, in this country and at this moment, to maintain, in our general education, a proper balance of subjects, and to secure that, while scientific and technical studies have full scope, a due efficacy shall be given also to the studies of literature and history.

We have no Academy of Letters in England, and, for my part, I am with those who hope that we never shall have one.   But no doubt we must desire to have what Mr Matthew Arnold called 'a public force of correct literary opinion, possessing within certain limits a clear sense of what is right and wrong, sound and unsound.'   In concluding this lecture, I would venture to say that such a force of correct literary opinion is just what an intelligent humanism should contribute to supply; not, as an Academy does, in a public or corporate form, but through the influence and example of individuals. Humanism can do that, if it is loyal to its best self; if it avoids a needless excess of technicality in the treatment of literature; if it cultivates sanity of judgment, and is careful that the exercise of ingenuity shall be controlled by the literary sense. Discoveries of a signal kind, such as mark the progress of the new sciences, can seldom now be expected in the province of humanism. In humanism the genuine originality must now consist, for the most part, in applying, by patient work, a more accurate knowledge and a more delicate perception at a number of particular points, in the hope of enabling each successive generation of students to apprehend classical antiquity in a more fruitful manner, with a greater distinctness and with a nearer approach to truth.

It has been a great privilege for me to address such an audience on this subject. I am well aware how little I have had to say that can be new to many of my hearers; but it may be good sometimes, in the case of studies which are so important for the intellectual well-being of the nation, to pause and think what they mean and where they stand; to look back and to look forward. The endeavour to do so, however defective the result may be, is at least one which cannot be foreign to the traditions or the genius of the place in which I have had the honour to speak.

CAMBRIDGE: PRINTED BY J. & C. F. CLAY, AT THE UNIVERSITY PRESS.

9 781113 771506

I dedicate this book to my grandchildren: Rebecca, Charlotte, Stephen, Lisa, James, Rachel and Emily.

Malcolm Roscow

HARRY

AUSTIN MACAULEY PUBLISHERS™

LONDON · CAMBRIDGE · NEW YORK · SHARJAH

A CIP catalogue record for this title is available from the British Library.

ISBN 9781788482424 (Paperback)
ISBN 9781788482431 (Hardback)
ISBN 9781788482448 (E-Book)
www.austinmacauley.com

First Published (2018)
Austin Macauley Publishers Ltd™
25 Canada Square
Canary Wharf
London
E14 5LQ

Acknowledgements

As always, the person I must thank first is my partner, Hil. She tailors her life around my writing and never, ever, complains about the amount of time I spend at my laptop. She is my first port of call when it comes to editing my work prior to submitting it to my publisher, making suggestions and pointing out errors, and she is rarely wrong. I would be lost without her.

I should also like to offer my sincere thanks to all those who have had a hand in the publication of this book at Austin Macauley. I had thought to thank everyone individually, but was told that the list would be a very long one.

This is the third novel Austin Macauley have published for me, and – as before – it has been a thoroughly enjoyable experience, not to mention the sheer quality of the work and level of professionalism from all concerned. I might write these stories, but the experts finish them, polish them and bring them to life.

Thank you to one and all.

Chapter 1

The annual Parents' Ball was in full swing. The prestigious Hertfordshire private school booked this stately-home venue for their black-tie event every year and it was always well attended. Every table in the ballroom of Knebworth House was taken. There were crisp white tablecloths on the tables and the lights were low.

Max had found a table for four. It was at the rear of the room about as far from the dance floor as it was possible to get, but it had been the only table available when he and Sue arrived. On the table was a bottle of Chateau-bottled Bordeaux and a bottle of a South African Chardonnay. Max was drinking the claret, or sipping it, since he was driving. Sue was on her second glass of Chardonnay.

Veronica and Henry were late. That was nothing new; they were almost always late. When they finally arrived, Max stood and raised his hand.

They spotted him and made their way over. The twelve-piece band was between numbers, and the dance floor was momentarily deserted. They took a shortcut and walked diagonally across it.

The conversation in the room was loud, and getting louder. Later in the evening, people would be dancing on the tables. It happened every year. These people needed no instructions on how to party. They were successful, well-heeled people, many running their own business.

Max got to his feet.

"Hello, you two," Veronica said, pecking Sue on the cheek. "Sorry we're late, my fault as usual. My, don't you look handsome," she said, patting Max on the cheek. "Evening dress suits you!"

Max grinned. "Flattery will get you everywhere." He shook Henry's hand. "Hello, Henry. You're looking well."

"Might say the same about you," Henry said.

Veronica was wearing a little black cocktail dress with a plunging neckline, and as he pulled out a chair for her, Max said, "Love your dress, Veronica."

Veronica gave him a beaming smile. "You see, Henry, at least *Max* notices what I wear."

Almost all the women in the room, including Sue, were wearing full-length ball gowns, but Veronica did as she pleased. She was a hugely wealthy, not to mention strikingly attractive woman, and if Veronica wanted to wear short, she wore short.

"She started getting ready at four o'clock this afternoon, for God's sake," Henry grumbled. "And she's changed her dress three times since. Max, do *you* know why women have to spend so much time getting ready? Because it's beyond me."

"I'm saying nothing," Max replied, wisely ducking the question.

"Ignore him, Veronica," Sue said. "All men have to do is shave, comb their hair and throw on a jacket."

"Red, Veronica?" Max said, reaching for the Bordeaux.

Veronica shook her head, her red hair bouncing around her face. "Not tonight, Max, thank you. I'm in the mood for white tonight."

"I'll have red," Henry said.

Max put the Bordeaux down and picked up the Chardonnay. He poured Veronica a glass before topping up his wife's glass. Then he picked up the Bordeaux again and poured Henry a glass, before putting another splash into his own glass.

They raised their glasses and clinked them. "Happy days." It was their usual toast.

The two bottles were getting dangerously low and Max caught the eye of a passing waiter. He pointed to the bottles and made a circular motion with his finger. The waiter got the message and went off to get replacements.

"So what have you two been up?" Henry asked.

"The usual boring stuff as far as I'm concerned," Sue replied. "I drive the children to school in the mornings and I pick them up again in the afternoons. Then, when Max is away on business, which seems to be most of the time these days, I take the children to their friends, or wherever else they want to go. I don't seem to be any more than their personal taxi service these days."

"Oh dear," Henry said, patting her hand sympathetically. "Poor you."

"What about you, Max?" Veronica said, picking up her glass. "Have you been away this week?" She took a sip of her wine.

"Yes, I was in Sweden this week," Max said. "I got back yesterday."

"Good trip?" Henry asked.

Max nodded. "I would say so, yes."

"Are you going to New York again in the near future?" Henry asked.

"Yes, the week after next." Max took a sip of his wine.

The waiter arrived with two more bottles of wine which, to make sure they were getting the same wine they were drinking, Max checked before the waiter uncorked them. He nodded. As the waiter uncorked them, Max emptied the remains of the original bottles into their glasses. The waiter then picked up the empties and left.

The band was playing a quickstep and people were making the most of it. The dance floor was packed to capacity.

"Are New York still paying the children's school fees, Max?" Henry asked.

"I assume so, Henry," Max replied, "since no one has said anything to the contrary. I don't even bother checking these days."

"That was a wonderful deal you negotiated with them when you joined them," Veronica said. "I don't know anybody else who has their children's school fees paid for them."

"Wasn't it, just?" Max agreed. "But that's what happens when you get headhunted. It puts you in the strongest position of all. I got everything I asked for, and then some."

A stockinged-foot began to slide up the inside of his calf sending a tingle up his spine. He glanced at Veronica, who was sitting across the table from him. She was toying with the stem of her wine glass, a picture of innocence.

The quickstep ended and the band segued into a foxtrot. Several couples left the floor, leaving room for more.

"They're playing our tune, Veronica," Max said jokingly. "May I have the pleasure?"

"I thought you'd never ask," Veronica replied, in the same jokey fashion. She removed her foot from Max's calf and slipped on her shoe.

"How about it, Sue?" Henry said. "Shall we?"

"Why not?" Sue said, getting to her feet.

At six-foot-one, Max was taller than his wife by a foot, but when he was dancing with Veronica all he had to do to dance cheek-to-cheek with her was dip his head slightly.

In the heady atmosphere and with the band playing a melody that brought back memories for both of them, neither Max nor Veronica felt the need to say anything. It had been some time since they had danced together, and they savoured the moment.

They had met at the school about eighteen months ago. Max had been having a rare day off work and he had been sitting in his car in the drive at the front of the school waiting for the children to come out. Veronica had pulled up behind him in her open Mercedes sports car. She had come to pick up her son, Randy. They had got out of their cars, introduced themselves and started chatting. The attraction had been instantaneous, for both of them. Veronica was on her third husband and was not of a mind to go for a fourth. Max was on his first marriage and wanted to keep it that way. Although it had been a struggle, for both of them, especially as they met up as a foursome on a fairly regular basis.

She moved in close and breathed in his ear, "I dressed for you tonight, Max."

"Veronica, *please*," Max croaked. "It's hard enough as it is. Don't make it even more difficult."

She pressed herself against him. "You know how I feel about you. And we can arrange things in such a way that Sue and Henry will never know."

"Veronica … we agreed."

"Every time I see you, I want you. It's driving me mad. I can't go on like this."

Distracted, Max almost danced them into Mr and Mrs Godley, the headmaster and his wife, who were moving along at a snail's pace having mobile conversations with parents.

Because of the amount of time he was away on business, Max rarely visited the school, but he had met the headmaster on a couple of occasions. "Good evening, headmaster," he said. He nodded and smiled at the headmaster's wife. "Mrs Godley."

"Good evening," the Godleys replied, in unison. The headmaster looked vague, as if unsure of who Max was.

Max helped him out. "Max Hughes," he said. "Harry, Amanda and Clarissa's father."

The penny dropped. "Ah, yes, of course. Very nice to see you again, Mr Hughes."

"You too, headmaster."

"It's nice to see the event so well-attended again," Mr Godley said.

"Indeed, it is," Max agreed.

The headmaster was a serious man who was not given to making small talk, and the conversation - whilst brief - was formal and awkward. Max steered Veronica away from them as soon as he could.

"Max, for God's sake *say* something."

"Veronica, what *can* I say? We've been through this before, several times. We both know the score."

"Well, I can't stand it any longer. I decided this morning that I was going to tell you tonight exactly how I feel about you. I'm besotted with you, Max. I've never felt this way about any other man."

Max steered them safely around a couple he knew slightly and forced himself to smile at them.

"You're not going off me, Max, are you?"

"Veronica, my feelings for you have not changed since the day we met. In fact, if anything, they're stronger."

"Then why haven't you done something about it?"

"You know the answer to that, Veronica. I haven't done anything about it because of our marriages, and our children."

"You're not seeing someone else, are you, Max?" Veronica asked suspiciously.

"Veronica, if I were seeing anyone else, it would be you. There's no one else."

"Am I wasting my time, Max?"

"Veronica, I should say yes to that question, but it isn't that simple because I feel the same way about you."

"I want you to make love to me tonight, Max. I don't care how we arrange it. I've waited long enough."

"And if it all went pear-shaped?"

"I can't think that far ahead. All I can think of is how I feel about you at this very moment. If I had the choice, I would have you take me outside right now and make love to me in the car park if necessary. That's how I feel about you."

Max was saved from having to think what to say by the band finishing the number they had been playing and people applauding and drifting back to their tables.

15

When they got back at their own table, Sue and Henry were embroiled in a conversation about the four of them taking a holiday together while the children were away in Italy with the school. Sue brought Max and Veronica up to speed, and then said, "Henry and I think it's a great idea. How do you two feel about it?"

"When is the school trip?" Max said, reaching for the bottle to top up Veronica's glass.

"The end of July," Sue said. "Do keep up, Max. I told you that the other day."

"I think it's wonderful idea," Veronica said. "Do say yes, Max?"

"Come on, old boy," Henry said. "We've been talking about going away together for ages. Surely you can find time in your busy schedule for a holiday, especially since we're talking almost four months ahead. And we're only talking about a week."

"Do say yes, Max," Veronica said.

"I'm sure I can manage a week," Max said. "Especially given that much notice. Did you have somewhere in mind?"

"Somewhere with some sun." Henry said, with feeling. "I need to get away from this awful English weather."

As they talked it through, Max suggested that, since they would only be going away for a week, they should avoid anywhere that would involve a serious time change, like Florida. "If we went to Florida, it would take us two days to get over the time change, and then it would be time to come home again. If we headed due south, like Spain, Portugal, or the Canaries, we'd be guaranteed sunshine and we wouldn't have a time change to worry about."

"What about Madeira?" Sue suggested. "It's a four-hour flight, but we'd be in the same time zone. We've been there several times, but Max and I have never stayed at Reid's. I've always wanted to give that a try."

"That wouldn't be much fun for Veronica and me," Henry said. "We've stayed at Reid's dozens of times. Why don't we try somewhere none of us has ever been?"

"That makes sense," Max said. "It's always nice to try somewhere new. Any ideas?"

"I'm sure we'll find something on the Internet," Veronica said.

"Yes, I'm sure we will," Sue agreed. "And, since I probably have more time on my hands than all of you busy people, why don't I check it out and see what I can come up with?"

General consensus was that this was an excellent idea.

While Max was dancing with Sue a little while later, he was thinking about his conversation with Veronica. The last thing he wanted was to lose Sue and cause a break-up in the family, but what Veronica had said about being besotted with him had bowled him over. The problem was, if it all went pear-shaped and ended up with Sue leaving him, what then? An affair was one thing, but a separation, or – God forbid – a divorce, was another thing altogether.

"You're very quiet, darling," Sue said, looking up into his eyes. "Is everything all right?"

"Everything's fine," he said, smiling at her. "I was just enjoying the music, and being with you."

As he spoke these words, Max realised that a lie such as this would be nothing compared to the lies he would have to tell if he started a relationship with Veronica. Life would be one long lie.

From then on, the four friends talked and laughed and danced the night away. They left the dancing on the tables to the more inebriated of the revellers. Since Henry had also driven to the venue, he, like Max, was drinking sparingly.

As protocol demanded, the four of them danced the last waltz with their respective spouses. Whenever Max happened to glance at Veronica, he would find her looking at him. And vice versa.

Henry had been talking recently of getting himself a Jaguar sports car, and as they joined the throng heading out into the car park, Max asked him if he had bought one yet.

"I certainly have," Henry said, beaming. "I bought it last week and she's a beauty. Come and have a look at her."

At the far end of the car park, tucked safely away from other cars, was a brand new Jaguar XKR coupe in metallic silver. There was a full moon and its image was reflected in the paintwork on the bonnet.

Sue walked round the car admiring its flowing lines. "She's a beauty, Henry. When are you going to give me a spin in her?"

"Well," Henry responded, "if Max has no objections, I'll take you for a spin right now. And then I'll drive you home."

Max knew this would mean him driving Veronica home, which – all things considered – he would have preferred not to do, but he knew he had no choice. He shrugged and said, "That's fine with me."

"Good," Henry said. "Then you take Veronica home."

"Yes, why don't you do that, Max?" Veronica said, stifling a grin. "Why don't you take me home?"

Max said nothing. He knew when he was beaten.

He and Veronica stood in the cool early-morning air and watched the sports car roar off into the distance. Then, Veronica slipped her arm through his and they walked to his car – a Jaguar saloon – with his arm pressed firmly against her breast.

Veronica had refreshed her perfume before leaving the building, and with her sitting next to him and toying with his emotions, Max found the atmosphere in the car almost overwhelming. He started the engine and let his window down in the hope some fresh air would help.

Before he put the car in gear, Veronica took his hand in hers. "You do realise, Max, that we have to make the most of this. We can't let the evening end with you just driving me home. We might never have another opportunity like this."

Max argued, "But if we did go somewhere and Sue and Henry got to your house before we did, how would we explain it?"

"We could say we went for a drive too, and that we obviously went for a longer drive than they did."

Max was struggling. If he took Veronica for a drive, it wouldn't end there. It would almost certainly result in them starting a full-blown affair, which could end in disaster. That wouldn't be fair on Sue, and it wouldn't be fair on the children. They had done nothing wrong.

"I'm sorry, Veronica," he said. "But as much as I would like to take you for a drive, and whatever that entailed, I think it would be better if I just drove you home."

"Alright, Max," Veronica said. "But don't expect me to stop trying. Because I won't."

The drive to the ivy-covered manor house that Henry and Veronica owned - or rather Veronica owned and Henry lived in - took no more than twenty minutes. Throughout the drive neither of them spoke. They were both breathing heavily and Veronica was making it difficult for Max to concentrate on his driving by running her fingernail up and down the back of his hand, which was sending tingles up and down his spine.

There was a high-walled courtyard at the front of the house, in the middle of which was a wishing well, around which was a turning circle. Max swung the car round it, stopped, put the automatic into park and put the handbrake on. He left the engine running.

"I suppose you leaving the engine running means you're not coming in," Veronica said.

"I'm afraid so."

"It's a shame it has to end like this when we have such an opportunity."

"I know, Veronica, but …"

"Couldn't you at least come in for a coffee?"

"What would be the point? You know what it would lead to."

"Do I at least get a kiss?"

Max leaned over and gave her a peck on the cheek.

"Well, I suppose that's better than nothing," Veronica said. She looked into his eyes and stroked his cheek. "You're a lovely man, Max. What a shame you weren't available before I married Henry."

Max gave her a long searching look, before climbing out of the car and walking round and opening her door for her. He waited until she had walked to the house and opened the front door, and then said, "Goodnight, Veronica. And I'm sorry, I really am."

"You're sure you won't come in?"

"Veronica, at the moment I'm not sure of anything."

Veronica stood in the doorway and watched him drive towards the courtyard gates. She blew him a kiss.

He didn't see it. He drove home with his emotions all over the place and desperately trying to hold it all together.

Chapter 2

Wanting to show Sue she was *not* just a taxi service for the children and that he *did* care and he *did* listen, Max had taken the afternoon off work and had driven up from his office in London to pick up the children. He was sitting in his car outside the school.

Max was a firm believer in giving his children the best education he could. He believed that your education is a part of you, a part that nobody can take away from you, a part that sets you up for life. When you leave school and start work, it is on your CV for all to see. It gives you confidence, and it provides a springboard to the future, opening up opportunities that would otherwise not be available to you.

The same had not been true of the education his father had given him. *He* had not been picked up from school and driven home in a Jaguar. For him to get home from school, which was in a grimy mill town in Lancashire, he had to take a bus, a train, and then another bus.

He looked at the lovely old building across the drive from where he sat. Once a stately home, with twelve acres of rolling meadows and centuries old hardwood trees, and now a private day and boarding school with a heated outdoor swimming pool and six tennis courts, it was a far cry from the brick and slate roofed school he had attended. He allowed himself a moment of pride for what he had achieved in life.

Many of the boarders were from overseas; the progeny of parents who lived in far-flung places and had no room in their busy lives for the children they had spawned, although some simply wanted their children to be educated at a very good English school. As to the day pupils, before the advent of the Internet many of these had been the progeny of local, and not so local, old money. But since the advent of the Internet, there was much more new money at the school than old, and it was easy to spot the difference. The new money picked up their offspring in brand new top-of-the range vehicles that they leased and changed every year, and in which they chattered incessantly into their mobile phones while waiting for their progeny to come out of school. The old money had nothing to prove to anybody. They were not concerned about what other people thought. They owned their cars and they kept them for years, changing them only when they were giving trouble. And they used their mobile phones only when absolutely necessary.

Parked behind him was a line of seven or eight expensive late-model cars and SUVs, all driven by relatively young women.

Immediately behind him was a space that had just been vacated by a woman whose child had just skipped merrily out of school, and in his offside wing mirror, Max watched a familiar Mercedes sports convertible slide smoothly into the space. As Veronica climbed out and started walking towards his car, Max's heart started thudding heavily in his chest. She knocked on his window.

He let the window down.

"What are you doing here?" she said.

"I took the afternoon off. I'm giving Sue a break."

"Well, wonders never cease. There may be hope for you yet."

He started to get out of the car.

"No, don't get out," Veronica said, pushing the door shut. "I'll get in." She walked round the car and climbed into the front passenger seat and closed the door.

She was wearing the same perfume she had worn to the school's Parent's Ball two weeks ago and the memory of how close he had come to losing control of himself came flooding back. He told himself to get a grip.

"Sue emailed me this morning about our holiday," Veronica said. "She was suggesting the Marbella Club in Spain and Henry and I think it's a wonderful idea. How about you and Sue coming over for dinner tomorrow evening, so we can talk about it? Will you be free tomorrow evening?"

"Yes, but I have a ten o'clock flight to New York the following morning," Max said. "So I'll need to get a reasonably early night."

"Fine, I'll have the meal ready for eight. I'll give Sue a call and let her know. Ah, there's Randy."

Red-haired like his mother, and already almost six feet tall, fifteen year-old Randy was coming out of the school with a tall slim blonde girl.

"I'll cook something I know you like," Veronica said. She opened the car door and was gone before Max had a chance to respond.

Randy spotted his mother and said a regretful goodbye to the girl he had been chatting up. He grinned at Max as he headed for his mother's car.

"How are you, Randy?" Max said through the open window.

"Fine thank you, Uncle Max," Randy said.

"My compliments on your taste in girls. She's very pretty."

Randy laughed.

No one had invited Randy to call Max *Uncle Max* and Sue *Auntie Sue*; Randy had just taken it upon himself to do so. But Max and Sue knew him so well and liked him so much that neither of them was offended by it. In fact, they had been flattered.

Randy had an easy laid-back air about him, but he was nobody's fool. He was into computers in a big way; his goal being to get an honours degree in IT – Information Technology – at Oxford, or Cambridge.

Max liked this kind of drive, especially in one so young, and he predicted Randy would go far in life.

When Harry, Max's son, walked - or rather sauntered indolently - out of the school building, Max actually felt quite ashamed of him. Harry had his school blazer over his arm, his sleeves rolled up and his shirt-tail hanging out of his trousers. His tie was half-way round his neck, and his hair looked like it had not been combed for a week. The laces on his shoes were undone and Max wondered if they come undone of their own accord, or he had undone them purposely. He suspected the latter. He reminded Max of *William* from the *Just William* series of novels penned by Richmal Crompton in the dim and distant past. When he was a boy, Max had been an avid reader of the Just William books.

Harry waited for a white Range Rover Vogue with blacked-out rear windows to pass, and then wandered across the drive as if he had all the time in the world. He climbed into the front seat of the car, slamming the door in the process.

Max frowned. He had never been able to get it into his son's head that Jaguar car doors did not need to be slammed, they just needed to be closed. He let it go.

"Good day, son?" he asked.

Harry shrugged. "It was okay, I suppose."

Max shook his head. *So much for the expensive education I'm giving you.* It had crossed Max's mind that Harry's attitude might have something to do with him being away so much of the time; the lack of a father figure. But short of changing his job, there was nothing much he could do about that.

Amanda strolled out of the school surrounded by a bevy of older boys, all vying for her attention. Blue-eyed, blonde, and extremely pretty, the thirteen year-old was almost an exact facsimile of her mother. She had also inherited her mother's penchant for always dressing well, even when at home. If anything, Amanda was even more fastidious about the way she looked than her mother. She actually made her school uniform looked like a fashion statement.

"Why are you picking us up today, Daddy?" she said, climbing into the rear seat behind her father. "Is Mummy not well?"

"She fine," Max said, eyeballing his daughter in the rear-view mirror. "I thought I'd give her a break for once and pick you up myself. You don't mind, do you?"

"Of course I don't mind." Amanda sat there for a few moments, deep in thought. Then she said, "Daddy?"

"Yes, sweetheart?"

"Daddy, may I have a new dress for Bernadette's birthday party?"

Max met her eyes in the mirror. "But wouldn't one of your other dresses do, sweetheart? You seem to have a wardrobe full of dresses you never seem to wear."

Amanda held his gaze. "But Daddy, all the other girls are having new dresses and you wouldn't want me going to the party not to be looking my best, *would* you?"

Max sighed. Amanda had been able to twist him around her little finger since she was a little girl. "No, of course I wouldn't, poppet. Yes, of course you can have a new dress."

Harry swivelled round in his seat and gave his sister one of his famous black looks.

Amanda stuck her tongue out at him.

Finally, the baby of the family, eight year-old Clarissa, skipped out of the school, climbed into the car and plonked herself on the rear seat next to her sister.

"Hello, pumpkin," her father said. "Have you had a good day?"

"Yes, thank you Daddy, I've had a lovely day. I got two more good conduct stars, today."

"Little creep," Harry muttered.

"I am *not* a little creep," Clarissa said indignantly. "And anyway, my friend Emily thinks you're a stinker."

When they got home, the children headed off to their bedrooms to do their homework.

Max joined Sue in the kitchen, where she was starting to prepare the evening meal. She thanked him for picking up the children. "It was such a nice break," she said. "It gave me the chance to get all kinds of things done."

Max parked himself on a stool at the breakfast bar. "No problem. Glad to be able to help. By the way, Harry seems to be getting worse. He was a pain in the neck in the car on the way home. He was picking a fight with his sisters all the way home."

Sue shook her head sadly. "I know. I do wish I knew what was making him so unhappy."

Max told her about bumping into Veronica at the school and her asking if they could go round for dinner tomorrow evening to talk about their holiday.

"Yes, she told me," Sue said. "She just got off the phone." She opened a cupboard and took out two packets of Basmati rice. "I told her we'd go if I could find a sitter. Tuesday night is not the best night of the week to find a sitter. She said not to worry, that she'd anticipated it might be difficult and she'd found us one. A friend of hers has a nineteen-year-old daughter, and she has her own car."

Max gave her a quizzical look. "Are you sure you're happy leaving the children with somebody you've never met?"

Sue rounded on him. With her hands on hips and her face set, she said, "Max, since you're hardly ever here, please don't question my judgement when it comes to the children. Okay? Veronica is my best friend, and I trust her implicitly. If she says the girl will be fine, I'm sure the girl will be fine."

Chapter 3

Veronica and Henry's house was built of a stone that had mellowed over the years to a warm, honey-coloured patina. It was sat on four acres of land and was reputed to be over two hundred and fifty years old. Apart from a small formal garden and an apple orchard, the land to the rear of the house was heavily wooded. The house had once belonged to a titled family.

Some years earlier, Henry had brought in contractors to redecorate the dining room. In the course of removing old wallpaper, a quantity of plaster had fallen off one of the walls to reveal murals of American Paint Horses, painted and signed by a well-known nineteenth-century artist. Henry had the paintings professionally removed and sold at auction, where they had realised a vast sum of money. The party Henry and Veronica had thrown for their friends to celebrate their windfall had everyone's liver aching for a week.

The kitchen still had the original stone floor, but the flooring in the rest of the downstairs of the house had been replaced by solid oak parquet flooring. In the dining room and the family room were working log fireplaces, and on most weekends in the summer, Henry was to be found out in the woodland with a chainsaw stocking up on logs and kindling. During the autumn and winter months, there was invariably the smell of wood smoke in and around the house.

Within the walled courtyard at the front of the house was garaging for three cars, over which was a dovecote with three pairs of doves. Henry often spoke of getting rid of the doves because their droppings made such a mess of their cars.

The courtyard was screened from the road by an eight-foot high brick wall, which made it impossible for people entering or leaving the courtyard to see what was coming the other way, and when Max and Sue arrived to take up their invitation to dinner the following evening, Max had to stand on his brakes as a black Porsche Carrera thundered out of the courtyard.

The two cars stopped side-by-side, driver-to-driver, their wing-mirrors a matter of inches apart.

Max knew the driver of the Porsche. Steve Porter was an estate agent with some of the most expensive properties in the area on his books. His son was in the same class as Harry at school. His son, whose name Max couldn't remember, was sitting in the passenger seat beside him.

Porter let down his window. "Sorry Max," he said, sheepishly. "I was showing off to Randy. Silly of me."

Randy had shoehorned himself into what was laughingly known as a back seat. He was sitting across the car with his knees under his chin. "Hi Uncle Max," he called. "Sorry, it was my fault. I was asking Mr Porter how fast the car would go."

"No problem," Max said, his pulse rate slowing to something like its normal rate.

"Hi Sue," Porter said. "How are you?"

"I'm fine, Steve. Tell Gloria I'll see her at the coffee morning next week."

"I will. Well, best be off. Nice to see you both and have a nice evening." Porter roared away, his tyres squealing

Despite it being early May and a pleasantly warm evening, white smoke was issuing from one of the house's numerous chimneys.

Veronica was in the kitchen preparing dinner. The kitchen overlooked the courtyard and she saw them arrive. She waved and went to let them in.

"Hi there," she said. "Did Maria arrive on time?"

"On the dot," Sue said. "And she seems very nice. The children certainly seemed to like her."

Veronica closed the solid oak front door. "I thought they would," she said. "She used to sit for Randy until recently, but he was getting too interested in her. And not as a babysitter, if you get my drift."

Max laughed. "I'm not surprised. She's a very attractive girl."

Veronica continued, "Nowadays, I use a seventy-year-old spinster who lives locally. That clips his wings, I can tell you."

"Spoilsport," Max said, chuckling.

"Well," Sue said, "Maria should be safe enough with Harry. He isn't showing the slightest interest in girls, yet."

"He's probably just a late starter," Max said. "Some boys are."

"Were you a later starter, Max?" Veronica asked mischievously.

"That depends on your point of view," Max replied. "I was thirteen when I kissed my first girl. And I impressed her so much that she refused to go out with me again."

Sue said, "The good news is, he's improved since then."

Veronica laughed. "I'm glad to hear it."

Henry clattered down the stairs. "Hello, you two. We've got the house to ourselves, tonight. Randy's staying overnight with friends."

"Yes, they were leaving as we arrived," Sue said. "In fact, we almost bumped into them."

"Literally," Max said. "They almost ran into us."

"Well you're obviously still in one piece, so come on through and I'll get some drinks organised." Henry set off down the long wide hall, his leather-soled brogues clumping heavily on the parquet floor.

"I'll just finish up in the kitchen," Veronica said. "I'll join you shortly."

"Anything I can do to help?" Sue said.

"No thanks, Sue. It's all under control. The meat will be done in twenty minutes. All I have to is put the vegetables on."

"Well, if you're sure."

"I'm sure."

Sue followed Henry down the hall.

Max hung back. "Smells like we're having beef," he said, sniffing the air.

"We are," Veronica said. "We're having Beef Wellington."

"My all-time favourite dish," Max said, rolling his eyes.

"I told you I'd cook you something you like. You go and get yourself a drink. I'll join you shortly."

The family room was a large, square, high-ceilinged room with heavy chintz curtains at windows which still had the original leading. There were two three-seater sofas, two armchairs, each with its own footstool, all of which were covered in the same material as the curtains. The room had beams, which - Henry was apt to point out to newcomers - had once been actual ships timbers. Hanging from the ceiling was a large brass chandelier replete with a couple of dozen candle-shaped light bulbs, while hunting scenes of signed original oils adorned the walls. The focal point of the room was a large stone fireplace, complete with antique brass furniture. Several large logs crackled and spat in the grate. The smell of wood smoke oozed from the very pores of the room.

As he walked passed the fireplace, Henry gave one of the logs a shove with the sole of his shoe, sending a shower of sparks cascading up the chimney.

A pair of leaded French windows led out on to a stone-built terrace at the rear of the house where Henry had set up a wet bar.

When Veronica entertained, she entertained in style, and her long and weathered oak table had been set with crisp white linen tablecloth, polished silver cutlery, gleaming crystal glasses and a pair of lighted candles in silver storm lanterns.

With Max standing alongside, watching, Henry grabbed a handful of ice cubes from a silver ice bucket and dumped them in a cut-crystal tumbler. He poured in a triple measure of Tanqueray Gin, and then squeezed a wedge of lemon into the glass, before dropping in the lemon. He topped up the glass with Schweppes Tonic Water, stirred it with a silver spoon and handed it to Max. "Give that to Veronica, would you, Max. Tell her from me she deserves it. She's been preparing for the evening since the middle of the afternoon."

Veronica was lifting the oven dish containing the meat out of the oven with a pair of oven gloves when Max walked in with her drink. Distracted by his presence, she accidentally tilted the oven dish and the juice spat and burned her arm.

She uttered an expletive Max had never heard her use before, and dumped the oven dish on the hob, before heading for the sink and the cold water tap.

Max put her drink down and got to the tap before her. He turned it on and stood by solicitously as she ran the cold water over her arm.

She let the water run for a few moments and then turned off the tap and patted her arm dry with a tea towel.

"Are you all right?" Max asked, anxiously.

Veronica nodded. "I'll live."

Max picked up her drink and handed it to her. "From Henry," he said. "He said you've been preparing for tonight all afternoon and you deserve it."

"Henry talks too much," Veronica said. She took a a large swallow of her drink. "Mmm, that's good. Well, Henry might talk too much, but he *does* know how to make a gin and tonic." She put the glass down. "I'll put the meat in the warming cupboard, and then you can help me carry the soup through."

"What soup are we having?"

"Chilled vichyssoise. And don't tell Henry I'm serving two of your favourite dishes tonight, because he might get the wrong idea."

"Or the right one," Max observed, dryly.

When Max walked out on to the terrace with a bowl of soup in each hand, Henry apologised for not yet getting him a drink.

"Don't worry about it," Max said. "I'll stick to tonic water tonight. I'm flying to New York first thing in the morning, and I hate flying with a hangover."

As they drank their soup, the conversation turned to the school visit to Italy. Because Max had been away on business so much recently he knew very little of what was going on, and he asked Sue which of their children were going.

She looked at him, exasperated. "Max, how many times do I have to tell you? Harry and Amanda are going to Italy, and Clarissa is boarding at the school so the four of us can go away on holiday together."

"Okay, okay. No need to bite my head off."

"Honestly, Max, I despair of you sometimes. Half the time you're not here, and when you are here, you're not listening. That's the third time I've told you what's happening!"

"Well now I know, don't I?" Max said, glaring at her. "What will they be doing in Italy?"

Sue threw her hands up in despair. "I give up!"

Veronica explained. "It's an educational visit, Max. It's to give the children an insight into Italian culture. They'll be studying the works of Michelangelo and Leonardo da Vinci. They are staying in an old monastery on a cliff top overlooking the Adriatic. The object of the visit is to broaden their minds."

"Right, so now I know. Thank you, Veronica."

"Got it now?" Sue said.

"Yes, thank you. You need to tell me these things when I don't have other things on my mind."

"Oh, *really*," Sue said crossly. "And when might that be? I sometimes think you don't think of *anything* but your precious job. I sometimes wish you'd give up the job and find something nearer home. At least, we'd see something of you."

Annoyed, Max retorted, "My *precious job*, as you call it, provides us with a standard of living most people can only dream of, not to mention it pays the children's school fees. So don't knock it."

"Hey, come on you two," Veronica said, "let's not spoil the evening." She got to her feet. "Max, would you mind carving the meat? Henry, why don't you top up everyone's glass? And then we need to finish talking about our holiday. From what Sue's told me, the villas in the grounds of the Marbella Club are like gold dust, and we need to move while we still can." She collected the empty soup bowls and walked into the house.

Max followed her.

When she got to the kitchen, Veronica put the soup bowls on a worktop. When Max walked in, she kicked the door shut and dragged him into a corner. "Kiss me, damn it!" she said, her eyes flashing. "And, this time, don't you *dare* refuse."

Max needed no second bidding. He threw his arms round her, crushed her to him and kissed her, hard.

A knock on the window startled them. They broke apart, panting.

It was Randy. He pulled a face that under normal circumstances would have made them both laugh, and spread his hands in a gesture of apology. He pointed to the front door.

"He's forgotten his house key, again," Veronica said. She nodded to her son to indicate she would let him in. "He's always forgetting his key."

Randy headed in the direction of the front door.

"He saw us, didn't he?" Max said.

"Yes, he saw us," Veronica confirmed. "But he won't tell."

"How do you know he won't tell?"

"Because I know my son," Veronica said. She went to let him in.

Max's pulse was racing. He tried to calm his breathing.

Veronica's voice drifted in from the hall. "Forget your key again?"

"Yes, sorry."

"But you've been gone for ages, sweetheart. You surely didn't come home just to get your key."

"I forgot my laptop. We got all the way to Chris's house, and then had to come all the way back again. I can't do my homework without it."

"Where is your laptop?"

"In my bedroom."

"Right. Well, we're in the middle of dinner, so close the door on your way out."

"I will." Randy called, "Hi, Uncle Max."

"Hi, Randy."

Randy took the stairs two at a time.

Veronica walked back into the kitchen.

"So much for us saying no-one would know if we started something," Max said.

"I told you," Veronica said. "There's nothing to worry about it. Randy won't tell."

Randy charged down the stairs, making a thunderous din. "I've got my key, Mum," he called.

"Alright, my darling," Veronica called. "See you in the morning. Love you."

"Love you too. Bye. Bye, Uncle Max."

"Bye, Randy."

There was the sound of the front door closing, then Randy ran past the kitchen window with his laptop under his arm. He waved.

"I think you're right," Max said, waving back. "I don't think he'll tell. Now, where's the carving knife?"

Chapter 4

"Mrs Hughes?"

The voice was vaguely familiar. "Speaking," Sue said into the phone.

"It's Mrs Godley ... from the school."

"Oh, hello, Mrs Godley. Well, this is a nice surprise. To what do I owe the pleasure?"

"I wondered if you would mind dropping in to see me at the school at your early convenience. There's something I'd like to talk to you about."

Sue's brain went into overdrive. This was the first time she had ever had a call from the headmaster's wife, and as reassuring as Mrs Godley sounded, she automatically thought there must be a problem.

"Yes, of course," she said. "May I know what it's about?"

"It's probably nothing to worry about, my dear, but…"

"It's Sue, Mrs Godley. Please, call me Sue."

"Thank you, my dear. Sue, it's just that my husband and I are concerned about Harry. He's developing something of an attitude. He used to be such fun, getting along with the other boys and getting into mischief from time to time, as boys of his age do, but he's changed. He used to be gregarious but now he seems to prefer his own company. We thought you should know about it, then perhaps between us we can nip in the bud whatever's bothering him."

"Well yes, of course, Mrs Godley," Sue said, her voice registering her concern. "My husband and I have noticed a change in him recently, but we had just put it down to his age. Do you think there may be more to it than that?"

"We do, actually."

"Then, yes, of course I'll drop in. When did you have in mind?"

"Would three o-clock tomorrow afternoon be suitable? Then you can collect the children immediately afterwards."

When Sue picked up the children from school that afternoon, she mentioned that Mrs Godley had called her and that she would be meeting her the following afternoon, although she didn't say what Mrs Godley wanted to talk to her about. She said that in the event the meeting went on longer than expected, they should wait by the car.

Harry frowned. "What does she want to see you about?" he asked, suspiciously.

"I don't know, Harry," Sue lied. "Perhaps she just wants a general chat about how the three of you are doing."

"It's not something I've done, Mummy, is it?" Clarissa said. "Because I do try to be good."

"Little creep," Harry muttered.

"Harry," Sue said sharply, "I won't have you talking to your sister like that. You apologise to Clarissa, this minute."

"I'm *sorry*," Harry said loudly. Under his breath, he repeated, "Little creep."

"That's better. And no, Clarissa, I'm sure it's nothing you've done."

"And I'm sure it's nothing I've done either," Amanda said. "So it must be something *you've* done, Harry."

Sue put the car in gear and sighed. "Children, can we *please* stop this bickering." She let off the handbrake and made a three-point turn in the drive.

"What are we having to eat tonight?" Harry asked.

"I haven't decided yet. What would you like to eat?" Sue accelerated down the school's private road towards the main road into Welwyn Garden City, which was some three or four hundred yards distant.

"I'd like beans on toast, Mummy," Clarissa said.

"That's all you *ever* want," Harry said.

Sue had had enough. "Harry, that's *enough*! I don't want to hear another word from you until we get home."

The following afternoon, Mrs Godley received Sue in the headmaster's study. She told Sue her husband was teaching an A-level mathematics class, so they would not be disturbed. She sat Sue down in one of a pair of comfortable-looking chairs by an open window. Outside, the school gardener had just cut the lawns and the sweet smell of newly-mown grass drifted in on the breeze.

Mrs Godley put a kettle on to boil and got out cups and saucers. "Earl Grey all right, my dear?" she said.

"Earl Grey's fine, thank you."

"Milk, or lemon?"

Sue took milk in tea, but then this *was* the headmaster's study and this *was* the headmaster's wife. "Lemon, please."

"A wise choice, if I may say so. I do think that milk ruins the flavour of Earl Grey. Wouldn't you agree, my dear?"

"I most certainly would." Sue drank Earl Grey so rarely that she didn't really have an opinion on the subject. At home, they used PG Tips in pyramid bags.

"Sugar?"

"No, thank you."

Sue watched Mrs Godley making the tea and found herself hoping she looked half as good when she got to her age. The head's wife was sixty-four, but her hair was still dark with only the merest traces of grey. Her face, apart from laughter lines at the corners of her eyes, was virtually unlined. She had high cheekbones, giving her an almost aristocratic appearance, and she had the kind of manner that put people immediately at their ease.

Her husband had been headmaster of the school when she had met and married him. She had, at the time, been the history teacher. After they were married, she had - of her own volition - taken on the mantle of surrogate mother to the children, especially to the boarders, some of whom rarely saw their parents. Mrs Godley was loved by everyone from the school governors down to the youngest of the children.

The school boarded children from as far afield as China, Russia, Saudi Arabia, et al and Mrs Godley was known to all and sundry as *Mutti*. She had no known German antecedents, and quite where this German-for-mother nickname came from nobody knew, but it fitted her like a glove and she wore it with pride.

While the children had often referred to Mrs Godley in conversation as *Mutti*, Sue had not known her well enough to call her *Mutti* herself, but as they sipped their tea and got better acquainted, Mrs Godley invited her to do so.

"After all, my dear, I *am* a surrogate mother to your children." Her eyebrows knitted in a frown. "Oh, I do hope that doesn't sound presumptuous."

"No, of course not," Sue said. She smiled and added, "Mutti."

Mrs Godley beamed. "Well my dear, since we've got together to talk about Harry, perhaps we should make a start."

Anxious to hear what the problem was, Sue sat forward in her chair and gave Mrs Godley her full attention.

"My husband and I find that in cases like this it often helps to start with what happens in the home."

Sue took this as an implied criticism. "Well, my husband and I are not child psychologists, and I'm sure we do get it wrong sometimes, but we do our best for our children."

"As do we all, my dear. That's what parenting is all about. But this is not meant as criticism. Let me ask you this; does Harry have his father's ear? I mean, does his father listen when Harry tries to talk to him?"

Sue shook her head. "The short answer to that is no, he doesn't. Well, not as a rule. Max is so wrapped up in his business these days that he hardly listens to anybody, including me."

"Then that may have something to do with it. My husband and I have found that fathers who have become very successful in life often have very little time for their sons. When they are very young, they play model trains and football with them, but when their sons get into their

43

middle teenage years, meaning Harry's age, they often seem to leave them to their own devices."

There was something disturbingly familiar about what Mrs Godley was saying, and Sue said, "Actually, Mutti, that describes my husband to a tee. And now I come to think of it, I have noticed Harry looking frustrated when he's trying to talk to his father and it's obvious Max isn't listening."

"Worth having word with your husband, do you think, my dear?"

"It certainly is, Mutti. I'm glad you mentioned it."

"And what about friends at home?" Mrs Godley asked. "Does Harry spend much time with boys of his own age at home?"

"Actually, Harry has no friends at home. But that's not really his fault. We live in a little village, and …"

"I know the village. I have a friend living there. In fact, I know your house. And a lovely house it is, too."

"Thank you, that's kind of you. As a matter of fact, the house may be a part of the problem. I say that because most of the villagers live in terraced cottages or very small houses, and their children don't seem to want to mix with ours. What about here at the school, Mutti? Does Harry have many friends here?"

"As far as my husband and I are aware, Harry has no friends here at the school."

"Apart from Randy, of course," Sue said, "Randy Hodson. They have been friends for ages. My husband and I are very friendly with Randy's parents. In fact, we're going on holiday with them when the children are in Italy."

Mrs Godley's face clouded. "Actually, my dear, that's something else I wanted to talk to you about. There was an altercation between Harry and Randy one day last week; Thursday, if memory serves. I didn't contact you at the time because these things happen from time to time and usually it's a storm in a teacup and is over with quickly. But perhaps in this case it has some relevance."

This was the first Sue had heard of it. "What kind of altercation are you talking about?"

"It seems that Randy punched Harry in the chest, and witnesses say that the punch was delivered with such force that it knocked Harry to the ground."

Sue's eyes opened wide in surprise. "Well, you *do* surprise me. I thought Harry and Randy were the best of friends. I wonder what brought that on."

"I think it might be worth trying to find out, my dear, because it may help identify what's bothering Harry."

"Yes, of course," Sue said. "I'll see what I can find out."

They were on the ground floor and there was the sound of desk lids banging and chairs being pushed back and shoes shuffling from the floor above.

"We should probably leave it at that, my dear," Mrs Godley said. "The children are coming out."

They got to their feet.

"Thank you for letting me know what's been going on, Mutti," Sue said, shaking Mrs Godley's hand, "I'll you let you know what I find out. It was nice getting to know you, and thank you for the tea."

When Sue walked out of the building, Harry was standing by the car waiting for her.

"Well," he demanded.

"Well what?" Sue said, annoyed by his attitude.

"Come on, Mum, you know what I'm talking about. What did Mrs Godley want to talk to you about?"

There were adults and children milling about and Sue had no desire to have anyone hear what they were talking about. "Let's sit in the car," she said. She pressed the remote to open the vehicle's doors and they climbed in. Harry sat in the front passenger seat beside her.

"It was me she wanted to talk about me, wasn't it?"

Sue saw no point in denying it. "Yes, Harry, it was. But it was only with your best interests in mind."

Harry glanced at his mother and then stared moodily through the windscreen.

This seemed like an ideal opportunity to bring up the incident with Randy, and Sue went for it. "What's this I hear about Randy punching you? I thought you two were the best of friends."

"We were, but we're not anymore."

"But why, Harry? Why did Randy punch you?"

"I don't want to talk about it."

At home that evening, Sue raised the subject again, and again she got the same response. Harry had raised his drawbridge, and it was clear he was not going to let it down again.

Later that evening, Max phoned from New York.

"Hello, you gorgeous creature," he said.

"Max, have you been drinking?"

He laughed. "No, why?"

"Because the last time you called me a gorgeous creature you were as drunk as a skunk."

He laughed again. "No, I haven't been drinking. I've just had some *very* good news."

"I'm always open to good news. So do tell."

"I've got a promotion. A big one."

"Just a second, Max," Sue said cautiously. "How can you get a promotion? You're already the managing director of the company's UK division; what else is there?"

"How does vice-president in charge of European operations grab you?" He sounded elated.

Sue was far from elated. "I'm not sure I like the sound of that, Max. That smacks of you being away from home even more than you are at the moment."

"Sue, it means a thirty percent increase in salary."

"So what? It's not more money we need, Max, it's the children and I seeing more of you. Tell me, if you accepted this promotion, how much more time would you need to be away from home than you are now?"

There was a pause, and then Max said quietly, "It's hard to say."

"So you would be away more than you are now. How could you possibly take on Europe and *not* be away more?"

"Sue, I won't be visiting customers in Europe. I'll be directing traffic, as it were."

"From where?"

"From my office in London. Although I will, of course, have to visit our European offices. Sue, we'll be able to buy ourselves a home in the sun. Wouldn't it be wonderful to have a holiday home in Spain, or Florida, even?"

"Max, we already have a holiday home in the Lake District. Why do we need another one?"

"Well, if for no other reason than that property is the best investment you can have. You can never have too many properties. And I get stock options. They could be worth a *fortune* in the future."

Sue frowned. "Stop right there, Max. What do you mean, *I get* stock options? Don't you mean you would get stock options if you took on the job."

There was a pause. "Sue, I *have* taken on the job. It's a done deal."

"I see," Sue said quietly. "There was a time, Max, when you would never even *consider* making a decision of such importance without discussing it with me first. Now, you just go ahead and do whatever you like."

"Sue, most women would give their eye teeth for a husband with a job like mine."

"In case you hadn't noticed, Max, I'm not most women. I'm *me*. By the way, while I have you on the phone, Mrs Godley from the school called me yesterday and asked me to drop in and see her."

"What did she want?"

"She wanted to tell me she and husband are worried about Harry."

"Sue, I'm sorry, but can this wait? I'm just about to go into a meeting. Can we talk about it when I get home? By the way, I won't be home until Sunday, now. They want me to fly out to Chicago, tomorrow. There's a big …"

Sue tuned him out. She let him finish what he had to say, without hearing a word, and then said, "Goodnight, Max," and put the phone down.

Chapter 5

Max and Sue's house was a twenty-minute drive from the school. It was out in the Hertfordshire countryside three miles east of Knebworth.

The house stood alongside a country lane. On the other side of the lane was a five-acre field in which horses and ponies grazed and in which the local annual gymkhana was held. Apart from their house, there were three other houses in a stretch of lane extending to a quarter of a mile, meaning it was quite a lonely place, especially at night.

The house was built on a plot of almost an acre, much of which was laid to lawn for ease of maintenance. The house, which had been built some twenty-five years earlier, had been built for a wealthy London merchant. It was a substantial property, built of brick with a Canadian shingle roof. At the front of the house was a semi-circular drive with hard standing for several cars. Attached to the right-hand end of the house was a double garage with individual electric up-and-over doors, which could be accessed from within the house.

As to the inside of the house, the downstairs accommodation comprised a through living room that extended from the front of the house to the back, a conservatory, a dining room, a small room that Max used as a study, and a large and well-equipped kitchen with a breakfast bar with seating for five. Connecting the kitchen and the front door to the living room and dining room, was a hall of about twenty feet in length by eight feet in width. In the hall was a window which allowed the occupants of the house to see anyone coming to the house, or vehicles driving past in the lane. Between the kitchen and front door was a cloakroom and toilet.

The upstairs accommodation comprised the master bedroom with its own en-suite bathroom, two further double bedrooms, and a single bedroom. The master bedroom was at the rear of the house overlooking a paved patio and the rear garden. Harry's room, which was the largest of the other double bedrooms, was at the front of the house, overlooking the drive. Amanda's room was at the opposite end of the landing. Clarissa's room – the small single room – was between her parent's room and the family bathroom.

On the morning after Sue's meeting with Mrs Godley, and her telephone conversation with Max, it was a warm and sunny morning and she and Veronica were having coffee on the patio at the rear of the house. They had bumped into each other at the school while dropping off their children, and Sue had invited Veronica round for coffee ostensibly to find out if she knew anything about Randy punching Harry.

The gardener, a grizzled seventy-one-year-old who had more or less come with the house, was mowing the lawn and the two women were watching in amazement at how straight he was making the lines. It was almost as if he had laid down string to guide him.

Veronica remarked on how lucky Sue was to have such a good gardener. "Our gardener is well past his prime," she said. "Henry keeps saying he's going to get rid of him and get somebody younger, but Basil's been with us for years and he's got a very sick wife. They need the money and there's no way I'm agreeing to Henry firing him. I'll fire Henry first."

A couple of hundred yards as the crow flies from where they were sitting stood a twelfth-century Norman church. It began to strike the hour. It struck ten times. The church was the focal point of the village, but the closest Sue and Max got to involvement in the church was sitting up in bed on a Sunday morning listening to the church bells summoning the villagers to the morning service while they drank their tea and read the newspapers.

Veronica took a sip her coffee and asked, "Have you heard from Max?"

"He phoned me last night," Sue replied, pulling a face.

"I take it the call didn't go too well, then. Do you want to talk about it?"

Sue told her about Max taking on Europe.

"But that's absolutely brilliant," Veronica said, "Well done, him."

"I'm glad you're pleased, because I'm not. In fact, I'm bloody furious."

Veronica looked surprised. "But why? Surely it's a promotion."

"It *is*, but what I'm angry about is he took it on without discussing it with me first."

"I'm sure he didn't mean anything by that, Sue. He probably took it for granted you'd be delighted with the news."

"More likely he took it on without telling me because he thought I would try and talk him out of it."

"Oh dear, I don't like the sound of that."

"I would go so far as to say his success could be the ruination of our marriage. It's odd, isn't it, Veronica; you think that once you get there and you're making lots of money, everything will be fine. But that's certainly not true in our case."

"Tell me about it." Veronica said, with feeling. "The more money Henry and I have, the unhappier we seem to become. Although in our case, money is not the only cause of the problem."

Sue looked at her friend in surprise. "You kept that quiet. I didn't realise you had a problem."

Veronica gave a little shrug. "Well, you know me. I don't like to wear my problems on my sleeve."

"Do you want to talk about it?"

"Not particularly."

They watched in silence as the gardener finished cutting the lawn. He shut the lawn mower down and brushed the grass cuttings off it, before putting it away in the garden shed. Then, cap in hand, he wandered over to them. He was sweating and he wiped the sweat from his brow with the back of his hand.

"All done, Cyril?" Sue said.

He nodded. "All done."

Sue got to her feet and made a show of inspecting his handiwork. She nodded approvingly. "Very nice, Cyril. Very nice indeed. My friend and I were wondering how you manage to get the lines so straight."

Cyril gave her a crooked little smile. "Put it down to fifty years of practice." He indicated the apple trees.

52

"Looks like there'll be a right good crop of apples again this year."

"Then, I'll bake you and your wife an apple pie again," Sue said.

"The missus and me will like that. We likes your apple pies."

"Good. See you again next week then, Cyril."

"Yes, see you next week." Cyril nodded courteously to the two women and then put his cap on and wandered off round the side of the house.

"Nice man," Veronica said.

"Yes, very." Sue sat down and settled back into her chair, "By the way, I had a call from Mrs Godley at the school yesterday."

"What did *she* want?"

"Amongst other things, to tell me that Harry and Randy had what she called an altercation recently?"

Veronica frowned. "What sort of altercation?"

"Well, apparently Randy punched Harry, and he punched him hard enough to knock him down. Harry hasn't said anything to me about it and I wondered if Randy had said anything to you about it."

Veronica looked genuinely surprised. "He hasn't said a thing to me about it, which is surprising because that's the sort of thing he would talk to me about. I thought they were still the best of friends."

"So did I, but according to Mrs Godley, apparently not."

"I shouldn't worry about it, Sue. I'm sure it was something and nothing. Probably some nonsense over a girl. That's what fifteen-year-old boys usually fall out over."

"I'm not sure about that," Sue said. "Harry doesn't seem all that interested in girls." She took a sip of her coffee. It was cold. "By the way, have you noticed a change in Harry's attitude recently? Because that's another thing Mrs Godley wanted to talk about. In fact, it was the main thing she wanted to talk about. She and Mr Godley have noticed a change in Harry's attitude recently and they were concerned about it."

"I can't say I've noticed," Veronica said. "I'll have a word with Randy. If I can get him to tell me why he punched Harry, perhaps that will throw some light on the subject."

That evening, Max called again from New York.

"Still mad at me?" he said.

"I'm not mad at you Max, I'm just disappointed that you chose to make a decision of that magnitude without consulting me first. It makes me feel I don't count anymore."

"Of course you count, sweetheart. You'll always count."

"I'm glad to hear it. Max, the last time you called I needed to talk to you about Harry and it was important. Do you have any idea how it felt to be brushed off with *can it wait till I get home*?"

"I'm sorry, Sue. That was remiss of me and I shouldn't have said that. Will you forgive me?"

"I'll forgive you if we can talk about it now."

"Sue, I'm sorry, but I can't. I'm just about to go into another meeting."

Sue sighed. "Max, if you didn't have the time to talk, why did you bother calling?"

"I called to apologise."

"Max, in case it happens to have slipped your notice, Harry is your *son*, and he has a problem. When *will* you have time to talk about it?"

"Soon, Sue. That's a promise. I'll call you as soon as I can, and then we'll talk about it."

Sue heard male voices in the background.

"Sue, I'm sorry, I have to go. I'll call you as soon as I can."

Sue found herself listening to the buzzing tone. "You do that, Max," she said, talking to herself as she put the phone down. "And one day you'll call, and I won't be here."

Chapter 6

"*HUGHES!*"

The bellow reverberated round the room, bouncing off the classroom's numerous hard surfaces - the floor, the walls, the windows, the ceiling, the desks.

The chalk hit Harry on the forehead fairly and squarely between his eyes. In truth, considering how far it had travelled and the fact that it had been thrown rather than fired from a weapon, it was an excellent shot and Harry's classmates clapped and cheered and yelled, "Good shot, sir!"

"*SILENCE!*"

Harry looked ruefully at the chalk, which was now lying on his desk. It was a brand new piece of chalk, out of the box just a few minutes ago, and – when thrown from a distance of twenty feet or so - a piece of solid chalk four and a half inches long and three eighths of an inch in diameter can hurt. Harry rubbed his head and fixed his gaze on the science master.

"What have I just said, Hughes?" Now he had Harry's attention, the science master reduced his decibel level to something more akin to a shout.

Necks craned and twenty-one pairs of adolescent male eyes looked first at Harry, then at the science master, and then again at Harry, as they waited for his response.

"I don't know, sir," In truth, Harry had not heard a word of what the science master had said since the lesson had begun.

The science master advanced on him, his weight causing the two-hundred-year-old floorboards to creak ominously.

All fidgeting in the room ceased as the boys waited to see what would happen next. In the ensuing silence, the sound of traffic could be heard from the main road half a mile away.

The science master stopped by the side of Harry's desk and looked disdainfully down at him. Bob Cunliffe was a big man, six feet three inches tall and weighing in at over nineteen stone. Someone had once described him as *'as large as life and twice as ugly'*, and the description fitted him to a tee.

"Stand up, Hughes!"

Harry got to his feet.

Towering head and shoulders above the errant schoolboy, Cunliffe enquired conversationally, "Do you know where I expect to see you end up in life, Hughes?"

"I can't imagine, sir. But I have the feeling you're just about to tell me."

Several of Harry's classmates tittered.

Cunliffe looked around the room and roared, "*SILENCE!*" He looked down at Harry again. "I expect to see you sweeping the streets, or driving a bus, Hughes."

"Well, you know what they say, sir. We're all entitled to our own opinion."

Several of his classmates tittered, again.

"*SILENCE*!" Not the fittest of men, the science master's face was now a dark shade of purple.

The school nickname for the science master was Boris, so named after Boris Karloff, star of the black and white horror movies of years gone by. If anything, Boris Karloff had been better looking. He certainly had better teeth. The science master's teeth were badly nicotine-stained from years of smoking three packets of cigarettes a day. The mints he sucked to try and cover up the fact that he had chronic halitosis made so little difference he could have saved his money.

"You think you're clever, don't you, Hughes?"

Harry stood his ground. "Averagely clever I would say, sir." He stared Boris out. "But that's not really for me to say, is it … *sir*?" He placed heavy emphasised on the *sir*.

Boris realised he had met his match and was not going to win. He said quietly, "Sit down, Hughes." He turned and walked back to the front of the classroom.

While Boris was still walking, and he himself was still on his feet, Harry had the urge to turn round and smirk at his classmates to show them how clever he was. But he realised that if he did this and they all began to laugh, Boris would realise something was going on and it could all come down on him like a ton of bricks. He decided discretion was the better art of valour and sat down.

He waited until Boris started writing on the blackboard, and then he called, "Excuse me, sir."

Boris stiffened visibly. He stopped writing and turned and looked at Harry. "What is it, Hughes?"

Harry held up the chalk for all to see. "You forgot the chalk, sir. Shall I throw it back to you?"

The tension in the air was palpable. Everybody wanted to laugh, but nobody dared. One look at the expression on Boris's face was enough to dissuade even the most foolhardy. Then one boy, who had been struggling to contain himself, broke wind loudly. The fart was worthy of an entry in the Guinness Book of Records and the classroom erupted. Soon, everyone was howling with laughter, their shoulders shaking, tears rolling down their cheeks and stamping their feet. It was absolute bedlam.

When the noise finally subsided and there was some semblance of order in the room, Boris said quietly, "Be at the headmaster's study at three-thirty, Hughes." He looked in the box for another piece of chalk. The box was empty. He walked back to Harry's desk and took the chalk from him. "One day, Hughes," he muttered darkly.

When Sue arrived to pick up the children that afternoon, Veronica's Mercedes was parked across from the school. The top was down and Veronica was in the driver's seat soaking up the sun and listening to classical music on her car's CD player. Sue parked behind her, switched off her engine, and got out of her car.

When Veronica saw the dress Sue was wearing, her eyebrows shot up and she sat bolt upright. "My God! Don't you look the bees' knees? Wherever did you buy that dress? I *love* it."

Sue gave her a twirl. "I'm glad you like it. I bought it from Harvey Nick's in London this morning. I figured that if Max can take on Europe without discussing it with me, I can buy myself a dress. He'll kill me when he finds out what it cost, but I'm past caring. And anyway, he can afford it."

"Attagirl!" Veronica raised her hand. "Girl power. High five."

They high-fived each other and burst into peals of laughter.

Veronica climbed out of the car and they stood by the side of the car talking.

"I had a word with Randy last night," she said, "and it took me over half an hour to even get him to admit he *had* punched Harry, let alone tell me *why*. I still think it has something to do with a girl, but who can tell with boys of their age?"

Children started to come out of the school.

Randy was one of the first out. As he approached his mother's car, he looked Sue up and down and said exactly what his mother had said, "Well, don't *you* look the bees' knees."

Sue beamed. "You know something, Veronica; I could get to like this son of yours."

Veronica laughed. "We have to go, Randy, I have things to do. Sue, I'll let you know if I learn any more about what we were talking about."

Sue thank her and waved them off. She walked back to her people carrier.

First of her brood out was Clarissa, as was usually the case. She skipped happily over to her mother's vehicle.

Sue leaned over and opened the front nearside door for her.

"Hello, precious. Had a good day?"

"Yes. Thank you, Mummy. You look very pretty today."

"Why thank you, my darling."

"Is that a new dress? I haven't seen it before."

"Yes, it is. I bought it this morning."

"It's lovely."

"Good, I'm glad you like it."

Amanda walked out of the school with three female friends. She knew perfectly well her mother was waiting for her, but she waited until her mother had tooted her horn before taking leave of her friends. Sue's vehicle was a seven-seater with three rows of seat and Amanda climbed into the seat immediately behind her mother.

"Mummy's got a new dress," Clarissa said.

"So I see," Amanda said. "It's a lovely dress, Mummy."

"Thank you, sweetheart. Where's Harry, by the way? He's usually first out."

"He's probably still in with the headmaster," Amanda replied.

Wondering what her son had been up to now, Sue's heart sank. She met her daughter's eyes in her rear-view mirror. "Why is he in with Mr Godley, Amanda?"

Amanda had no desire to snitch on her brother. "I don't think that's for me to say, Mummy. I think you'd better ask him."

Harry walked out of the school a little after 4pm. His head was hanging and his shoulders were drooping. He looked as if he could burst into tears at any moment.

A boarder, a boy of about his age, was hanging around near the school entrance, and he saw Harry and called, "Nice one this morning, Harry."

Harry scowled at him. "Who asked you for your opinion?"

"Hey, come on, Harry," the boy said. "I'm on your side."

"Get lost."

By dint of his usually being the first out of school, Harry invariably had the first choice of seat in his mother's vehicle and he usually sat in the front passenger seat next to her. When he opened the front door on the passenger side and found Clarissa sitting there he was far from pleased. "That's my seat," he said. "So scoot."

"I got here first and Mummy said I can sit here, so there." Clarissa stuck her tongue out at him.

"Harry, that seat is for whoever gets out of school first and wants to sit there," Sue said. "And when it's *your* car, *you* can decide who sits where."

Harry realised he wasn't going to get his own way. With a face almost long enough to trip over, he slammed the front door and climbed into the rear of the vehicle and threw himself into one of the seats in the third row.

Sue had her window down and she had heard what he had said to the other boy. She eyed her son in her rear-view mirror. "What on earth was all that about, Harry? That boy was just trying to be nice. There was no need to bite his head off."

Harry ignored her and looked away.

Sue swivelled round in her seat. "And why did Mr Godley want to see you?"

"I don't want to talk about it."

"Well, I do. And this car isn't going anywhere until you tell me why the headmaster wanted see you."

"I had a run in with Boris."

"Do you mean Mr Cunliffe? The science master?"

"Yes, Mr Cunliffe. Boris." Under his breath Harry muttered, "Silly old goat."

"And?"

"I just had a run in with him, that's all. It was no big deal."

Sue looked to Amanda for guidance. "Amanda, do you know what happened?"

"Mummy, I'm sorry but I don't think it's for me to say."

"I can tell you what happened, Mummy?" Clarissa said. "Everybody in the school knows what happened. They've all been talking about it."

"Shut up, you little creep," Harry hissed.

"Harry, I won't tell you again, you do not talk to your sister like that! No thank you, Clarissa. I'll let Amanda tell me what happened. So, Amanda, you have the floor. What happened?"

Amanda knew she had no choice. "Well, I wasn't there, but as I understand it, Harry wasn't listening to Boris, and ..."

"Mr Cunliffe, if you please, Amanda."

Amanda corrected herself. "Mr Cunliffe. Well Mr Cunliffe threw a piece of chalk at Harry, but it backfired on him because Harry made a complete fool of him. The whole school's been talking about it all day."

Sue sighed. Addressing Harry through her rear-view mirror, she said, "What *are* we going to do with you, Harry? Teachers are not people to be made fools of, they are highly educated people who are there to be respected. Haven't we brought you up to at least understand that?"

"Well he started it," Harry huffed. "He shouldn't have thrown a piece of chalk at me. That was stupid. I could have him for assault."

"No, Harry, *you* started it. You should have been listening. I happen to know Mr Cunliffe is a Cambridge graduate and he's probably been teaching since long before you were born. I won't have you treating him like a fool. Do you understand, Harry?"

"Yes, I understand," Harry said in a voice his mother had to strain to hear.

"What did Mr Godley say?"

"He said what you just said. Can we go home now? I'm hungry."

Sue knew she wasn't going to get any more out of him and she sighed and shook her head at the futility of even trying. She switched on the engine and put the vehicle in gear. Before she drove away, she eyeballed Harry in her mirror and said sternly, "When we get home, young man, you are going straight to your room and you're staying there. There'll be no TV, and no surfing the net. And I'm putting a call in to your father in New York this evening. We'll see what he has to say."

"See if I care," Harry kept his voice low enough that his mother would not be able to hear him.

That evening, Sue managed to contact Max at a little after 9pm UK time. Fortunately, she caught him when he had time to talk. He listened in silence as she told him what had happened.

"Put him on," Max said. He sounded annoyed.

Sue carried the phone to the foot of the stairs. "Harry, your father wants to talk to you."

The door to Harry's bedroom opened and Harry walked out. Sue could see even from down here that he was ashen-faced. He walked slowly down the stairs and, avoiding eye contact with his mother, took the phone from her.

Sue walked away. She had tears in her eyes. She hated doing this, but Harry had to be told and he wasn't listening to her.

Harry waited until he was sure his mother was out of earshot, and then said quietly into the phone, "It's Harry, Dad. Mum said you wanted a word with me."

Chapter 7

Harry's father had come down on him hard on the phone, and Harry felt a certain sense of satisfaction that, when he went missing, his father would feel responsible. And serve him right. But what Harry was doing had nothing to do with his father, and he wasn't leaving home, he was just going away for a few days.

He knew his mother would be worried when she came in to wake him for school in the morning and found he wasn't there, but he didn't plan to have her worrying for long. As soon as he was settled in at Paul's parents' house in Surrey, he would switch on his mobile and call her and tell her where he was and when he was coming home.

For a sixteen year-old, Paul seemed wise beyond his years, and while no one else seemed to understand him, Paul understood him perfectly. It was Paul who had suggested it might be better if he did not tell his parents what he was doing or where he was going, his thinking being that since he and Harry had never met, they would probably not let him go.

Getting away from the hassle he had been getting from home and school was just what the doctor ordered, and Harry was looking forward to spending a few days away from it all. Paul's parent's house in Surrey sounded amazing, with its heated outdoor swimming pool, stables and tennis court.

Since his father had chewed him out on the phone, Harry's mother had come into his room three times to see if he was alright. Each time, she had tried to get him to tell her what his father had said to him, and each time he had told her he didn't want to talk about it.

For the last hour and a half, Harry had been lying in bed in his jeans, T-shirt and socks, with his duvet pulled up under his chin, pretending to be asleep.

His black leather sports bag lay on the carpet on the far side of his bed. In it were a clean T-shirt, three pairs of underpants, a clean pair of pyjamas, a spare pair of socks and his toiletries, which comprised his toothbrush, a tube of toothpaste, a roll-on deodorant and his comb. On the carpet next to his sports bag lay his brown leather bomber jacket, which his parents had bought him for his fifteenth birthday and which he loved. Next to that lay his Timberland boat shoes, which were the most comfortable shoes he possessed. His mobile phone, which was fully charged, lay nestled in one of his shoes together with its charger, while in the other shoe lay his house keys and his wallet. He had organised everything like this so he would know where to find them in the dark when it was time to leave.

His mother had got into bed just after 11pm and, as usual, she had read for half an hour or so, before switching off her bedside lamp.

Now, the house was in darkness. The only sound Harry could hear was Clarissa talking in her sleep.

Earlier, a dog fox had barked. There were a lot of foxes in the area and the family had lived in the house long enough for Harry to be able to distinguish between the bark of a dog fox, and a vixen. And an owl had hooted twice. It sounded to have come from the big old beech tree at the foot of the drive. Ten minutes or so ago, Harry had heard a car in the distance. But now the night was still and quiet.

It was time to go.

He desperately needed a pee, but it would have to wait. He considered it would be tempting providence to use the family bathroom along the landing. How would he explain being fully dressed at a quarter-to-one in the morning in the event Amanda or Clarissa got up to use the loo? He had the option to use the downstairs loo, but he had been brought up to always flush the loo after he had used it, and the downstairs loo had a particularly noisy flush. But there were hedges almost all the way to Knebworth and at this time of night there would be nobody around to see him relieving himself.

He climbed out of bed and fumbled around in the darkness for his shoes. He took out of them the items he had put in them and put his mobile in the left-hand pocket of his jeans, his house keys in the right-hand pocket and his wallet in the back pocket. Then he put on his shoes and tied the leather laces, before standing up and putting on his bomber jacket. He loved his bomber jacket. He loved the softness and the smell of the leather. It was lined with wool and it was warm, almost like wearing a warm blanket. Then, he picked up his sports bag which was zipped and ready to go.

He felt his way around his bed and crept to the door. He opened the door and stepped silently out on to the landing. He always slept with his door closed, so he closed it quietly behind him.

He crept silently downstairs, walked across the carpeted hall, opened the front door and stepped out into the chilly night air. The front door had a Yale lock and he knew that if he didn't use the key to close the door the lock would click as it engaged. He didn't want to risk waking someone, so he used his key.

The owl hooted. He had been right; it *was* in the tree at the foot of the drive. He told himself it was hooting because it was glad of his company, and – despite the fact that he couldn't see the bird - he grinned up at it.

His composite-soled shoes made no sound on the tarmac drive, and a couple of minutes later he was breathing a sigh of relief as he relieved himself against a hedge a couple of hundred yards from the house.

It took him a little over twenty-five minutes to walk to Knebworth, and in that time the only sign of life he saw was a fox chasing a rabbit in a field. He walked by the light of a three-quarter moon in an otherwise cloudless sky.

The lane led him to the junction with the road from Stevenage to Welwyn Garden City in the middle of Knebworth, where he stopped to take stock.

His ultimate objective was to get to London's King's Cross railway station, and to do that he needed to take a train. Two hundred yards down the road ahead of him was Knebworth station, but Harry knew that the train he was planning to catch did not stop at Knebworth; he would have to catch it at Welwyn Garden City, which was five miles away. The question was, how was he going to get to Welwyn Garden City? Ideally, he would thumb a lift, always assuming of course there was a lift to be had, and there was sign of any traffic at the moment. Failing that, he would have to walk. He had calculated he could walk it in a little over an hour.

He was on the point of starting to walk, when he saw the lights of a car coming from the direction of Stevenage. As luck would have it, it was a taxi, and its light was on, which meant it was available, Harry flagged it down.

The driver let the nearside window down and leant over and asked in a kindly tone of voice, "Does your mother know you're out at this time of night?"

"I don't mean to be rude," Harry said, "but I don't think that's any of your business."

"Where do you want to go?"

"The train station in Welwyn Garden City. Will you take me, or shall I walk?"

"I'll take you. I can't have someone of your age walking the streets at this time of night."

Harry opened the back door and climbed in.

The route to Welwyn Garden City took them past the school and in his rear-view mirror the driver noticed Harry looking at it.

"Is that your school?" he asked.

Harry nodded. "Yes, it is."

"Who, or what, are you running away from?"

"Who says I'm running away?" Harry said. From then on he declined to answer any more of the driver's questions.

When they got to the train station, the driver told Harry the fare would be £20.

Harry's father had instilled in him that it was better to make a friend than an enemy, and that unless there was some reason not to, such as poor service, to tip generously.

He had told Harry that he usually tipped ten percent, and Harry handed the driver a £20 note and two pound-coins.

The driver handed the two pound-coins back to him. "You keep them," he said. "You might need them. And you watch yourself out there. Not everybody's as nice as I am."

Hardly surprisingly, given the time of night, the station was deserted. And, with the exception of an isolated light here and there, it was in darkness.

Harry had taken the train into London from here on a number of occasions with his mother and he knew from which platform London-bound trains left. He made his way to the platform by means of the covered footbridge and when he got there he checked his watch to see how long he would have to wait. It was 1.47am, which meant he had almost two hours to wait.

There was a hot drink dispenser on the platform, and using the two pound coins the taxi driver had given back to him, he got himself a hot chocolate. He sat down on a bench to drink it.

It was way past his bedtime and he was struggling to stay awake. After making sure there were no undesirables lurking in the dark inner recesses of the station, he made himself a bed on the bench using his sports bag as a pillow. He set the alarm on his mobile for 4am, and lay down and closed his eyes.

He slept soundly until his mobile woke him. Ten minutes later, he was boarding the train to London.

Chapter 8

Brrring ... brrring ... brrring ... brrring ... brrring.

"Hullo." It was 2.15am New York time, and Max's voice was dark brown with sleep.

"Max, Harry's gone." It was 7.15am UK time and there was no disguising the panic in Sue's voice.

"*What*?" His voice was clearer now, sharper. "What do you mean, he's *gone*?"

"Max, for heaven's sake, what do you *think* I mean? He's gone. He's left home."

"Are you sure?"

"Would I be waking you up in the middle of the night if I wasn't? Of course, I'm sure. He's taken his sports bag, underwear, a spare T-shirt, his bomber jacket, his Timberland shoes, his toothbrush and the spare tube of toothpaste from the family bathroom. I'm telling you, Max, he's gone."

"Sue, give me a second to think about this." Max sat up in his hotel bed and switched on a bedside lamp. "How long has he been gone?"

"I don't know. His bed was cold when I went in to wake him for school this morning. He must have gone sometime during the night."

"So his bed *had* been slept in."

"Yes, it had. He was in bed and asleep when I popped my head round his door before I went to bed at eleven o'clock. At least I *thought* he was asleep. What on earth did you say to him last night?"

"I told him he should be grateful he's attending a school of that calibre, and that money doesn't grow on trees. I told him he should thank his lucky stars he's getting the education he's getting and that I didn't get anything *like* the start in life he's getting. And I told him that if he didn't buck up his ideas I might have to think about taking him out of the school."

"Well, that's just brilliant, Max. When he needs his father's support the most, you come down on him like a ton of bricks."

"Sue, that's not fair. I'm three thousand miles away and you phone me up and tell me there's a problem and you want me to do something about it, and then when I do something about it, you criticise me for how I handled it. If you had told me how you wanted me to play it ..."

"You should *know* how to play it, Max."

"Ah, here we go again. Because I'm his father, you mean."

"Absentee father more like."

"Oh, *please*. Sue, this isn't getting us anywhere. What do you plan to do?"

"What do *I* plan to do?"

"Come on, Sue. I can't do anything from here. Especially at twenty-past-two in the morning."

"You could tell me you were going to take the next plane home."

"Sue, I *can't* come home. Well, not at the moment. There's too much going on here."

"No, of course you can't. Silly of me to even suggest it. Your business is much more important than your son. Don't worry, Max. I'll take care of it. I always do." She slammed the phone down.

A minute later, Max called back.

"He's probably doing it to teach me a lesson. I admit I was a bit heavy-handed with him, but he's a sensible boy, and I'm sure he's not going to do anything silly. I assume you've called the police."

"I haven't called them yet. We've both been giving him a hard time recently and I thought he might just be trying to scare us, so I thought I'd wait until after I'd dropped the girls off at the school before I called them. Just in case he might be there."

"Sounds like a plan. Sue, I'm sorry but I need to get some sleep. I have a busy day tomorrow. Keep me posted. Okay?"

Sue sighed. "Alright, Max. I'll keep you posted." She put the phone down.

When Sue and the girls climbed into the people carrier to go to school, Clarissa, who had been in tears since learning her brother was missing, asked her mother if she could stay at home and help her look for him.

"Better not, poppet," Sue said. "I've no idea what's going to happen today, and it's probably better that I'm on my own. But I'll tell you all about it when I pick you up from school this afternoon. That's a promise."

When they got to the school, Sue let the girls get out of the car and then hurried into the school to find Mrs Godley.

Mrs Godley greeted her with a smile. "Hello, my dear. This is a nice surprise."

Sue tried to keep the panic out of her voice. "Mutti, Harry isn't here, is he? He wasn't in his bed when I went in to wake him for school this morning and he seems to have left home."

"Oh my dear, I'm so very sorry," Mrs Godley said, concern written all over her face. "As to whether he's here at the school, not to my knowledge he isn't. I'm sure I would know if he were." Her face clouded. "I do hope it has nothing to do with what my husband said to him yesterday."

"I'm sure it was nothing your husband said, Mutti. More likely what his father said to him later." Sue told her what Max had said to Harry over the phone.

"Have you informed the police, Sue?"

"Not yet, I wanted to check with you, first." Sue bit back a sob. "Oh God! I hope we find him."

Mrs Godley put her arm round Sue's shoulder and gave her a little hug. "Chin up, my dear. I'm sure he'll turn up safe and sound very soon."

Sue couldn't decide whether to drive straight to the police station, or drive home and call them. In case Harry had come home in her absence, she chose the latter option.

The police said they would send someone straight round.

Shortly after she had called the police, Veronica phoned. "I've just heard. It's all over the school. Could you use some company?"

Tears welled up in Sue's eyes. "Bless you, Veronica. I'd love some company."

"I'll be right over. Have you called the police?"

"They're on their way."

"Is Max coming home?"

"What do you think?"

Veronica was round within fifteen minutes. Sue was letting her into the house when a marked police car pulled into the drive and parked behind Veronica's car. Two uniformed officers got out, one male, one female. The policewoman looked so young that Sue was reminded of the adage that you realise you're getting older when the police start looking younger.

After they had all introduced themselves, Sue led the way into the house and then into the living room.

Veronica excused herself, saying that since they didn't need her for this she would make them all some tea. She headed off to the kitchen.

The policewoman, who had introduced herself as Kate, took charge. As they all sat down, she took a pad and pencil from the breast pocket of her uniform. "As I understand it, Mrs Hughes, you reported your son missing at 8.50am this morning."

"Yes, I first realised he was missing when I went to wake him for school just after 7am. I went to the school before I called you to make sure he hadn't stayed the night there."

"The school being?"

Sue gave her the name of the school.

The officers looked at each other.

Kate asked, "Had his bed been slept in?"

"Yes it had, but it was cold, so he must have been gone for some time."

"When did you last see your son?"

"At around 11pm last night. I popped my head round the door just before I went to bed. He was in bed, sleeping. Or at least, he seemed to be."

"Has your son … it's Harry, isn't it?"

"Yes, Harry."

"Has Harry ever done anything like this before?"

"No, he hasn't. But …"

Kate looked up from her notes. "But what?"

Sue sighed. "I'd better start at the beginning. It started yesterday morning when Harry wasn't listening in class and the science master threw a piece of chalk at him. Harry's response earned him a visit to the headmaster's study. I got on at him about it, then last evening, my husband, Harry's father, who's in New York on business, gave him a hard time about it over the phone. Max, my husband, thinks Harry might have done this to teach him a lesson for being heavy handed with him."

Kate made a note. "Was anything else bothering Harry?"

"There *has* been something bothering him, and for some time now, but he refuses to say what it is."

Sue had just finished explaining about the problems they had been having with Harry when Veronica walked in with tea on a tray. She put the tray on the coffee table. "Milk everyone?"

"And two sugars for me," the policeman said.

"Milk, but no sugar for me, thank you," Kate said.

After Veronica had handed everyone their tea, Sue suggested she might want to sit in on this as her input might be useful.

"Fine," Veronica said, taking a seat.

"Could it be a problem over a girl?" Kate asked.

"We don't think so," Sue said. "Do we, Veronica?"

"No, we don't," Veronica said, shaking her head. "But there is something bothering him. He and my son Randy are in the same class at school, and they used to be the best of friends, but for some reason neither he nor Randy seem to want to talk about, Randy knocked Harry down recently."

"It could be something and nothing," Kate said. She made a note anyway.

"Does your son have a mobile, Mrs Hughes?" the policeman asked.

"Yes, he does. And before you ask, I *have* tried calling him. I've been calling him every fifteen minutes since I realised he was missing. His phone's switched off."

"Isn't it possible to locate someone through a mobile phone even when it's switched off?" Veronica asked.

"If the battery hasn't been taken out of it, yes it is," the policeman replied.

"We'll look into that," Kate said, making another note. "What's his mobile number, Mrs Hughes?"

Kate checked the list in her own mobile to find Harry's number.

Kate wrote it down, and then asked, "How does Harry get on with his father? As a rule, I mean."

"He gets on all right with him, I suppose," Sue replied. "But his father is away so often that they don't really know each other."

"I assume Harry took some money with him," Kate said. "Would you happen to know how much?"

"Not offhand I wouldn't, but I know how I can find out. He keeps his money in an old Quality Street tin in his bedroom, and I know how much he had in it two days ago."

Kate said, "I assume he has a computer."

"Yes, he has a computer. That's in his bedroom, too."

"Then before we do anything else, I think we should take a look at it."

Sue led the way upstairs.

Harry kept his Quality Street tin behind his sweaters on the top shelf of a fitted wardrobe that ran the full length of the wall. When Sue opened it, Kate remarked on what a tidy boy Harry was.

"He always has been," Sue said. "If the rest of the family were half as tidy as Harry, it would make my job a good deal easier." She moved the sweaters to one side and took the tin down. "There should be over four hundred pounds in here," she said. "I know that because I needed to pay my cleaner the other day and I didn't have enough money in my purse. Harry lent me thirty pounds. He counted it out in front of me."

The tin was empty.

"So he has about four hundred pounds on him," Kate said.

Sue nodded. "Yes."

"Is this Harry?" the policeman said, picking up a silver-framed photograph of a tousle-haired teenaged boy with freckles on his nose. He was wearing a school blazer, which the two officers could see was hanging in his wardrobe.

Sue smiled fondly at the photograph. "Yes, that's Harry. That picture was taken at the school prize-giving last year. He won a prize for being the most improved pupil in the school. We were so proud of him. I wish we knew what had gone wrong between then and now. He's a different boy, today."

"Could we take the picture with us?" The policeman asked. "We'll let you have it back in due course."

"Yes, of course you can."

There was the sound of the phone ringing in the hall downstairs.

Veronica was sitting in the living room reading a magazine. She put the magazine down, got to her feet, walked into the hall and called, "Shall I get that, Sue?"

"Please, Veronica. Tell whoever it is that I'll call them back."

Sue pointed out Harry's laptop.

The policeman asked if the computer was password protected.

"Yes, it is, but I know the password. It's my mother's middle name, Gwendolyn."

Kate sat down at Harry's desk and raised the lid on the laptop. She switched it on. When the screen came to life and asked for the password, she entered it.

Veronica called, "Sue, it's Max."

"That's my husband," Sue said. "He's calling from New York. I'd better take it." She hurried down the stairs and took the phone, mouthing *thank you* to Veronica. "Yes, Max?"

"I was worried and I couldn't sleep. Are you all right?"

"I'm fine. The police are here."

"Do they have any ideas?"

"Not yet. They're still asking questions. Harry's taken everything he had in his Quality Street tin, which was about four hundred pounds, so it looks as if he isn't planning to come home any time soon."

"Perhaps a search of his computer will yield something."

"They're looking at it as we speak."

"Good. Well, I just called to check you were okay. I'd better go, Sue, I need to try and get back to sleep. I'll call you again later in the day." He hung up.

Sue put the phone down and went back upstairs.

The two police officers were looking at emails on Harry's laptop, and they were staring intently at the screen.

"It fits," Kate was saying to her colleague.

"Like a glove," her colleague said.

Kate glanced at her watch. "Shute! We need to call this in, there's not a moment to lose."

The policeman headed for the bedroom door.

"What fits?" Sue said.

Kate quickly closed the lid on the laptop and got to her feet. "A taxi driver reported picking up a boy of about Harry's age in Knebworth at around 1.00am this morning. He said the boy told him he was going to London, and asked him to take him to the train station in Welwyn Garden City. He said the boy admitted that the school they passed on the way was the school he attended. It was the school you mentioned earlier, and we've found emails corroborating Harry's trip to London. We need to call this in urgently. I have to go, Mrs Hughes. I'll call you as soon as we know something"

The policeman spoke into the phone-unit attached to the shoulder of his uniform as he raced down the stairs, Kate hard at his heels.

Chapter 9

Harry stood on the main concourse at London's King's Cross station with his sports bag at his feet. He had spruced himself up in the men's toilet; taking off his T-shirt and washing his face and under his arms, before brushing his teeth and combing his hair.

Since he had got off the train from Welwyn Garden City, he had tried to sleep on several occasions, but each time he had laid down on a bench, a member of the station staff had moved him on. He was beginning to understand how a vagrant must feel.

He couldn't wait to meet Paul. He was so interesting and it was amazing how much he knew. Whatever subject Harry had brought up over the six weeks they had been exchanging messages on an Internet chat room site, Paul had an answer. It was a pity he hadn't been able to email a photograph of himself, but if he didn't have a digital camera, he didn't have a digital camera. Harry had emailed him a picture of himself, the one in the silver frame in his bedroom. He had taken it out of its frame, and scanned it into his computer, before emailing it to him. So when he got off the train, at least Paul would know what *he* looked like, so there should be no difficulty linking up.

The 10.47am arrival from Edinburgh was due in less than ten minutes. The arrangement was that Harry would wait by the ticket collector's barrier. He had already checked at which platform the train would arrive and he wandered over. The morning rush hour had been over for some time, and there were now very few people about.

Harry had no qualms whatsoever about meeting Paul. He was even comfortable with the thought of meeting Paul's parents, whom he felt sure would be very nice people. Even though he had never met Paul, he saw him as his new best friend. At least he had never given him any aggravation. When Paul had suggested getting together, Harry had willingly given him his mobile phone number. He had asked Paul for his mobile number, but Paul had explained that he had lost his mobile and had not got around to replacing it. He had said he should have a new mobile by the time they met.

The Edinburgh train arrived on time and Harry stood and watched until the last passenger had disembarked. No-one resembling the description Paul had given him of himself had disembarked and Harry was beginning to think he had missed the train. Either that, or he had decided not to come.

Harry was standing there wondering what to do, when a man in a business suit approached him. He had walked into the station from the entrance that led to the taxi rank.

"Hello, Harry," he said, smiling broadly, "I'm Paul's father. Paul's missed the train. He called me from Edinburgh and asked me to meet you. He sends his apologies and said to tell you he'll be on the next train and that he's looking forward to meeting you this evening. So, if you're ready, I have a car waiting outside."

To Harry, something didn't feel right. In Paul's emails, he had spoken of attending a private school in Edinburgh, and he had talked a lot about Scotland, as if he knew it well. He had also talked a lot about his father and, while he had never actually said his father was Scottish, Harry had always assumed this to be the case. But there was nothing remotely Scottish about this man. He did have an accent, but it certainly wasn't a Scottish one. With his short dark curly hair and his swarthy complexion, Harry thought he looked more like an Arab, than a Scotsman.

As he stood there assessing the situation, a piece of advice his father had given him came to mind, *If you're not sure of something, follow your gut feeling. If it doesn't feel right, don't do it.* And Harry's gut feeling was telling him that something was definitely not right. In fact, alarm bells were ringing loudly in his brain. Instead of following the man, who had turned to leave, he said, "How do I know you are who you say you are?"

The man turned back and nodded approvingly. "Paul was right," he said, "you *are* a bright boy. And you're right to be cautious. So you know I am who I say I am, I've brought copies of some of the emails you and Paul have been exchanging. Paul emailed them down to me after he missed his train this morning." From the inside pocket of his jacket, the man withdrew what Harry could see were copies of Yahoo emails. He used Yahoo email himself, and he knew Paul did too, but he still wasn't convinced. He declined to take them.

Suddenly, there was the pounding of heavy feet and they were surrounded by large uniformed police officers.

A man in a business suit strolled over and smiled at the man claiming to be Paul's father. "I'll take those, Achmed," he said, taking the emails from the man's hand.

"So, DCI Schembri, we meet again," the man said, seemingly unfazed at being the object of interest of so many police officers. "This is beginning to feel like déjà vu. And you're still wasting your time, and you know it."

"We'll see about that," Schembri said. He read a couple of the emails. "So, you're Paul this time, and you're sixteen and you're Scottish. The last time we met, you were Alex, you were fifteen and you were English. I can't remember what you were the time before that. I'll say one thing for you, Achmed; no-one can accuse you of not having a vivid imagination."

"So what," Achmed said with a shrug. "You know there's nothing you can do."

The detective smiled grimly. "If you're referring to your diplomatic immunity, you can forget it. It won't work for you this time. Not with evidence like this." He waved the emails in the Arab's face. "And in case you're thinking of claiming you don't know where these came from, or that we planted them on you, we have evidence on film of every move you made since you got out of the Mercedes outside the station. This time, my friend, you are going down. I'm arresting you on suspicion of grooming a minor." He read him his rights and instructed one of his officers to, "Cuff him."

"Hands behind your back," a burly policeman growled.

"Did we get the two in the Mercedes?" Schembri asked.

"Yes, we got them," another officer said.

Harry was thoroughly bewildered. "Would somebody mind telling me what's going on?"

Sue had heard nothing since the two police officers had hurried away from the house earlier that morning, and she was frantic with worry.

To give her moral support, Veronica had stayed all morning, and for lunch, which in Sue's case had amounted to a cup of tea and a piece of toast and marmalade. She had no appetite for food. Veronica had not been gone for more than a few minutes, when the phone rang.

Hoping it was news about Harry, she ran into the hall and snatched it up.

"Hello, yes?"

"Mrs Hughes?" It was a man's voice; a voice she didn't recognise.

"Speaking."

"It's DCI Bob Schembri, of Covent Garden CID."

"Have you found Harry?"

"Yes, we've found him. And I'm pleased to tell you that he's absolutely fine."

The adrenaline rush Sue experienced made her feel quite faint. "Oh, thank God! I've been frantic. You've no idea what's been going through my mind. He's not in any trouble, is he?"

The detective chuckled. "No, he's not in any trouble. Quite the contrary, in fact. He's actually being very useful to us."

"Sorry?"

"It's complicated. Mrs Hughes, I wonder if you could come up to London."

"Yes, of course. When?"

"Today. As soon as possible, in fact. I'd like you and Harry here together, because there's something you both should know."

"Right, well I have to pick up my daughters from school at 3.30pm, but I can drop them off at a friend's and take the train. I should be able to get into London by 5.00/5.30pm, depending on the times of the trains."

"5.00/5.30pm will be fine. In the meantime, we'll continue to pick Harry's brains. He's a very clever boy, Mrs Hughes. You and your husband must be very proud of him. And speaking of your husband, I understand from Harry that he's away on business. I'll need to speak to him when he gets back."

"He'll be back in his office on Monday morning. Chief Inspector, would you pass on a message to Harry for me?"

"Yes, of course."

"Would you tell him that as far as I'm concerned, he's not in any trouble?"

"I'll be happy to. I'm sure he'll be happy to hear that. He's been worried about what you're going to say to him."

After Sue had hung up, she dialled Max's mobile. It went into voice mail, so she dialled the number of the company's head office. She told the switchboard operator who she was, and asked to speak to her husband.

"He's in the morning meeting with the president of the company, Mrs Hughes. And the president doesn't like his meetings to be interrupted. May I ask if it's important?"

"It's important to me," Sue said. "And I would hope it will be to Max."

"I can give him a message when he gets out of the meeting."

"Please do. Tell him that Harry's been found and that he's safe and well."

"I assume he'll know who Harry is?"

"He should do, although I sometimes think he forgets. Harry's his son."

Sue hung up and phoned the school.

Mrs Godley was delighted with the news. "Oh, my dear, I'm so pleased. Would you like me to pass on the news to Amanda and Clarissa?"

"That's kind of you, Mutti, but I think I'd rather tell them myself. I'm sure there'll be floods of tears when they hear that Harry is safe, especially from Clarissa."

Then she phoned Veronica. "They've found him."

"Oh, thank God! Is he all right?"

"He's fine."

"Where did they find him?"

"They haven't said, but he's at Covent Garden police station and I've been asked to go up there."

"Do you want me to pick up the girls? I can keep them here while you're in town."

"Thanks for the offer, but I think it would better if I picked them up myself. There'll be floods of tears when Clarissa hears the news. But I will drop them off and leave them with you, if that's okay. I'll pick them up again when I get back from London."

"Of course, it's okay. I'll feed them, so you've no need to worry about that. I bet Max was relieved."

"I couldn't get hold of him. He was in a meeting. I had to leave a message with their receptionist."

"Oh Sue, how *frustrating* for you."

"Tell me about it!"

Sue hated tube trains, especially in the rush hour, and when she got to London she took a taxi from King's Cross to Covent Garden police station.

When Harry saw her, he threw his arms round her and wept. "I'm sorry, Mum. I'll never do anything like that again. It was a stupid thing to do."

Sue brushed away his tears with her thumb. "Never mind, sweetheart. You're safe now."

Schembri introduced himself and pulled out a chair for her. He had someone organise coffee.

"Where did you find him?" Sue asked.

"At King's Cross station. He was waiting for somebody he thought was a boy of his own age to get off a train from Edinburgh, and this is why I wanted to talk to you face-to-face. Your son has had a very lucky escape. He was actually met by a middle-aged Arab who had been pretending to be a sixteen-year-old schoolboy. This man is part of a gang operating out of an embassy in London under the cover of diplomatic immunity. They have been grooming boys of Harry's age for the sex trade in the Middle East, and if we hadn't got there when we did, Harry would have been drugged, whisked off in a waiting car, driven out to a private airfield in Essex, and flown out of the country, probably never to be seen again."

The colour drained from Sue's face.

Schembri had not previously told Harry what he had just told his mother, preferring to wait until his mother was there so he could tell them together. "You see, Harry," he said. "You see what might have happened to you?"

Harry nodded glumly.

Now over the initial shock, Sue said, "Harry, I know things have been difficult for you recently, but why did you feel the need to run away?"

"I wasn't running away," Harry protested.

"If I could explain," Schembri said. "Like boys who have not been as lucky as Harry and have been caught out, Harry had been exchanging messages over an Internet chat line with someone he thought was a boy of his own age. These people are very clever and very plausible, and I certainly don't blame Harry. He just happened to be in the wrong place at the wrong time."

"Is Dad angry with me?" Harry said.

Sue shook her head. "No, Harry, he's not angry with you. He's just relieved you're safe and well. Just as I am."

The detective leaned forward in his chair, his expression deadly serious. "Mrs Hughes, I can't impress on you enough the seriousness of what might have happened if we hadn't turned up when we did. In the last fifteen months, thirteen boys of Harry's age have been abducted from the Home Counties, and even though we've had Interpol and all the other international police networks working with us, they have vanished without trace."

Sue turned to her son. "You see, Harry. You see what might have happened."

"I know." Harry looked a picture of abject misery.

"The thing is, Mrs Hughes," the detective continued, "we have three people in custody as a result of Harry's quick thinking, all of them known to us, and the problem is that they have diplomatic immunity. We need to put them away this time. To cut to the chase, I need to know if you and your husband would be agreeable to Harry being called as a witness. The lawyers representing these people will be using the considerable means they have at their disposal to get their clients released. We've been after these people for a long time now, and we finally have the evidence to put them away. But we need Harry in the witness box."

"But if these are such determined people, Chief Inspector, wouldn't putting Harry in the witness box put him at risk?"

"I'd be lying if I didn't say that was a possibility, Mrs Hughes, but we can do something about that. My immediate concern is that if we don't inform the Criminal Prosecution Service we have someone prepared to enter the witness box, they might not agree to a trial, in which case these people could slip through our fingers again. The fact that they have diplomatic immunity can be a real problem in cases like this."

"So if we don't agree to Harry going in the witness box, these abductions are likely to continue?"

"It's a distinct possibility."

Sue had heard enough. "Then, yes, of course Harry must go in the witness box."

"Do you think your husband will see it that way?"

"Well, I can't speak for my husband, but I would be very surprised if he didn't."

The detective turned to Harry. "How would *you* feel about going in the witness box, Harry?"

Harry shrugged. "I'm with Mum. If it would mean you having to let them go if I didn't, I have to. We can't let it happen to anybody else."

Schembri smiled. "Good! Well, I think that about wraps things up for the moment." He got a business card from a box on his desk and handed it to Sue. "If you'd have your husband call me on this number at the earliest opportunity. As I said, there's no time to lose."

That evening, Sue phoned Max and told him what had happened. And she told him what Schembri had said about putting Harry in the witness box. "He didn't think the CPS would agree to a trial unless we agreed to it."

"Which, knowing the kind of people we're dealing with, could be putting Harry at risk," Max said.

"Well, yes, but it could be putting other boys at risk if we didn't. They have to be stopped, Max."

"Does Harry have an opinion on the subject?"

"The detective asked him that, and Harry agrees he should do it."

"How is he, after today's experience?"

"Well, he's obviously had a stressful day, but he seems none the worse for his adventure. It's certainly taught him a lesson. He won't be going on Internet chat sites again in a hurry."

"I'm glad to hear it. Is he there?"

"He went to bed early. He hardy got any sleep last night and he's worn out."

"Tell him I'm proud of him."

"It would carry a lot more weight if you told him yourself. Why don't you make time in your busy schedule to call him after school tomorrow? It would really make his day if he knew he would be talking to you when he got home."

"I'm sorry, Sue, but I can't tomorrow. I'm going to be busy. There are some heavy hitters coming in from out of state."

"Could you call him the next day. You surely won't be working on a Saturday?"

"I'm afraid not. The president of the company has invited me to his home in the Hamptons for a barbecue lunch. He wants me to meet his family. And he's taking me sailing afterwards. By the time I get back to New York, it will be time to catch the overnight flight back to London."

Sue wasn't going to let it go. "Then call him on your mobile during the day. I'm sure the president of the company won't object to you talking to your son, especially after what Harry's been through. If fact, if he knew what Harry had been through, he would probably *insist* on you talking to him."

"Sue, I'll be home on Sunday morning. There'll be plenty of time to talk to Harry then. I'm sorry, Sue, I have to go." He hung up before Sue had a chance to respond.

As Sue put the phone down, she muttered, "If you're having steak for dinner this evening, Max, make sure you chew it properly. I would hate it to choke you."

Chapter 10

On the Sunday morning, Max arrived home to the sound of the church bells summoning the villagers to the morning service.

Sue, who was vacuuming the hall carpet, saw the Jaguar pull into the drive. She switched off the vacuum cleaner and walked to the foot of the stairs. "Harry, your dad's home." She opened the front door and stepped outside.

Harry took the stairs, two at a time. He charged out of the house as his father was getting out of his car. "Hi, Dad. Can I help you with your suitcase?"

Max looked at him in astonishment. He could scarcely believe the change in him. He seemed like a different boy. There was no sign of the surly attitude now.

Sue smiled. "I said you'd see a change in him."

Max ruffled Harry's hair." Of course you can help me with my suitcase. But I warn you, it's heavy." He walked to the rear of the car and opened the boot.

"I'm in the newspapers," Harry said, struggling to lift his father's heavy suitcase.

Max frowned.

"There's an article about him in the morning paper," Sue explained.

Max looked at her in a way that suggested he thought she was somehow responsible for Harry being in the papers.

"Don't look at me like that," she huffed. "I'm not responsible for what they put in the papers."

Clarissa ran out of the house, followed closely by Amanda.

"Daddy, Daddy." Clarissa raised her arms for a hug.

"Hello, young lady." Max picked her up and hugged her.

"Did you bring me a present?"

"I'm sorry, poppet, I didn't have time. I've been really busy. I'll bring you one from my next trip, I promise."

"Hello, Daddy," Amanda said. "Congratulations on your new appointment."

"Thank you, sweetheart," Max said, giving her a hug.

"Does it mean you'll be away from home even more now, Dad?" Harry asked, lugging his father's suitcase towards the house.

Max ducked the question. He pecked Sue on the cheek.

"Is that the best you can do after you've been away a week," she said.

He grinned. "Sorry." He took her in his arms and gave her a proper kiss.

After they gone into the house and closed the door, Harry asked, "Do you want to read the article now, Dad?"

"Harry, why don't you let your father get some sleep first," Sue said. "He's been travelling all night; he must be exhausted."

"Ooh," Harry wailed.

Sue mouthed '*Try and be nice to him*' at her husband.

Max got the message. "Your mother's right, Harry, I *am* tired. I'll read it when I wake up, and I promise you it will have my undivided attention." He went upstairs, undressed and got straight into bed. He was asleep almost before his head hit the pillow.

When he finally surfaced, five hours later, Sue was doing some ironing in the kitchen. She heard him call, "Did somebody mention coffee?"

Harry was doing his homework on the kitchen table. His ears pricked up. "Dad's awake."

Sue stood the iron on its stand and switched it off at the plug. "Harry, why don't you get me the newspaper? Your father can read it while he's having his coffee."

Harry punched the air. "*Yes!* Can I be there when he's reading it?"

"I'm not sure that's such a good idea, Harry. I don't think I want you to hear his language when he sees what they've written"

"Ooh," Harry wailed.

"It's not what they've written about you he's going to be upset about, because he's going to be very proud of you; it's the information they've given out about the school he's going to be upset about."

Sue took Max's coffee and the newspaper upstairs to find him sitting up in bed with the curtains still closed. "Welcome to the land of the living," she said. She put his coffee on the nightstand beside him and dropped the newspaper on the bed. She drew back the curtains and opened a window to let in some fresh air,

Max yawned. "I'm so bloody tired I don't know what day of the week it is."

Sue had him sit forward so she could plump up his pillows for him.

He settled back and reached for his coffee. He took a sip. "Mmm, that's nice." He put his coffee down again and picked up the newspaper. It was the Sunday Telegraph. "So he's hit the nationals," he observed.

"Which is a pity," Sue said, "because knowing how these things can escalate, it wouldn't surprise me to see journalists camping on our doorstep before long."

Max pulled a face. "That's the last thing we need."

Sue had opened the paper at the appropriate page and Max began to read the article. It was entitled:

'SCHOOLBOY OUTWITS ARAB GANG INVOLVED IN ABDUCTIONS: POLICE SAY DIPLOMATIC IMMUNITY WON'T SAVE THEM THIS TIME.'

"I don't believe it!" Max said, snapping the paper angrily. "Jesus Christ! Are these people out of their minds?" He read on.

'A fifteen-year-old schoolboy from an exclusive private school twenty-five miles north of London has inadvertently provided police with the evidence they have been seeking to break up an Arab gang responsible for kidnapping British schoolboys and shipping them off to the sex trade in the Middle East.

"For Christ's sake," Max exclaimed, "there *is* only one school fitting that description twenty-five miles north of London. Now they know which school he attends." He read on.

'James, not his real name – we've given him this name to protect his identity...

"To protect his identity?" Max snorted. "Who are they trying to kid? Now they've identified the school, and given his age, they might just as well have given his full name and what he likes for breakfast."

He took another sip of his coffee and read on.

'*James refused to accept that the man who confronted him at London's Kings Cross station was the man he had been corresponding with through an Internet chat room. He believed he was meeting a sixteen year-old Scottish boy off a train from Edinburgh, but a man claiming to be the sixteen year-old's father came instead. The man, who is of Middle Eastern origin, is employed by an embassy in London and is known to the police, showed James copies of emails he had been exchanging with him to try and convince him he was who he had said he was, but James was having none of it.*

Max nodded approvingly. "Good for Harry."

'*The police had seen the exchange of emails on the fifteen year-old's laptop at his Hertfordshire home, and they were lying in wait. They videotaped the forty-eight year-old Arab as he walked into the station and showed James the emails.*

On being informed of his rights, the man is reported to have laughed, telling the police that, because of his diplomatic immunity, there was nothing they could do. But the police are confident that, this time, his diplomatic immunity will not help him, or the other two employees of the same embassy who were sitting in a waiting Mercedes outside the station. It is thought that if James had not stood his ground, he would have been drugged and driven to a private landing strip in Essex and flown out of the country.

The police believe that this gang may have abducted as many as thirteen Home Counties schoolboys in the last fifteen months.

Parents anxious for information about missing sons have been contacting the police, after being approached by this newspaper.

Well done, James. This paper salutes you.'

"Damn fool journalists," Max growled. He lowered the paper. "What was that detective's name again?"

"DCI Schembri," Sue said. "He gave me his card."

"Good. Because after this," Max slapped the newspaper with the back of his hand, "unless I'm very much mistaken, Harry's going to need police protection."

Chapter 11

The following day, Monday, Sue had just dropped the children off at school and was about to drive away, when Mrs Godley hurried out, a look of concern on her face.

Sue let her window down. "Good morning, Mutti. You look worried. Is something wrong?"

"Sue, thank goodness I caught you. The school is awash with the news of the article about Harry in the papers, and there's a journalist sniffing around. Don't look now, my dear, but he's standing by the silver car under the oak tree. He has a photographer with him, although I'm not sure where he is. Oh, I see him. He's sitting in the car."

Sue adjusted her electrically-controlled wing mirror so she could see the man. He was leaning against the car with his arms folded, watching vehicles arriving and dropping off children. He displayed the attitude of someone who felt he had every right to be there. He looked relaxed enough, but it was obvious he was missing nothing.

"They turned up while the boarders were having breakfast," Mrs Godley continued. "My husband asked them to leave, but they refused, saying they had as much right to be there as anybody, and that the story was in the public interest. If they don't leave soon, my husband's going to call the police. My dear, they obviously don't know who you are and they obviously haven't identified Harry, so why don't you slip away while the going's good. I'll phone you if there are any developments I think you should know about."

As Sue made a three-point turn, without being obvious about it she watched Mrs Godley walk over and speak to the journalist.

He was a short, skinny man in a rumpled suit. He listened to what Mrs Godley had to say and then shrugged and raised his hands in a gesture suggesting he was asking her what she expected him to do about it.

Mrs Godley looked furious. She turned and marched into the school.

Sue was approaching the main road at the bottom of the drive when Veronica's car turned in. Randy was in the seat beside her.

They both stopped and let their windows down.

"Morning," Veronica said. "We saw the article about Harry. Not good news, that."

"Tell me about it," Sue said. "There's a journalist and a photographer snooping round, at the school."

"Have they called the police?"

They were blocking the drive and a Range Rover with blacked-out windows pulled up behind Veronica, its headlights flashing. The young female driver sat impatiently tapping her steering wheel with her fingernail and glaring at them.

"Do you fancy some coffee?" Veronica asked.

"I'd love some."

"Right, I'll drop Randy off and I'll see you at home in ten minutes."

There was a long continuous blast from a set of twin-tone horns from the Range Rover, almost deafening them.

"All right, all right," Veronica said, looking in her rear-view mirror to see who was making all the fuss. She recognised the driver. "Oh, it's her. Well *she* can wait."

"We'd better move," Sue said. "See you shortly." She took her foot off the brake.

"Bye, Auntie Sue," Randy called. "And well done to Harry."

Sue gave him a sad little smile. "If only it were that simple, Randy."

The recommended speed limit for the drive was 10 mph. Veronica drove at 7 mph, leaving the woman in the Range Rover unable to pass and flashing her lights and fuming.

When Max got to his office, he took DCI Schembri's business card out of his wallet and phoned him.

The detective thanked him for contacting him so promptly.

"No problem," Max said, slipping his jacket off and hanging it on the back of his chair. "Have you seen the article about Harry, in the paper?" He sat down at his desk.

"Yes, I've seen it," Schembri confirmed. "It was unfortunate, but not entirely unexpected."

"Is it something we need to be worried about?"

"Not at this stage, I wouldn't have thought."

"Well, you understand these things better than I do. By the way, Chief Inspector, my wife called me while I was on the train and told me there was a journalist and a photographer sniffing round at the school."

"That's too bad," Schembri said, "but I can't say I'm surprised. Once the media get a sniff of something, they go at it like a dog with a bone. Has Mrs Hughes spoken to you about putting Harry in the witness box?"

"Yes, she has. And I agree with her. As far as I'm concerned, it's a no-brainer. How could we *not* agree? These people have to be stopped."

"I was hoping you would say that," Schembri said. "Now I have your decision, we can go to the CPS and try and persuade them to agree to take it to trial."

"What are the chances?"

"Hard to say. Best guess, seventy/thirty, our favour."

"I hope you've got them locked safely away in the meantime."

"Have no fear. Short of somebody rolling up with a division of Sherman tanks, they're not going anywhere."

"So where do we go from here, Chief Inspector?"

"I think that for the moment, Mr Hughes, all you and I need to do is keep in touch. Perhaps you would let me have your mobile phone number."

Sue spent the rest of the morning with Veronica, and she stayed for lunch. On her way home, she stopped off at the local butcher's for some lamb chops for the family's evening meal.

As she was about to turn into the drive at home, she was surprised to see a small grey car in the drive. It was not a car she recognised, and neither was the man who was ringing the front doorbell. He was a huge, shaven-headed individual with the build of an all-in wrestler. He reminded Sue of the character *Odd Job* in the James Bond movie *Goldfinger*. She could see he wasn't alone. There was another man sitting at the wheel of the car. She had the presence of mind to drive straight on.

There were two pubs in the village: the Red Lion, which was just down the lane from the house, and the Pig and Whistle, which was on the other side of the village. Deeming it prudent to get as far from the house as possible, before calling Max and asking him what she should do, she drove to the Pig and Whistle, where she parked in the car park at the rear of the pub. It was 1.35pm and the thatched-roofed pub was plying its busy lunchtime trade, with several other cars in the car park. She parked in such a way that she could not be seen from the lane. She switched off her engine and phoned Max.

After she had told him what she had seen, he asked her to describe the car.

"Do you remember when we all went out for dinner on Harry's fifteenth birthday?" she said.

"Yes?"

"And Harry showed us the car he would like, on his mobile?"

"A Subaru Impreza. Yes?"

"Well, it looked like one of those. It was a grey one."

"I don't like the sound of that," Max said. "Apart from boy racers, the only people who drive cars like that are people who feel the need to outrun the police. I think I'd better have a word with DCI Schembri,"

"Have you spoken to him, Max?"

"Yes, I called him when I got to the office."

"What shall I do?"

"I suggest you sit tight for a few minutes, and then drive back to the house. If they're still there, drive straight on and call me again. If they're still there, I'll dial 999. Leave it for about ten minutes. They'll probably have realised by then that nobody's home and hopefully they'll have gone."

"I hope you're right," Sue said. "I didn't like the look of them at all."

As Max had suggested, Sue left it for ten minutes and then drove back to the house. There was no sign of the grey car, or the men, but thinking it could be tempting providence to leave her vehicle on view in case they came back, she put it straight in the garage, closing the electrically-operated up-and-over door from the remote she kept in the car, before switching off her engine and getting out of the vehicle.

She was just about to go through the connecting door that led into the house, when she heard a car in the drive.

Convinced the two men had come back again, she froze. She heard the car engine die, followed momentarily by two male voices. Sue was quite well-travelled, but they were speaking in a language that was totally unfamiliar to her. She heard footsteps on the drive, and then she heard the doorbell ring in the house.

She felt certain that the man at the door earlier had not been a journalist, he had looked much too threatening to be a journalist, and she was convinced it was him again. Her heart began to thump painfully in her chest.

There was a window in the garage, and it occurred to her that, unless she moved from where she stood, if they walked round the house and looked in through the window they would see her. So she knelt down on the blind side of her vehicle.

She heard the doorbell ring again.

Her knee was hurting from kneeling on the hard concrete floor, but she didn't dare move in case they heard her. In fact, she hardly dared to breathe.

The doorbell rang again.

After what seemed an age, she heard footsteps on the drive again, then two doors slam and a car engine start up. She heard them drive away, the exhaust note sounding like that of a sports car.

With her heart still pounding, but finally able to breathe again, she got to her feet. She stretched her aching back and rubbed her sore knee. She let herself into the house and checked through the window in the hall to make sure the car had gone, before phoning Max and telling him what had just happened.

"Sue, I can't come back immediately," he said, "but if anybody comes to the door from now on, check who it is - without letting them see you, if possible – and, if it's them, or somebody you're not sure about, dial 999. I'll get home as soon as I can, but it won't be before this evening. I'm up to the eyes in it, here."

Sue felt better for hearing his voice. Her heart was getting back to its normal rhythm and, after they had ended the call, she put the kettle on to make herself some tea. The kettle had just boiled when Mrs Godley phoned.

"I've been trying to get hold of you, my dear," she said.

"Sorry, Mutti, I've been out since I left the school this morning, and I've only just got back. Has something happened?"

"I'm afraid it has, my dear. The police removed the journalist and his photographer soon after you left this morning, but they came back while the children were at lunch. They marched into the dining room as bold as brass and marched straight over to Harry's table. Consensus among the teachers who were present was that somebody had pointed him out to them. Before anyone knew what was happening, they had taken a photograph of him. They even had him smile for the camera. So, I'm afraid Harry's picture is now going to be in the papers, too."

Sue let Mrs Godley continue without saying a word. After what had happened since she got out of bed this morning, nothing would surprise her.

"And to top it all, as they walked out of the dining room, the journalist told a member of staff, and I quote his words verbatim: '*This will put the school on the map.*' The cheek of the man! I'm so very sorry, my dear. We are simply not equipped to handle this kind of thing."

Mrs Godley sounded so upset that, despite how stressed she was feeling herself, Sue felt quite sorry for her. "Don't give it another thought, Mutti," she said. "If Princess Di couldn't keep the paparazzi at bay, what hope is there for mere mortals like us?"

Max didn't get home until after 8pm. He apologised for being late, blaming it on having to clear a week's worth of work because of his trip to New York.

Sue grilled him a lamp chop and steamed some vegetables, and sat with him while he ate. As they talked, he told her he had phoned Schembri after she had called him the second time that afternoon.

"And what did he say?"

"He said that, since we didn't actually know who the two men were, and they had not actually done anything wrong, there wasn't much he could say, above and beyond

107

to keep him informed and to dial 999 if you feel worried, or threatened."

"It's alright for him," Sue said. "He spends his time surrounded by police officers. Did he say anything else of interest?"

Max stared at her, wondering if he should tell her what Schembri had told him that afternoon. He decided she should know. "Well, I wasn't sure I was going to tell you this, Sue, but Schembri told me that in the car the Arabs had waiting to whisk Harry away, they found a syringe containing enough drugs to knock out a full-grown man for up to twenty-four hours."

He was just in time to catch Sue as she collapsed in a dead faint.

Chapter 12

Max put his briefcase on the overhead rack and settled himself into a forward-facing seat. Every year, he bought himself a first-class season ticket because at peak times this was the only way he was guaranteed a seat. The other occupants of the carriage were businessmen with their faces buried in their newspapers, and they ignored him, as he ignored them. It was a daily ritual, an unwritten rule, and anyone daring to break it by opening his mouth got either an energetic snap of a paper, or a raised eyebrow for his pains. This had been going on ever since Max had started commuting, and rather than being irritated by it, as he once had, he was now amused by it.

There were two reasons Max took the train to the office, one of them being that it was less stressful than driving. Driving into London at peak times was a nightmare. The other reason was that it gave him a chance to read a newspaper and see what was going on in the world.

As usual, he had bought a Daily Telegraph at Welwyn Garden City station. The Telegraph had been his paper of choice for some time. From his perspective, it reported the news as it was, not with some agenda behind it. As the train gathered speed, he settled down to read.

There was nothing of interest on the front page, or the second, but when he saw what was on the third page, he swore under his breath. There, as large as life, was Harry sitting at a table in his school uniform in what was clearly the school dining room.

The caption read: **Harry Hughes – School Hero: Fifteen Year-old Fools Abductors.**

In the picture, Harry was laughing, and because of the way in which the picture and the caption had been presented, it looked as if he were laughing at how clever he had been in fooling his would-be abductors; as if he were thumbing his nose at them.

The article gave his age, his form, and how long he had been a pupil at the school. It also stated that he had two sisters at the school. Mercifully, it had not named Amanda or Clarissa.

Max was travelling in a quiet coach, so he got up and walked to the standing area near the toilet at the end of the carriage. Planting his feet to steady himself against the rocking motion of the speeding train, he phoned Sue.

"Don't these idiots *realise* the danger they're putting people in?" he ranted. "Are they *insane*? Don't they *care*?" He stepped aside to let someone pass. "Sue, I think we should consider taking Harry out of school. At least until this blows over."

"But what about his schooling, Max? DCI Schembri said it could go on for ages. Think what it would do to his education."

Max sighed. "You're right. Forget I said that, it was just a knee-jerk reaction. Do you still think we should put Harry in the witness box?"

"Of course, I do. Why should I have changed my mind about that? Why do you ask?"

"Sue, I was thinking of you. You're the one with strange men coming to the door."

When Sue dropped the children off at school that morning, Mrs Godley hurried out.

Sue let the window down. "Good morning, Mutti."

Mrs Godley dispensed with pleasantries. "Have you seen the paper today?"

Sue knocked her vehicle out of gear and put the handbrake on. "I haven't," she said, "but Max has. And he's absolutely furious. His initial reaction was that we might have to think about taking Harry out of school. But from what we've been told, this thing could drag on for ages and we have his education to think of."

"That's what I wanted to talk to you about, my dear. My husband and I have an idea that you and your husband might want to think about. It occurs to us that with all the information the media has published about Harry, it might be worth thinking about boarding him here at the school?"

Sue switched her engine off. "But that could put the school in the firing line, Mutti. Would you want that responsibility?"

"My husband and I are aware of that, my dear, but we're prepared to take that chance. It's Harry's education we're thinking of. If he boarded, he would never be alone; there's always someone here. And there's a police station less than a mile away."

Sue thought the idea was certainly worth considering. "Thank you, Mutti," she said. "I'll have a word with Max about it."

When she got home, Sue put a call through to Max's office, but she was told he was in a meeting. His secretary offered to interrupt the meeting, but Sue told her not to bother, that it could wait until he got home.

The phone in the hall was a cordless model that sat on its base on a table across the hall from the window. On the wall over the table was a mirror, and as Sue put the phone back in its cradle, a movement in the mirror caught her eye.

What she saw scared the living daylights out of her.

The grey car that had been parked in the drive the previous day was pulling into the drive.

Her immediate thought was to pretend she wasn't in, but that wasn't an option, because apart from the fact that her vehicle was parked in the drive, the man who had been ringing the doorbell the previous day was sitting in the front passenger seat and he was looking straight at her.

She moved quickly away from the window and stood there frozen, not knowing what to do. She was like a deer caught in car headlights.

When the doorbell rang, even though she had been expecting it to ring, she almost jumped out of her skin. She had no option but to answer it.

The man at the door was a Romanian by the name of Constantin Boguescu. He and the driver of the car, his cousin Nicu, were members of a gang of thugs-for-hire. Their speciality was intimidation, in all its forms. They had access to firearms and were not afraid to use them. Boguescu was a fit and muscular thirty-one-year-old, and were it not for the knife scar running from the side of his eye to the side of his mouth, he would be a good-looking man. He wore jeans that were torn at the knees, T-shirt, and a well-worn leather jacket.

Max was a big man, but this man made mincemeat of him.

"Mrs Hughes?" he said.

There seemed no point in denying that she was indeed Mrs Hughes. "Yes, I'm Mrs Hughes."

Boguescu smiled, tight scar tissue pulling up the corner of his mouth and turning his smile into a leer. "Nice picture of Harry in paper."

Sue wanted to slam the door in his face, but she knew a foot in the door would prevent it.

"I bring message for you. Message is Harry must not—repeat, *not*—appear in witness box."

A bright light flashed, and Sue realised that the driver of the car was now standing in the drive and had taken a photograph of her.

Boguescu's eyes were hard. "If we forced to come back…" He left the sentence unfinished, but the way he drew his finger across his throat left no doubt as to what he was getting at. As if that were not enough, he added, "You have nice home, and it would be shame if house burned down while family sleeping."

The police were there within minutes of Sue calling them. It was Kate, the young policewoman who had been instrumental in finding the vital emails on Harry's laptop when he went missing, and her male colleague again.

"You look as white as a sheet," Kate said, as Sue led them into the living room. "Can I make you some tea?"

Sue wailed, "They threatened to burn the house down while the family was sleeping, and they took a picture of me."

Kate put her arm around her. "I'm sure they don't mean it; they're just trying to scare you. Let me make you that tea."

Sue dabbed the tears from her eyes with a tissue. "I'll make it," she said. "You don't know where anything is."

Kate was having none of it. "Then, I'll just have to find it, won't I? You sit down and tell Gary what happened."

Sue and Gary sat in adjacent armchairs and Gary produced a pad and pencil. "Mrs Hughes, when you called it in, you mentioned that the two men had also come yesterday. Why didn't you call it in then?"

"They came twice yesterday," Sue said. She explained the circumstances. "I suppose I didn't call it in because they hadn't actually done anything wrong. Looking back on it, it was stupid not to. But that's being wise after the event."

"Can you describe them?"

Sue described Boguescu in detail. When it came to the other man, the man who was driving the car, because she had barely seen him, there wasn't much she could say about him except that he was tall and thin and he was wearing a shabby dark blue suit.

"And you say you thought the accent of the man at the door was Eastern European."

"Yes. I can't be sure, but I had the feeling he might be Bulgarian, or Romanian. He had that Slavic look about him and his voice had that kind of lilt."

Gary wrote it all down. "Can you describe the car?"

Sue described the car in as much detail as she could remember.

"When I described it to my husband, he said it sounded like a Subaru Impreza."

"Finding that shouldn't be too difficult. There are very few Subaru Imprezas in this neck of the woods, let alone light grey ones. I don't suppose you got the registration number."

"No, I'm sorry. I only saw it twice, and then only briefly."

There was a rattle of crockery from the kitchen.

"Apart from the colour, can you tell me anything else about the car?"

"Such as?"

"Well, was it new? Old? Good condition? Poor condition?"

"I couldn't tell you what condition it was in, but it certainly didn't look like a new car."

"Did you notice anything else about it? Anything unusual?"

When Sue cast her mind back and concentrated, she *did* remember something unusual about the car. "Yes, there was something unusual about it," she said. "They had parked it in such a way that I got a look at the back of the car, and it had a square rear number plate."

Gary looked up from his notes. "Are you sure about that, Mrs Hughes? Please, think carefully. This could be important."

"Yes, I'm a hundred percent sure. It had a square number plate. It didn't register at the time, but when I think back, it struck me as odd because most cars have rectangular number plates."

"I wish everyone was as observant as you are," Gary said.

Kate walked in with the tea. She had found a tray and she put it on the coffee table.

Gary got to his feet. "I've got a description of the car, Kate, and I need to call it in. It sounds like a grey import from Japan."

"That should make it easier to find," Kate said.

Sue and Kate sipped their tea while Gary made his call.

"Harry's becoming quite a celebrity in the media," Kate observed.

"Yes, he is," Sue agreed. "And more's the pity."

"Was he any the worse for his early morning jaunt into London?"

"He was tired, because he'd had very little sleep the night before and it had been an exhausting day for him, but otherwise he was fine. Interestingly, what happened in London seems to have done him some good. Before it kicked off, he was quiet and introverted. Now we can't shut him up."

Sue had called Max immediately after calling the police, and he got home a couple of hours after the police had left. In order to get home as quickly as possible, he had taken a taxi instead of the train.

"So what do we do now?" he said, throwing himself into a chair.

"Heaven only knows," Sue replied. "Have you spoken to DCI Schembri?"

"Yes, I have. I called him from the taxi."

"And what did he say?"

"He said that things are happening far more quickly than he expected, and that we need to meet. He's driving up to see us this evening. He said to expect him around eight o'clock."

Sue looked Max in the eye. "Max, I hope you're not planning to make any trips in the foreseeable future,

116

because after what happened today, I'm not staying in this house if you're not here."

Chapter 13

DCI Schembri had told Max to expect him around 8pm, but it was almost 9pm when he finally arrived.

Max answered the door.

Schembri, who had a colleague with him, said, "Sorry, we're late. We couldn't get away from the office any earlier. One way or another, things are a bit hectic at the moment."

"No problem." Max let them in and closed the door. He extended his hand. "Max Hughes."

Schembri shook the outstretched hand. "Bob Schembri. And this is DS Patterson, who specialises in cases involving diplomatic immunity."

"Good evening, sir," Patterson said.

"Good evening, sergeant."

Sue walked down the hall from the living room and gave Schembri a warm smile. "So we meet again, Chief Inspector."

"Indeed we do, Mrs Hughes. And it's nice to see you again." Schembri introduced DS Patterson.

Sue nodded politely to Patterson. "Good evening, sergeant."

"Good evening, madam."

"Come on through, gentleman," Sue said, leading the way to the living room. "And thank you for coming all this way to see us, and especially at such short notice."

"No problem" Schembri said. "Things are happening a lot more quickly than I expected and, as I see it, there's no time to lose."

"Can I get you a drink, gentlemen?" Sue said. "Tea … coffee?"

"A glass of water for me, if I may," Schembri said.

"Sergeant?"

"Nothing for me, thank you."

Max sat the two detectives down while Sue went off to the kitchen.

Schembri looked round the spacious and well-appointed room. "You have a lovely home, Mr Hughes."

Max acknowledged the compliment with a smile and a thank you. "And it's Max, by the way. Which side of the River do you live on, Bob?" He was referring of course to the River Thames.

"I live on the south side," Schembri replied. "Close to Selsdon Park, in Surrey."

"I know Selsdon Park," Max said. "I've played golf there and I've entertained at the hotel. Lovely complex. Do you play golf, Bob?"

Schembri shook his head. "I've never had the time. I've always been too busy trying to catch criminals."

Sue came back with his glass of water.

Schembri thanked her and took a sip, before putting the glass down on a leather coaster on the coffee table.

"And speaking of criminals," Max said. "How's it going with the Arabs you have in custody?"

"So far, so good," Schembri replied. "They are still languishing at Her Majesty's pleasure. We have a meeting with their legal team in the morning."

"We're trying to get their diplomatic immunity waived," Patterson explained.

"How does that work?" Max asked.

Patterson sat forward in his chair with his elbows on his knees. "How it works, Mr Hughes, is that when a person with diplomatic immunity commits a serious offence, a serious offence being defined as an offence that might carry a custodial sentence of over twelve months …"

"Which, in the case of the three we have in custody will certainly be the case," Schembri interjected. "They'll be going down for a long time when this thing is sorted out. Sorry Dick, you were saying?"

Patterson did not seem to take offence at being interrupted. "As I was saying, when a person with diplomatic immunity commits a serious offence, a police officer, in this case DCI Schembri, submits a report to the DPG, which is the Diplomatic Protection Group of the Metropolitan Police, and a copy is forwarded to the Protocol Directorate at the FCO, which is the Foreign and Commonwealth Office. The Chief Crown Prosecutor will then review the case and decide whether the criteria for prosecution are satisfied. And that's where we are at the moment; waiting for his decision."

"And the Arabs' legal team are doing their level best to make sure we don't get it," Schembri said.

"They seem remarkably well-connected," Max said.

"They are," Schembri said. "We know enough about them to know that they are part of a well-funded organisation with tentacles extending all over Europe."

Sue said, "But Bob, if these people in the Middle East want boys for sex, why don't they just pick up boys locally? I've never been to the Middle East, but I'm sure they have rent boys over there. Why go to the trouble of abducting boys from England?"

"That's an interesting question, Sue. I'm sorry, may I call you Sue?"

"Yes, of course, you may."

"Well, probably the best way I can answer that is to liken it to how some men need a trophy wife they can parade around to impress their friends. These people in the Middle East need good-looking, well-educated boys from good homes. Boys they can parade in front of their friends without fear of them embarrassing them."

"Does that mean they look after the boys?" Sue asked.

Schembri slowly shook his head. "Not in the sense you mean. It's probably true that the boys will live in luxurious surroundings and will want for nothing, but in truth they will be nothing more than sex slaves, there to do their master's bidding."

"And when their master gets tired of them?" Max asked.

"Are you sure you really want to know?" Schembri said, glancing at Sue.

Sue's face was beginning to turn pale. "Can we change the subject?" she said, "This is beginning to make me feel sick."

"Sorry, darling," Max said, "Yes, of course, we can. Bob, what about the men who have been coming to the house?"

"It's because of them that I've driven straight up to see you," Schembri said. "The fact that they have been coming to the house in broad daylight, and so soon after we picked up the Arabs, demonstrates how serious these people are, and we need to be talking about getting you all into a secure location. And it's not just Harry I'm talking about; I mean all of you. If they are as determined as they seem to be, any one of you could be snatched."

Max was horrified. "Hang on a second, Bob," he said. "It's not that simple. We can't just up sticks, and leave. I have a business in London to run, and we have the children's schooling to think of."

"Mrs Godley's offer might go some way towards solving the problem?" Sue said. "At least, as far as the children are concerned."

Schembri asked her to explain what she was talking about.

Sue explained about Mrs Godley's offer to board Harry at the school. And then she added, "And it occurred to me that we could board Amanda and Clarissa as well."

Max threw his hands up in the air. "Whoa, whoa, whoa. Boarding Harry at the school is one thing, but boarding the girls as well is another matter entirely. If we are talking about boarding them until the Arabs come to trial, it could cost a fortune. I'm not made of money."

Sue looked him squarely in the eye. "What's more important Max, money, or the safety of your children?"

"Come on, Sue. That's not fair."

"Let's consider boarding the children at the school, *for the moment*," Schembri said. "I would have to check the school's security arrangements, talk to the headmaster, and discuss the idea with the local police, but the idea is not without merit."

Max said. "But what about you, Sue? If we did board all three children at the school, that would leave you on your own when I'm not here. I'm sure you realise that I can't put my business life on hold until this thing is over with, which means I *will* have to travel. How would we protect you?"

"I was just thinking about that," Sue said. "I'll have a word with Veronica. Perhaps she would let me stay with her while you're away."

"Which just leaves you, Max," Schembri said. "You shouldn't be on your own, either."

"You've no need to worry about me," Max said airily. "I can look after myself."

"You didn't see the size of the man at the door," Sue said.

Schembri looked at his watch. "I'm sorry, but Dick and I are going to have to love you and leave you. I have to drop Dick off on the way home, and I have to be in the office early in the morning to get briefed for the meeting with the Arab's lawyers. I'll call you in the morning, Max."

"Fine, I'll be in my office all day tomorrow."

"Okay. By the way, is Harry still up? I wouldn't want to leave without saying hello to him."

"He's in his room," Sue said, "I'll get him."

Harry came down in his pyjamas and dressing gown.

"Hey there, partner," Schembri said, raising his hand.

Harry grinned and slapped a high-five with him.

Schembri chatted with Harry for a couple of minutes before ruffling his hair and saying, "Sorry, partner, I have to go. But there was just one thing I wanted to say, and that is no more smiling for the camera. OK?"

Harry got the message. "OK."

Max saw the two detectives to their car.

It was a warm and pleasant evening and Schembri stopped by his car and cocked his head on one side, listening to the quietness of the countryside. Then, he sniffed the air.

"I envy you living out here," he told Max, "very few people, clean air and no traffic. I sometimes get tired of the madness of London."

He took his car key from his pocket and pressed the remote to unlock the doors. The indicator lights on the Audi flashed twice.

Patterson shook hands with Max and wished him goodnight.

"Goodnight, Dick," Max said, "It was nice meeting you."

"You too, sir."

Schembri climbed into the driving seat and let down the window before closing the door. "I'll call you tomorrow, Max," he said. He started the engine and put the car in gear.

"Thanks for coming, Bob," Max said. "Drive safely."

He stood and waved them off. The horse in the field across the lane looked at him and whinnied softly, as if in greeting. Max walked across the lane and stroked its neck. "If only our lives were as simple as yours," he murmured.

He stayed outside for a while, enjoying the late evening air.

When he got back into the house, Harry looked as if he had been crying.

Sue explained, "He's just beginning to realise the danger he's put the family in."

Harry looked at his father. "I'm sorry, Dad." A tear rolled down his cheek.

Max gave him a hug. "I should probably be apologising to you, Harry, because I'm partly to blame. If I'd spend more time with you … Shall we call it quits?"

"Please," Harry said.

Sue smiled, pleased with the reconciliation between father and son. "Off to bed now, Harry," she said. "Your father and I have a lot to talk about."

Chapter 14

The next morning, Sue dropped the children off at school and went in to find Mrs Godley.

"My dear, *of course,* you can board all three children," Mrs Godley said, beaming. "We would be *delighted* to have them." She took Sue's arm. "Let's talk in my husband's study."

When they were sitting comfortably, Sue said, "Mutti, it's subject to final approval by the Metropolitan Police. They say they will need to visit the school to check security, and talk to your husband, and the local police."

"Yes, of course. But my dear, what about you? After the dreadful experience you had yesterday, I do hope you won't be staying in that big house alone."

"I won't be alone," Sue assured her. "I expect to have something organised by the end of the day. At least, I hope so." She showed Mrs Godley a pair of crossed fingers.

Mrs Godley asked if Harry and Amanda would still be going to Italy with the school "You'll understand that I need to know if there will be any change to the numbers," she explained.

"Yes, of course," Sue said. "But at this stage, Mutti, I just don't know. I'll have to get back to you on that."

Before taking the children to school, Sue had called Veronica to ask if it would be convenient if she called round after dropping the children off, saying there was something she needed to talk to her about.

Veronica had said that, of course, it would be convenient and she would expect her a little after 9am.

It was a warm and sunny day and when Sue got to Veronica's they talked over coffee on the terrace at the rear of the property. Even though no fire had been lit, there was still the sweet smell of wood smoke. It seemed to ooze out of the very pores of the house.

Veronica listened open-mouthed as Sue told her about the two men coming to the house the previous day, and the detectives driving up from London later. After she had heard the whole story, Veronica exclaimed, "But *of course* you can stay here! In fact, I absolutely *insist* on it!"

"It will mean me sleeping here, *and* being with you during the day," Sue said. "Could you stand that much of my company?"

"You *idiot*, of course I could. In any case, Henry's hardly ever here and I would welcome the company. You can have the bedroom at the back of the house. It's got a lovely view over the woods. It's a bit draughty, because it's an old house, but the bed's comfortable. When would you want this arrangement to start?"

"Well, *now* really," Sue said. "I'm not supposed to be alone from now on. Will that be a problem?"

"Absolutely not."

"Will you need to discuss it with Henry first?"

Veronica shook her head. "Henry does as he's told. But he'll be delighted to have you stay, I know he will. Hey, I've just had an idea. Since you obviously have nothing planned for the rest of the day, and I certainly don't, what do you say we take a train into London, have lunch and a glass or two of wine somewhere nice, and then do a little *retail therapy* at Harvey Nick's."

"Sounds good to me," Sue said. "And when we've done that, why don't we drop in on Max? You've never seen his office, have you?"

"No, I haven't," Veronica said. "That sounds like a wonderful idea!"

"We'll need to be back in time to pick up the children from school."

"You're right. We'd better skip lunch, or just have a sandwich somewhere. Which car shall we take to the station? Yours, or mine?"

"No contest," Sue said. "I'll take a Mercedes sports car over a people carrier any day of the week."

As the inter-city express left Welwyn Garden City station and started to pick up speed, Sue brought up the subject of Mrs Godley asking if they still planned to go ahead with their holiday while the children were in Italy.

"I don't see why we shouldn't," Veronica said. "Especially since the villa's already been booked and we've paid a deposit on it. I can't see those morons who paid you a visit yesterday following the children to Italy, can you? And we adults should have nothing to worry about, because there'll be four of us."

Just as Veronica said this, the door to their first-class compartment slid open a few inches and a man tossed something about the size of a postcard into the compartment. He then walked on rapidly towards the front of the train. It had happened so quickly that neither of them had got a good look at him. Apart from him being tall and thin, the only thing they had noticed was that he was wearing a light-grey suit.

The object had landed face down on the floor and Veronica bent down and picked it up. She turned it over. "It's a picture of you," she said, handing it to Sue.

It was the picture one of the two men had taken of her when they came to the house the previous day. At the time, Sue had been terrified, but now she was sick and tired of feeling threatened and she was angry.

"You realise what this means," Veronica said.

"I know *exactly* what it means. It means they're following me. It also means they want me to *know* they're following me. I've had enough of this."

"Meaning?" Veronica said.

"Meaning I'm planning to put a stop to this nonsense, once and for all." Sue took her mobile out of her handbag. "How soon before we get to King's Cross, do you think? Half an hour?"

Veronica glanced out of the window. She took the train into London often enough to know pretty much where they were. "We passed Brookmans Park a couple of minutes ago. We should get to King's Cross in about twenty-five minutes."

Sue had put DCI Schembri's mobile number in her speed-dial list and she scrolled down the list and pressed the number.

Similarly, Schembri had Sue's number in his speed-dial list. He answered on the second ring. "Morning, Sue? What's up? I know you didn't call to talk about the weather."

"No, I didn't. Bob, a friend and I are on a train travelling from Welwyn Garden City to King's Cross." She explained about what had happened.

"Right," Schembri said, in a brisk business-like voice. 'Where's the train now?"

"We've just passed Brookman's Park. We should be at King's Cross in about twenty-five minutes."

"Give me a second ..."

Sue heard him barking instructions.

"Is the train crowded, Sue?"

"I've no idea, Bob. But it's an inter-city train, so I should think there'll be quite a lot people on it."

"Just give me a second ..." Schembri barked more instructions. "You still there?" He sounded to be breathing heavily, as if he were walking rapidly.

"Yes, I'm still here."

"Did you see who threw the picture?"

"We didn't see his face, because it happened too quickly. But we noticed it was a tall thin man and that he was wearing a light-grey suit."

"Does the train stop before it gets to Kings Cross?"

"Hang on a second. Veronica, do you happen to know if this train stops at Finsbury Park? I know some of them do."

"I can't be certain," Veronica replied. "But I think most of the inter-city trains do stop there, so I should think it probably will."

"We think it will stop at Finsbury Park, Bob, but we can't be certain."

"That won't help," Schembri said, "I can't get men to Finsbury Park in time. We'll just have to hope that the train doesn't stop there, or, if it does, that he doesn't get off there." He was now breathing very heavily. "Just a second, Sue." Sue heard car doors slamming, and then Schembri ordering, "King's Cross, and don't spare the horses! Put the blues and twos on. You still there, Sue?"

"Yes, I'm still here."

"Sue, I don't think you're in any danger. I think he threw the picture in to let you know he was there and to intimidate you. I can't see him doing anything silly on a crowded train. By the way, which way did he go? Did he go towards the front of the train, or the rear?"

Sue heard the sound of police sirens over the phone. "He went towards the front."

"And where in the train is your carriage situated? Is it at the front, the middle, or the rear?"

"I haven't a clue," Sue said. "I didn't notice. Do you have any idea where we are in the train, Veronica?"

"I've no idea," Veronica said, "I wasn't paying particular attention. At a guess, I'd say we are about in the middle."

"We think we're about in the middle of the train, Bob."

"All right, Sue. Now stay calm ..."

"I am calm. I'm just angry."

"Good, you stay that way. But, listen, don't go doing something you might live to regret. These are dangerous people we're dealing with. Now, here's what you do."

Sue listened carefully to what Schembri had to say, and then said, "Right, see you there." She ended the call and put her mobile back in her handbag.

"What's happening?" Veronica asked.

Sue was already on her feet. "We have to make our way to the front of the train. I'll explain on the way."

"Isn't this exciting," Veronica said, getting to her feet. "I haven't had this much fun in ages."

Sue saw a face she recognised after they had walked the length of four carriages. It was the man who had taken the photograph of her the previous day. He was sitting at the far end of the carriage and he was travelling with his back to the engine, meaning he was facing her. When he had taken the picture he had been wearing a blue suit; today he was wearing a light grey suit, but there was no doubting it was the same man. She had been so scared when he had taken the picture that she had thought she would never forget his face as long as she lived, but now, she felt nothing but contempt for him.

Like all the other economy-class carriages had been, the carriage was busy, with every seat taken and luggage everywhere, including on some of the tables.

Sue knew the man had seen her. The moment she had spotted him she could see that he had spotted her. He had then averted his eyes and stared through the window as if the suburbs of North London offered some morbid fascination for him.

He was sitting in an aisle seat right next to the door at the end of the carriage, which meant that when she stopped to open the sliding door into the next carriage, she would be standing right beside him. As she walked through the carriage, with Veronica immediately behind her, she forced herself not to look at him. When she stopped to press the illuminated button to open the door, she was standing a matter of inches from him. Angry or not, there was nothing she could do to stop her heart from beating almost uncontrollably.

He sat staring through the window, seemingly oblivious.

As she pressed the button to open the door, she glanced down at him. She noticed that his face was pockmarked and his hair was greasy. She also noticed there was a strong smell of body odour coming off him and the notion that his body odour might indicate he was as nervous as she was crossed her mind, a notion which; since he was obviously as hard as nails, she dismissed as ludicrous. She pressed the illuminated button and the door slid open. She stepped through.

Veronica stepped through behind her.

When the door had closed behind them, Veronica asked Sue if she had seen him.

"We just passed him."

"Do you mean the nasty piece of work next to the door? The one with the body odour?"

"That's the one."

"And he took the photograph?"

"Yep."

"God! He's awful. Do you think he saw you?"

"He saw me the moment we stepped into the carriage."

"And he just got a good look at me," Veronica said. "When you had stepped through the door, he stared at me as if committing my face to memory. I'm not surprised you were scared out there in the countryside when he came to the house yesterday. I would have run a mile."

"I had nowhere to run," Sue said.

They were standing in the area of the train in which people gathered prior to disembarkation, and it was evident they were at the front of the train because what would have been the door into the next carriage had been blocked off. They were first at the door, which meant they would be first off the train.

They were coming into Kings' Cross station and Veronica looked through the window to make sure they were on the side next to the platform. They were. People were now coming thick and fast behind them and a lengthy queue had begun to form.

Sue looked back to see what the man was doing. She could see the top of his head, which meant he had not yet left his seat. This was good news, because she and Veronica needed to get off the train as far ahead of him as possible, and there was no way he would get through the mass of humanity standing next to him. He would have to wait for the crush to disperse.

She watched him finally struggle to his feet, and it was a struggle because no one would make way for him. And then, when he did manage to get to his feet, for some inexplicable reason he tried to make his way towards the rear of the train, perhaps to leave the train at the opposite end of the carriage. Watching him struggle to get through the crush gave Sue a moment of intense pleasure. No one seemed to want to let him pass, and for the first time in her entire life, she was glad of the bloody-mindedness of the British public.

The train was now travelling very slowly and its brakes were starting to screech. There was a train parked on the other side of the platform ahead of them, which meant they were getting close to the buffers. Sue stood with her finger on the button, in readiness to press it the moment the train stopped.

The train stopped with a lurch and one last screech of brakes. The moment the light on the button came on, Sue pushed it, hard. The door hissed opened and she leapt out on to the platform.

Veronica leapt out immediately behind her.

In a smart dark blue two-piece suit, DCI Schembri looked like any another businessman waiting for a colleague off a train. He was standing on the other side of the ticket barrier. Standing a few feet away from him, and hidden behind hoardings, were six tall and heavily-built uniformed police officers.

Sue and Veronica were both wearing heels, but they sprinted for the ticket barrier like athletes in pursuit of an Olympic gold medal.

Once they were through the barrier, Schembri took them to one side. "Did you see him?" he asked Sue.

"Yes, I saw him," she panted.

"Describe him to me."

"He's tall and thin, with dark greasy hair and a pock-marked face. He's wearing a light-grey suit."

"Point him out to me when you see him. But don't let him see you. We don't want to spook him."

They stepped behind the hoarding, out of sight. Next to some of the uniformed officers, even Veronica looked small.

"You need to introduce me to your Chief Inspector," Veronica whispered in Sue's ear. "He's *very* good looking. Do you happen to know if he's married?"

Sue had to laugh. "Behave yourself." She peeped round the hoarding. People were flowing down the platform like a river of ants, but there was no sign yet of the man in the grey suit.

Nicu Boguescu finally made an appearance when most of the other passengers had left the train. He got off and caught up with an expensively-dressed and rather haughty-looking lady who was walking hand-in-hand with a well-dressed little girl with pigtails. He was trying to make conversation with, as if to give the impression he was travelling with her. She was studiously ignoring him, while the little girl was casting curious glances at him.

Sue caught Schembri's attention. "That's him," she said. "It's the man with the woman with the little girl with the pigtails."

"You're sure?"

"I'm absolutely certain. I won't forget *his* face in a hurry."

Schembri waited until Boguescu had passed through the ticket barrier, and then he stepped forward. "Excuse me, sir," he said. "I'd like a word with you."

Before Boguescu realised what was happening, his arms had been forced behind his back and he had been handcuffed.

The lady with the little girl walked on by. "Silly man," she said, giving Boguescu a disdainful look.

"Who was he, Grandmama?" the little girl asked.

"He was nobody, my darling. Nobody at all."

"Well, that's one less thug to worry about," Schembri said, as Boguescu was led away. "He won't have a team of lawyers trying to get *him* off."

"Speaking of lawyers," Sue said, "how was your meeting with the Arabs lawyers this morning?"

"It was a waste of their time and mine," Schembri said. "They're clutching at straws."

Sue introduced Schembri to Veronica and told him she would be staying with her when Max was away. "So you have no need to worry about me from now on," she said.

"So I see," Schembri said, smiling shrewdly. "From what I've seen today, it's not you I should be worried about, it's the thugs."

Chapter 15

Addressing her offspring in a hall strewn with school bags and suitcases, Sue said, "Now, children, you *do* understand what's happening?"

"Yes, Mum." Harry sighed. He sounded bored.

"Yes, Mummy," Amanda said.

"You'll be boarding until further notice. Mutti will take care of you, and …"

"But I want to stay with *you*, Mummy," Clarissa wailed. "*Please*, Mummy. *Please* don't send me away." Her eyes were brimming with tears.

Sue knelt down and hugged her. "I'm not sending you away, my darling. It's so we know you'll be safe, and it's only until those nasty men have gone away."

"But I won't be able to talk to you if I need you," Clarissa wailed. "Why can't I have a mobile? Harry and Amanda have mobiles."

Sue brushed a wayward lock of hair away from her daughter's eye. "I think you're too young to have a mobile, poppet. I'll buy you one when you're older." She got to her feet again. "What was I saying? Oh yes, as I've told you, I'll be staying with Auntie Veronica when Daddy's not here, and when she drops Randy off at school in the mornings I'll come in with her. And when Daddy gets home from work in the evenings and picks me up from Auntie Veronica's, we'll both come to the school. So we'll see each other twice a day. There won't be a problem with any of this because it's all been cleared with Mutti. If there are any changes to the plan, I'll text you. And if you need to contact me, text me, or call me. Now, are your mobiles charged? Harry?"

Harry sighed again. It was all so boring. "Yes, Mum." He drew out the *yes*.

Sue was getting tired of Harry's attitude. After perking up while he was the school hero, he had once again become sullen and uncooperative. "For goodness sake, Harry," she said, "you of all people should understand why this is necessary, so less of the attitude. Okay?"

Harry shrugged. "Whatever."

"Amanda, is your mobile charged?"

"Yes, Mummy. I charged it last night."

"And is your charger in your suitcase, Harry?"

"No, it's in my school bag."

Sue counted to five under her breath. "Amanda, do you have your charger."

"In my suitcase."

"But what if a bad man comes and takes me away?" Clarissa wailed. "How will I be able to tell you?"

Sue brushed the obstinate lock of hair from her daughter's eye again. It immediately bounced back. "No-one is coming to take you away, my darling, because I won't let them. Harry, I want you to look out for your sisters. You're plenty old enough to do that, now. Is that understood?"

"Loud and clear," Harry said. This was a phrase he had picked up from his father recently. He thought it sounded

139

cool, and he had been using it whenever the opportunity presented itself.

"Amanda, since Clarissa will be in the same dormitory building as you, I want you to keep a special eye on her. Will you do that for me?"

"Of course, I will, Mummy. We'll have fun won't we, sweetie?"

Clarissa's bottom lip was quivering.

"Right, if everybody's ready, let's get you off to school."

When Max and Sue got to the school that evening, there was a marked police car parked under the oak tree. There were two uniformed officers on board, and while Sue went into the school to find the children, Max walked over to have a word with them. He introduced himself and told them he was glad to see them there. They told him there would be a police presence throughout the night, and that a car would be dropping in on a regular basis during daylight hours.

Max and Sue stayed with the children for a while and then drove home.

While Max put the car in the garage, Sue opened the front door to let herself into the house. She found three business cards on the mat under the letterbox in the hall. Two were from journalists representing tabloid newspapers, the gutter press as Max called them when he saw the cards; the third was from a journalist representing a national broadsheet paper. On the back of each card was a handwritten message asking for someone to please call the telephone number on the card, saying in each case that it would be to their financial benefit to do so. Max ripped the cards up and tossed them in the wastepaper basket.

And there were two messages on the answering machine, both from newspapers, and both asking for someone to please return their call. Max deleted them.

They had a meal in the kitchen, put the dishes in the dishwasher, made themselves a coffee, and then, remarking on how quiet the house was without the kids, walked down the hall into the living room to watch TV.

Coronation Street was just beginning, and being from the Manchester area, Max was a fan. As, nowadays, was Sue. They settled down to watch it.

When the adverts came on, Max took the opportunity to use the loo. He used the one in the cloakroom by the front door. When he came out of the cloakroom, there was a photograph lying on the mat behind the front door. It had not been there prior to him using the loo, which meant it had only just been pushed through the letterbox. He opened the door and stepped outside and took a look around. There was no one in sight.

He closed the door and bent down and picked up the photograph. It was a picture of Sue walking down the crowded carriage of a train, with Veronica immediately behind her. Max knew immediately what it was because Sue and Veronica had dropped in on him at his office, carrying Harvey Nichol's shopping bags and smelling of gin, and told him what had happened on the train. The clincher was that, in the picture, they were wearing what they had worn when they dropped in on him.

He took the photograph back into the living room, where Sue was sprawled on the sofa watching the advertisements. "Look what I've found," he said, handing her the photograph. "It's just been pushed through the letterbox."

"I didn't hear a car," Sue said.

"Neither did I," Max said.

When Sue saw what was in the photograph, the implication was clear and her face paled. "Oh my God!" she said. "There must have two of them."

"What are you talking about?" Max said.

"There must have been two of them on the train. If the man Bob took into custody had taken it, I would have seen him take it." She looked at the photograph again. "And this has been taken from halfway down the carriage; the man Bob picked up was sitting at the far end of the carriage." She marvelled at the irony of it. "Here we were congratulating ourselves on outsmarting him, and all the time there were two of them on the train."

In the early hours of the next morning, Max was awakened by cold steel pressed hard against his neck. He knew immediately what it was, because he could feel the two barrels. The sawn-off shotgun was being pressed against his neck with such force that Max had the impression that the man holding the weapon was seriously pissed off with him about something, rather than just trying to frighten him.

"Give me reason to pull trigger," a voice that sounded like it had been dug from the bottom of a gravel pit growled.

Max could smell stale cigarette smoke on the man's breath, and on his clothes. He positively reeked of it. For some reason he was keeping his voice low, as if trying not to wake Sue, who, if her deep and even breathing was anything to go by, was soundly asleep.

Apart from a dull green glow from the electric clock/radio on the nightstand on Sue's side of the bed, the room was in darkness. Out here in the country, darkness meant absolute darkness, which meant that even though Max had his eyes open, he could see nothing. "Take it easy," he said quietly. "I'm not going to do anything, silly."

He listened carefully, wondering if the man was alone. He could hear no movement from within the house, but in the stillness he could just hear the sound of a car engine idling outside in the drive. Which probably meant there were at least two of them, the other one sitting at the wheel of the car ready to make a quick getaway.

"What do you want?" he whispered.

"You know what we want," the voice said.

"Refresh my memory," Max said, wincing as the shotgun was pressed even harder against his neck. He knew he was going to have one hell of a bruise on his neck when he woke up in the morning.

"Not good time to try to make jokes," the voice growled. "We want Harry not go in witness box."

Max felt the warmth of the man's breath on his cheek. He also got a faint whiff of gun oil and prayed that the safety catch was on. All it would take in a highly charged situation like this would be the twitch of a nervous finger on a sensitive trigger. And if that happened at this range, it would not only be he who would be heading for the pearly gates; Sue would be heading there as well.

"Is message clear?" Constantin Boguescu asked.

"Loud and clear," Max whispered.

"Good, because this is last warning. Next time …" He left the sentence unfinished. The gun was removed from Max's neck. "Do not try to follow, or I come back and shoot you, and then wife. Capiche?"

Max knew it was just a threat; he and Sue would have been dead already if it hadn't been, but he wasn't about to put it to the test. "I won't move a muscle," he promised.

He lay there until he heard the front door open and close, and then he slipped out of bed and hurried into Harry's room. Before he reached the window, he heard a car engine race, a car door slam, and tyres screech.

Even though there were no children in the house, out of habit Sue had drawn the curtains in Harry's room, and in the darkness Max couldn't find the middle of the curtains. Finally, he grabbed one of them and yanked it back. He looked down on to the drive, but he was too late. The car had gone. He opened the window and put his head out. He could hear the car tearing down the lane. The sound was rapidly receding.

He had left his mobile on charge in the kitchen, and making as little noise as possible, he hurried downstairs and into the kitchen. He closed the door so that when he switched the light on it wouldn't disturb Sue. He grabbed his mobile and yanked the charger cable out of it. He found Schembri's number on his speed-dial list and pressed it. While he waited for the detective to answer, he checked the time on the illuminated clock on the front of the cooker. It was 1.17am.

Schembri answered on the third ring. Even though it was early morning and he had been sound asleep, his voice was sharp. "Yes, Max?"

144

"Bob, we've just had a visitor and he brought a shotgun with him. I'll probably have a bruise the size of an egg on the neck in the morning to prove it."

"Christ almighty! Are you all right?"

"I'm fine. God knows why, but he kept his voice down and Sue didn't know a thing about it. She's still asleep. I hate to think what she'll say when I tell her."

"Tell me what happened."

Max explained exactly what had happened, including what had been said.

"Did you see anything?"

"Not a thing. It's pitch black out here at this time of night, unless there's a moon, and there's no moon tonight. I think he was Romanian, Bob. In fact, I'm sure of it. I've travelled in that part of the world."

"That figures. The guy we picked up at King's Cross was Romanian."

"Speaking of the guy you picked up at King's Cross, Bob, it seems there were two of them on the train." Max explained about the photograph that had been dropped through the letterbox earlier in the evening, and what Sue had said about it.

"This changes everything," Schembri said. "There's no time to lose, Max. You and I need to get together, and I mean without delay. Can you come to my office first thing in the morning?"

"I'll come straight from King's Cross when I get off the train."

"I'll be expecting you."

Seven hours later, Schembri was inspecting a bruise the size of a duck egg on Max's neck. "Are you ready for that safe house now?" he asked.

Max shook his head. "We're not giving in to them, Bob."

"Then all we can do is secure your house. And I do mean *secure* it. It'll cost you, Max, but with what I have in mind, to get in the house after it's been done they would have to ram-raid it."

"I'm not sure there's much point, Bob."

"Why do you say that?"

"Because when I told Sue what had happened in the night, she told me she won't spend another night in the house. She wants me to put it on the market."

Chapter 16

"Veronica, its Max."

"Oh, hi …"

"Don't mention my name," Max interjected hurriedly. "I don't want Sue to know I'm calling."

"Oh, okay. Where are you speaking from?"

"I'm in London, at my office. Is she within hearing distance?"

"No, she's in the kitchen. She's making smoked salmon and cucumber sandwiches for our lunch."

"Lucky you. Where are you?"

"In relation to what?"

"Where are you in the house?"

"I'm in the hall."

"Can you take the phone somewhere private, like out in the garden? So she doesn't know it's me you're speaking to."

"Just a second," Veronica carried the cordless phone through to the kitchen, where Sue was buttering thinly sliced brown bread. A side of smoked salmon lay on a silver-trimmed fish-shaped carving board on the worktop next to the sink. Half a cucumber in a cellophane wrapper lay beside it. "Sue, I need to take this. I'll be out in the garden."

"Are you sure you can trust me with all this smoked salmon?" Sue said mischievously. "I might scoff the lot."

Veronica laughed. "You'll be as sick as a dog if you do. I won't be long." She carried the phone out into the garden and sat with her back to the house. "Right," she said. "I'm all yours."

"I wish you were," Max said, intending it as a joke.

Veronica paused. "Do you mean that, Max?"

Max realised she had taken him seriously and kicked himself for being so stupid.

"Because if you did, Max, you need to let me know. You know how I feel about you."

"I was actually calling to ask your advice on how to approach Sue about something," Max said, wishing now he had never made the call.

"Well don't *I* wish the ground would open up and swallow me?" Veronica said, the disappointment in her voice clearly evident.

Max winced. "Did she tell you we had a visitor in the middle of the night?"

"Yes, she did."

"Well, what I was calling about was that, when I told her about our visitor, she told me she wanted me to put the house on the market."

"And if I'd had a man with a shotgun in my bedroom at the dead of night, I'd probably want to move, too. So what did you want my advice on?"

"I don't want to sell the house and I wanted your advice on how to talk her out of it."

"You're a grown man, Max. I'm sure you can figure that out for yourself. Was there something else?"

Max knew he should end the call, but her reminding him how she felt about him had got his juices flowing. Like a testosterone-fuelled teenager, he ploughed on, "Are you saying you still feel the same way about me as you did on the night of the school dance?"

"What kind of question is that? Of course, I am. I can't turn my feelings on and off like a tap. But when you don't feel the same way about me, what's the point?"

"How do you know I don't feel the same way about you?"

"Don't play games with me, Max. It's hard enough for me as it is."

"I'm not playing games with you, Veronica. I *do* feel the same way about you."

"Then you have a very funny way of showing it."

"Well, in case you hadn't noticed, Veronica, I do have some rather pressing matters on my mind at the moment, like thugs from Eastern Europe scaring the life out of my family. And there's still the question of the effect us having an affair would have on Sue, Henry, and the kids."

"You can forget about Henry. His dolly birds keep *him* happy."

"His *what*!"

"His dolly birds; his bright young things. Didn't you know he was into young women in their late teens and early twenties? They seem to find him irresistible, although I can't imagine why."

Max was staggered. He thought he knew Henry. "I most certainly didn't know. Well, I *am* surprised. You've kept that quiet."

"We're not ones to wash our dirty linen in public. To put it in a nutshell, our marriage is a sham and has been for

149

years. But it suits me to have him around. He's useful around the house, and he's good company, when he's not out gallivanting, that is. That's why I've never done anything about it."

"What about your relationship with Sue, Veronica? Could you handle the guilt if you and I had an affair?"

"*Guilt*?" Veronica snorted. "What guilt? *She's* not whiter than white."

"What's that supposed to mean?"

"It means that she and Henry had an affair."

"They *what*?"

"They had an affair."

"You're *kidding*!"

"No, I'm not."

"How the hell did I miss that? I had no idea."

"Probably because you're never home."

"When was this, Veronica?"

"It started in March of the year before last, and it went on for almost a year."

"Good grief, I thought I knew her. I can't believe I didn't suspect anything. Why have you never told me?"

"There's never been any reason to. Now, there is."

"You're not just *saying* that, Veronica? Sue really *did* have an affair with Henry?"

"Yes, Max, she really did."

"Does she know you know?"

"Not that I'm aware of. And neither does Henry. As far as you and I are concerned, if we did start something we would simply be redressing the balance. Now what was it you wanted me to ask her, again?"

"Forget it. It doesn't seem important now."

Chapter 17

Veronica was dressed to the nines. Her make-up was impeccable, and she was wearing a perfume Sue had never known her wear before. Judging by the lightness and subtlety of the fragrance it must have cost a small fortune. They were standing in the hall by the open front door of Veronica's house. A taxi was waiting outside in the courtyard with its engine running.

"Don't wait up, Sue," Veronica said. "My friend and I can talk for England, once we get started. Henry said he would be in by ten, and Randy will steer you through the TV remote. Make sure you watch what you want to watch, otherwise he'll have you watching recordings of *Top Gear* all evening."

"I must be really cramping his style," Sue said. "In fact, I must be cramping everybody's style by now. You must all be sick of the sight of me."

"Sue, you're not cramping anybody's style. We're only too happy to have you. Now, you know where everything is. Help yourself to wine; that Cabernet Sauvignon Henry brought home yesterday should be a nice one."

"Thanks, but I think I'll give alcohol a miss tonight. I'm drinking far too much at the moment. I'm sure my liver would welcome a rest."

"Well it's up to you, but I don't think anyone would blame you for drinking too much at the moment, given what *you* have on your plate."

Veronica had had her hair done that morning. In fact, since they were of necessity joined at the hip at the moment, she and Sue had had their hair done together. Sitting in the chair beside her at the hairdressers, Veronica had surprised Sue by having the long bouncy style she had worn all the time she had known her cut short. She had handed the hairdresser a cutting from a magazine to show her what she had in mind, and her hair was now short, chic, and very sophisticated.

Sue had wondered at the time what had brought on this radical change of appearance, and she suspected there might be a man in the picture. Standing there in the hall, she stepped back and looked Veronica up and down. "Are you *sure* you're only meeting a friend, Veronica?" she said, an amused look in her eye.

Veronica shrugged. "My friend's a very snazzy dresser, and you know how I hate someone being better dressed than me." She looked at her watch. "Well, I mustn't keep her waiting, so I'd better be off."

Veronica climbed out of the taxi at the Radisson Edwardian Hotel at Heathrow Airport at 8.45pm His plane was due in at 8.20pm and there was no point her getting there too early. It would take time getting through the formalities at the airport, and a taxi to the hotel would take fifteen to twenty minutes.

When the uniformed commissionaire wished her a good evening and opened the hotel door for her, there was something in his manner that made her feel uncomfortable. She had a pretty good idea what it was: a woman dressed to kill walking into a hotel near a major international airport on her own at this time of evening? She had always avoided walking into a hotel or restaurant on her own for this very reason. She tried to put it out of her mind, but this hotel catered mainly for visiting businessmen, many of who were from overseas and on virtually unlimited expense accounts, and when she walked into the large marble-floored lobby, she was immediately aware she was getting the wrong kind of attention from some of the men sitting in there.

The man she was meeting walked into the hotel at 9.05pm. In his charcoal grey pinstripe suit, white shirt with button-down collar, striped tie, and gleaming black shoes, he looked every inch the successful businessman he was.

As he strode to the reception desk, Veronica watched him look casually round the lobby. When his eyes met hers, they crinkled into a smile. He put his overnight bag down, checked in, and handed the receptionist a credit card, which she wiped. She handed him a key card. He asked her something and she pointed to a bank of lifts.

To get to the lifts he had to pass Veronica's chair, and as he passed her, he murmured out of the corner of his mouth, "Room 319."

Veronica left it a few minutes before getting to her feet and click-clacking her way across the lobby to the lifts. She took the lift to the third floor, and followed the signs down the lushly carpeted hallway to room 319, where, to let him know it was her, she adopted their pre-arranged, and she thought rather ridiculous, signal of knocking three times, and then twice more. When he had suggested this, she had almost asked *why don't I knock three times and ask for Joe?*

He opened the door. He had taken off his jacket and tie and he was grinning like the proverbial Cheshire cat. "Hi there," he said. "Come on in."

"I don't know what you're grinning at," she said, walking into the room. "I've been propositioned twice while I've been waiting for you, and the commissionaire was giving me very nasty looks. I thought at one point he was going to ask me to leave. I'm not going through this again, Max. I felt like a hooker down there."

Max gave her a hug. "I'm sorry," he said. "It won't happen again." He looked up and down the hallway and then stepped back into the room and closed the door. "Did Sue suspect anything?"

Veronica took her coat off and draped it over a chair. "I don't think so. I told her I was meeting a girlfriend."

She looked different and Max noticed she had had her hair cut. "I love your hair, Veronica. It really suits you like that. It emphasises your high cheekbones and the colour of your eyes. It's absolutely gorgeous."

Veronica smiled. "Flattery will get you everywhere. I think Sue wondered why I'd had it cut short."

"And just as matter of interest, why did you?"

She looked into his eyes. "I did it for you. Just as I dressed for you on the evening of the school dance."

"Well, thank you," Max said. "Now, I'm the one to be flattered."

"You're welcome, and you *should* be flattered. I've never gone to this much trouble for a man in my entire life, and I include my husbands." She flopped into a chair.

"Drink, Veronica?"

"Yes, and make it a large one. I need it after what I've just been through."

"The usual?"

"Please."

Max walked to the mini bar accompanied by the distant and muted roar of a jet aircraft taking off. He opened the minibar and took out two miniatures of Gordon's Gin and two small cans of Schweppes Tonic Water. "There's no ice. But there may be an ice dispenser down the hall if you need it."

"I don't need ice. Just pour. I need something to settle my nerves," She shook her head crossly. "This is not how I wanted our first time to be, Max. I wanted it to be romantic. As it is, I feel I should be quoting you my price."

Max handed her her drink and grinned. "I'm glad you're not. I probably couldn't afford you."

"Oh, very droll." She took the drink off him.

"No seriously, Veronica. I'm not surprised men were propositioning you. You look absolutely stunning."

"Well that's all right then." She held up her glass. "What shall we drink to?"

"Under normal circumstances I might have suggested drinking to absent friends," Max said. "But under present circumstances, that might not be appropriate."

"Then, let's drink to happy days."

"Happy days it is."

They touched glasses.

Veronica took a sip of her drink. "How's Paris?"

Max shrugged. "Same old, same old. When you're there on business, it's just another city in just another country. If you and I were there together, on the other hand, it would be a different matter entirely. I hope we can set that up at some point."

Back at Veronica's house, Henry held the now only one-third full bottle of Cabernet Sauvignon over Sue's glass. "Top you up?" he asked.

"Oh, go on then," Sue said. "I wasn't planning to have more than one glass, but why not. It's a lovely wine."

"Attagirl." Henry stopped pouring when the wine was within a fraction of an inch of the rim of the glass.

Sue asked suspiciously, "You wouldn't be trying to get me drunk by any chance, would you?"

"Would I do such a thing?" Henry said, a picture of innocence.

"Yes, you would, you old reprobate! You forget how well I know you."

"So what if you do get drunk?" Henry sat on the sofa beside her. "What would it matter? The boss won't be back until the early hours, and Randy's up in his room surfing the net, so he won't bother us. What do you say, Sue, for old time's sake?" He put his hand on her leg.

Sue removed his hand. "I don't think so, Henry."

"But why not?"

"For two reasons," Sue said, glancing at him. "One of them being Veronica, the other being Max."

"That didn't stop you before." He took a gulp of his wine.

"Things are different, now."

"How are they different? You and I are the same people we were back then."

"They just are." Sue inched away from him. She sipped her wine.

"And how do you know our respective spouses are not shacked up in some hotel room going at it like rabbits even as we speak?"

"Because Max is in Paris, and Sue's in London with a friend."

"How do you know she is? People do tell lies, y'know."

"I've never known Veronica tell me a lie."

"And what about Max? Paris is only two hundred miles from London, and a couple of hundred miles never stopped a man who wanted to get his leg over." Henry took another slurp of his wine.

"Max isn't like that."

"How do you know he isn't? He's a man isn't he?"

"They're not all like you, Henry."

"How would you know?" Henry scoffed. "How many men do *you* know? Take it from one who knows, Sue, men are all the same. They only ever think of one thing. It's an appetite. It doesn't have to mean anything; it's just sex."

"Well that might be all it means to you, Henry, but it's not all it means to me. There has to be more. So, as far as your offer is concerned, thanks, but no thanks."

At the Radisson, Max and Veronica were naked on the super king-size bed.

He hovered over her.

"Be gentle with me," Veronica murmured. "At least, to begin with. I want our first time to be special."

157

"I will," Max promised. He lowered himself on to her.

It was 3.30am when Veronica finally got home, and she was exhausted. Max had worn her out. She had no idea he had so much energy. He had awakened in her something that had been dormant for far too long and she had ridden home in the back of the taxi with a big smile on her face.

And, as far as she was concerned, this was just the beginning.

Chapter 18

Veronica was still smiling when she went down to breakfast the next morning.

Sue and Randy had started breakfast without her, and when Veronica waltzed into the room, Sue asked her what she was looking so pleased about.

"I'm smiling at something my friend said last night," Veronica lied, sitting down at the table. "Would you pass the toast please, Randy?"

Later that morning, Veronica got a text message from Max. It raised another smile. '*Safely back in Paris and you were fantastic last night! I can't wait till next time*'.

Her reply read, '*And so were you. I won't be able to walk for a week.*'

That afternoon, Sue and Veronica drove to the school to pick Randy up and they left a little earlier than usual because the children had now been boarding for three weeks and Sue wanted an update from Mrs Godley on how there were settling in. It was mid-June, it was a hot and sunny day and Veronica had the top down on her car.

When they got to the school, Veronica asked Sue if she would mind her joining her in her meeting with Mrs Godley, explaining that she hardly knew Mrs Godley and would welcome the opportunity to get to know her a little better. Sue had no objections and happily agreed.

During the half hour or so they spent with the headmaster's wife, Mrs Godley and Veronica got on like the proverbial house on fire and were soon on first name terms, or *Mutti* in Mrs Godley's case.

When it came to discussing Sue's children, Mrs Godley reported that they had settled in well, adding, "If anything, Clarissa has settled in rather better than her siblings, which, knowing how close she is to you, rather surprised me. She seems to be treating it as a huge adventure."

After they had finished talking to Mrs Godley, Sue and Veronica went and rounded up the children. Randy joined them and Sue was delighted to see that he and Harry seemed to be on good terms again, albeit perhaps not quite such good terms as had previously been the case.

The two friends chatted with the children for an hour or so, and then said their goodbyes and walked out of the building with Randy. It was after 5pm. By now, the other mothers had collected their charges and driven away, and Veronica's Mercedes was the only car in the drive. A marked police car had been parked in the drive when they had arrived, but as the police had informed Max when the children first started boarding, during daylight hours they were only maintaining a presence on a sporadic basis.

Randy was first at the car. There was a photograph on the driver's seat and he leant in and picked it up. It was a picture of his mother and Auntie Sue walking through the crowded carriage of a train. He handed the photograph to his mother, who looked at it, uttered an expletive under her breath, and handed it to Sue.

It was a copy of the same photograph that had been pushed through Sue's letterbox three weeks ago. "So!" Sue said, "now they have you in their sights as well."

"So it would seem," Veronica said. "Well, I'll say one thing for them, they're nothing if not persistent."

Randy knew nothing about what had happened on the train, because his mother had not wanted to scare him, but since it was all now coming alarmingly close to home, she explained what had happened while they were driving home.

"So you see, my darling," she said as they pulled into the courtyard at the house, "we all need to be vigilant now, including you. From now on, no talking to strangers, and no getting into cars with people you don't know."

When they got into the house, Sue gave Bob Schembri a call and told him about Veronica getting a copy of the photograph.

Max was due back from his trip to France that evening. The arrangement was that he would pick up his car from the long term car park at Heathrow and pick Sue up from Veronica's on his way home. This was to be their first night in their own home since the contractors had finished securing the house, and Sue was having mixed feelings about it. The bedroom she was using at Veronica's was cold and draughty, even at this time of the year. It had leaded windows that let in the wind, a creaky floor, and a bed that had been handed down from Veronica's grandmother. It was a vast bed, with an ancient brass headboard, and it sagged badly in the middle, resulting in Sue waking with an aching back each morning. She was looking forward to sleeping in her own bed again, but she was still having nightmares about men with shotguns in her bedroom.

In a phone call from Paris a few days earlier, Max had told her not to worry, saying that the security contractors had told him it would take nothing short of a tank to break into the house now, which had not entirely reassured her.

Max had phoned the security firm from Paris, and he had asked them to drop off the new keys at Veronica's. Both sets of keys, his and hers, were now safely ensconced in Sue's handbag. They didn't look like any house keys Sue had ever seen; more like something out of a science fiction movie.

She was upstairs packing at Veronica's when Bob Schembri arrived.

Henry answered the door. Never having met Schembri before, he asked to see his ID.

Schembri showed him his warrant card, and Henry introduced himself and let him in.

"Some house," Schembri said, stepping into the hall.

Pleased with the compliment, Henry said, "She's a draughty old pile, but we like her. Get you a drink, Chief Inspector?"

"Not while I'm working, thanks."

Sue heard Schembri's voice and walked out on to landing and looked down. "Hello, Bob," she said.

He looked up. "Hello, Sue. They're not letting up, are they?"

"No, they're not," Sue said, walking down the stairs.

Henry led the way into the family room. "My wife's in the garden. She's picking vegetables for our evening meal, but she should be in shortly. Take a seat, Chief Inspector."

"It's Bob," Schembri said, sitting down.

"And I'm Henry. Sure about that drink? Not even a small one?" He held his thumb and forefinger an inch apart and grinned.

Schembri laughed. "That looks like a large one to me. And the answer's still the same. I'm sorry it's come to having to make your house secure as well as Max and Sue's, but it's better to be safe than sorry."

"It will cost a king's ransom to make this pile secure," Henry grumbled.

At that moment, Veronica walked in from the garden with an armful of fresh vegetables. She had heard what Henry had said and she said pointedly, "Your point being? Since I'm the one who'll be paying for it, why should that bother you? Hello again, Chief Inspector. Sorry to have to drag you all the way out here."

"No problem. And please, call me Bob."

"I will. And I'm Veronica. Let me put these vegetables in the kitchen and then we can talk. Have you offered our guest a drink, Henry?"

"Of course, I've offered him a drink," Henry said, miffed at Veronica putting him down in front of a visitor. "Are you suggesting I don't know how to look after a guest?"

"I *have* been offered a drink, thanks," Schembri said, anxious to take the heat out of the situation.

"Right, back in a sec," Veronica headed off in the direction of the kitchen.

When Veronica came back, Henry was saying: "But I still don't understand why we should secure *our* house. *We* haven't been threatened."

"What do you call the photograph on the seat of my car if not a threat?" Veronica retorted. "It didn't get there of its own accord. Somebody put it there. You might not feel threatened, Henry, but I certainly do."

"She's right, I'm afraid," Schembri said.

"It's scary to think there might be someone out there watching the house even as we speak," Sue said. "You didn't see a car loitering suspiciously when you got here, did you, Bob?"

"I didn't see a thing," Schembri said. "And believe me, I *was* looking. To answer your question, Henry, the reason your house must be made secure is that these people have demonstrated how easily they can break into a house at the dead of night without disturbing the occupants, and their willingness to threaten people in their beds with shotguns. And considering the speed at which this is ramping up, the sooner your house is made secure, the better."

"I couldn't agree with you more," Veronica said. "So, please, Bob, get it organised, and the sooner the better. And to hell with the cost."

That evening, despite Veronica pleading with him to stay in, Henry went out. He told her he was going out because of the way she had spoken to him when her *detective friend* was there, that he wasn't letting a bunch of thugs rule *his* life, and that she wouldn't be alone because *her son* would be here. "You'll just have to make do with *him*, won't you?"

Max arrived just before 10pm. Veronica was in the kitchen and she saw his car pull into the courtyard. As was always the case when she saw him, her heart skipped a beat. She went to let him in.

When she opened the door, Max took a quick look behind her to make sure no one was there, and then stepped forward to kiss her.

She put a gentle hand against his chest to stop him and gave a little shake of her head. "It's not a good time, Max. We've had another upset today, and Sue's just down the hall."

"Oh, right," Max said. "I didn't know. What was the upset?"

"Come on in and we'll tell you."

Max stepped into the house and Veronica closed the door behind him. Then she called, "Sue, Max is here."

Sue hurried out of the living room. "I didn't hear the bell."

"I was in the kitchen and I saw him arrive," Veronica explained.

Sue threw her arms round Max's neck. "I've missed you," she said, kissing him long and hard.

"I've missed you too," he said, when she had finally let go of him.

She looked up into his face. "You look tired. Have you had a tough trip?"

"I have, actually. I've been all over France and I've been in a different hotel almost every night."

Sue frowned. "But why, Max? You told me that when you were heading up Europe, you wouldn't have to do all that. To use your words, you said you would be *directing traffic*. I thought you would be staying in Paris and letting somebody else do the donkey work."

"I know I did," Max said, "and that was the plan. But there's a new man in the Paris office and I thought he would benefit from my experience, so I made a swing of the market with him."

"I see," Sue said, her eyes flashing dangerously. "And are you going to be giving every country in Europe *the benefit of your experience*? Am I going to be seeing *anything* of you in the future, Max? You've conned me, haven't you?"

"Sue, please. This is neither the time …"

Sue turned to Veronica. "Thank you for having me, Veronica, and I'll see you again on Monday morning. Max, my suitcase is in the bedroom at the back of the house. Would you please get it for me? Did you lock the car?"

"No, I didn't lock it. I thought …"

"I'll wait in the car."

While Max went to get her suitcase, Sue went to say goodbye to Randy. "I'll see you on Monday morning," she said.

"Goodbye, Auntie Sue. Yes, see you Monday. Have a nice weekend."

"Thanks. You too!"

Sue gave Veronica a hug.

"Keep your chin up, sweetie," Veronica said. "You know where I am if you need me."

Max and Sue made the trip home without a word being spoken.

Chapter 19

As they approached the house, Max spoke for the first time since they had left Veronica's.

"Have you got the keys?"

Sue fished in her handbag for the new keys and handed him a set.

On first impression, the contractors appeared to have done an excellent job. The curtains had been drawn electronically in all the rooms at the front of the house and timers had switched lamps on. While there was actually no one in the house, it looked very much like a family was at home.

When Max swung the Jaguar into the drive, powerful arc lights flooded the drive and the sides of the house with enough light to host a five-a-side football match.

While the house had primarily been secured to prevent nefarious characters with shotguns breaking in at the dead of night, it would also serve to deter burglars. As to there being no cars in the drive, he reasoned that, since there were two garages, the cars could have been put away for the night. No one would know if they had, or had not, been put away, unless they looked through the window at the side of the garage, and the arc lights would have come on and scared the living daylights out of them long before they reached the window.

Angry though she was with Max, Sue had to admit he had been right in agreeing to have the house secured, even though it had cost a small fortune. No one in their right mind would dare even set foot on the drive after dark now. If they did, they would very soon realise their mistake.

Max stopped the car by the front door and got out and walked round the house to make sure the contractors had put lights on the back of the house as well. They had, and they all came on.

Sue waited in the car for him to come back. She had to put the sun visor down to keep the glare from the arc lights out of her eyes.

Max came back grinning. "There's so much light back there that we'll be able to have a barbecue in the middle of the night."

"Oh good," Sue said sarcastically, "I've always wanted to have a barbecue in the middle of the night."

"Hey, come on, Sue," Max protested. "I've done this as much for you as anyone. In fact, more so, since you were the one who didn't want to spend another night in the house."

The house was now sporting a new front door, this one made of heavy duty PVC which, the contractors had claimed, not even the police would be able to break into. And the contractors had said that installing new locks, would not per se make a door secure unless the frame was also secure, and the new door had been set in a stout hardwood frame. Sue had always liked the front door, and Max had asked the contractors to make sure the new one looked as much like the old one as possible. And they had succeeded because, to him, it looked exactly like the old one. He put it to the test by asking Sue how she liked the new door.

Sue shaded her eyes with her hand against the glare from the arc lights so she could get a better look at it. "It looks very much like the old one," she said. "Except that it's a slightly different shade of white."

Pleased, Max said, "Let me show you how the new lock works."

They stepped up to the door.

Max selected a key from the ring of three keys Sue had given him and inserted it in the lock. "The door has five deadbolts, and to disengage them you have to turn the key two and half turns to the right," he explained. He turned the key to the right, counting aloud for Sue's benefit, "One, two, two and a half. So the key is now upside down." He took a half step back so that Sue could see that the key was, indeed, upside down. "If you don't follow the *exact* procedure, the door won't open and you'll set the alarm off. Now we've turned the key, we have to press the handle down like this. Are you watching?"

Sue sighed. "Yes, Max. I'm watching."

"When you press the handle down, the deadbolts withdraw. And the contractors told me you should be able to hear them withdraw, so I'm going to press it now. Are you listening?"

Sue sighed again, wishing he would just get on with it. "Yes, Max. I'm listening."

Judging by the *clunk* the deadbolts made, the door was substantial enough to have secured the vault at the Bank of England.

169

When Max pushed the door open, there was a buzzing noise reminiscent of a swarm of angry bees. It was so loud that that, in itself, would have been enough to scare off the average burglar. "That's to tell us we have fifteen seconds to get to the keypad."

The contractor had informed Max that the keypad was located behind the door in the cloakroom, and he stepped quickly into the house and switched on the hall light. "We'll have to be quick, otherwise the alarm will go off."

By now, Sue's senses were off the radar. The house might have *looked* the same, but it didn't *feel* the same. It felt more like a fortress than a house. She hurried into the cloakroom behind Max. "What happens if you don't get there in time?" she asked.

"A SWAT team and a police helicopter arrive," Max said, intending it as a joke.

Sue was trying to imagine how on earth she was going to remember everything he was saying. She had heard him say something, but she hadn't heard *what* he had said. "That's nice," she said.

Max punched four numbers into the keypad and the buzzing stopped. "I didn't think you were listening," he said, turning to face her. "You really do need to listen, Sue, because otherwise you're going to get caught out when I'm not here. And to answer your question, what happens if you don't switch the alarm off, is that, within five minutes a police car will arrive with its blue lights flashing and its siren wailing. I'll write the numbers down for you, and you'll need to memorise them. And make sure you don't let anybody else see them."

The condescending side of her husband was the side Sue liked the least. "Give me credit, Max," she said crossly. "I'm not *entirely* stupid."

Max spent the next half hour walking Sue round the house and explaining what had been done, and what she must, and must not, do.

The police had found that the intruder with the shotgun had gained entry into the house by jemmying one of the windows in the conservatory, and extensive work had been carried out to ensure that this could not happen again.

To Sue, the house didn't feel like home any more, it felt alien. She knew that if she were in the house on her own, she would be afraid to go out in case she hadn't set the alarm properly and it went off. And she knew she would be afraid to open a window, in case she didn't close it properly later and the alarm went off when she set it for the night. And she knew that if she forgot where the sensors under the carpets were, and she stepped on one of them during the night when she couldn't sleep and had got up to make herself a cup of tea, which was not unusual when Max was away, the alarm would go off and the police would be there, waking up the entire village with their sirens. That is unless the alarm had not already woken them.

It was an odd and disturbing feeling. When they had been on the outside of the house and Max had been explaining how the alarm worked, the house had felt like a fortress. Now she was on the inside and worried about how she would get out without setting off the alarm, it felt more like a prison.

She wanted to yell, *I don't want all this security, Max. I want my home back.* Instead, she said meekly, "Would you like a cup of tea, darling?"

That, at least, was something she didn't need instructions on.

Chapter 20

Since he had got back from Paris, Max had seemed distant and preoccupied, as if he had something on his mind. And his behaviour had changed. Sue said nothing about it until they were having breakfast on the Monday morning, and then she came right out with it.

"Max, have you met someone?"

Max looked up from buttering his toast. "What do you mean, have I met someone? I meet a lot of people."

"Don't play games with me, Max. You know what I mean. Your behaviour's been different since you got back from Paris. Are you having an affair?"

"Come off it, Sue. When do I have the time to have an affair?" He spread some marmalade on his toast and bit into it.

"Then, why have you been so quiet this weekend? The only time you seemed to want to engage in conversation with me was when we spent time with the children."

Max manufactured a hurt look. "Sue, in case it had slipped your notice, I have just taken on a lot of additional responsibility. I have a lot on my mind."

"Does that mean you're not having an affair?"

"No, I am not having an affair." Max looked at his watch and then dabbed at his lips with his napkin. "We'd better go. I'll be late for my train."

On the way to Veronica's, Max talked almost non-stop, which was most unlike him. He seemed to be making a determined attempt to say everything he hadn't said over the weekend. And when they got to Veronica's, rather than leaning across the car and giving Sue a perfunctory peck on the cheek, he got out of the car, opened her door for her, hugged her, kissed her full on the mouth and told her he was looking forward to seeing her again in the evening, which he had never ever said to her before.

Veronica let her into the house and, as she made coffee in the kitchen, she asked Sue how she had got on with the new security at home. "Did you manage to avoid setting off the alarm?"

"Yes, we managed to avoid setting off the alarm. Max took care of that. But I hate what they've done. The house doesn't feel like home anymore; it feels more like a fortress, or a prison."

Veronica got cups and saucers out of a cupboard, and then milk and sweeteners. "Did you see the children over the weekend?"

"Yes, we saw them on Saturday afternoon, and again yesterday. We took them out for a meal, last evening. We went to that new restaurant at Watton-at-Stone."

"I hear it's very good."

"It is; it's excellent."

"Good, then we must go there together sometime."

A high-pressure area had been sitting over the UK for the last couple of weeks and it was another perfect day, so they took their coffee out into the garden, sitting with a little wrought iron table between them.

"How's Max?" Veronica asked casually. "That was some kiss he gave you when he dropped you off. I saw you through the kitchen window," she added by way of explanation.

"I'm not actually sure *how* he is," Sue replied.

"What do you mean?" Veronica said, eyeing her friend quizzically.

"I think he's having an affair."

Veronica looked at her seemingly incredulously. "I don't believe it for a second. For one thing, when would he have the time? He's never here."

"That's what he said when I broached the subject this morning?"

"What makes you think he's having an affair?" Veronica took a sip of her coffee.

There was the hum of traffic from the A1(M) motorway a half mile or so away. If Veronica's house had a weakness, it was that, apart from late at night and the early hours of the morning, there was an almost continuous hum of traffic from the motorway, which was a main arterial route into London.

"Well, for one thing," Sue said, "apart from when we were with the children, he hardly had two words to say to me, and I mean all weekend. He seemed preoccupied, as if he had something on his mind."

"He could have been preoccupied with business," Veronica said. "When all's said and done, he *has* just taken on a lot more responsibility."

"That's what he said when I brought up the subject this morning. But he did something else this weekend that he's never done before; he played golf twice. He played on Saturday morning, *and* Sunday morning. He's never done that before. When he's been away for a week or more previously, he has only *ever* played one round of golf at the weekend, which is out of consideration for me. And there were times during the weekend that I got the feeling he wasn't with me; that he was somewhere else. But what *really* got me thinking he had met somebody was that twice over the weekend he turned me down in bed. I can't remember the last time *he* turned *me* down. *I'm* usually the one turning *him* down."

Veronica's mind slipped back to her tryst with Max and she had to hide a smile. She knew something about his appetite for sex. He had been insatiable. "You're lucky he's only turned you down twice," she said. "The only time Henry even comes into my bedroom is when he wants to know where his clean pyjamas are."

Sue got back to what she had been saying. "On Saturday night he made the excuse that he was tired ..."

"Which I imagine he would have been after travelling all over France all week."

Sue frowned. "Whose side are you on, Veronica? Why are you making excuses for him?"

"I'm on your side, sweetie," Veronica said smoothly. "You know that. Go on with what you were saying."

"Where was I? Oh yes, and when I started showing interest in bed last night, he got out of bed and went downstairs and made himself a cup of tea. I was so mad I was willing him to step on one of the pressure pads and set the alarm off."

Veronica threw her head back and burst into a peal of laughter.

"No, I'm telling you, Veronica, he's met somebody. Somebody, he's smitten with."

"You could be wrong, Sue."

"I don't think so. I actually wouldn't mind him having the odd one-night stand while he's out of the country, providing he doesn't let me find out about it; what I don't know won't hurt me, so to speak. But it's the thought of him falling in love with another woman that bothers me. It would destroy everything we've built together, not to mention what it would do to the children."

"Do you have any idea who it might be?"

Sue shook her head. "I've been racking my brains, but I can't think of anybody. Certainly nobody I know. He's only been behaving strangely since he came back from Paris, so it could be someone he met there."

"How often will he have to go to Paris?"

"I don't know," Sue said. "Probably not all that often, since he has the rest of Europe to take care of as well."

"Well, if he *has* met somebody in Paris, it might amount to nothing. He won't be able to see her all that often, and she could be married and have no intention of leaving her husband. What are you planning to do about it?"

"I don't know," Sue said. "I haven't had time to think about it; probably nothing for the moment. There are too many other things going on in my life to contemplate a break-up in my marriage. I might just have to accept it for the time being and see how things pan out."

"That sounds like a plan," Veronica said. "By the way, while we're on the subject of relationships, have *you* ever had an affair, Sue?"

177

When Sue didn't immediately answer her question, Veronica smiled. "I'll take it that's a yes. Come on, sweetie, spill the beans; you know it won't go any further."

Sue spent a few moments thinking about whether to admit to her friend something she had never admitted to anyone. She felt on safe ground and decided to go for it. "Well, it was a long time ago and it didn't amount to anything, so I don't see why I shouldn't tell you. It was actually a one-night stand, not an affair. It was after the Christmas party of a company I was working for in London two years after Max and I got married. He was a director of the company, a very attractive man, and I got drunk and, well …" She shrugged. "One thing led to another. You know how it goes."

"Of course, I do. We've all been there. Does Max know?"

Sue shook her head. "No, Max doesn't know. Back then, when I was still feeling guilty about it, I did think about telling him, to get it off my chest, but for some reason I never got around to it. And I wouldn't want to tell him now, unless there was a very good reason for it."

"Was that the only time you strayed?" Veronica asked.

Sue reddened. "No, there was another time, but I'd rather not talk about it."

Veronica knew from the way Sue had reddened that she was referring to her affair with Henry. "Is it still raw?" she asked.

Sue shifted uncomfortably in her seat. "Not really. I'd just rather not talk about it."

"Was he married?"

"Veronica, do you mind if we talk about something else?"

Chapter 21

"When can I see you again?"

"Max," Veronica said into the phone, "I don't know. It's difficult with Sue here all the time."

"Where is she, now? She can't hear you, can she?"

"No, she can't hear me. She's in the garden, enjoying the sunshine."

"I'm going to Italy next week. I could nip back one night. We could do what we did last time."

"Were you not listening last time?"

"Listening to what?"

"I didn't think you were. I told you last time that I would never sit in a hotel lobby waiting for you ever again."

"Then *you* suggest something."

"I don't think so, Max."

"Don't tell me you're cooling off. We've only just begun."

"I'm not cooling off, Max. It's just that it's complicated."

"Why, because Sue's staying with you? She was staying with you last time."

Veronica was using the phone in the hall and it wasn't a cordless model. She stepped back so she could see the patio through the open French windows in the living room. She could see the patio, but she couldn't see the chair in which Sue was sitting. To be on the safe side, she lowered her voice. "This is not a good time, Max. Sue could walk in. We were just about to go food shopping. In any case, I've been doing a lot of thinking this morning, and I think we should call it off."

"What is this, Veronica? Guilty conscience?"

"You can call it what you like, Max, but the fact is that Sue has more than enough on her plate at the moment and I have no desire to add to her problems. She is, when all is said and done, my best friend. I just think we should leave it where it is."

"So just like that …" Veronica heard Max snap his fingers, "you take the unilateral decision to break it off."

"There's nothing to break off, Max. We met once, and we had a good time. Let's leave it at that."

"But *you* were the one who wanted us to have an affair, Veronica. I didn't start it, you did."

"I know I did, and I'm sorry. It was a mistake, and I shouldn't have."

Max spoke evenly and without rancour. "Veronica, when you told me at the school dance that you wanted to have an affair with me, I said that despite fancying you rotten I wouldn't start a relationship with you because of the effect it would have on our families. And now you've got me hooked, you're dumping me. How would you feel if I did that to you?"

Veronica stepped back to check the patio again. "Max, Sue *knows* you've met someone. She told me all about it after you dropped her off here this morning."

"How *can* she know? I haven't told her, and you obviously haven't. And no one saw us together. We couldn't have been more careful."

"Women have intuition, Max."

"Oh, do me a favour."

"Max, take it from me, Sue *knows* you've met someone. This morning, she described to me in detail how your behaviour had changed over the weekend, and she was right when she said it could only mean one thing. She just doesn't know it's me."

"Veronica, if I promised to be more careful in future, would you see me again?"

"I don't know, Max; I'd have to give that some thought. But I certainly wouldn't agree to see you again unless I was convinced that Sue wouldn't …"

There was an anguished wail from behind her.

Veronica turned to see Sue running barefoot through the family room towards the French windows, stumbling and almost falling in her haste to get away. She scooped up her handbag from the coffee table and her shoes from the patio.

"Oh, *God*!" Veronica yelled into the phone, "It's Sue. She must have heard me. Max, I have to go." She slammed the phone down and raced through the family room and out into the garden. She heard Sue's people carrier start up.

The wrought-iron gate into the courtyard was open and Veronica raced towards it. There was the sound of a car engine racing and tyres squealing and she got to the gate just in time to see the rear end of Sue's people carrier careering through the courtyard entrance. Running as hard as she could, and yelling Sue's name and imploring her to stop, Veronica followed her out of the courtyard.

Bordering Veronica's house was a three-acre green on which a local cricket club played weekend matches. On the far side of the green was a duck pond, and a row of thatched cottages. Running parallel to the courtyard wall was a Category-B road that led into Welwyn Garden City, and a hundred yards to the left of the courtyard entrance, and partly hidden by a large tree, sat a Subaru Impreza with two men on board. Veronica noticed the car when she heard its engine start up.

She recognised the make of car because Randy was always talking about them, and he had shown her pictures on his laptop. It was the car he wanted when he was old enough to drive, which Veronica was dead against, because she knew it to be favoured by boy racers.

As Sue hurtled down the B-road, heading in the direction of Welwyn Garden City, the Subaru's engine howled and the car leapt forward.

As it snarled past her, Veronica recognised the man in the passenger seat from the description Sue had given her. Sue had told her that when he came to the house he had scared the living daylights out of her, and now Veronica knew why. He was *huge*.

Her blood ran cold and she turned and raced back to the house to get to the phone.

Chapter 22

With tears pouring down her cheeks, Sue cried, "How *could* you?" She slammed her hand on the steering wheel. "How *could* you?" She slammed the steering wheel again. "I thought you were my friend."

She drove blindly, neither knowing nor caring where she was going. All she wanted to do was get as far away from Veronica as possible.

After a while her rage subsided and she started to concentrate on her driving. When she looked around her, she saw nothing even remotely familiar and realised she had no idea where she was. She had a feeling she was north of Welwyn Garden City, because she vaguely remembered turning left soon after passing over the A1 (M), and the town was to the right. She was on a two-lane country road with hedges on both sides.

She had been aware of a car behind her, and now she was concentrating she realised it was following her. To put it to the test, she speeded up. The car speeded up. She slowed down, and the car slowed down. Whatever she did, the car stayed with her. It had been following at a distance of forty to fifty yards, but it suddenly moved to within twenty to thirty yards of her. It was at this point that she recognised the car and the man sitting beside the driver.

How could she not recognise a man who had come to her house and scared the living daylights out of her?

Rather than feeling afraid, Sue felt angry. Furious even. How *dare* they do this to her after just learning that her husband was having an affair with her best friend? She felt like jamming her brakes on and having them run into the back of her vehicle, just to teach them a lesson.

She could see that both men were smoking. Occasionally, one of them would put his hand out of an open window and flick ash off his cigarette. She remembered Max telling her that the man with the shotgun had reeked of cigarette smoke.

She glanced in her rear-view mirror again, and the driver of the Subaru grinned and wiggled his fingers at her. Then, the two men looked at each other and laughed.

Her mobile rang. It was inside her handbag on the seat beside her. Thinking it was probably Veronica, she let it ring.

She glanced in her mirror again, and both men waved to her. They must have eyes like hawks to be able to see her eyes at this distance.

The phone stopped ringing. And then it started again.

Sue negotiated a bend in the road to reveal a relatively wide stretch of road that ran virtually straight for several hundred yards. She checked her mobile to see who was calling. It *was* Veronica. She has nothing to say to *her,* and certainly not at a time like this. She dropped the phone on the seat beside her, where it continued to ring.

She realised this was an obvious place for the Subaru to pass her, which was the last thing she needed. While they were behind her there was nothing they could do to her, but if they got ahead of her ...? This didn't bear thinking about. The only option she seemed to have was to try and outrun them. She knew it was a pious hope, because her vehicle was built for carrying nine people, not outrunning high performance cars, but she had to do something. She stood on the accelerator pedal. The vehicle accelerated, but maddeningly slowly. She was almost jumping up and down in her seat to make it to go faster.

Her mobile stopped ringing.

She looked in her rear-view mirror again, and blinked in surprise. The car was no longer there. She soon found out where it was when she heard the howl of a high-performance engine immediately beside her. By now, she was doing almost sixty-five miles per hour.

The car pulled ahead of her, and then fell back. When it repeated the procedure twice, she knew they were playing with her. When it next drew alongside, she found herself looking into the eyes of the man who had terrified her at her own front door. Constantin Boguescu leered at her.

The two vehicles were now within a couple of hundred yards of the end of the straight stretch, and the distance was closing fast.

Sue's brain went into overdrive. She knew that a blip of the Subaru's throttle would get the car ahead of her in no time at all, and she was running out of space, and options.

A thought occurred to her. She had watched American police programmes on TV with the children when Max had been away, and she had seen them perform what they called their PIT - Pursuit Intervention Technique - manoeuvre when they wanted to bring a dangerous car chase to an end, and it occurred to her that if she could somehow disable their car, she would have a chance to get away from them. It was worth a try.

Realising he was running out of road, the Subaru driver started to increase his speed, and when Sue found herself looking at the rear wing of the car, she swung her people carrier hard over to the right, at the same time standing on her brakes.

As the right front wing of her vehicle struck the left rear wing of the Subaru, her head was whipped forward, and she felt an excruciating pain in her neck. She was still standing on her brakes and her vehicle ground to a halt and the engine stalled.

The effect of the collision on the Subaru was catastrophic. The rear of the car slewed to the right, and then to the left, and then to the right again, finally slewing sideways some thirty to forty yards ahead of Sue's vehicle with smoke pouring off its tyres.

Through a windscreen that now had a long diagonal crack across it, Sue could see that the man who had terrified her at her front door was no longer grinning. His face had taken on a look of absolute horror.

Because of the speed at which the car had been travelling, it still had considerable forward momentum and it rolled over, sideways. It rolled once, and then again, and then again, each time bouncing up into the air. Great clods of earth flew up from the roadside verge each time it crashed to the ground, and Sue watched it change shape like Plasticine in the hands of a child each time it landed. Bits of metal and fragments of glass rained down on the road. The car finally came to rest, on its wheels, and lay still. A cloud of steam hissed from under a bonnet that was now crumpled beyond recognition.

The two men sat upright in their seats, their faces buried in airbags that were now in the process of deflating. The roof of the car had been stove in, and Sue could see that the necks of the two men were set at impossible angles. There was no sign of life from either of them.

After the noise and the carnage, the peace and tranquillity of the Hertfordshire countryside was pure bliss, especially when Sue realised she was no longer in danger. There was a hollow sound in her ears and she fancied she heard a helicopter approaching. She realised she was listening to her own heartbeat. She lost consciousness.

She woke to the sound of her mobile ringing. None of what was happening seemed real. It was as if she were in a dream, and the phone ringing was a part of it. It was only when it continued to ring that she came to her senses and answered it. When she spoke, her words sounded hollow in her ears.

It was Bob Schembri. "Sue, thank God! I've been trying to get hold of you for ages. Are you all right?"

"I'm not sure, Bob. My neck hurts, and I can hear my heart beating in my ears."

"Sue, we know you've been involved in an accident. There was a witness and we know what happened and we know where you are. So hang in there, the emergency services are on the way."

"I think I've killed them, Bob."

"Sue, you haven't killed anybody. It was an accident, plain and simple. According to the witness, who I imagine is still at the scene, the two men in the car were hassling you and you panicked and lost control of your vehicle. And that's what I want you to tell the police when they get there, because I don't want them going off half-cocked. Do you understand, Sue?"

"I understand, Bob."

"I'll get there as soon as I can. Sue, I'm going to hang up now, because I want to get on my way. And don't go thinking you've done anything wrong, because you haven't. Okay? Don't forget, there was a witness."

"All right, Bob."

They ended the call.

While she had been talking to Schembri, Sue had been watching a man in a suit wandering around what was left of the Subaru, and she assumed he was the witness Schembri had been talking about. She tooted her horn at him.

He walked over and smiled at her, before opening the door. The door had been damaged in the collision and he had to force it open. He looked like a nice man. Probably in his early to mid-thirties, he looked like the kind of man who would have a wife and children. In her side mirror, she could see a silver BMW parked behind her with its hazard lights flashing.

He gave her a warm smile. "Welcome back to the land of the living. The emergency services are on their way. I was driving behind those idiots in the Subaru and I saw what happened. I'm not surprised you lost control of your vehicle. Are you all right?"

"I think I'll live," Sue said. "Are they dead?"

He glanced at the wreckage of the car. "I'm not a doctor, but I think so. I can't see any sign of life."

Sue tried to undo her seatbelt. It was a struggle because as a result of the collision it had tightened around her. She had just managed to release it when her mobile rang again.

"I'll leave you to your call," the man said, turning and walking away.

There was the sound of sirens approaching.

It was Max, and he sounded frantic. "Sue, I've only just got the message. I was in a meeting. Look, head for the nearest police station, and whatever you do don't stop until you get there. Go through red lights if you have to. Just don't stop."

"You're too late, Max," Sue said wearily. "It's all over."

"Sorry?"

Sue told him about the crash.

"Oh my God! Are you all right, darling?"

"No, Max, I'm not all right. I've hurt my neck. And I'm not sure I want to talk to you."

"Sue, *please*. I know what you heard at Veronica's, but …"

"Max, I don't want to talk about it now. We'll talk about it later. Now if you don't mind, I'm going to hang up. I really don't feel well," she ended the call.

A police car with its blue lights flashing raced up on the other side of the Subaru, and skidded to a stop by the wreckage. Two uniformed officers jumped out. One of them hurried to the wreckage to check for signs of life, while the other one hurried over to check on Sue.

A minute or so later, an ambulance arrived. Two paramedics got out and hurried to the wreckage. They took one look at the occupants, and then looked at each other and shook their heads.

"Mrs Hughes?" the policeman said, glancing at the damage to her vehicle.

Sue nodded, and winced. "Yes, I'm Mrs Hughes."

He noticed her wincing. "Neck hurting?"

She nodded, wincing again. "Yes, a lot."

"You've probably got whiplash," the policeman said. "And I'm not surprised, after an accident like this." He raised a hand and called "*Over here!*" to the paramedics. He turned back to Sue. "We've been looking for you over half of Hertfordshire." He gestured at the Subaru, a smile on his lips. "But from what I can see, you were managing pretty well without us."

Chapter 23

There were now three police cars, an ambulance, and a fire engine at the scene. The police, who knew the whole story, were making no bones about letting the paramedics and the fire crew know what Sue had been through. And the witness, whom the police had asked to hang around, was voicing loudly what he had witnessed to whoever would listen as the fire crew went about their grisly task of extricating the bodies from the wreckage. At a result, no one was shedding a tear for the two men in the Subaru.

Because the wreckage of the Subaru was blocking much of the road, the ambulance could not get close to Sue's vehicle, and the paramedics had to squeeze through with a wheelchair. For Sue, every movement: being helped out of her vehicle, the four steps she had to take to get to the wheelchair, and then sitting in the wheelchair, was agonising.

By the time Bob Schembri caught up with her, Sue was sitting up in bed in a private room in the Lister Hospital in Stevenage. She had been given morphine for the pain, and she was wearing a neck brace.

"Well," he said, "considering the state of your vehicle, you look in remarkably good shape. And by the way, are you trying to make me redundant? That's now three people you've taken out of the equation."

"Just doing my bit to help the cause," Sue remarked dryly. She lowered her voice. "Bob, between you and I, I was just trying to disable their vehicle so I could get away. I knew that if I let them pass me, I would be at their mercy."

"I had a feeling that was what happened," Schembri said. "And that will be our secret. And thank God you didn't let them pass you. Who knows what might have happened if you had. Did the local police ask you what happened?"

"Actually, no, nobody did. They were too busy taking care of me."

"Good." There was one chair in the room and Schembri asked if he could sit.

"Of course you can," Sue said.

Schembri sat down and crossed his legs. "Max called me while I was on my way up here."

Sue didn't particularly want to hear about Max. "Did he?" she asked, disinterestedly.

"It's none of my business, but he seemed to be choosing his words more carefully than usual. Have you two fallen out about something?"

"It's nothing you need worry about. Bob, with three of these thugs out of the way, do you think we're out of the woods now?"

"As long as the Arabs are in jail, Sue, I'm afraid not. There's no shortage of thugs for hire out there, that's for sure."

"Do you have any idea who the men in the car were?"

"We do, as it happens. They had ID on them. One was Romanian, the other was Bulgarian, and – surprise, surprise - they were in the country illegally."

That afternoon, the police officer who had been first on the scene dropped in. He asked her how she was feeling.

"I'm fine, apart from my neck," she said.

"You're lucky to get away with just an injured neck," he said. "Your vehicle's a write-off."

"It didn't seem that badly damaged to me," Sue said, surprised. "But then I didn't exactly hang around to take a look at it."

"You can't always tell from just looking at the external damage. But in this case, even if it were repaired, no insurance company would touch it. Do you feel up to making a statement, Mrs Hughes?"

"Yes, of course. Might as well get it over with."

"May I sit down?"

"Please do."

The officer moved the chair to accommodate his long legs, and sat down. He took out a notebook and pencil. "This shouldn't take long, because we know from the witness statement what happened up to the time of the accident. We need to know, in your own words, why you swerved into the Subaru when it was overtaking you."

"I didn't swerve," Sue said, "I panicked. And they were harassing me rather than overtaking me. They were speeding up and slowing down. And the man in the passenger seat had come to my house and threatened me. I was absolutely *terrified*. I'm sure anybody who had been through what I've been through would have been. I panicked and I lost control of my vehicle? I don't know what else I can tell you."

"So you panicked and lost control of your vehicle?" the officer repeated, while writing it down. "Are you saying that was what happened?"

"That's exactly what I'm saying."

The officer nodded. "Thank you, Mrs Hughes, that's all I need to know." He put his notebook and pencil away and got to his feet.

"Am I in trouble?" Sue asked.

He smiled at her. "No, you're not in trouble. It will be written up an accident. You'll need to inform your insurance company. I hope you're soon feeling better." As he left the room, he grinned, gave her the thumbs up sign and mouthed, '*Well done, you.*'

The hospital had told Sue that they wanted to keep her in overnight for observation, which left her with a problem: all she had to wear were the clothes she had been wearing at the time of the accident, and what she had in her handbag, meaning her lipstick. She would need her makeup and clean underwear for the morning, and it was all at Veronica's. She had already decided she was not going to let what had happened between Veronica and Max ruin her relationship with Veronica, but she was not ready to talk about it yet, so she was not going to ask Veronica to bring her her things. Max would have to bring them.

She sent him a text.

'*I'm in the Lister Hospital, in Stevenage and they are keeping me in for observation overnight. I assume you'll be coming to see me tonight and, when you do, would you please collect my makeup and some clean underwear for me from Veronica's? Veronica will know where to find them.'* Contrary to her normal procedure when sending Max a message, she left her message unsigned.

Max responded almost immediately.

'Bob Schembri's been in touch, so I'm up to speed, and I'm relieved to hear you're okay. I'll be happy to bring your things. See you this evening. Love you, Max.'

When Max arrived that evening, Sue had not bargained on him bringing Veronica with him.

They walked in together and stood by the bed. Neither of them seemed to know what to say. Max was carrying an overnight bag that Sue had never seen before, and she assumed it belonged to Veronica. Veronica was carrying a large bouquet of flowers.

After a brief and slightly embarrassing silence, Veronica made the running. "We thought it would be better if we came together," she said, "because this seemed as good a time as any to get what's happened between us squared away."

Max put the bag down beside the bed and bent over to kiss his wife. "How are you feeling, darling?"

"I'm fine," she said, turning her face away. "Look, you two, I'm not taking the pair of you on at the same time in the condition I'm in. One of you had better make yourself scarce."

"Would you mind, Max?" Veronica said.

"I'll find myself a coffee," Max said. He turned and walked out of the room, closing the door behind him.

Veronica looked for a vase into which to put the flowers. There wasn't one. She stood by the bed looking lost. "I can't begin to tell you how sorry I am, Sue," she said. "If you hadn't overheard my phone conversation with Max this morning, none of this would have happened and you wouldn't have had an accident and you wouldn't be here in hospital. I wish I knew what to say to put things right."

Sue felt weary: not so much from the effects of the crash, more from the emotion welling up inside her. She could see how sorry Veronica was and how much she wanted to make amends, and she actually felt quite sorry for her. "How long has it been going on, Veronica? And sit down for heaven's sake, you're making the place look untidy."

Her levity was offered as an olive branch and Veronica took it and smiled. She sat down and laid the flowers across her lap. "It only happened once, Sue, and I give you my cast-iron guarantee that it will never happen again. And I know Max will tell you the same, because we discussed it in the car on the way here. We are both horrified about what happened."

"Who started it, Veronica?"

"Since we're being honest with each other, I have to admit that I did."

"But why, Veronica? Knowing how much I have on my plate at the moment, you are the *last* person I would have expected to make a play for my husband."

"Well since you ask, Sue, I saw it as a way of redressing the balance for you having an affair with Henry."

Sue had no idea Veronica knew about her affair with Henry and she was momentarily nonplussed. She closed her eyes, as if it would make the affair go away.

"In fairness to Max," Veronica continued, "he only agreed to meet me after I'd told him about your affair with Henry."

Sue sighed. "It looks like I got what I deserved, then. How long have you known?"

"I think I knew more or less as soon as it began. I saw the change in you, and I saw the change in Henry. And I saw how you were with each other when we were all together. It was really just a question of adding two and two."

"Then why, for heaven's sake, didn't you say something? You could have nipped it in the bud."

Veronica looked slightly shamefaced. "This is so difficult," she said. "Hands on heart, it was for purely selfish reasons that I didn't say anything. I'd always fancied Max, and I planned to save it until I could use it to persuade him to have an affair with me."

"Well, all things considered, I don't suppose I can blame you for that. He is a very attractive man. As a matter of interest, Veronica, when did you sleep with him?"

Not wanting to answer the question, Veronica studied her fingernails. Finally, she said, "Does it matter?"

"Yes, it does. It matters to me."

"I slept with him the night I told you I was going to meet a friend in London."

"But Max was in Paris that night. Or at least he was supposed to be. Did he lie to me about being in Paris?"

"No, he didn't lie to you. He *was* in Paris. He flew back that evening and we met at a hotel at Heathrow. He flew back to Paris the next morning."

"I see," Sue said. "Veronica, I need to know that this is the end of it. Because if it isn't, it's the end of us as friends."

"As I said earlier, it's the end of it for me, and I know it's the end of it for Max, too. He's mortified about what happened today. I think he realises how close he came to losing you."

At that moment, there was a knock on the door. The door opened and Max put his head round it. "Can I come in?"

"Yes, you can come in," Sue said.

Max walked in and stood by the end of the bed, his demeanour that of a schoolboy standing outside the headmaster's study, waiting to be punished.

Sue said, "Max, Veronica and I have talked it through, and as far as I'm concerned it's over and done with. But I have something say to both of you, and that is that if there's any more nonsense from either of you I'll put the pair of you over my knee and spank you."

Max relaxed visibly. He grinned. "I'll have some of that."

"Max, I'm trying to be serious."

"I know. And I'm sorry, Sue, I really am."

"And so am I," Veronica said.

"Then give me a hug, the pair of you. And watch my neck, because it hurts like hell."

Chapter 24

The man had got on the same train as Max in Welwyn Garden City and Max had noticed him because, when the train was pulling into the station, he had caught the man looking directly at him. Max had got into a first-class carriage; the man had got into the second-class carriage immediately behind it.

Max had not given the man another thought until he was walking to his office and caught the man's reflection in the window of a corner shop on Southampton Row. He didn't feel threatened, because it was rush hour and the streets were teeming with people hurrying to their place of work, but he mentally kicked himself for not listening to Bob Schembri's warnings that he was just as vulnerable as any other member of the family, more so in fact since he was the only member of the family out and about unaccompanied, and to take different trains, and walk different streets to his office. He had convinced himself he was invincible, and he had continued with his normal daily routine.

Max had no recollection of *ever* feeling physically threatened, apart from once at school when he was about fifteen when a fellow pupil, a young thug with a gang of cronies behind him, had seen fit to start bullying him. Max had let it go on for a few days, and he had then given the boy the hiding of his life in front of his pals. The bullying had stopped, immediately. Max had always thought that his physical size had put people off trying anything on with him. He was over six feet tall, and by dint of three years of serious bodybuilding when he was in his late teens, he was broad in the shoulder and deep in the chest.

But the next time he caught a glimpse of the man in a shop window, the man was no longer alone. There were now two of them, which put a completely different complexion on things.

Max realised that it was entirely possible that the man who had travelled on his train actually lived in the Welwyn Garden City area and that he took the train to London every morning, and that he had bumped into the man who now accompanied him quite by chance, but by dint of the use of angled shop windows, he didn't think so, because when he stopped, they stopped; when he started, they started, and when he crossed the road, they crossed the road.

Even so, he still couldn't be certain they were following him. To be certain, he stepped through the next open shop door, which happened to be a shop specialising in pipe tobacco, and cigars. For the next couple of minutes, he wandered round the shop breathing in the rich aroma of tobacco and pretending he was looking for something, while keeping a watchful eye on the door to the street, and the shop window. He reasoned that if the men walked past the shop, the chances were that they were simply going about their daily business. If, on the other hand, they did not walk past the shop, the chances were that he had been right, and that they were indeed following him.

Eventually, the shop's proprietor, an elderly gentleman who was dressed like a character out of a Charles Dickens novel and who had owned and run the shop for the last fifty years, asked him if he could help him find what he was looking for. Max told him thank you, no, that he was fine. But the elderly gentleman persisted, enquiring after his health and venturing his opinion on the state of the weather, and finally, more out of a feeling of guilt than anything, Max picked up a tin of pipe tobacco. Checking to see if the two men were following him cost him £25 for a tin of tobacco he had absolutely no use for. He had not smoked in years, and even then he had only smoked cigarettes. He had never smoked a pipe and he had no intention of starting now. He and the elderly gentleman thanked each other and wished each other good morning, and he carried his purchase out into the street in a little paper bag the proprietor had provided.

Out in the street, he took a quick look to his right and almost burst out laughing. The two men were gazing intently into the window of the next-but-one shop window, which happened to be a shop selling ladies' lingerie. How obvious was that!

Twenty yards or so to his left, meaning the direction in which he wanted to go, was a zebra crossing, and crossing the road seemed like a good idea. This was not only because his office was on the other side of the road, albeit still some half mile distant, if the two men also crossed the road it would provide further evidence that they were following him.

He walked to the crossing. A group of people stood complaining about having to wait for a double-decker bus that had found itself stranded over the crossing by the traffic in front of it stopping suddenly. The driver of the bus was making gestures of apology and pointing to the vehicle in front of him.

Max stood at the back of the queue and looked to his right. The two men had detached themselves from the window of the lingerie shop and were now making their way towards him. They were not looking in his direction, seemingly deep in conversation with each other.

The traffic ahead of the bus slowly started to move and the bus crawled off the crossing with a roar of its engine and an oily smell of diesel from its exhaust pipe. The group walked across the crossing, and Max walked across with them.

With so many people around, Max felt in no immediate danger, but he felt it prudent to get off the street and call Bob Schembri. On the far side of the crossing was a delicatessen, into which Max stepped, at the same time taking a quick look back.

The two men were crossing the road, still apparently deep in conversation with each other.

The delicatessen was busy and the atmosphere was warm and inviting, with a wonderful smell of coffee and of bread being toasted. Three people were serving behind the counter. There were five tables, four of which were occupied by people drinking coffee and eating breakfast before going to work. There was an empty table by the window. Max positioned himself at the back of the queue at the counter, and looked back. There was no sign of the two men, and he assumed they were hanging around in the street out of sight. He bought a cappuccino and carried it to the empty table by the window. He sat down, took out his mobile and pressed Bob Schembri's number on his speed-dial list.

To his surprise, and dismay, he got a recorded message informing him that the number he had dialled was temporarily unavailable and suggesting he either leave a message, or try again later. Try later? *Jesus Christ*! For all he knew he could be tied up with duct tape and lying in the boot of a car later. He flipped the phone shut and sat there with the instrument in his hand wondering what to do.

He had just taken a sip of his cappuccino when his mobile rang. It was set to ring and vibrate, and the vibration gave him the sensation of a mild electric shock.

It was Schembri. "Sorry, Max, I was in a meeting with the top brass, and they don't like mobiles going off while they're talking. What's up?"

"I'm being followed, Bob."

"*Right* …" Schembri drew out the word, as if he were not entirely surprised to hear it.

This was not the reaction Max had expected. "Did you not hear what I said, Bob? I'm being followed."

"What makes you think you're being followed?"

Max gave him chapter and verse about everything that had happened, from seeing the man at Welwyn Garden City station, to seeing his reflection in windows, and everything he had done to check that he was being followed. "I'm telling you, Bob, I'm being followed."

"Can you describe him?" Schembri said.

"What do you mean, *him*? There are two of them, at least *now* there are."

"*Two* of them?" The detective's voice took on an urgent tone. "Where are you, Max?"

"I'm in a delicatessen on Southampton Road. It's across the road from a tobacconist's shop." He glanced through the window and read the sign over the tobacconist's shop. "The shop is called Murray's, Purveyors of Fine Tobacco."

"Stay put, Max." Schembri's voice was now urgent. "And don't hang up."

Max took another sip of his cappuccino and sat looking out on to Southampton Row with his phone to his ear.

Suddenly, the two men appeared. They had been standing by a dry cleaning establishment a few yards away, waiting for Max to come out of the delicatessen. One of them had a mobile to his ear and he waved to Max.

Schembri came back on the line. "You still there, Max?"

"Yes, I'm still here. What the hell's going on, Bob? One of the guys just waved to me."

"I know, I told him to. He's the man I've had following you."

"He's the *what*! For crying out loud, Bob, why didn't you tell me you've had someone following me?"

"I didn't tell you, Max, because I didn't want you to relax your guard. He lives in the Welwyn Garden City area and he takes the same train to work as you."

"How long have you been having me followed?"

"Since you had the shotgun put to your neck."

"Then you owe me twenty-five quid."

"Why do I owe you twenty-five quid?"

"Because I spent twenty-five quid on tobacco in the tobacconist's shop. I went in there to check if they were following me, and the owner was such a nice man I felt I had to buy something. And I don't smoke."

"Couldn't you just have bought a box of matches?"

"How could I justify looking round the entire shop just for a box of matches? The proprietor would have thought I was mad."

"You're English, you could have talked about the weather."

Max chuckled. "When I came out of the shop, they were looking through the window of a ladies' lingerie shop. That was the clincher for me. I mean, what man in his right mind stands in the street looking in a ladies' lingerie shop?"

"I can explain that," Schembri said. "The guy from Welwyn Garden City is planning to buy his wife some lingerie for her birthday. We've been kidding him about it."

Duh! "Who's the second guy?"

"He's another one of ours. They bumped into each other in Russell Square, and, since your tail didn't know he'd been spotted - until you started playing super sleuth - they decided to walk you to your office together."

Max looked through the window again. The second man had gone. The one from Welwyn Garden City was standing there looking embarrassed at having been caught out. "I have a question for you, Bob. Do you have me tailed when I go home in the evening?"

"I wish you hadn't asked me that, Max."

"By which I take it you don't."

"The powers that be wouldn't wear it. It's easy in the morning because you always take the same train, but you and our guy go home at different times and we don't have the resources to have someone standing around waiting for you to leave your office."

"Then let's hope the clowns who have been making our lives a misery don't have the resources either. It would be ironic if you protected me on my way to my office, and they nabbed me on my way home."

Chapter 25

As expected, the insurance company had written Sue's vehicle off, and they had told her she could go ahead and find herself a replacement. As to replacement value, they had said that they would only provide compensation equal to the value of the vehicle at the time of the accident.

Max had bought the five-year-old Citroen Grand Picasso three years ago, and while it had been properly maintained and cleaned at least once every two weeks, its value had plummeted. Max knew that to find Sue a suitable replacement, he was going to have to dig deep.

He had been to the garage to which the Citroen had been taken and he had seen the damage from what Sue had described to him as *not that much of an impact*. The damage was, in fact, so extensive that he had realised how close he had come to losing her and it had brought tears to his eyes. As the policeman who had come to the hospital to take her statement had said, she had been lucky to get away from the collision with nothing worse than a sore neck. In addition to this, Max was experiencing pangs of remorse over the fact that, had he not slept with Veronica, Sue would not have gone haring off and the accident would not have happened. He was anxious to make amends.

As to what her next vehicle would be, it would, of necessity, need to be another form of people carrier, because - one day - life would be back to normal and she would once again be providing a free taxi service for the children and their friends.

Max had always been a fan of Toyota. Over the years, he had owned a Supra, Toyota's powerful three-litre sports car, and one of their big Lexus saloons, and in terms of quality and reliability, he rated them higher than Mercedes. And he had always been a big fan of their seven-seat Land Cruiser. In thinking about what had happened to Sue, he thought that a Land Cruiser might be an ideal vehicle for her. Not that he expected that what had happened to her would ever happen to her again, but better to be safe than sorry.

The *clowns*, as Max had taken to calling them, seemed to have quietened down since Sue had put paid to two of them – three, if you included the one on the train – but Max knew that this was no reason for complacency. Bob Schembri was certainly advising against complacency. He was still having Max followed, albeit only on his way to work, not on his way home.

The Land Cruiser was a big heavy vehicle, which would offer Sue excellent protection in the event of an accident. It had a high driving position, which would allow her to see over hedges and other vehicles, and it had a big V-8 engine, which would give her far more power than the Citroen had been able to deliver. Max had driven a Land Cruiser and it had been a thoroughly enjoyable experience. It was a behemoth of a vehicle, and he knew it wouldn't fit their garage, but it was the protection it would afford Sue that was uppermost in his mind.

When he broached the subject with Sue, she had no idea what a Land Cruiser looked like, so he brought up Toyota's official website on his laptop and showed her a picture of one. She said she liked the look of it, and he checked the dealer network on the website and found that there was a dealership in Letchworth, which was about twelve miles away. He checked the dealer's website and discovered that they had a brand new vehicle in metallic silver with black leather upholstery in stock.

Land Cruisers were far from cheap, and initially Max had had in mind to buy Sue a low-mileage second-hand one, but the more he thought about it, the more he thought he should buy her a new one. Sue had never had a brand new vehicle, and he thought that buying her a new one might go some way towards making up for his indiscretion with Veronica. He phoned the dealership and booked a date and time for he and Sue to go and see the vehicle.

Sue fell in love with the vehicle the moment she saw it. Max had always been the one to drive the luxury vehicle in the family, she being relegated to driving whatever the family requirements dictated at the time, and the thought of being able to call this gorgeous new vehicle her own, made her heart sing. While Max listened to what the salesman was saying, she heard none of it. She was too busy visualising herself up there in the driving seat.

When the salesman had finished his spiel, he asked, "Would madam like to see the inside of the vehicle?"

Max answered for her, "Judging by the look on her face, I'm sure *madam* would love to see the inside of the vehicle."

Not realising that getting into a Land Cruiser would entail having to climb up into it, Sue had worn a straight skirt, and when the salesman opened the door for her, he apologised, saying, "It's quite a step up, I'm afraid."

Undaunted, Sue hitched up her skirt and climbed up, remarking, "I see I'm going to have to wear trousers when I drive this."

She was still wearing a neck brace, and Max warned her to watch her neck.

The pain in her neck had now settled down to a dull ache, and the hospital had told her that all being well she should be able to take the brace off in a week or so.

Max was standing by her side of the vehicle, and when she settled into the driver's seat, her eyes were level with his. Normally, whether she was standing beside him, or sitting in a vehicle, she had to look up to him, and this made a nice change.

"I'm going to enjoy this high driving position," she said, looking around the cavernous interior of the vehicle and then out over its long bonnet.

"If I may, let me show you how to adjust the seat and the steering wheel," the salesman said. He excused himself and leaned in and put the key in the ignition. He turned it and the engine fired with a roar.

With the seat and steering wheel adjusted to Sue's liking, the salesman walked around the vehicle and climbed up into the seat beside her. He explained how the four-wheel drive arrangement worked, and then showed her how to turn on the lights, the windscreen wipers, screen wash, indicators, etc. He then added what he proudly referred to as his *piece de resistance*, "She's *very* easy to drive."

It was his referring to the vehicle as *she* on top of all the other things Sue liked about it, that she decided that, come what may, she was going to have it.

The salesman then had her climb up into the rear of the vehicle to show her the seven seats, the legroom, the huge luggage area, and the TV screens which were set into the back of the front seat headrests. Sue thought these would be ideal for keeping the children occupied on long trips, such as the four-hour drive to their holiday home in the Lake District.

When the salesman had finished telling Sue everything he wanted to tell her, Max said, "Well, darling, what do you think?"

"Need you ask?" she replied, her eyes twinkling.

"Are you happy with the colour?"

"It's perfect in every respect. I wouldn't want to change a thing."

The salesman was standing with the fingers of both hands crossed behind his back. He hadn't made a sale for three days, and before they had arrived, his boss, the sales manager, had been all over him to make sure he made this one.

"What can you do on the price?" Max asked him.

"That will depend on how you will be paying for the vehicle, sir."

The salesman's *will be* paying for the vehicle, as if it were a done deal, was not lost on Max. But he didn't hold it against him. He was a salesman too, and he would probably have said something similar had he been in his position. Sue telling the salesman how much she liked the vehicle every time he had shown her something had not exactly helped his negotiating position, but he didn't mind because he could see how excited she was. He had told the salesman they were looking for a vehicle to replace one written off in an accident, and he said, "It will be part cheque from the insurance company, with the balance by banker's draft drawn on my bank."

"Then, I can give you a five percent discount, sir."

"What do you think, Sue?"

"It's up to you, Max. It's your money."

"Yes, but it's your vehicle, darling. If you want it, you can have it."

"Then, I'll have it. Thank you, darling, I love it."

As they went through the paperwork in the office, Max spotted something in the printed blurb that made him smile. It read: *Short of something armoured, nothing will get you into, and, more importantly, out of, a hostile place than a Toyota 4 x 4*. He pointed it out to Sue, joking, "There's nothing you won't be able to knock off the road in this one."

His joke fell on stony ground. "Max, I know you're buying me a lovely car, but after what I went through, that isn't even remotely funny."

Chapter 26

"More coffee, Sue?"

"Have we time?"

Veronica glanced at the cuckoo clock on the breakfast room wall. "I think so. If we leave in ten minutes we should get to the school on time."

"Would you like to go in the Land Cruiser this morning, Randy?"

"Oh, could we, Auntie Sue? I was hoping you'd ask."

"Of course, we can."

"Oh, cool." Randy, who was in his stocking feet, swallowed what was left of his orange juice in a gulp and got to his feet. "I'll get my things."

"Have you cleaned your shoes?" his mother asked.

"I cleaned them last night."

"Have you done your homework?"

"*Mother!* You *know* I've done my homework. I *always* do my homework." He only called Veronica 'Mother' when he was exasperated with her. Otherwise it was Mum.

"Off you go then. And don't forget to clean your teeth."

"*Mother!*"

As Randy ran up the stairs, making an unholy row, Veronica poured Sue some more coffee.

Sue took a sip and said, "Wasn't that fun, yesterday?" She was referring to she and Veronica celebrating getting her new Land Cruiser by driving to London in it to shop for clothes for their forthcoming holiday.

Veronica smiled. "Wasn't it just? But if our husbands knew how much money we'd spent, I doubt whether they would see it that way."

"Max would have a fit," Sue said. "I won't be letting *him* see my credit card statement at the end of the month, that's for sure."

"But we needed new things for our holiday, didn't we, sweetie?" Veronica said. "I mean, I didn't have a *thing* to wear. And we're worth it, aren't we?"

"Of course, we are," Sue said.

"Our husbands don't know how lucky they are having us as their wives," Veronica said. "And speaking of husbands, Sue, how are things between you and Max now?"

Sue pulled a face "So so. He was fine until a couple of days after he bought me the Land Cruiser, and then he switched me off again. I swear he thinks more of his business than he does of me."

"When's he getting back from Slovenia?"

"I don't know for certain. The last time I spoke to him he said it would be either Thursday night or Saturday morning, depending on some meetings he was trying to set up."

"I don't know how you stand him being away so much," Veronica said. "I know I couldn't. It would drive me crazy."

215

"I don't know how I stand it either," Sue said. "It never gets any easier. I sometimes think I would be prepared to give it all up to have a man who had a nine-to-five job."

"I'll be outside," Randy called, clattering down the stairs.

"We'd better go," Veronica said, glancing at the clock again. "I'll just refresh my lipstick."

"And I'll get my bag," Sue said.

When Randy got to the Land Cruiser his hand flew to his mouth. He stared at it, horrified, and then walked back into the house. "Auntie Sue," he said, "I think you'd better see this."

"See what?" Sue said.

"Your new Land Cruiser!"

"What about it?"

"I think you'd better take a look at it."

The word HARRY had been gouged out of the rear nearside door of the Land Cruiser in letters six inches high. It had been gouged out with such force that the metal around the lettering had been severely dented. A line had been gouged under the word, and under this line the words WITNESS BOX had been gouged. Then there was an equals sign followed by a stick figure dangling from a gallows, to form a crude arithmetic equation. The meaning of the message was clear: if Harry takes the witness box, he is a dead man. The force with which the message had been gouged into the bodywork told a message of its own. On the ground by the side of the vehicle were the flakes of metal that had been gouged out.

Veronica stepped out of the house and closed the door. "Right," she said. "I'm ready. Let's go." She saw the damage to Sue's new vehicle and her hand flew to her mouth. "The *bastards*," she cried. "The absolute *bastards*."

"They haven't gone away, have they?" Sue said quietly. "They've been regrouping. Bob was right when he said we shouldn't relax our guard."

"This must have been done during the night," Veronica said. "I'm sure they'll be long gone by now, but Randy see if there are any cars by the green, or people you don't recognise."

"Right." Randy hared off down the courtyard and out through the gate.

Veronica bent down to inspect the damage. "Good thing you didn't let them get their hands on you when they were chasing you, Sue."

Sue winced. "Oh, don't."

Randy ran back into the courtyard. "There's nobody out there who shouldn't be," he panted.

"Take a look in the garden," his mother said. "And round the house. And check the orchard, and the woods. For all we know, somebody could be watching us from the trees."

Randy raced across the courtyard and through the wrought iron gate leading to the back garden.

Sue stood by the Land Cruiser deep in thought. "You and I are going to have to do something about this, Veronica," she said, "because I'm not having this. And it's clear the police can't protect us."

"What did you have in mind?" Veronica asked.

"I don't know; I need to think about it. But I do know one thing; they're not getting away with this."

"Shouldn't we leave it to the police?" Veronica said. "I know you don't think they can protect us, but they're much better equipped to deal with this than we are."

But Sue was adamant. "I'll call Bob and the local police to tell them what's happened, but then you and I should sit down and do some serious brainstorming. We'd better take Randy in your car and leave the Land Cruiser here. I'll call the police on our way."

Soon after they got back from dropping Randy off at school, a marked police car pulled in the courtyard and two uniformed officers got out to inspect the damage to the Land Cruiser. Sue and Veronica went out to speak to them.

One of the officers said it looked like a screwdriver had been used. "We'll have forensics come over and take a look," he said, "but I wouldn't hold your breath."

When the police had left, Veronica and Sue headed back into the house.

"Max is going to be livid about this," Sue said, as Veronica closed the front door.

Veronica looked at her in surprise. "But why, Sue? It wasn't your fault."

"He won't see it that way." Sue checked her watch. "Slovenia's two hours ahead of us. I might just get him at lunch if I call him now. I might as well get it over with. It will only spoil my day thinking about what he's going to say, if I don't. I'll call him from the garden."

She was right, Max was not at all pleased. "What on earth were you thinking of? That's a very expensive vehicle."

"Max, it was parked in the courtyard at Veronica's. It's not as if I had left in out in a rough part of town. And it

218

was done overnight. Am I supposed to stay up all night to make sure nobody goes near it?"

"But still."

"But still *what,* Max? Are you blaming *me* for them coming at the dead of night and carving chunks out of my nice new car? Do you think I *invited* them to come and damage it?"

"No, of course not, but ..."

"Well, thanks for your support, Max. Now, I wish I hadn't bothered calling you. Just so you know, I'm calling the dealer and asking them to come and collect it tomorrow afternoon. The police said the forensics people should have finished with it by then. When are you coming home?"

"I'm not sure. I had thought I would be home on Saturday, but it might be Monday now."

"Max, why do you even bother coming home? You'll only be gone again as soon as you get here. Why don't you just stay on the Continent?"

"Sue, that's silly."

"Yes, of course it is. That's how you *see* me, isn't it, Max? Just a silly woman."

"Sue, can we do this some other time. I'm in a restaurant. I'm with people."

"Who are these people?"

"What does it matter who they are?"

"Are they customers, or members of the company?"

"They're from our Ljubljana office."

"So they report to you."

"Well yes, but ..."

"Then, *I* should be more important to you than they are."

Max sighed. "Sue, can I call you later?"

"You swore it wouldn't be like this when you took on Europe, Max. All you ever think of is your precious job. I don't count anymore."

"Of course, you do."

"Well, it doesn't feel like it to me. I feel like an inconvenience"

"Sue, please."

"One day, you'll come home from one of your trips and I won't be here."

"Sue ..."

Sue switched the phone off and walked back into the house. "I don't know about you, Veronica, but I need a drink."

Veronica gave her a sympathetic smile. "Bad as that?"

"He's hopeless."

"Gin and tonic?"

"Yes, please. A *large* one. In fact, make it a triple."

"Sounds good to me. I'll have one too."

At 2.15pm, Bob Schembri phoned Sue on her mobile. "Sue, in view of what's just happened, I'm having the local boys increase the frequency of their visits to Veronica's house."

"Couldn't you put a man on the house full-time, Bob?" Sue said. She and Veronica had been drinking since 11.15 that morning, and her voice was slurring slightly.

Veronica nodded enthusiastically at Sue's suggestion and then picked up her glass and had another drink.

"I realise," Sue continued, "that they would need rocket-powered grenades to get into the house now it's been secured, but Veronica and I still have to walk to our cars and you can only see a third of the courtyard from the kitchen window."

"I know, Sue, and I would if I could, but with all the cuts going on at the moment my hands are tied. Perhaps we should think about putting closed circuit TV outside the house. That's about the only thing that hasn't been done. Otherwise, all I can suggest is that you call me day or night if you have a problem. Wake me up in the middle of the night, if necessary."

When Sue had ended the call, Veronica said, "He's sweet on you."

"Oh, come on. He isn't sweet on me; he's just doing his job."

"Yes, he is. I've seen it in the way he looks at you. And his voice softens when he speaks to you."

"No, it doesn't. Well if it does, I hadn't noticed."

"Yes, it does, and, yes, you had. And you flush when you're talking to him."

"I do not."

"Yes, you do. You're flushed, now. Go and take a look in a mirror. You look as if you've gone too heavy on the blusher."

Sue realised the game was up. "I didn't realise it was *that* obvious?" She shrugged. "Well, I will admit that I do quite like him. But there's nothing I can do about it, so there's no point in even thinking about it." She took a sip of her drink.

"You can meet him for a drink," Veronica said. "With Max away and the kids boarding, who would know? I won't tell."

"What about Randy?"

"He spends so much time on his computer in his room that I doubt he would even notice you were missing."

"What about Henry?"

"We could choose a night when he isn't coming home. He always tells me in advance when he's not coming home, because it makes him feel less guilty. You could arrange to see Bob, if you wanted to."

Sue cast a suspicious eye at her. "Is there some reason why you are trying to drive me into the arms of another man? Max, for example, I hope you're not still sweet on him."

"Heaven's, no, I've learned my lesson there. It's just that I hate to see you so unhappy."

Sue said wistfully, "I will admit that I've found myself thinking about Bob, recently. In fact, I almost called him the other evening."

"You should have done. You could do worse. Think about it, Sue: he's not married, he must make a pretty good salary, and he's hellishly attractive. Truth to tell, I quite fancy him myself."

"That much was obvious when you first met him at King's Cross."

"Then you'd better get on with it before I get there before you, hadn't you?"

"You know something," Sue said, draining the contents of her glass. "I might just do that." She waggled her glass at Veronica. "How about another one of these?"

That evening, Henry walked in from a tiring day at his factory to a most unusual scenario: a quiet house. Usually, when he got home, the house was a hive of activity: music on the radio, Veronica in the kitchen preparing the evening meal, Sue helping her, and Randy upstairs in his room doing whatever Randy did in his room. The only sound was the ticking of the grandfather clock in the hall. As he closed the front door, it started to chime the hour. It was 6pm He knew Veronica and Sue were home, because Veronica's Mercedes was in the courtyard, as was Sue's new Land Cruiser. He had missed the damage to the vehicle when he had gone to work that morning, but he had seen it now and he had stood looking at it and shaking his head.

There was a red light flashing on the phone in the hall, indicating there was a message on the answering machine. He ignored it. He put his briefcase down by his bureau at the far end of the hall. "Veronica?" he called. There was no reply. "Where the hell is everybody?" he muttered. He needed a drink and he headed for the kitchen where he kept a bottle of twenty-year old Macallan single malt scotch in a cupboard. As he walked back down the hall, he heard snoring. It was coming from the drawing room, a room they normally only used for entertaining. He walked in to find Veronica sprawled on one of two silk sofas, with Sue sprawled on the other. Both were sound asleep. Veronica was lying on her back with her mouth open, snoring loudly. An empty tumbler lay on its side on the sofa by her outstretched hand. A slice of lemon lay in the glass. There was a stain on the sofa where the contents of the glass had spilt when she had lost consciousness. Sue was lying on her side with one arm dangling over the edge of the sofa. Her empty glass stood upright on the carpet.

A bottle of Tanqueray gin stood on the coffee table, its cap nowhere in sight. A half-inch of gin remained in the bottle. Henry had only bought the bottle yesterday. He usually only drank Gordon's, but his local off-licence was doing a special promotion on Tanqueray and he had bought three bottles for the price of two. None of them had been opened, until now. The room smelt like a distillery.

Some of his watermarked handmade stationery lay on the carpet by the sofa on which Veronica was sleeping, and several sheets with pencil-written notes on them were scattered around.

Henry would normally have gone ballistic about the stain on the sofa, not to mention his personal stationery being used without his permission, but not this time. He knew these women well enough to know that this kind of behaviour was out of character, and he suspected it had much to do with the damage to the Land Cruiser. He collected the bottle and the glasses and carried them into the kitchen.

The glasses clinking in the kitchen sink woke Veronica. "Is that you, Randy?" she called, her voice husky from sleep, and alcohol.

"No, it's me," Henry called.

"Is Randy home?"

"I've no idea. I've only just got in."

"What time is it?"

Henry glanced at the cuckoo clock. "It's just after six." Since he had a bottle of gin in his hand, he decided on a gin and tonic instead of a scotch, and he took a tumbler from a cupboard and emptied the balance of the contents of the bottle of Tanqueray into it. He cut a slice of lemon and dropped it into the glass, and then half-filled the glass with ice cubes from the automatic ice dispenser in the front of the fridge door.

Veronica lay listening to the sounds from the kitchen. She had a vague feeling something was wrong, but

224

couldn't think what it was. She tried to sit up, and groaned as bright white lights flashed before her eyes. As her head began to clear, she realised what was wrong - they hadn't picked Randy up. "Henry," she called. "Is Randy in his room?"

Henry was opening a bottle of Schweppes Tonic Water. "I've no idea."

"Well would you check, please?"

"When I've finished making my drink."

"*Now* please, Henry."

Muttering "What did your last servant die of?" Henry walked out into the hall and clumped up the stairs, making as much noise as he could to express his displeasure at being ordered around. He walked along the landing and stuck his head round the door of Randy's room. There was no sign of Randy. He walked back on to the landing, and called, "No, he's not in his room."

The commotion woke Sue, who – inebriated though she was – immediately realised they hadn't picked Randy up. She looked across at Veronica, "We haven't picked Randy up." Her tongue was so swollen she was having difficulty forming her words.

Henry walked down the stairs and called, "Drink, you two?" Adding under his breath, "If you haven't had enough already."

Veronica and Sue stared at each other. They looked like wrecks. Their clothes looked like they had been sleeping in them, which – in point of fact - they had, and their normally immaculately turned out hairstyles looked anything but immaculate. Under any other circumstances they would have dissolved into fits of laughter at the sight of each other, but not this time. Even if Randy had not been picked up, he should have been home long since. Before the trouble had begun, he had walked home from school in twenty-five minutes on any number of occasions.

Veronica's mobile lay on the carpet by the sofa on which she was sitting, and she picked it up and speed-dialled Randy's number. "It's ringing," she said. The number rang and rang, but there was no reply. Veronica knew that his mobile was set to activate the voicemail facility after seven rings, but it continued to ring long after this. When it was obvious that Randy was not going to answer, Veronica ended the call and turned to Sue. "Why would he switch off his voicemail facility?" she said. "He's never done that before. What are we going to do?"

"Well, the one thing we're *not* going to do is panic," Sue said. "Try his number again."
Veronica pressed Randy's speed-dial number again, and this time she got a recorded message saying that the number was temporarily unavailable and to try again later. This meant that, since she had first phoned the number and now, the phone had been switched off. "His phone's switched off now," she told Sue. "I don't like this one bit. He *never* switches his phone off. We need to get to the school."

"It would be quicker to phone," Sue said.

Veronica shook her head. "I need to go there."

"Right." Sue got to her feet and groaned. "My head! I might just give up drinking after this."

Veronica had a problem with her feet swelling after a bout of heavy drinking and she was struggling to get her shoes on. "Henry," she called, "you need to take us to the school."

Henry had just finished mixing his drink and the glass was halfway to his lips. "Why?"

"Because Randy should have been home by now, and his phone's been switched off. He never switches his phone off."

Henry knew this to be true and he realised from the tone of his wife's voice something was seriously wrong. He put his drink down. "I'll get the car started."

Veronica hobbled into the kitchen.

"You'd better run a comb through your hair," Henry said. "You don't want people seeing you looking like that."

"I'll comb it in the car. Are you ready, Sue?"

"Be with you in a minute," Sue called. She made a quick visit to the bathroom, ran a comb through her hair, grabbed her handbag and rushed out of the house, locking the door.

Veronica and Henry were sitting in the car with the engine running.

By breaking speed limits all the way, they made it to the school in five minutes. Henry skidded the car to a stop on the drive, and the two women climbed out and made their way unsteadily into the building.

Mrs Godley saw the worried looks on their faces, and said, "Randy hasn't come home, has he?"

"No, he hasn't," Veronica said. "And his mobile's switched off. Mutti, he *never* switches his mobile off." She was close to tears.

If Mrs Godley had noticed the strong smell of alcohol on their breath, she made no mention of it. "When you didn't turn up, I told him that if he could wait until five o'clock I would drive him home. I had to meet a couple of new parents first. He said he didn't want to trouble me and he could be home in twenty minutes if he ran. I didn't want to let him go, but he wouldn't take no for an answer. I phoned you on your house phone when he left, but there was no reply, so I left a message on the answering machine. And I know he'd called you at least twice on your mobile."

By now, Veronica was looking on the point of collapse, and Sue took charge. "Thank you, Mutti; we'll take it from here." She took Veronica's arm. "Come on, we need to call Bob Schembri."

"Please keep me posted, my dear," Mrs Godley said.

"Of course," Sue responded.

Sue phoned Schembri as they walked to the car.

"Bob, Randy's gone missing."

Chapter 27

'GET POLICE TO RELEASE MEN THEY HOLDING AND WE NOT HURT RANDY.'

The words looked to have been cut from four different publications: a glossy magazine, a paperback book, and two newspapers, one of which was pink – probably the Financial Times. They had been pasted on a sheet of A4 copy paper, which had been folded so it would fit through the letterbox.

Henry had found the message on the mat behind the front door when he had come down to make Veronica a cup of tea at 5am. She had not slept a wink and Henry had been making her cups of tea regularly throughout the night.

The previous evening, the local police had been there until 8pm and Bob Schembri and his colleague DS Johnson had left an hour or so later. None of them had had an appetite for food, and dinner had never materialised. Sue had sustained them with cups of tea, coffee and biscuits, and had made sandwiches when Schembri had left. Veronica had spent most of the evening in her room, nursing the mother of all migraines.

During the evening, Henry had agreed to closed circuit TV being installed around the outside of the house, and he had called his factory manager on his home phone to say not to expect him until later in the morning.

Breakfast had been a sombre affair, with Veronica – who looked to have aged ten years - finally making an appearance, but only managing to eat a piece of buttered toast.

During breakfast, Sue had been aware that Veronica had been casting glances at her, and she found out what was on Veronica's mind about mid-morning when they were having yet another cup of coffee in the family room.

Veronica came right out with it. "Sue, I'm sorry, and you're probably going to hate me for this, but knowing what might be happening to Randy, I need you to change your mind about putting Harry in the witness box."

Sue understood where Veronica was coming from, but after all she and her family had been through to ensure that the people the police were holding were put away where they belonged, asking her to throw it all away was incomprehensible. It would be giving in to them; letting them win. And she couldn't do that. But what could she say to Veronica?

Henry gave her a sympathetic smile, as if he understood her predicament.

Sue stalled for time. "There might be something else Bob can do," she said. "Let me have a word with him. I'll call him from the garden." Sue picked up her mobile and stepped out on to the patio. So she wouldn't be overheard from the house, she walked to the bottom of the garden. She had no idea what she was going to say to Schembri, but she needn't have worried, because the moment she got through to him there was a loud shriek from inside the house.

"*RANDY!*"

Sue said quickly into the phone, "Bob, I'll have to call you back. It sounds like Randy's home." She shut off the phone and ran back into the house.

Veronica was in the hall with her arms round her son. She was sobbing tears of pure joy.

Randy's face was red, he was sweating profusely, and his chest was heaving. He had his school blazer clutched in his hand, and his tie was half way round his neck. His shirt-tails were hanging out of his trousers. "Hi, Auntie Sue," he said, grinning at her.

"Randy! Thank *God* you're back." Sue joined them in a group hug. As she hugged them, she shed a few tears of her own.

Henry joined them. He shook Randy's hand vigorously. "I'm glad to see you back, my boy." Even *his* eyes were moist.

"Thanks, Henry," Randy said. "It's good to *be* back."

"Let me run you a bath," Veronica said. "Then, what do you say to a full English breakfast?"

"Yes, please. I'm *starving*."

"I'll call Bob," Sue said.

After his bath, Randy ate his breakfast as if his life depended on it.

Schembri arrived a couple of hours later. DC Johnson was with him. He shook Randy's hand. "I'm glad to see you home safely," he said briskly. "They treat you well enough?"

"They didn't *mistreat* me," Randy replied.

"Good. Conference time! Where do we sit, Veronica?"

The only table big enough to accommodate them all was the ten-seat table in the dining room. It was an antique table that had belonged to Veronica's maternal grandmother and, while Sue went to make coffee, Veronica threw a green baize cloth over it.

When Sue came back with the coffee, Schembri positioned himself at the head of the table, putting Randy at the other end of the table, facing him.

DC Johnson got out a pad and pencil.

"Right," Schembri said, "let's get things started, and let's begin at the beginning. Tell us what happened after you'd decided to run home from school, Randy."

Randy cleared his throat. "Well, nothing happened until I was two-thirds of the way home, and then I heard a car in the lane behind me. I heard it stop, and then I heard people running. The next thing I knew I'd been grabbed from behind and a black hood had been pulled over my head."

Johnson, who didn't take shorthand, was writing furiously.

"So you didn't see who grabbed you," Schembri said.

Randy shook his head. "I didn't see a thing."

"Could you see anything through the hood?" Schembri asked. "Shapes, images, that sort of thing."

"No, nothing," Randy replied. "It was pitch black in the hood. I didn't see a thing until they pushed me into the bedroom of the house they kept me at overnight. And even then I didn't see anything, because they only took the hood off when they pushed me into the room. And then they closed the door, and locked it."

"Oh, my poor darling," Veronica said.

"Describe the bedroom, Randy," Schembri said.

Randy shrugged. "There's not much to say about it really. It was just an ordinary room."

232

"I need more than that, Randy. Cast your mind back. *Think*. How big a room was it?"

"It was a square room about ten feet by ten."

"High ceiling? Low ceiling?"

Randy looked up at the ceiling. "Lower than this room. About eight feet, I would say."

"Anything else about the room?"

"The paper was peeling off the walls."

"Go on."

Starting to get the hang of what the detective was looking for, Randy said, "It had bare floor boards, which creaked when I walked on them, and it had a single bed, a very narrow one. More of a cot really, for a child."

"Any other furniture in the room?"

"No. There was no table, no chair. And there was nowhere to hang anything except for a plastic hook on the back of the door. And there was a naked light bulb hanging from the centre of the ceiling. I had the feeling it might have been an old council house. And I would say it hadn't been used for some time."

"Why do you say that, Randy?" Schembri said.

"It smelt damp, and musty."

"Is there anything else you remember about the house?"

"It had a narrow staircase,"

"How narrow, Randy? No detail is too small, so think back."

"Narrow enough that while I had my right hand on the rail, the back of my left hand was brushing the wall. And the wall felt damp."

Schembri changed tack. "I assume you had to use the bathroom while you were there, so what about that? Did it have a window, and did it have a view from the window?"

"I did have to use the bathroom, but I didn't see it because they put the hood over my head before they let me use it."

"Was there no chance of taking the hood off while you were in the toilet?"

Randy shook his head. "No, because they didn't close the door. I think the man was standing in the doorway, watching me."

"*Bastards*!" Henry growled.

"Anything else you remember about the bathroom, Randy?"

"Only that there was no toilet paper. I was given a few pieces of what felt like newspaper."

"Oh, my poor darling," Veronica said again.

"How did you let them know you needed to use the bathroom?"

"I stamped on the floor and shouted."

"Let's get back to the bedroom, Randy? I assume there was a window."

"Yes, there was a window. And some moth-eaten old curtains."

"What could you see from the window?"

"A field. Trees. Hedges. Some birds. Blue sky."

"Was there anything in the field? Cattle? Horses?"

"Some cows, black and white ones. And there was a handful of sheep. And I saw a couple of foxes."

"Any people?"

"No, no people."

"Were you at the front of the house, or the back?"

"I would say I was at the back. I didn't see any other houses. Just open countryside."

"I assume you couldn't open the window. They wouldn't be stupid enough to put you in a room with a window you could open."

"No, I couldn't open the window. It had a metal frame, and it had been screwed shut. I would have needed a screwdriver to open it."

"You say they picked you up close to home, Randy. Tell us how long it took to drive from there to the house they kept you at."

Veronica interrupted his flow. "Did they feed you, Randy?"

"They gave me bread and cheese last night, and water to drink. No food this morning, just water."

"I wish I could get my hands on them!" Henry growled.

"How far was the house from where they picked you up, Randy?" Schembri said, mildly irritated by his flow being interrupted, but understanding that Randy's mother and stepfather had spent the night under extreme stress. "I realise you can't be exact, and a rough estimate will be fine."

"I would say it was a drive of about twenty minutes, and it was all twists and turns. No motorways."

"So all country roads, would you say?"

Randy nodded. "Yes, I would say so."

"Was the driver driving quickly?"

"Not particularly."

"So four or five miles?" Schembri ventured. "Give or take?"

Randy thought about it for a moment, and then nodded. "Sounds about right. It took me almost two hours to get back, but then I wasn't running in a straight line. I was running behind hedges, because I knew they would be out looking for me."

"Good thinking," Schembri said.

"And it's a good thing you have that sense of direction of yours," Henry said. "You could put Randy in the middle of the Gobi Desert and he would find his way out of it," he announced proudly.

"I got that from you, didn't I, Mum?" Randy said, grinning at his mother.

Veronica smiled fondly at him. "Yes, you did, my darling. And thank goodness you did."

Johnson took the opportunity to rub his aching wrist.

Schembri continued, "Randy, when you were finding your way home this morning, in which direction were you travelling? East, west, north, or south?"

"I would say I was heading east, because I was running directly into the sun."

"So the house must be west of here. Let's take a break everyone, I need to call this in." Schembri got to his feet. "Stay put everybody, please." He went out into the garden to make his call.

While his boss was gone, Johnson took the opportunity to sharpen his pencil and rub his aching wrist again.

Henry asked him if he had ever thought of using a portable dictating machine.

Schembri was back within a few minutes, and the questioning began again.

"And at no time did you see any of their faces, Randy?"

Randy shook his head. "They always made sure I had the hood over my head."

"Did they bring your food, such as it was, to your room?"

"Yes, they did. A hand came round the door and put the food on the floor."

"Did you hear any of their voices?"

"I heard one soon after they snatched me," Randy said. "The driver had to do an emergency stop, and he came out with a mouthful."

"In English?"

"Yes, but in an accent I'd never heard before."

"Unusual that," Schembri mused, "a foreigner swearing in a language other than his own. Might indicate he'd been in England for some time. So you didn't see any of them, Randy, but do you have any idea how many of them there were?"

"Well, two of them grabbed me, one on each arm, and they stayed with me in the back of the car. And there had to be a driver, so there had to be at least three of them."

"Any idea what kind of car it was?"

"I do as it happens. It was a black Lexus LS400, an old one. I got a quick look at it when I got away from them this morning. It had grey leather upholstery."

"I don't suppose you got a look at the number plate."

"Sorry. I was more interested in getting away than looking at the number plate."

"I don't blame you for that. Anything else you remember about the car?"

"Only that the interior stank of beer, and cigarette smoke. And there were empty beer cans all over the floor. I felt them under my feet, yesterday."

"I need to call this in as well," Schembri said, getting to his feet. "Stay put again everyone, please."

Henry piped up, "Bob, do you need me? I seem to be surplus to requirements here, and I have a factory to run. Would you mind if I left?"

"I think we can manage without you," Schembri said. "Oh, before I forget, the CCTV people will be getting in touch with you shortly about putting cameras outside the house."

"Let's hope you catch those morons before that becomes necessary," Henry responded.

Schembri came back, sat down and got right on with his questions. "Randy, with bare floorboards in the room they kept you in, sounds from downstairs would carry. Are you sure you didn't hear voices?"

"I *did* hear voices,' Randy said, "but I couldn't hear what they were saying. They were playing loud music on a radio, and there was a lot of laughter. And then at one stage there were raised voices and it sounded like they were having an argument. The noise went on until just after midnight."

"What happened then?"

"The radio went off and I heard car doors slam. Then I heard a car start up and drive away. I assumed it was the Lexus."

"Did they leave somebody in the house with you?"

"Yes, they did. There was movement until about one o'clock. And then I heard snoring."

"Did you manage to get some sleep, Randy," Sue asked.

"Very little, Auntie Sue. I might have dozed off for an hour or two, but the bed was lumpy and I couldn't get comfortable."

DC Johnson rubbed his wrist and cracked his fingers, earning him a frown from the DCI.

"Randy, let's get to how you escaped."

"I escaped when they were taking me to the car."

"I assume they'd put the hood on you."

"Yes, they had. I had a man on each arm, as before, but when we got to the car one of them let go of me. I assume to get into the other side of the car."

"I think I know what's coming," Schembri said, a ghost of a smile appearing on his lips.

Randy grinned. "I whipped the hood off, twisted round and ducked under the arm of the other man, and ran off into the field."

Schembri slapped the table in triumph. "Well done, you! Bloody amateurs. I knew they'd slip up sooner or later. Did you see any of their faces at this point?"

"No, I was too busy trying to get away."

"And nobody could blame you for that. Randy, let's backtrack. What about when the car came back to the house this morning? What time did it come back, and what happened when it did?"

"It came back at about a quarter to seven. Soon after that one of them came upstairs and let me use the toilet."

"Same procedure as before; hood on and bathroom door open?"

"Yes to the first question, and no to the second."

"You mean he closed the door?"

"Yes, he did. Which I thought was strange, because I could have taken the hood off."

239

"And did you take the hood off?"

"No, I didn't think it would have achieved anything, except to annoy him. And he'd brought me a glass of water. He'd left it on the floor in the bedroom. I found it when he took me back to the room."

"And he didn't say anything?"

"Wait a second," Randy said. "I've just realised … he *did* say something."

Schembri's ears pricked up. "What did he say?"

"He asked me if I was all right, and he called me Randy."

Schembri leaned forward in his chair. "How was his English?"

"He *was* English."

"Are you sure about that?"

"I'm absolutely certain." The grandfather clock in the hall started chiming the hour. Randy looked up and grinned. "I know who it was."

"Who was it?"

"It was the locum sports master at school."

"Are you sure, Randy?"

"I'm absolutely certain. I've been spending time with him on the running track, and it was definitely him. I can't think why it didn't occur to me at the time."

"Sometimes it takes something to jog the memory," Schembri said.

"It makes sense," Sue said. "The photograph left on the seat of Veronica's car at the school, and them knowing when Randy was leaving the school to run home yesterday. They didn't need someone to be watching the school; they had a spy within the school. It all fits perfectly."

Schembri's brain was in overdrive. "Randy, is there any chance he would know you had clocked him?"

"Since I didn't know myself at the time, I don't see why he would."

Schembri got to his feet. "I need to get to the school. If he doesn't know Randy's on to him, he's probably there now."

Sue saw an opportunity to spend some time alone with the detective. "Would you mind if I came with you?" she asked. She glanced at Veronica.

Veronica's eyes crinkled in a smile.

"Not at all," Schembri said. "Johnson, call it in and tell the local boys to contact the unit at the school and have them pick up the locum sports master. And then stay here and see if there's anything else Randy can tell you. What's the locum sports master's name, Randy?"

"It's Tony, Tony Grantham."

Sue climbed into the front passenger seat of the unmarked police car and stared at the array of technical paraphernalia. From the outside, the car looked like a normal 7-series Volvo, but on the inside it bristled with technology. "Which one's the siren?" she asked.

Schembri started the car and pointed to a switch. "It's that one." He let the handbrake off and steered the car through the courtyard gate. "But don't touch it. Sound carries, and I don't want to spook Grantham before the local boys have had a chance to apprehend him."

For the next few minutes, Sue learned something about police driving. Schembri drove like the wind, but at no time did she feel unsafe.

When they got to the school, two uniformed officers were escorting a young man in a tracksuit out of the building. Neither officer was holding him, and he seemed to be accompanying them willingly. In fact, to Sue, he actually seemed relieved that he was being apprehended.

"Interesting they haven't seen fit to cuff him," Schembri said, bringing the car to a halt, and switching off the engine. "You stay her, Sue." He got out of the car, walked across the drive and showed the two officers his warrant card.

To Sue's surprise, the locum sports master offered Schembri his hand, which Schembri declined.

One of the officers then spent several minutes explaining something to the detective, who slowly shook his head. When the officer had stopped talking, Schembri offered the young man his hand, which the young man, took. To Sue's amazement, Schembri then put his arms round him and hugged him.

The young man then said something to the detective who, after a moment's thought, nodded and led him over to his car. He led him to Sue's side of the car, and opened the door. "He has something he'd like to say to you," he told her.

The locum sports master bent down to look her in the eye. There was deep sorrow in his eyes. "Mrs Hughes, I know how this must look, but I think that when you've heard the full story you'll understand. I just wanted to assure you that I would never have allowed anything to happen to Harry, or his sisters."

Not knowing what was going on, Sue was nonplussed. "I'm glad to hear it," she said. "But the same can't be said of Randy, can it? What you did to him was despicable. His mother has aged ten years overnight."

"There was nothing I could do about it. But I did let him escape when I got the chance."

"I think that's enough for now," Schembri said. He led the young man back to the marked police car, where one of the officers helped him into the back seat. Schembri had a quick word with them before walking back to his own car.

"What was all that about?" Sue said.

Schembri shook his head. "I can't imagine what he's been going through. They're holding his wife, and they threatened to kill her if he didn't do as he was told. They forced him to watch three of them raping her, to show him they were serious."

Sue closed her eyes. "Oh, God, that's *awful*. But, Bob, if they're holding his wife, is he going to tell you anything anyway?"

"He said that snatching Randy and forcing him to go with them has sickened him, and he's ready to tell us everything he knows. And he thinks they've already killed his wife, so he feels he has nothing left to lose." Schembri looked across the car at Sue. "One thing's for certain, there'll be a police presence at Veronica's house 24/7 from now on, even if CCTV *has* been installed. I'm not having those animals getting their hands on *you*."

Chapter 28

The atmosphere in the interview room at Covent Garden police station was formal, but congenial.

This was to be the first formal interview with Tony Grantham, the locum sports master – or, more accurately, the *ex*-locum sports master, since the school had been informed that Grantham would not be coming back. He couldn't have gone back if he had wanted to, because for the foreseeable future he would be in the care of the Witness Protection Programme.

Overnight, the police had made him as comfortable as they could in a cell within the building. The plan was to find out everything he knew and then whisk him away to the safe house they had earmarked for him. The charge against him was kidnap, which was a mere formality and would ultimately be dropped.

The headmaster had been informed of the circumstances of Grantham's arrest and Mr Godley had expressed profound sorrow at the news that his locum sports master's wife had been abducted, and profound regret that Grantham would not be coming back to the school. Mr Godley had said, "During the four-month period he was with us, Tony did such a good job and was so popular with the students and the rest of the staff, that I was thinking of offering him a permanent position." Mr Godley had asked that the best wishes of everyone at the school be passed on to Grantham, and to tell him that they were all thinking of him and praying for the safe return of his wife.

Now, sitting in the interview room in Covent Garden, Schembri asked Grantham if he wanted to have a solicitor present.

Grantham shook his head. "Why would I need a solicitor when all I want to do is tell you what happened and what I know? Then, I'd like to get some sleep. It's been twenty-three days since my wife was abducted, and I haven't had a decent night's sleep since."

The tape was switched on.

Schembri began the interview by identifying everyone present: himself, DC Johnson, and Tony Grantham. He then said, "Tony, for the benefit of the tape, would you please tell us how you first came into contact with the men you believe to be holding your wife."

"Don't you mean the men who *were* holding my wife?" Grantham said. Since his arrest the previous day, he had stated on a number of occasions that it was his firm belief that the men who had taken his wife had already killed her

"We don't know for certain your wife is dead, Tony," Schembri said gently.

"No, but I'm ninety-nine percent certain she is. Getting back to your question, Chief Inspector, my wife and I were doing our weekly food shop at the Tesco Extra supermarket, in Hatfield, when ..."

"Tony, for the benefit of the tape, would you please give us the date and time of the event in question."

"It was Saturday, the seventh of June, 2014. At around two-thirty in the afternoon."

"Thank you. And what happened at two-thirty in the afternoon on the day in question?"

"We'd done the shopping and we were walking back to the car. I was pushing the trolley, and Alice was walking beside me. She was carrying some flowers she had bought her mother for her birthday." Grantham paused, clearly distressed at having to relive the events of that day.

"Take your time, Tony" Schembri said.

Grantham took some deep breaths, wiped a tear from his eye, and continued. "A big black Lexus drove past us and pulled into the space beside our car."

"Did you happen to notice who was in the Lexus?"

"I wasn't paying too much attention at the time, but I've gone over it a million times since then, and I'm fairly certain there were three men in it. Two in the front, and one in the back."

"And what happened then, Tony?"

Grantham took another deep breath. He was clearly struggling. "We got to the car and I unlocked it with the remote and started putting the shopping in the boot."

"And the Lexus was parked next to you."

"It was as near to me as you are now."

"Did the men stay in the car, or did they get out?"

"They stayed in the car. At least, I think they did. I wasn't paying them any attention, at that point."

"Go on, Tony?"

"I finished putting the shopping in the boot, and then I pushed the trolley to the covered trolley park."

"And where was your wife while you were taking the trolley back?"

"I assumed she was getting into the car. That was the usual procedure. She would wait until I had put everything in the boot, and then she would get in the car while I took the trolley back."

"And how long do you think it took you to walk to the trolley park, and back."

Grantham shrugged. "A minute, two at the most. It was no more than thirty yards away."

"And what did you find when you got back to the car?"

"That my wife was nowhere to be seen."

"So she wasn't in the car?"

"No, she wasn't."

"And the Lexus?"

"That was nowhere to be seen either. It had gone."

"What did you do then, Tony?"

"I didn't know what to do. At first, I thought Alice might have gone back into the store because she had forgotten something, but she wouldn't have gone back into the store without waiting for me to come back first and telling me. And then I thought she might have seen someone she knew and had gone to have a word with them. And then I noticed a note tucked under the windscreen wiper on the driver's side of our car, which was the side the Lexus had been parked next to. When I walked around the car to see what it said, I stepped on the flowers my wife had bought for her mother. Then I knew something was wrong," Grantham's eyes began to fill up.

"Do you need a moment?" Schembri said.

"No, I'm fine," Grantham angrily brushed the tears away. "Damn! I told myself I wouldn't cry again. I've done nothing but cry for the last three weeks."

"Well, nobody could blame you for that, Tony. I think you're doing remarkably well. Tony, for the benefit of the tape, what did the note say?"

Schembri handed Grantham the actual note.

Grantham took the note, but declined to read it. He had no need to read it. What it said was etched on his memory, and would probably remain there for the rest of his life. He looked Schembri in the eye and said bravely, "It said, *Contact police and we kill your wife.*"

"And did you contact the police?"

"What do you think I am?" Grantham snapped. "Stupid?"

"I'm sorry, Tony. I had to ask, for the tape. Let's move on. Did somebody then contact you?"

"Yes, they did."

"*When* did they contact you?"

"At two o'clock the next morning. They sent a message to my mobile."

"And what did the message say?"

Grantham looked on the point of bursting into tears.

"I'm sorry, Tony. I know how hard this must be for you, but we need to know what the message said for the tape."

Tears welled up in Grantham's eyes. "It didn't *say* anything. It was video footage of a man raping my wife. She was naked and she was screaming, and two other men were standing there, waiting to rape her. And they were all laughing into the camera." Grantham began to sob uncontrollably.

Schembri said, "Let's take a break. Interview suspended at eleven forty-five a.m." He nodded to DC

Johnson, who switched the tape off. "Are you all right, Tony?"

Tears were cascading down Grantham's cheeks and his shoulders were shaking. "How could they do that to Alice?" he choked. "She was the sweetest, kindest, most unassuming woman you could wish to meet. In all the time I knew her she never had a wrong word to say about anyone."

Schembri walked round the table and helped Grantham to his feet. "Come on," he said kindly, "let's get some food into you. That should make you feel better. I know you haven't been eating enough. We'll reconvene at 2pm."

Before the tape was switched on again that afternoon, Schembri asked Grantham if he was up to continuing.

"I'm fine now, thank you," Grantham said. "Having some food helped. I've had no appetite since Alice was taken. I've been living on sandwiches, and beans on toast."

The tape was switched on, and Schembri began the questioning again.

"Tony, we were talking earlier about you getting the video footage on your mobile. Tell us what happened next."

"About lunchtime that day ..."

"Which was the Sunday?"

"Yes, the Sunday. I got a call from them, on my mobile."

The police had relieved Grantham of his mobile when they had arrested him, and now Schembri handed it back to him. "For the benefit of the tape," he said, "I am now handing Mr Grantham his mobile back."

Grantham found the message and nodded to Schembri, who said, "For the benefit of the tape, what comes next is a record of the actual phone conversation Tony Grantham had with one of the men who had kidnapped his wife. Go ahead, Tony."

Grantham turned the phone's volume up to full, set it to loudspeaker, selected *play*, and put the phone on the table.

The voice came over loud and clear. '*Did you get message?*' It was the voice of a peasant. Uneducated, rough, and with a heavy Eastern European accent.

'Yes, I got the message.' This was clearly recognisable as the voice of Tony Grantham.

'*You do what we want, yes?*'

'Before I agree to anything, I want to know how my wife is.'

'*Your wife okay ... for now. You give us information, she stay that way.*'

"What kind of information?"

'*When police, and Harry Hughes' mother, arrive at school, and when they leave again.*'

'And if I choose not to give you this information?'

'*That would not be wise. First we have fun with your wife, who very pretty lady, then she meet with unfortunate accident.*'

'You bastard!'

'*Sure, I bastard. Nasty bastard.*' This was followed by a throaty laugh.

There was a pause, and then Tony Grantham said, 'All right, I'll give you the information. Just don't hurt my wife. All right?'

'*You have pencil?*'

'Wait a second. Okay, I have a pencil.'

'*Take down phone number?*' A mobile phone number was dictated.

There was a pause, and then Grantham's voice said, 'And when do you want me to call this number?'

'*Call every day, at seven in evening. You not call, wife in big trouble.*'

As this point, the call ended abruptly, and Tony Grantham leaned forward and switched the phone off.

"So what happened next?" Schembri asked him.

Grantham shrugged. "I did what I was told. I placed a call every evening, at seven."

"Did they ever let you speak to your wife?"

Grantham shook his head. "No, they didn't. Not once. I asked to speak to her every time I called, but they just kept making excuses as to why I couldn't."

"Did you ever meet them? Apart from when Randy was snatched, that is."

"No, that was the only time I met them."

"So, Tony, let's talk about the set-up at the school and how Randy's abduction was arranged."

Grantham shifted on the hard plastic chair to make himself more comfortable. "As to the set up at the school, my room, broom cupboard really, was at the front of the building overlooking the drive, so it was easy for me to see who was coming and going."

"But how did you manage to let them know that Randy had not been picked up and that he had set off running. He told us he could make it home in twenty minutes. That would give you very little time."

"I sent them a text. Chief Inspector, you know all this. Must I keep answering the same questions?"

"It's for the benefit of the tape, Tony. Please answer the question."

"The arrangement was that if I saw certain people alone and unaccompanied, Randy being one of them, I was to send them a text immediately."

Schembri understood the difficult situation Grantham had been in at the time, but he couldn't help asking, "And how did letting them know Randy was alone and unaccompanied make you feel, Tony?"

"How do you think it made me feel? It made me feel sick to the stomach. But what else could I do? They were holding my wife."

"And for the benefit of the tape, Tony, were you with him when they snatched him?"

"I had to be. They didn't know him from Adam, and how would it have gone for my wife if they'd snatched the wrong boy? I had to point him out to them."

"How did you know where they would be?"

"They had told me where they would be. When the school was coming out, they always parked in the same place."

"Which was where, exactly?"

"In a lane not far from Randy's house."

"Go on."

"I caught Randy up halfway up the lane, and I slowed down and kept my distance so he wouldn't hear my car and turn round and recognise it."

"And their car was parked where? I assume it was the black Lexus?"

"Yes, the black Lexus. It was parked in a passing place further up the lane. Harry walked right past it. When I got to it, I stopped my car, jumped out and jumped into the

Lexus, which took off immediately, and I pointed Randy out to them."

"Randy said two people grabbed him. Were you one of them?"

Grantham shook his head. "No, I was in the front seat, so I could point him out to them. The two men in the back of the car grabbed him."

"Where did you take him?"

"To a derelict council house midway between Welwyn Garden City and Harpenden."

"Randy said that the car left the house shortly after midnight and that one person stayed. Would that person happen to be you?"

"Yes, it would. I insisted on it. They didn't want to let me stay, but I pointed out that I wasn't going to do anything stupid while they were holding my wife, and when I yelled at them, they seemed to get the point."

Schembri had an idea. When he had all the information he needed, and the tape had been switched off, he asked Tony Grantham one last question, "Tony, apart from the call you missed making at seven o'clock last night, which you missed because we had your phone, have you missed making any other call to them?"

"No, that was the only one I missed."

"Right, then you call them on your mobile at seven o'clock this evening, and this is what you tell them …"

Chapter 29

On Schembri's instructions, and despite there now being CCTV coverage and movement-sensing floodlights on all four corners of the house, a marked police car with two uniformed officers on board was now parked in Veronica's courtyard 24/7. When the lights were on, the courtyard and the grounds within fifty feet of the house were lit up like broad daylight, and movement from anything bigger than a field mouse would set them off.

Sue's Land Cruiser was back, together with a brand new rear door, and the courtyard was becoming very congested, especially at night when Henry was home. The police had got into the habit of reversing into the courtyard and parking facing the gate in case they had to leave in a hurry. This meant parking immediately under the dovecote, and they were not best pleased to have to keep cleaning bird droppings off the roof of their car.

Tony Grantham was safely ensconced in a safe house well away from London. He had been right about his wife being killed. A woman out walking her dog had found her naked body in a shallow ditch on the outskirts of Hatfield. She had been strangled. A post mortem had revealed evidence of serious sexual abuse, and consensus had it that she had probably been strangled while being raped. When Grantham was given the news, he had had to be sedated.

Schembri was beside himself with rage at what had happened to Grantham's wife, and at not yet being able to apprehend the perpetrators, but the phone call Grantham had made to the perpetrators after his interview had set certain things in motion, and Schembri felt sure they would catch them soon.

When Schembri had phoned Sue to give her the news about Tony Grantham's wife, Sue had been appalled. "That's absolutely *dreadful*! The poor girl. How she must have suffered. And *he* must have been devastated."

"He was. Sue, until we catch these people, I don't want you to go out of the house on your own. I mean even into the courtyard. It's all right to go out into the courtyard if the police are there, but don't even go out into the back garden for a breath of air unaccompanied. Do you understand me, Sue? We have no idea what these people might get up to next. They are capable of anything."

"I understand, Bob."

"Sue …" He hesitated.

"Yes?"

"I wondered if …" He hesitated again.

"If what?"

"I probably shouldn't ask, but …"

Sue laughed. "Spit it out, Bob. Whatever it is I'm not going to bite your head off."

Schembri took the plunge. "I wondered if you would let me buy you dinner when this is over with."

Max had now been away for two weeks and in that time he had only phoned her once. This was so out of character for him that Sue was convinced he had met someone on the Continent and was having an affair, and she saw no reason why she should not have dinner with the detective. After all, what was good for the goose was good for the gander. And as Veronica had pointed out, Max would never know.

"I would be delighted to have dinner with you, Bob," she said. "And I see no reason why we should wait until this is over, so sooner, rather than later."

Sue was desperately unhappy with the amount of time Max was spending away from home, and more and more often she found herself thinking of leaving him. Uppermost in her mind was how she would manage to look after herself and the children if she did.

She knew that if she did leave him she would have to rein in her horns financially, but she was still young enough to get herself a job and she knew Max well enough to know that he would continue to pay the children's school fees. And if this separation ended in divorce, she felt she would do well out of the settlement.

She had no idea what shares or other investments Max had, because he had never talked about them, but she knew that if she got half the house and half their holiday home in the Lake District, she would be quite well off. And a good lawyer should be able to get her a sizeable portion of his income. She had no idea what his income was, either, but from the way they were living and the freedom he seemed to have with money, it must be substantial.

She confided in Veronica, who told her that if it did come to a separation and she needed a roof over her head until things were sorted out, she and the children could stay with her as long as it took to find somewhere to live.

When Max finally got back from his trip, he picked Sue up from Veronica's and they left her Land Cruiser in the courtyard and drove home in his car.

On the way home, he hardly said a word. Max was a master of the long silence, having acquired the habit from his mother and perfected it over the years, but over the weekend the silence became the longest yet.

He had come home on the Saturday morning, and Sue left it until after they had eaten dinner on the Sunday evening before walking into his study and demanding, "Max, how long do you intend keeping this up?"

Max put his pen down and sat back in his chair. "Keeping what up?"

When he was in this mood, his constantly answering a question with a question was irritating in the extreme, and Sue felt like slapping him. But she kept her cool. "I'm talking about the long silence. Thirty-six hours is stretching it, even by your standards."

"I might ask you the same question," Max replied.

"What do you mean?"

"I mean how long do *you* intend to keep it up? You've hardly said a word to me since I got home."

"Yes, I have. I asked you if you'd had a good trip when you picked me up from Veronica's."

"And apart from that, and when we picked the children up from school and took them out to lunch today, that's about all you've said to me all weekend. And even then you couldn't look at me when you were speaking to me."

"That's because I was angry with you for being away so long. Max, when you took on Europe, you told me ..."

"Here we go again. You're beginning to sound like a broken record. Sue, instead of standing there with your hands on your hips and glaring at me, why don't you sit down and we'll try and talk this thing through!"

Sue sat down in a wing chair beside his desk.

Max pushed back his chair, stretched out his legs and put his hands behind his head, interlocking his fingers. "Right, let's have it. What's wrong?"

"There are so many things going through my mind that I don't know where to begin."

"I can't help you there, Sue. Only you know what's going through your mind."

Sue thought for a moment, and then said, "Right, I'll start with who went on your trip with you?"

Max raised an eyebrow in surprise. "Nobody went with me. I went on my own. What makes you think somebody went with me?"

"Did Geraldine go with you?"

Max frowned. "Who's Geraldine?"

"The brunette you didn't bother to introduce me to when Veronica and I dropped in on you at the office on the afternoon of the incident on the train."

"Oh, her," Max said airily. "I didn't introduce you to her because she was a temp. My secretary was on holiday. Geraldine was only with me for two weeks."

"Why didn't you give me an itinerary this time? You've always given me one before. Did you not want me to know where you were?"

"Sue, I didn't have an itinerary myself until I got to where I was going. Geraldine had messed several things up, that being one of them."

"Why didn't you ask her to email me one?"

"I did, and I had assumed she had. If she didn't, then I'm sorry. Joan's back from holiday now, and she'll send you an itinerary on future trips, as usual. But you could have called me. You know I never switch my mobile off when I'm travelling. Is there something else you're not happy about?"

"Yes, there is. Why have you stopped calling me in the evenings? You used to call me every evening, regardless of where you were in the world."

"That's easy to explain. I haven't been calling because I didn't want to have my head bitten off every time I called."

"I haven't been biting your head off."

"Yes, you have."

"No, I haven't."

"Well, what would *you* call it? I should have recorded our conversations, then you could have heard yourself. You were so nasty with me at times that I was convinced you were trying to drive me away."

"That's silly. Of course I wasn't trying to drive you away."

Max sat up and pulled his chair closer to his desk. "Sue, if there's nothing else, I have things to do."

"There *is* something else. Next time you change your plans, like when you're coming home, please don't inform me by text. Knowing you couldn't even be bothered phoning me to let know really hurt."

"Well, I'm sorry it hurt, but I sent you a text rather than calling you because I knew you'd be annoyed and I didn't want to get my head bitten off again. And the reason I didn't come home last weekend was because New York asked me to stay and clean up after a guy they had just let go. They let him go because he was doing a lousy job, and if *I* do a lousy job they'll let *me* go too. They're not paying me a quarter of a million dollars a year for nothing."

Sue's jaw dropped. "They're paying you *how* much?"

"Sue, ask yourself this; if I were having an affair, which your questions seem to imply, would I be telling you how much I was making?"

"No, I don't suppose you would."

"Of course, I wouldn't. Now let me ask *you* a question; when was the last time you showed the slightest interest in my business?"

In thinking about this, Sue realised he was right. It had been some time, and she admitted it.

"Not just some time," Max responded, "more like a hell of a long time. I've found myself thinking recently that you don't actually care what I do for a living, as long as I continue to keep you in the style to which you have become accustomed, and pay the children's school fees."

"Max, I can assure you it isn't like that at all. And if you could hear the way I talk about you to the other mothers at the school, you would know that. I'm actually very proud of you, and what you've achieved."

Max nodded. "Well, that's all right, then. And apology accepted."

"Max, while we're getting things off our chests, whenever you've come back from an extended trip in the past you've given me a hug and a kiss. Why didn't you do that this time?"

"Because of the way you were looking at me when I picked you up at Veronica's. Honestly, Sue, if looks could kill."

"Then it's my turn to apologise."

"Apology accepted. Is there anything else you'd like to get off your chest?"

"Yes there is. When you called me the first week you were away, why didn't you ask how the children were getting on with their end-of-term exams? Are you not interested in your children anymore?"

"What kind of question is that? Of course, I'm interested in the children. I probably had a lot on my mind, at the time."

"All right, I accept that. Max, while we're on the subject of getting things off our chests, there's another thing. Why did you have your laundry done? You've never done that before."

"Christ almighty, Sue! You're surely not complaining about that. I would have thought most wives would have been happy not to have to do his laundry when their husband came home from a two-week trip."

"I'd got it into my head you'd had your laundry done because you had lipstick on your collar, or perfume down the front of your shirt, and you'd had it done so I wouldn't find out you'd been seeing somebody."

"If you were thinking that, things have really off track between us. It was nothing like that. I had it done because after being away for two weeks there was a lot of it and I didn't want you to have to do it." Max was getting tired of the inquisition. "Sue, is there something else, or are we about done here?"

Sue shook her head. "No, I think that about covers it."

"Right, then I have a question to ask you. What's going on between you and Bob Schembri?"

The blood rushed to Sue's neck, and then to her cheeks. Her face felt to be on fire. She tried to brazen it out. "Why should something be going on between Bob and I?"

"Because I got a call from Henry while I was away, and he told me that if I valued my marriage I'd better do something about you and Bob Schembri. Because, as he put it, the two of you were getting *cosy*."

"Max, there's nothing going on between Bob and I."

"Come off it, Sue. I've seen the way the two of you look at each other. And when I mentioned his name, you turned the colour of beetroot."

"I did *not*!" It was a pointless denial because her face was now bright red.

"Yes, you did. You forget how well I know you. So what's going on?"

"He's … he's asked me out to dinner. That's all."

"Has he, now? So, while he's supposed to be protecting us, he's been making a move on you. Perhaps I should report him to his superiors. I think they would take a dim view of that."

Sue was horrified. "Max, you *mustn't*."

"Relax, Sue, I'm just making a point. I wouldn't dream of trying to get Bob into trouble after what he's done for us. Sue, can we start again? I probably haven't told you this anything like often enough recently, but I really do love you, and the last thing I would want is for something to go wrong between us. What do you say? Do we have a deal?"

Sue got up and walked round his desk. She threw her arms round his neck and gave him a long, drawn-out and very passionate kiss. "That's better," she said, when she finally let him up for air. "All you had to do was tell me you love me. Of course, we have a deal. And I love you, too."

Chapter 30

"Oh, sorry, Max," Schembri said. "I was trying to get hold of Sue. I must have pressed your number by mistake."

"You dialled the right number, Bob. I picked up her phone."

"You're home from your trip, then."

"Yes, I got home a couple of days ago. Can I help? Sue's upstairs taking a bath at the moment."

Sue was up to her chin in Chanel bath-foam Max had bought her in London that afternoon. She was surrounded by scented candles he had lit for her. She called, "Was that my phone, darling?"

"Hang on a second, Bob." Max put his hand over the mouthpiece, and called, "It's Bob Schembri. He wants a word with you. Shall I tell him you'll call him back?"

"See what he wants, darling."

"Bob, she can't come to the phone at the moment. Is there something I can help you with?"

"I just called to let her know we've caught the bad guys."

"You're *kidding*! My God, it's been going on for so long I thought it would never happen. Bob, that's fantastic news. Let me tell Sue. She's going to be over the moon. Hang on a second." Max put his hand over the mouthpiece again, and called. "Sue, they've caught them. They've caught the bad guys."

Sue climbed out of the bath and reached for a towel. "Keep him on the phone, Max. I'll come down."

"She's coming down, Bob. But while I have you on the phone, does this mean we're off the hook? That we can get on with our lives?"

"Hopefully, yes. But we mustn't forget that Harry is our only witness. Without him, our case collapses. By the way, the CPS has agreed to the Arabs going to trial."

"They took their time."

"These diplomatic immunity cases are always difficult. And this one has been particularly difficult."

"What about the school trip, Bob?"

"To be on the safe side I'm sending a man along with them. The headmaster's in the loop, and I'll make sure the Italian police are briefed so they can monitor the situation while the children are there."

"I'll tell Sue," Max said.

"She already knows."

Max realised that a lot of things had been going on in his absence, but things were fine between he and Sue now and he wasn't about to disturb anything, so he merely said, "Understood."

Sue was hurrying to dry herself with her towel. "I'll be down in a minute," she called. "Don't let him go."

"She'll be down in a minute, Bob. But in the meantime, I just want you to know how much I appreciate everything you've done for us. And especially the way you've looked after Sue while I've been away."

"I was just doing my job, Max. But thank you, anyway."

265

Sue walked down the stairs fastening her dressing gown.

"She's here, Bob. I'll hand you over."

Sue looked into Max's eyes as she took the phone. Keeping her voice down, she said, "I *love* my bath foam."

He grinned. "Then when you've finished talking to Bob, let's have an early night." He patted her on the rump and headed off to his study.

Sue carried the phone into the conservatory, speaking as she went. "Hi, Bob."

"Hello, Sue. How are you?"

"I'm absolutely fine, Bob. This is *amazing* news. I hadn't expected you to catch them anything like so quickly."

"We have Tony Grantham to thank for that."

Sue sat down in a rattan chair, kicked off her slippers and tucked her feet up underneath her. "How's he holding up?"

"He's putting a brave face on it, but I know he's suffering."

"Poor man, I really feel for him. Are you getting anything out of them?"

"One of them is talking. He's English and he was driving the car when they snatched Randy. We can't actually shut him up. It seems they forced him to rape Tony's wife and smile for the camera when they were making the video they sent to Grantham's mobile. I've been feeling like a priest hearing a confession. He seems to be a decent person who got in with the wrong company."

"Decent people don't rape defenceless women, Bob. Even under duress. But that's by the by. Where does that leave us?"

"I suppose that depends on when Max will be away again. I can make myself available more or less any evening, barring police emergencies."

Sue realised he had misunderstood her question. She chewed her bottom lip as she thought how to respond. Then she said gently, "Bob, I'm sorry, but there isn't going to be any *us*. Max and I have settled our differences."

"But what about all the time he spends away from home, Sue?"

"It's always been that way, Bob, and I suppose it always will be. I'm just going to have to live with it."

Schembri sighed. "I knew I was punching way above my weight. There's no way I can give you what Max can give you."

"It's not a question of what Max can give me, Bob. He and I have been together a long time, not to mention we have three children and a lot of history together, most of it good. If we *hadn't* settled our differences, it would have been a different story. I'm sorry if I raised your hopes."

"I'll get over it. Thank you for being honest with me."

"Bob, should I continue to stay at Veronica's? I mean, is this thing *really* over now?"

"I can't be absolutely certain, Sue. The English guy told us that no other people are involved, and we *think* he's telling us the truth. He would gain nothing by lying to us at this stage. But to be on the safe side, I suggest we leave things as they are until you go away on holiday and the children go to Italy. I don't see the need of a police presence at Veronica's now, so I'll cancel that arrangement. Just continue to be vigilant, and make sure you always have your mobile with you. And make sure the battery's always charged."

"What about Clarissa, Bob? Will you still have a presence at the school when we adults are in Spain, and Harry and Amanda are in Italy."

"Yes, we will. A patrol car will make regular visits to the school. Even though the English guy has told us no other people were involved, with three people dead already we're not taking any chances."

Chapter 31

It was the day the school broke up for the summer holiday and the family were spending the night at home together. It would be the first time since they had started boarding that the children had slept in their own beds. Max and Sue were determined to make it a happy family reunion, and had planned a little treat for them.

Max left his office early and took the train to Welwyn Garden City station, where Sue picked him up. It was the first time in six weeks that she had driven unaccompanied, and she was reminded of how she had felt when she had first driven unaccompanied after passing her driving test at the age of seventeen. She had realised when she climbed into the Land Cruiser at Veronica's that she was taking a slight risk driving alone, but it was a drive of no more than ten minutes to the station, and she locked the doors and kept her mobile on the seat beside her, just in case.

As Max climbed up into the vehicle, Sue joked, "Are you sure the office can manage without you for a week?"

"They'll manage," he said, closing the door and swivelling round and putting his briefcase on a back seat. "And I've told them in no uncertain terms that if they disturb me on holiday they'll be in serious trouble when I get back."

"Wow!" Sue said in mock delight. She turned the ignition key and the big vee-engine howled into life. "Does that mean I've got you to myself for a *whole week*?"

"I'm afraid so," Max said. "Of course, if you can't handle it …"

"I'll handle it," Sue said, smiling at him. "Come on, let's go and pick up the children."

Because it was the start of the school holidays, it was bedlam at the school with twice as many cars as usual as parents whose offspring had been boarding came to collect them. People were blocking the drive by standing in little groups renewing acquaintances with people they hadn't met for a year, there was luggage all over the place, and there were hordes of excited children for whom, for the next six weeks, school would be completely forgotten. A marked police car sat under the old oak tree.

At first, it looked as if Sue wouldn't be able to find anywhere to park, but as luck would have it a black Range Rover pulled out of a space just across from the school building and she nipped smartly into it. She went into the school to find the children, while Max went to have a word with the two officers in the police car.

As he approached, the driver let his window down. Max introduced himself.

"Hello, sir," the driver said. "Looking forward to having your family home again?"

"Very much so," Max said, "although it's only for the evening."

"I understand you and Mrs Hughes are going away on holiday tomorrow. Spain, isn't it?"

"Spain, yes. A hotel on the beach near Marbella."

"And very nice, too. I expect we'll be seeing you in the morning."

"You certainly will. We'll be dropping Harry and Amanda off."

"I'll bet they're looking forward to going to Italy."

"Amanda is. I'm not so sure about Harry."

"The buses will be leaving for the airport at 9am."

"So I understand," Max said. "We'll be here in good time."

"Well, enjoy your evening, sir."

"Thank you, officer. We plan to."

Harry and Amanda walked out of school with their school bags strapped to their backs and wheeling their suitcases behind them. Clarissa skipped out carrying her school bag, leaving her mother to wheel her suitcase for her.

When everyone was safely strapped in, Max turned round in his seat and announced, "Right, you lot, special treat tonight. A bucket load of chicken and the biggest bag of French fries you have ever seen, from KFC."

There was a round of cheers from the back of the vehicle.

"No French fries for me, Dad," Amanda said. "I have my figure to think of. I'll have a coleslaw instead, a small one."

"I'll have Amanda's fries," Harry said.

"Can I have a chocolate milk shake as well, please, Daddy?" Clarissa said.

"Of course, you can, pumpkin," Max said. "Tonight you can have whatever you like." He slapped Sue good-naturedly on the thigh. "Whenever you're ready, driver."

Sue stuck her tongue out at him and started the engine. With so much congestion, she had to do a five-point turn to turn the vehicle round. When they were pointing in the right direction, Harry asked his mother to stop at the police car, and she stopped alongside it.

Harry let his window down and motioned for the driver of the police car to do the same.

The officer obliged and grinned up at him. "How's it going, Harry?"

"It's going just great, Nick," Harry said. "No school for six weeks. How cool is that?"

The two officers laughed.

"How about putting the blues on for me, Nick?"

"Anything for you, Harry." The officer flicked a switch and the blue lights on the roof of the car sprang into life. Reflections of blue light bounced off the windows of the school and the vehicles around them. The officer left the blues on for a moment or two, and then turned them off again.

"Are you and Alec on duty in the morning?" Harry asked.

"Yes, we'll be here until the buses leave for the airport."

"Great, see you then."

"Yes, see you then, Harry."

Amanda and Clarissa scooted across, and Amanda called, "Hi, Nick. Hi, Alec."

The officers waved at them. "Hi, Amanda. Hi Clarissa."

Max had also lowered his window. "See you in the morning, gentleman," he said, raising his window again.

Sue waved to the two policemen and then pulled away. The police car followed them down to the main road. On the dual carriageway, it roared past them and sped off, the officers waving to them.

When they got home, Sue showed the children the clothes she had bought them for their trip. When she saw what her mother had bought her, Amanda's face lit up. "Thank you, Mummy, they're lovely. I love the dress."

Harry reacted with rather less enthusiasm. "I don't know why you bothered. In fact, I don't know why I'm going. I'd rather stay at home."

Sue counted to five under her breath. "Harry, you're going whether you like it or not. And you're going because it's part of your education. You're going to learn something of Italian culture. What on earth's the matter with you, Harry? One minute you're up, the next minute you're down."

"Nothing's the matter with me," Harry grumbled. They were in his parent's bedroom, and he headed for the door.

"Where do you think you're going?" Sue said.

"I'm going to watch TV."

"Oh, no, you're not, young man! You're going to do your packing. There'll be no TV until I say there will."

Harry wandered into his bedroom muttering about the unfairness of life.

Max was downstairs; he was cleaning shoes in the utility room. Sue went down to have a word with him. "Max, when you go for the chicken, take Harry with you. See if you can find out what's wrong with him. He's up and down like a yo-yo and I just can't get through to him."

"Okay," Max said, "I'll see what I can do."

So Clarissa wouldn't feel left out, Sue had bought her a kilt, which Clarissa was delighted with. A particular friend of hers at school was a Singaporean girl, a boarder, and Clarissa was even more delighted to learn that her mother had bought her friend a very pretty blouse. Mrs Godley had told Sue that the Singaporean girl's family had not made contact with her for over a year, and Sue wanted the little girl to know that somebody cared.

When it was time to go for the food, Max went up to Harry's room, where Harry was packing, and asked him to go with him. "It's been a while since we had a chat, and it will give us a chance to do some catching up."

Harry asked if they could go in the Land Cruiser.

"If you like," Max said.

"Cool. Then I'll come."

On the way, Max found common ground with Harry when he started to talk to him about cars, and he soon realised that Harry was quite knowledgeable on the subject. It also made him realise how little he knew about his son.

The KFC outlet was busy, with queues at all four tills. They joined the nearest queue, which also happened to be the shortest.

As they waited, Harry asked his father how his job was going since he had taken on Europe.

"It's going very well, Harry." Max was pleased that Harry had asked the question, because it showed he was making progress towards getting through to him. "Europe is a big territory to cover, but I've always liked a challenge and I'm really enjoying it."

"What about all the travelling you have to do? Do you enjoy that?"

"I've always enjoyed travelling, Harry. I regard it as one of the perks of the job. The only thing I don't like is the amount of time I have to spend away from you, your mother, and your sisters."

"Mum doesn't like you being away so much."

"I know she doesn't. But there's not much I can do about it; it goes with the job."

The line shuffled forward and they shuffled forward with it.

"And by the way, Harry, speaking of jobs, I realise you still have three more years of school, but have you given any thought as to what you would like to do when you leave school?"

"Not really," Harry said. "I do know I don't want to go to university."

"Why is that, Harry? I never had the chance to go university, but you do."

"Because I hate school and I *know* I would hate university."

The person at the head of the line was served and the line shuffled forward again.

"Why do you hate school, Harry?"

"I don't know, Dad. It's not the schoolwork, because I quite like that. I think it's because I don't seem to be able to make friends."

"But I thought that since the episode with the French master and the chalk, you were the school hero."

"That was then," Harry said. "Things are back to how they were before, now."

"And why do you think that is, Harry?"

"I don't know, Dad."

Max was making a lot more progress than he had anticipated, and he decided to strike while the iron was hot. "Harry, don't take this the wrong way, but your mother and I are worried about you. You seem to be up one minute and down the next, and you seem to be unhappy about something. Would it help to talk about it? I think you'll find I'm a good listener."

This was the first time that Harry had ever had the opportunity to talk to his father about his problem, and he opened his mouth to speak. But the line moved forward again, leaving just one person between them and the counter and his father said, "We'd better think about what we're going to order."

They looked at the range of offers on the board overhead, and Max said, "What do you say we go for the nineteen-piece bucket of chicken, and fries for five? With Amanda's portion as well, that will give you enough French fries, won't it?"

"More than enough."

"And what was it your sisters wanted?"

"A small coleslaw for Amanda and a chocolate milk shake for Clarissa."

Harry was disappointed he had missed the opportunity to seek his father's advice, and realised he was going to have to continue dealing with his problem himself.

Harry carried the sack of food to the Land Cruiser, strapped himself in, and sat in silence while his father started the engine. The food was warm on his lap and it smelt wonderful.

Max checked there was nothing coming and pulled smoothly out into the road, pointing the vehicle in the direction of home. Knowing this would be his last chance of finding out what Harry's problem was, at least until Harry got home from Italy, he decided to try again.

"Harry, just before we ordered, you were about to say something. What was it you were about to say?"

But the moment had passed and Harry's mood had passed with it. He didn't want to go there again. "It was nothing, Dad. Don't worry about it."

"All right, son. But if you change your mind …"

"I know."

They drove the rest of the way in silence.

As part of the treat, Sue had said they could eat off trays in the living room. The grown-ups had decided that this would be an evening to get to know each other again, to make up for lost time, and with the TV firmly switched off, they made a start on a veritable mountain of food.

As they ate, Max regaled them with tales of funny things that had happened to him on business trips, and then Amanda took over and started to tell them about some of the things that went on in the girls' dormitory after lights-out. She was careful about what she said, because of Clarissa, but she had them all in fits.

Sue had been educated at an all-girls boarding school and she knew all about what happened in a girls' dormitory after light's out. She was more amused by Max's frequent and incredulous, "*You're kidding*!" than she was by what Amanda was saying.

Clarissa surprised them by then throwing in her two-pennyworth; not so much because she had anything particularly funny to say, but because she had never previously shown any inclination to speak up for herself. Boarding at the school had clearly done her a lot more good, than harm. She now seemed more confident and just that little bit more mature.

Max tried several times to get Harry to say something, but Harry wasn't interested. He had retreated into his cave and no amount of coaxing would persuade him out of it.

When they had finished eating, they cleared away the debris and put the dishes in the dishwasher. And since they were all going away tomorrow, they switched the dishwasher on.

Max and Sue then left the children watching TV while they went upstairs to start packing.

Amanda came up just before 10pm to tell them that Clarissa had fallen asleep in a chair. Max went down and carried her up to her room. He left Sue to put her in her pyjamas and put her into bed while he went back into the master bedroom to get on with his packing. Clarissa slept soundly throughout.

Sue tucked her in, and then stood by her bed looking down at her. Sleeping peacefully with her long blonde hair tumbling about her face, Clarissa looked like a little angel, and Sue went to fetch Max. They stood by her bed and Sue laid her head against her husband's chest. "Max, it would destroy her if anything went wrong between you and I."

"Nothing's going to go wrong between us," Max said, bending down and planting a kiss on his wife's forehead. "Because I won't let it."

They walked back to their bedroom with their arms around each other.

As she undressed, Sue asked Max if he had had a chance to talk to Harry about what was bothering him.

"There was a moment just before we ordered the food that I thought he was going to tell me," Max replied,

278

unbuttoning his shirt, "but he was distracted and the moment passed. I tried again in the car on the way home, but he didn't want to know. I'm sorry, darling. I did try."

Chapter 32

The buses taking the children to the airport were a matching pair of large luxury air-conditioned coaches, their registration plates being the only noticeable difference about them. Their side-loading luggage doors were open and their drivers were rapidly filling their cavernous holds with the children's suitcases.

The police car was there, with the same crew on board as yesterday, and as Max got the children's suitcases out of the Land Cruiser's luggage compartment, the driver of the police car caught the eye of a slim, fit-looking man standing at the rear of the second bus. He indicated Max with a nod of his head.

As Sue walked to the buses with the children, Harry and Amanda wheeling their suitcases behind them, the casually dressed thirty-something-year-old walked over to Max to introduce himself. He waited until Max had closed the Land Cruiser's tailgate, and then enquired, "Mr Hughes?"

"Yes?"

"I'm DC James Cooper." The detective showed Max his warrant card. "I'm going to Italy with the children. DCI Schembri may have mentioned me."

"Ah, yes," Max said, shaking Cooper's hand. "Bob did say he was sending someone with the children, but he didn't mention you by name. Nice to meet you."

"It's nice to meet you, too, sir."

"Is it Jim?"

"I prefer James."

"James; it is." Max instinctively liked the detective, and it was not only because of the firmness of his handshake. Within a couple of inches of being as tall as himself, Cooper had pale blue eyes, fair hair that was certainly longer than most policemen wore, and an easy laid-back air about him. He also had an air of quiet competence, giving the impression that he was a man to whom you could give a job and know that the job would be done well. He was wearing a T-shirt and jeans and could easily have been taken for one of the teachers, all of whom were casually dressed. In no respect did he look like a policeman which, given why he was going on the trip, was good. Max thought Schembri had chosen well.

Sue called that the children were ready to board.

"Coming," Max called. He asked the detective if he needed his mobile number, adding, "Just in case."

Cooper shook his head. "The arrangement is that if I need to get in touch, I call DCI Schembri on his mobile. And I assume he will phone you. I assume he has your number."

"Yes, he does."

The detective gave Max a tight smile. "Let's hope we won't need to meet again."

Max knew what he meant. "Yes, let's hope we won't. Well, enjoy your trip. And take good care of my children."

"Don't worry," Cooper assured him. "I intend to."

They shook hands again, as if to seal the deal, and then walked across the drive together.

The luggage holds had been closed and the drivers had boarded their vehicles. Most of the other children had already boarded.

Amanda hugged and kissed Clarissa, and then her parents, and then she jumped on the first bus, walking to the back of the bus where her friends were calling that they had saved her a seat.

Max gave Harry a hug. "Have a great time, Harry. And when you get back, you and I are going to spend some quality time together and get to know each other. Okay?"

"I'd like that," Harry said. "Bye, Dad. Bye, Mum." He hugged his mother and blew Clarissa a kiss. "Bye, shrimp."

"Bye, tadpole," Clarissa replied, blowing him a kiss back.

Veronica and Henry were there with Randy, and Randy hugged and kissed his mother, before shaking hands with his stepfather. Before boarding, he turned to Max and Sue. "Bye, Auntie Sue. Bye, Uncle Max. I'll keep my eye on Harry and Amanda for you."

"Thank you, Randy," Max said. "And don't be too hard on the Italian girls."

Randy raised his eyebrows in mock astonishment. "Who, me?"

"Have a lovely trip, Randy," Sue said. "And we'll see you in a week."

Harry headed towards the second bus, but Cooper stopped him and told him he wanted him on the same bus as his sister. Harry saw the look in his eye and boarded the first bus. Cooper boarded behind him.

The doors hissed shut and the drivers started their engines. As the buses pulled away, there were waves and blown kisses and calls of, "Have a wonderful time," and then people began to drift towards their cars.

Max told Veronica and Henry that he and Sue wanted to have a word with Mr and Mrs Godley, who were standing on the school steps talking to a couple whose child had left on one of the buses.

Henry looked at his watch. It was 9.20am. "Okay, but we need to be at Heathrow two hours before the flight, which means leaving our house no later than 10.15am."

"Okay," Max said, "we'll keep it short."

Henry and Veronica walked to Henry's Jaguar and drove off.

While they waited for the headmaster and his wife to finish talking to the two parents, Clarissa's little Singaporean friend came out of the school. She saw Clarissa and ran gaily across, a happy smile on her face.

Clarissa introduced her to her parents.

"I'm very pleased to meet you, Changying," Sue said. "And what a lovely name you have." Knowing that Chinese names often had meanings, she asked, "Does it have a special meaning?"

Changying had a lisp and she smiled self-consciously, "Yeth, it doth. It meanth, flourithing and luthtrouth."

Clarissa handed her the gift her mother had bought for her. "This is for you, Changying," she said, "from my mummy." The blouse had been gift-wrapped, and the tape had a little pink bow.

Changying looked at Sue as if she couldn't believe her ears. "For *me*?"

Sue smiled at her. "Yes, Changying, for *you*."

"May I open it now?"

"If you like."

Changying carefully untied the bow and unwrapped the paper. When she saw the blouse, her eyes filled up. "Oh, thank you. I don't know what to thay."

Sue found the little girl's lisp enchanting. "You've already said it. Thank you is all you need to say. Are you and Clarissa going to have a lovely time together?"

"Oh, yeth, we're going to have a thuper time together."

Clarissa lifted her face to her parents to be kissed, and then skipped into the school with her friend.

Mr and Mrs Godley were now free and Mrs Godley smiled after the two girls. "Changying is such a sweet little girl," she said. "Clarissa is going to be just fine with her."

"I'm glad to have the opportunity to have a word, Mr Hughes," the headmaster said, shaking Max's hand. "Because I wanted to tell you how very sorry I am that we added to your problems."

Mrs Godley could see from the look on Max's face that he had no idea what her husband was talking about. "My husband is referring to the locum sports master," she explained. "If we hadn't hired him …"

Max waived the headmaster's apology aside. "What happened was hardly your fault. In fact, now we know the facts, it wasn't his fault either."

"All the same," the headmaster said.

Sue could see that the headmaster genuinely felt responsible for what had happened, and she tried to help ease his burden by shifting the emphasis. "By all accounts, he was a very good sports master."

"Indeed he was," the headmaster said, looking visibly relieved. "Actually, I probably shouldn't be saying this, but he was rather better than our permanent sports master. I was sorry to lose him."

"The poor man," Mrs Godley said, "and such an awful thing to happen to his wife." She shuddered.

They talked for few minutes, and then, knowing they were running out of time, Max pointedly looked at his watch. The arrangement was that they pick up Veronica and Henry at their house and drive to Heathrow in the Land Cruiser. "I'm sorry, headmaster, but we have to go. We have a plane to catch."

"Yes, of course," the headmaster said.

"Have a wonderful holiday, and don't worry about Clarissa," Mrs Godley said. "I shall look after her as if she were my own."

"I know you will, Mutti," Sue said, touching Mrs Godley's arm. "You have my mobile number, don't you?"

"Yes, I have it."

"I'll call you about the middle of next week, if that's all right; just to check that Clarissa is okay. And don't hesitate to call me, if you feel the need."

"I won't call unless it's absolutely necessary. Now off you go, my dear, and have a wonderful holiday. After everything you've been through; nobody deserves a holiday more."

Chapter 33

If Harry thought the accommodation at school was basic, it was five-star compared to the accommodation the monastery on the Amalfi coast of Italy provided.

At least, he had a room to himself. That is, if you could call what had once been a monk's cell and was no more than eight feet long by six feet wide, with a stone floor, a primitive wooden bunk, a chest of drawers that was riddled with woodworm, and, affixed to the back of the door, a strip of wood three feet long into which six hooks had been screwed to provide somewhere to hang things in lieu of a wardrobe, a room.

Hanging from the ceiling in roughly the centre of the room was a light bulb encased in a cheap-looking paper shade. The only other means of night-time illumination, was a bedside lamp on the chest of drawers. Harry could see that this was so far out of reach of the bed, it would necessitate having to get out of bed to switch it on, or off. When he switched it on, to check that the bulb was working, it gave off so little light that he knew that reading in bed would not be an option.

He opened his suitcase and hung what needed hanging on the hooks on the back of the door, leaving everything else in his suitcase on the floor in a corner of the room. As to his mobile, despite being reminded by his mother to make sure that his phone was fully charged, Harry had been in a bad mood at the time and had neglected to do so. On checking the battery, he found that the charge was down to eight percent, so he looked for a plug socket into which he could plug the two-pronged South-European adaptor his father had lent him. He found that the only socket in the room, apart from the one into which the lamp was plugged, was so old and looked so unsafe, that he decided against using it. Better that than have his phone go up in smoke and have to ask his parents to buy him a new one when he got home. He told himself that since he was not planning to make calls while he was here anyway, it didn't really matter. In any case, he could always use Amanda's phone. Her phone was always charged.

The monastery was eight hundred years old, and the bathroom and shower facilities, which were separated by gender, were a two-minute walk down a draughty stone-floored corridor. Harry had not brought his bedroom slippers, which meant he either had to walk down the corridor in his socks, or his bare feet. The washbasins had hot and cold running water, but the showers had only cold water. This was no doubt fine for monks back in the dark ages, but it was not fine for pampered kids from private schools, and many were complaining.

With no noticeable form of heating in the rooms, or the corridors, it was difficult to see how they would be able to use the monastery during the winter. Fortunately, the temperature when the Hertfordshire group had arrived was 36 degrees Centigrade, and the temperature in Harry's room was comfortable. That is, until the middle of the night, when, to keep warm, he had to get up and throw his dressing gown over his sheet and threadbare blanket, to give him another layer. There was no picking up the phone and calling room service and asking for another blanket here, since room service, or even phones in rooms, had never even been considered.

The monastery was perched on the edge of a sheer two-hundred-foot cliff and when Harry went to bed he left the window open and fell asleep listening to the roar of the mighty waves of the Adriatic Sea pounding on the rocks far below. If he stood on tiptoe, he could just see the rocks. It was a terrifying sight because he suffered from vertigo, and it was only because of the thickness of the walls that he felt safe. Had he not been so awed by the view, he would have asked for a room on the side of the building that overlooked the cobbled square of the village from which the monastery took its name.

Meals were served in a huge cave, its walls hewn from solid rock, and seating was at communal tables. There were students from three other schools in attendance: one from Zurich, Switzerland; one from Madrid, Spain, and one from Buenos Aires, Argentina. The common language was English, and the teachers from all four schools actively encouraged their students to mingle with the students from the other schools, which was another reason why these trips were so successful. Rather than merely learning something of Italian culture, it also taught students to mix with students from other countries.

The Hertfordshire group had arrived late on the Friday evening. On the Saturday, Harry had spent most of the day on his own, including reading for several hours in his room. On the Sunday morning, Amanda insisted he spend at least the morning with her. This was because her mother had instructed her not to let Harry be alone any more than was absolutely necessary. Up until then, she had only seen her brother in the distance.

The chefs only came in twice a day, once to cook lunch, and then to cook dinner. Breakfast was a self-service buffet. The emphasis was on healthy eating, and on offer were: a range of cereals, freshly-squeezed juices, hard boiled eggs, a selection of breads, toast, a variety of cold meats, a selection of cheeses, tomatoes, and fresh fruit. There was tea and coffee to drink. The coffee was fine, but the English contingent could have taught the Italians a thing or two about how to make tea.

That morning, Amanda followed Harry round tables groaning with food. While Harry loaded his plate, she chose sparingly, before leading him to the table at which she had been sitting before he came down.

"How's your room?" she asked, taking a sip of her orange juice.

"Don't you mean my cell?" Harry replied, buttering a piece of brown toast.

Amanda laughed. "I know what you mean. Mine's the same. Which floor are you on?"

"The fourth. And you?"

"The third. Do you have a sea view?"

"Yes, you?"

"No, but I wish I did. I overlook the village square and the church bells woke me at six this morning. They were deafening."

"All I heard when I woke up were the waves pounding on the rocks," Harry said smugly.

As they ate, Amanda asked Harry what plans he had for the day. Sunday was a free day, as had been the previous day. Classes started tomorrow, Monday.

"I'd like to get Dad a card," Harry said.

"There's a card shop in the village," Amanda said. "I bought mine yesterday."

On their table were students from the Swiss and Spanish schools and Amanda took the opportunity to practice her German and Spanish on them. She was taking both subjects at school. She was getting on particularly well with a girl from the Swiss school, whom she had met the previous day. Elizabeth had close-cropped blonde hair, bright blue eyes, and the kind of personality that made people warm to her immediately.

Amanda introduced her to Harry.

Elizabeth put her knife and fork down and reached across the table. "Hello, Harry. I'm very pleased to meet you." Her native tongue was German, but she spoke English with barely a trace of an accent.

Harry shook her hand and said a brief hello and then got back to his meal.

Embarrassed by his rudeness, Amanda said, "Sorry, Elizabeth. My brother seems to have got out of bed on the wrong side this morning."

Elizabeth laughed at the expression Amanda had used, and she repeated it and shared it with some of the others on the table. None of them had heard it before and they all laughed. One of them said, "The English have such quaint expressions."

While Amanda chatted happily with her new friends, Harry finished his meal in silence. Then he got to his feet, and said, "I'm going to get Dad a card."

Amanda, who had already finished her meal, said, "I'll come with you." She got to her feet. "It was lovely to see you again, Elizabeth. Can we get together later?"

"I'd like that," Elizabeth said. She smiled at Harry. "Perhaps I'll see you later, too, Harry."

Harry mumbled something unintelligible and walked away.

Amanda caught up with him and rounded furiously on him. "Why must you be so rude, Harry? Elizabeth was only trying to be nice."

"Leave it," Harry said, "I'm not interested."

"I despair of you, sometimes," Amanda said, shaking her head.

The bells of the church in the square were ringing to summon parishioners to morning Mass, and as Amanda had said, they were deafening. The square was full of people making their way to the church, many in family groups spanning generations. Almost all the older women wore black. Local people whose lives revolved around the church. Staunch Catholics who would kneel in the confessional once a month and confess they had thought bad things of someone, or uttered a bad word, earning them five Hail Mary's and the warning that if they wanted to go to heaven they needed to mend their ways.

In one of the groups was a youth who, on first sight, stopped Harry in his tracks. Not realising he was no longer with her, Amanda carried on walking.

Harry had heard the expression love at first sight, but he had never before believed it existed. Until now. He was smitten. The good-looking Italian youth looked about twenty years of age.

Amanda finally realised she was talking to herself, and she stopped, turned, and looked back. Harry was standing with his back to her watching a family walk towards the church. "Harry," she called crossly, "what on earth are you doing?"

His emotions all over the place, Harry caught up with her and apologised, making the feeble excuse that something had crossed his mind and he had stopped to think about it. Still annoyed with his behaviour at the breakfast table, Amanda curtly informed him that most people could think and walk at the same time.

Reflecting that he had got on best with his father when they had talked cars, Harry bought his father a card with a picture of a red Ferrari on it. For his mother and Clarissa, he bought cards with pictures of local scenes on them.

The previous day, Amanda had bought cards for her parents, Clarissa, and several friends. She had already written them and sent them.

After they had left the card shop, Amanda asked Harry what he would like to do next. Harry told her he would like to hang around the square for a while, to get a taste of the local life. Muttering under her breath that she had at least *tried* to spend some time with him, Amanda left him there and went off to do her own thing.

When Mass ended and the youth and his family came out of the church, the postcards Harry had bought were no longer fit for purpose. Nervous and excited at the prospect of seeing the youth again, and wondering how he was going to approach him when he would be in the bosom of his family, his hot sticky hands had reduced the cards to virtual waste paper. He watched the youth walk towards, and then past him, and then walk down a narrow cobbled side street. Desolate at the thought he would probably never see him again, Harry walked miserably back to the card shop and bought replacement cards.

That afternoon, Harry decided to take a walk along the cliff top. He got his camera from his room, declined an invitation from Randy and some of the others from school to join them, and set off.

As he walked along the cliff top, there were regular booms from breakers hitting the rocks below, and at one point he ventured close to the edge and took a quick look down. Great slabs of rock had fallen from the face of the cliff, and breakers were racing in off the sea at the speed of an express train, curling themselves into huge white-topped waves, and crashing on to the rocks, making a loud boom and sending plumes of spray high into the air. Nervous at being so close to the edge, Harry took a few quick photographs, and then retreated to safer ground.

It was a hot day and Harry had eaten rather more roast lamb over lunch than he had intended, and as he wandered along the cliff top he began to feel sleepy. There were very few people around and he found himself a patch of grass well away from the edge of the cliff, and sat down. Soon, his eyelids were getting heavy, and he lay down to take a nap.

He had not been asleep long when a sudden change in air temperature caused him to wake up. He opened his eyes to find himself in the shadow of someone standing over him, blotting out the sun. At first he thought it was DC Cooper, who had been following him along the cliff top at a respectful distance, but as his eyes became accustomed to the light he realised it was the youth he had seen in the square that morning and had thought had been lost to him forever. His heart leapt.

The youth helped him to his feet, and said, "I Giuseppe Lucas."

"Harry Hughes."

They shook hands. Harry, whose father had always impressed on him the importance of a firm, dry handshake, couldn't help noticing that the Italian's hand was damp, and his handshake was weak and flabby.

"I see you in village with girl, this morning," Lucca said.

"My sister," Harry explained.

"Si, she look like you. And you wait for me to come out of church later."

Not realising he had been so obvious, Harry flushed. To make conversation he said, "And you were with your family." He added the only Italian word he felt comfortable with, "Si?"

"Si, my family. Why you want see me again?"

"I just thought we could be friends."

Lucca shrugged. "Okay, so now we friends. You stay at monastery?"

"Yes. Si."

"How long you stay?"

"Until Friday." Harry held up a hand with the fingers spread. "Five days."

"So now we friends, what we do next?"

What Harry wanted to do more than anything else in the world was kiss him. "How about showing me some more of the cliff top?" he said.

Lucca shrugged. "No problem," He gestured towards DC Cooper. "Who your friend?"

"He's one of our teachers from school," Harry lied. "He's just out taking a stroll. Don't worry about him."

"You sure he not policeman?" Lucca said, glancing in the direction of the detective. "To me, he look like policeman."

"He's not a policeman," Harry said. "Look, if it makes you feel more comfortable, I'll go and ask him to leave us alone. Okay?"

"Si. Okay."

Harry got to his feet and jogged over to the detective.

Cooper had been sitting on the grass, watching them. He got lithely to his feet. "What are you up to, Harry?" he asked suspiciously.

"I'm not up to anything," Harry replied. "James, would you mind leaving us alone?"

"To do what?"

"Just to take a walk along the cliff top with my friend."

"He's not your friend, Harry. You've only just met him. I saw the way you looked at him in the village square this morning, and I don't like the look of him."

"James, please."

"Harry, I made your father a solemn promise that I would look after you, and that's exactly what I intend to do. I suggest you go back and tell that young man that whatever he's suggesting you're not interested. And then I think that you and I should make our way back to the monastery."

"James, can't I at least talk to him?"

"About what, Harry? You'll be going home on Friday, so what's the point?"

"James, I promise that all we'll do is talk."

"I suspect you have other things in mind than just talking, Harry," the detective said.

"James, would you at least give me a few minutes with him? *Please*, thirty minutes. I can't get into any trouble in half an hour."

"I suspect you could get into trouble in half a minute if you set your mind to it, Harry."

"What about fifteen minutes then? Please, James." There was an outcrop of rock about fifty yards beyond where Lucca was standing, and Harry pointed to it. "If we just stay on the other side of that outcrop of rock and I promise not to do anything but talk … Please, James. Fifteen minutes is not too much to ask, is it?"

More to shut him up than anything, Cooper said, "All right, Harry, fifteen minutes. But if you let me down …"

"I won't let you down, James, I promise." Harry made the sign of the cross over his heart. "Cross my heart and hope to die."

"All right, Harry, fifteen minutes, and that's it. I'll be standing on this side of that outcrop of rock, and when your fifteen minutes is up I'll be coming round that rock with all guns blazing, so you'd better make sure you're not doing anything other than talking. Do I make myself clear, Harry?"

"As crystal," Harry said. He gave the detective a hug. "Thank you, James. You won't regret it, I promise you."

"I'd better not," Cooper said. He looked at his watch. "Right, your time starts now. Fifteen …"

Harry raced back to Giuseppe Lucca, gave him a cock-and-bull story about having to be back at the monastery in forty-five minutes, and allowed the Italian to lead him round the outcrop of rock.

As soon as they were out of sight of the detective, Lucca leaned back against the rock and posed seductively. "You want kiss me?"

Harry's pulse quickened. "Yes, I do. More than anything."

"First you pay me."

Harry laughed. "For *what*? *A kiss*? Don't be ridiculous."

"You pay me, otherwise I no kiss you."

"I couldn't pay you if I wanted to," Harry said. "I didn't bring any money with me." He was beginning to think Cooper had been right, and that this was not such a good idea. "Giuseppe," he said, "I'm sorry, but I think I'll just go back to the monastery."

"First, I take watch."

Harry was wearing a short-sleeved shirt and the expensive watch his father had given him for his fifteenth birthday was plainly visible. "You're not having my watch," he said. "It was a present from my father."

"Your father rich?"

Harry was getting annoyed. "I don't think that's any of your business."

"Maybe I kidnap you."

"I'd like to see you try," Harry said, now well and truly annoyed.

Lucca took a step forward and tried to snatch Harry's watch.

But Harry was too quick for him. He backed away.

Lucca lunged forward again ...

On the other side of the outcrop of rock, Cooper paced the ground anxiously. He knew he had made a mistake, but out of consideration for Harry he gave him an extra two minutes. Then, over the boom of the breakers from below, he yelled, "Time's up, Harry!"

When Harry did not appear, Cooper thought he might not have heard him over the bedlam from below, so he yelled again, louder this time. "Harry, can you hear me?" When Harry still did not appear, Cooper began to panic. He yelled at the top of his voice, "Harry, I'm coming round." He hurried round the outcrop of rock …

There was no one there.

Chapter 34

Max and Sue and Veronica and Henry had lunched in style under a large candy-striped awning on the beach; lunch being served by a dinner-jacketed waiter from the hotel's main restaurant. It was now 3pm and the lunch things had long since been cleared away. It was hot, 38 degrees Centigrade, and Henry had just asked Max if he would like another Pina Colada.

"No thanks, Henry," Max said. "Two is more than enough in this heat. I'm actually thinking of going back to the villa and taking a nap."

"Yes, perhaps you should," Sue said, peering over her sunglasses at her husband. "Your face is the colour of a lobster."

Max got to his feet. "Are you coming?" he said, looking down at his wife, who was stretched out on a recliner in shorts and a cotton top reading a Jilly Cooper novel.

Sue shook her head. "No, I'm going to stay here, darling. I'm enjoying the heat, and I've just got to an interesting place in my book."

"I think I'll forget that drink and take a nap myself shortly," Henry said.

"And I might join you," Veronica added.

"Right, see you all in a while, then," Max said, heading off towards their villa.

Their villa, which stood in walled grounds within the confines of the landscaped acreage owned by the world-renowned Marbella Club Hotel, boasted four bedrooms, each with en-suite bathroom, and its own swimming pool, in which all four of them had swum on more than one occasion since arriving two days ago. The villa had tiled floors throughout and was fully air-conditioned. To ensure guests were kept cool in the heat of a Costa del Sol summer, it also had a ceiling fan in every room.

Before entering the villa, Max bent down and brushed the sand off the soles of his feet with his hand. He then padded across the villa's large and expensively furnished living room, up its ornate sweeping staircase, and along a landing that opened on to the living room below and into their bedroom, closing the door behind him. Before lying down on the bed, he closed the shutters on the windows so the room would be dark.

He was dropping off to sleep when he heard Veronica and Henry talking in hushed tones as they came into the villa and climbed the stairs, and he was asleep within moments of hearing the door to their room close.

Sometime later, Max was woken from a deep sleep by his mobile ringing on the nightstand beside him. He reached over and picked it up. The time on the face of the instrument told him that it was 4.14pm, which meant he had been asleep for over an hour. He frowned when he saw who was calling, knowing for certain that Bob Schembri would not be disturbing him on holiday unless it was something important.

Before taking the call, he climbed off the bed and opened the shutters at the windows to let in some light. From where he stood, he could see Sue. She didn't look to have moved. She was still stretched out on her recliner reading her book.

"Bob, why do I have the feeling I'm not going to like what you're going to tell me?" he said into the phone.

"Are you sitting down, Max?" Schembri's voice was sombre.

When Max had been asked that question in the past, it had only ever meant one thing, and he sat down on the bed and prepared himself for bad news. "All right, Bob, I'm sitting down. Whatever it is, let's have it."

There was a pause, and then Schembri said, "There's been an accident."

"What kind of accident?"

There was another pause. "Harry's fallen off a cliff."

"Oh, dear God! Is he badly hurt?"

"It's more serious than that, I'm afraid."

Max felt himself go cold. "You don't mean …"

"I'm afraid so. I can't begin to tell you how sorry I am."

Max's mind went blank. He was having difficulty taking in what Schembri had told him. It had only been two days since he had promised Harry that when he got back from Italy they would spend some time getting to know each other. And now Harry was dead and that was never going to happen. Max immediately thought of Sue, and he looked through the window at her. She was laughing, probably at something she had just read in her book. How was he going to tell her? She and Harry had been as close as a mother and son could be. She was going to be devastated.

"What happened, Bob?" he asked quietly.

Schembri gave him chapter and verse on what DC Cooper had told him over the phone a little over an hour ago. When he had realised the importance of what Cooper was telling him, Schembri had asked Cooper to start again and he had recorded the conversation. He had then spent forty-five minutes writing down the salient facts before phoning Max.

Schembri told Max what Cooper had said about how Harry had reacted when he had seen the Italian youth in the village square that morning; about how the youth had turned up on the cliff top that afternoon; about Harry asking to be allowed to spend some time with the youth and refusing to take no for an answer, and about Cooper finally giving into him and giving him fifteen minutes. And Schembri told Max about Cooper hurrying round the outcrop of rock in a panic, only to find there was no one there.

Despite knowing his job was probably on the line, Cooper had not held back. He had told Schembri everything, leaving nothing out, and Schembri passed everything on to Max.

Max had long since adopted the philosophy that if something was meant to happen, it will. And the more he thought about it, the more he thought this was one of those cases. He sighed. "When did this happen, Bob?"

"It happened just after three o'clock this afternoon. The first thing Cooper did was look over the cliff, and he saw Harry's body lying on the rocks below. He didn't stand a chance, Max. The cliff is two hundred feet high."

Max let all the air out of his lungs and covered his face with his hands. It took several deep breaths before he felt able to continue the conversation. "I don't know what to say, Bob." A thought struck him. "Bob, is Amanda aware of what's happened?"

"I don't know, Max. *I* haven't told her. I thought you should be the first to know. Cooper might have told her, but on the other hand, he might not."

"I'd better call her. I'd rather she heard it from me than from somebody else."

"I can't begin to tell you how sorry I am, Max. We were supposed to be protecting him."

"Yes, but not against something like this. This sounds like something Harry brought on himself. I'm certainly not blaming you, or DC Cooper. What about this Italian youth, Bob? Is anything known about him?"

"There is, actually. He lives in the village, and he's been in trouble with the police before, for theft."

"How are the police treating this? As an accident, or a suspicious death?"

"Cooper said they are keeping open minds. They are out looking for the youth, as we speak."

"So," Max said quietly, "it looks like Harry was gay."

"Apparently, it was well known within the school."

"Really? Sue and I never suspected a thing. I just thought he was a late starter with girls. Some boys are. It would explain a lot: what was bothering him, his mood swings. It would also explain why he was on an Internet chat room site exchanging messages with someone he thought was a boy of his own age, and going to London to meet him. Speaking of which, Bob, you've lost your witness, haven't you?"

"Yes, I have. But that's my problem, Max, not yours. You have more than enough on your plate."

"Will you have to let the Arabs go?"

"I expect so. I can't see the CPS agreeing to a trial without a witness."

"I'm sorry to hear that, Bob."

"Don't be, Max. You and Sue did everything humanly possible to help, and I shall always be grateful to you for that. By the way, the Italian police will want somebody to identify the body, and I'm sure you wouldn't want Amanda to have to do that."

"Heaven forbid! That would probably finish her off. Sue and I will have to go over there. By the way, Bob, before I forget, will you tell DC Cooper that in no way do I hold him responsible for what happened. I know how difficult and headstrong Harry can …" he corrected himself, "*could* be, and I wouldn't want it sitting on Cooper's conscience for the rest of his life. It wasn't his fault."

"That's kind of you, Max. And I'm sure Cooper will appreciate it."

"Will it cost him his job?"

"Not if I have anything to do with it, it won't. He's too good a copper to lose over one bad decision. He'll probably get off with a stern warning."

Max thanked Schembri for everything he had done to protect the family and they wound up the conversation and ended the call.

Next, Max needed to call Amanda, and he was dreading it. He brought her number up on his mobile, took a deep breath, and pressed it.

Amanda answered on the second ring. "Hello, Daddy," she said cheerfully. "This is a nice surprise. Are you and Mummy having a lovely holiday?" There was youthful laughter in the background.

"Sweetheart, I can hear voices. Can you talk?"

"I'm with some friends, but yes I can talk. You sound serious, Daddy. Is something wrong?"

"You'd better prepare yourself for a shock, Amanda. Harry's had an accident. He's fallen off a cliff."

"Oh, Daddy, no. Is he badly hurt?"

Max took a deep breath. "I'm afraid it's worse than that, sweetheart. He didn't survive the fall."

At first Amanda didn't react, as if she hadn't understood what her father had told her. And then she broke down and sobbed.

Max sat with his phone to his ear, his heart going out to his daughter and wishing he could be there to put his arm round her and comfort her. There was no sound of laughter in the background now, just the sound of his daughter breaking her heart.

Eventually, Amanda calmed down. She said to her father in a very subdued voice, "I can't believe it, Daddy. I was only having lunch with him a few hours ago. When did it happen?"

"At around three o'clock this afternoon."

"How did Mummy take it?"

"I haven't told her yet. I wanted to tell you first, because I didn't want you hearing the news from somebody else. Your mother and I will need to identify the body, so we'll be coming over."

At the mention of the word *body*, Amanda burst into tears again.

Max wanted to get off the phone so he could give Sue the news, but he stayed with the phone glued to his ear until Amanda had calmed down again. "I'm all right now, Daddy," she said. "When you tell Mummy, would you please tell her I love her?"

"Of course, I will."

"Daddy …"

"Yes, sweetheart?"

"Who's going to tell Clarissa?"

Max had not had time to think about Clarissa. "I think your mother would be the best person to tell Clarissa," he said.

"I think you're right. Tell Mummy I'm thinking of her."

"I will. Stay strong, sweetheart, and we'll see you soon."

"I love you, Daddy."

"I love you too. sweetheart."

Max ended the call, got off the bed and slipped his mobile into the pocket of his shorts in case he needed it again. He padded across the room, opened the door, and stepped out on to the landing just as Veronica and Henry were coming out of their room.

"Enjoy your nap?" Henry said.

Veronica took one look at Max and exclaimed, "Max, whatever's the matter? You're as white as a sheet."

Max explained what had happened.

Veronica's hand flew to her mouth and she and Henry said, more or less in unison, "Oh my God!"

"I'm so sorry, old boy," Henry said.

"Does Sue know?" Veronica asked.

Max shook his head. "I haven't told her yet. I've just told Amanda. I didn't want her hearing it from somebody else."

"How did she take it?" Veronica said.

"She sobbed her heart out," Max replied. "Sue and I will have to go over there. They'll need us to identify the body."

Veronica said immediately, "We'll go with you."

"Yes, of course, we will," Henry said.

"There's no need for you to do that," Max said. "We're booked in here until Friday. Stay and enjoy the rest of your holiday."

"If you think we're letting you go through all that on your own, you've got another think coming," Veronica said.

"I agree," Henry said. "So let's hear no more about it. Now, what can we do to help, Max?"

"One thing you could do, Henry, is ask the concierge about flights to Italy. From what I can remember of that part of Italy, the nearest airport would be Salerno. And you might want to let reception know we'll be leaving. I suggest we try for flights leaving mid to late morning tomorrow."

"I'll get on with that right away," Henry said. He hurried off down the stairs.

"I'll come with you to tell Sue," Veronica said, slipping her arm through Max's in a gesture of support. "When you give her the news, she's going to need all the support she can get."

Chapter 35

There were no direct flights between Alicante and Salerno, and from leaving the Marbella Club Hotel it took them seven hours to get to the monastery.

They arrived late afternoon and were met by an attractive woman by the name of Adriana. When she knew which of the two couples were Harry's parents, she offered Max and Sue condolences on behalf of the company owning the monastery. She spoke in heavily accented, but easily understood, English.

She showed them into a small conference room off the reception area, and offered them coffee. After a three-hour taxi ride from Rome's Leonardo da Vinci airport, her offer was gratefully accepted.

While they were in the taxi, Max had received a phone call from Mr Godley at the school saying how upset he and Mrs Godley had been to hear the news, and offering condolences on behalf of the school. He had said that, as a mark of respect, he had been thinking of cutting the children's visit short and bringing them home. After a quick word with Sue about it, Max had thanked Mr Godley for the thought, but had told him that he and Sue would rather he didn't do that as the children would be disappointed if they had to go home early, and a change of flight would incur more expense for all the parents, and that wouldn't be fair to them.

When Adriana came back with the coffee, Sue asked if it would be possible for Amanda to join them.

"Si, of course," Adriana said. "We ask if she want to be excused classes, but she say she prefer to carry on, to stay busy." She checked her watch. "At the moment, she in pre-Raphaelite art class. I bring her to you."

Veronica asked if it would be possible to bring Randy as well.

"Si, of course. Your family name again, please? Sorry, I not good with foreign names."

"Hodson, Mrs Hodson. But my son's name is Williamson, Randy Williamson. He's my son from a previous marriage."

When Amanda saw her mother, she burst into tears and ran across the room and threw her arms round her neck. "I'm sorry, Mummy. I did try to spend some time with him, but he just wanted to be on his own."

"Shh," Sue said, stroking her daughter's hair. "No one's blaming you, my darling. I know you did your best."

Amanda threw her arms round her father's neck. "Daddy, I'm so sorry."

"I know you are, sweetheart. But as your mother said, no one's blaming you. It was just one of those things."

Amanda apologised to Veronica and Henry for their holiday being ruined.

"It hasn't been ruined at all," Veronica said, giving her a hug. "We can take a holiday any time we like. Being here with you at a time like this is much more important."

Henry greeted Amanda in the way he usually greeted her, with a gentle pat on the cheek. "I'm sorry for your loss," he said.

Amanda gave him a quick peck on the cheek. "Thank you, Uncle Henry."

Randy seemed to be holding up well. There was no sign of tears and his voice was strong. After kissing his mother and shaking hands with his stepfather, he told Max and Sue he was sorry for their loss, and then pulled a chair out for Amanda and sat down beside her.

Amanda's emotions were all over the place, and without thinking, she blurted out, "If Harry hadn't been gay, this would never have happened."

Max's stomach lurched. He had not found the right moment to tell Sue that Harry had been gay.

"Don't be silly, Amanda," Sue said. "Harry wasn't gay. I'm his mother, and I would know."

"I'm afraid he was, Auntie Sue," Randy said.

Veronica said sharply. "*Randy*, don't speak to ..."

Max didn't let her finish. "Let him speak, Veronica."

Randy looked to his stepfather for guidance.

Henry said, "If you have something to say on the subject, Randy, now's the time to say it."

Randy looked at his mother. "Do you remember when I punched Harry and I wouldn't tell you why?"

"How could I forget, when you and he had always been the best of friends?" Veronica replied.

"Well, the reason I punched him is that he had been following me round school telling me he loved me."

"Oh, yuk!" Amanda exclaimed.

"That's quite enough of that, Amanda," Max said. "Have some respect for your brother."

"Sorry, Daddy." Amanda hung her head in shame.

"At first, it didn't bother me," Randy continued, "but he wouldn't stop doing it."

"But that doesn't mean he was gay, Randy," Sue said. "Friends tell each other they love them all the time."

Henry said gently, "That might be the case with girls, Sue, but it's not the case with boys. At least not any boys I've ever met."

Randy continued, "And finally I warned him that if he didn't stop I would punch him. And he didn't stop, so I punched him. I'm really sorry, Auntie Sue. He left me no choice. He was saying it in front of the others, and it was getting embarrassing."

Max had heard more than enough on the subject. He wanted to move on. He wanted to hear what had happened from the only person other than Harry who had been there at the time, and he asked Amanda to find Adriana and have her bring DC Cooper to see them.

Ten minutes later, Cooper came into the room looking decidedly nervous.

To put him at his ease, Max got up, walked round the table, and shook his hand and told him he did not hold him responsible for what had happened.

"I do," Sue said. "He was supposed to be looking after him."

Cooper was suffering and it showed in his eyes. "I'm very sorry for your loss, Mrs Hughes," he said, offering her his hand.

Sue ignored his hand and pointedly refused to make eye contact with him.

Max introduced him to Veronica and Henry, who both stood to shake hands with him.

Randy greeted the detective with a friendly, "Hi James."

"Hello, Randy. How are you holding up?"

"It's still raw," Randy replied. "But I'm getting there."

"Hello, James," Amanda said.

"Hello, Amanda. Are you okay, now? I've been worried about you."

"I am now my parents are here," Amanda replied.

Max pointed to the only vacant chair at the table, and Cooper sat down. Max then asked him to tell them in his own words what had happened.

Cooper sat forward in his chair, cleared his throat, and began by telling them how yesterday morning he had followed Harry and Amanda out of the monastery and had followed them at a discreet distance as they crossed the village square. He told them how Harry had suddenly stopped in his tracks, leaving Amanda walking on alone.

"Yes, it was really annoying," Amanda said. "We were on our way to buy postcards, and one minute he was there, and the next minute I was talking to myself."

"Let DC Cooper go on with his story, Amanda," Max said.

"Sorry, Daddy."

"At first, I couldn't think why Harry had stopped like that," Cooper continued, "and then I realised he was staring at a group of people on their way to morning Mass. He watched them pass him by, and then he turned and watched until they had walked into the church."

"And the bells were deafening," Amanda said. "Weren't they, James?"

Cooper smiled at her. "Yes, they were, Amanda. They were very loud."

312

"So what was so special about this group that made Harry stop and watch them?" Max asked. He knew the answer to this question from his conversation of the previous day with Bob Schembri, and he had asked the question for Sue's benefit, hoping Cooper's answer would help her to accept that Harry had been gay.

"Well, I'd heard on the coach on the way to the airport that Harry was gay ..."

"Harry was *not* gay," Sue said, her throat turning bright red with anger. "Will people *please* stop saying my son was gay."

Max said, "Darling, please, let him finish. Go ahead, James."

Cooper apologised, saying, "I'm sorry, Mrs Hughes, I'm only passing on what I heard. If I can just explain; there was only one member of the group that Harry could possibly have been interested in, and that was a youth of about twenty. The rest of the group consisted of two elderly ladies, both of whom were dressed in black and I took to be his grandmothers; a man and woman in their mid-to-late forties, who I took to be his parents, and a heavily pregnant woman who looked to be in her mid-twenties. She was walking arm-in-arm with a man I took to be her husband, and I took her to be the youth's sister."

"And what happened on the cliff top?" Max said.

Cooper described in detail what had happened, ending up with how he had looked over the cliff and seen Harry's body lying on the rocks. It was the first time anyone but Max had heard the full story, and he ended his dissertation to stunned silence.

Randy, who had been listening quietly, was close to tears. He had known Harry was gay since long before the problems with the Arabs had begun, and he blamed himself for what had happened. If he had told his mother why he had punched Harry, Harry might still be alive today.

Sue caught him looking at her and she gave him a supportive little smile.

Her simple little act of kindness was too much to bear, and Randy burst into tears. He got to his feet, shoved his chair back, sending it crashing to the floor, and ran from the room, sobbing.

Veronica jumped to her feet. "I'd better go after him. And you'd better come too, Henry. Max and Sue don't need us for this. It's none of our business." They hurried out of the room.

Amanda asked, "Daddy, if you don't need me for anything, can I leave too? I'd like to get back to my studies."

"Yes, off you go," Max said. He waited until Amanda had left the room, and then picked up the fallen chair, and put it back under the table. He walked back to his own chair and sat down. "So where do we go from here, James?" he asked.

"Can I make a suggestion, Mr Hughes?" Cooper said.

"Of course, you can."

"It might put things in perspective if I showed you where it happened. Assuming, of course, you would like to see where it happened."

"I was just about to ask you to show us where it happened," Max said. "Do you feel up to it, Sue?"

"Yes, I'd like to see where it happened," Sue replied. "But first, I'd like to see the room in which my son spent the last night of his life."

Chapter 36

When Max saw the room in which his son had spent his last night on God's earth, he rolled his eyes. "What a dump!"

Sue's eyes flashed. "Max, for God's sake! What does it matter if it's a bit primitive? It's the room your son spent the last night of his life in, so have a little respect."

"Calling this room primitive would make that the understatement of the year." Max peered through the window. "Spectacular view, though."

While Harry had had to stand on the bed to see the rocks below, Max was tall enough to be able to see the rocks by just standing at the window.

There was a storm brewing and the sky was laden with heavy black clouds. The white tops the wind was whipping up stood out in stark contrast against the blackness of the sea.

Because of the strength of the wind, the incoming waves were bigger than usual, and they were building to huge heights and then curling and smashing on to the rocks with enormous *booms*, sending spray high into the air. It was easy to see why Harry's body had had to be recovered by Coast Guard helicopter.

Sue wandered around the room looking at her son's things. Most of the things she had packed for him were still in his suitcase, which lay open on the floor. Typical of Harry, his bed had not been made. Over the years, Sue had tried, pleaded with and cajoled Harry to make his bed, and she had always ended up making it herself. Now she wished she hadn't been so hard on him. She remained dry-eyed until she picked up his pyjamas and buried her face in them. She was reminded of how he had smelt as a baby, and her resolve deserted her and she sat on the bed and sobbed.

Max knelt down beside her and wrapped his arms around her. He stroked her hair and whispered words of comfort as she wept against his shoulder.

When she could cry no more, she looked at him with eyes red and still brimming with tears, and told him she was ready to go and see where he died.

Large drops of rain were falling as James Cooper led them along the cliff top. There would have been no point taking an umbrella; it would either have been turned inside out, or the unfortunate person holding it would have done a Mary Poppins and been carried off by the wind, probably never to be seen again.

Despite its strength, the wind was warm. And it carried the salty tang you remember from the time you first see the sea as a child until you go off to meet your maker.

As they walked along the cliff top, they heard the same *booms* Harry had heard the previous day, only louder, on account of the waves being bigger.

It was a walk of perhaps half a mile to the outcrop of rock, and no one spoke until they got there.

One thing Max had not counted on was the sheer beauty of the place: the dramatic cloud formations, the huge waves, the strength of the wind, the booms from below, the sensational view. To him, it was a consolation of sorts. Harry could have met his death in much worse places.

Sue saw things differently. She saw none of the beauty. To her, this was an awful place because this was the place where her son had met his death.

Yelling to make himself heard over the wind, Cooper walked them around the outcrop of rock and explained how horrified he had been when he walked around the outcrop of rock yesterday afternoon to find there was no one there, and how he had felt when he had looked over the edge of the cliff and seen Harry's body on the rocks two hundred feet below. "It's a sight I shall carry to my grave," he said.

The outcrop of rock was causing the wind to swirl dangerously, and when Sue ventured close to the edge of the cliff, with a view to looking down to see where Harry had fallen, Max yelled at her to come back, yelling that one death in the family was more than enough.

Seeing Harry's room, and then seeing where he had met his death, had brought a closure of sorts, and it was a calmer and more resigned group that made its way through the wind and the now driving rain back to the monastery.

Chapter 37

Harry's corpse had been taken to the morgue in Salerno, and the next morning Max and Sue took a taxi from their hotel. Veronica and Henry had taken a taxi to the airport to fly home.

A young male morgue assistant, who spoke only a smattering of English, led them into the bowels of the building.

Sue was carrying a long-stemmed red rose.

Along one wall of a cold, white-tiled room, with an unpleasant odour of chemicals, stood a bank of stainless steel doors. The assistant swung one of them open to reveal the soles of a pair of feet. A label was tied to the big toe of one of the feet. He pulled the tray out. The body was covered with a white sheet. Only the feet were visible.

Max took Sue's hand. "Are you ready for this, darling?"

Sue shook her head. "No, I'm not. But it has to be done."

The morgue assistant looked at them expectantly.

Max nodded.

The morgue assistant lifted the sheet at the top end of the corpse and pulled it down just enough to reveal its face.

Harry looked younger than his fifteen years.

Max peered at his face. "He looks if as if he's smiling."

The corpse *did* look as if it were smiling.

"Perhaps he's gone to a better place," Sue said.

There was a little curl of hair at the corpse's right temple that had been there since Harry was a child. Sue tried, as she had tried a thousand times before, to push it back in place. But, as it had always done, it sprang stubbornly back again. It had been a joke between them. She had always told him that the girls would love him for his curl. Now, she knew different.

She bent over and kissed the corpse on the forehead. Its skin was icy cold. She laid the rose beside Harry's head, and murmured, "Rest in peace, my darling." She looked up at her husband. "Max, will you do something for me?"

"Of course, darling. Anything."

"Take me home."

EPILOGUE

Stephen's mother called, "Stephen, I won't tell you again. Get off that computer and come down and get your meal. It's on the table and it's getting cold."

Stephen reread the email he had just received. '*Hello, Stephen, since we have so much in common, I would like to invite you to my parents' house in Surrey for a few days. You'll love the house. It has a swimming pool, a tennis court and stables, and there are places to walk in the woods. I suggest you don't tell your parents I've invited you because they probably won't let you come without meeting me first. Let me know as soon as you can. Your new best friend, William.*'

Stephen sent a quick reply. '*William, I have to go. My mum's getting upset because my meal's on the table and it's getting cold. Your parents' house sounds great and I'd love to see it. I'll think about how I can get away and get back to you. I can't wait to meet you. Your friend, Stephen.*'

He pressed *send*, closed the lid on his laptop, got to his feet, and called, "Coming, Mum."

The End

BLIND
TARGET

A Codi Sanders Thriller

BRENT LADD

This is a work of fiction. All of the characters, names, incidents, organizations, and dialogue in this novel are either the products of the author's imagination or are used fictitiously.

Archway Publishing books may be ordered through booksellers or by contacting:

Archway Publishing
1663 Liberty Drive
Bloomington, IN 47403
www.archwaypublishing.com
1 (888) 242-5904

ISBN: 978-1-4808-7843-3 (sc)
ISBN: 978-1-4808-7844-0 (hc)
ISBN: 978-1-4808-7845-7 (e)

Library of Congress Control Number: 2019906619

Print information available on the last page.

Archway Publishing rev. date: 06/10/2019

Dedicated to my wife Leesa, for whom
love has no conditions.

1

OCTOBER 1957 – UMNAK ISLAND,
ALEUTIAN ISLANDS, ALASKA — 4:14 A.M.

Engineer Marshal Sergei Popov swallowed back the bile that pushed at the back of his esophagus. Twenty minutes of bobbing up and down in an inflatable raft waiting for the all clear was taking its toll. His moss green face seemed to glow in the dwindling moonlight, as he tried to concentrate on the nodding coastline in the distance. His round face and large eyes made him look frog-like, but his aberrant fear of the water had him clinging to the craft's seat with rigid white knuckles.

A thin, black, mottled silhouette in the distance buoyed up and down with the shadowy sea. It was a land beyond desolate, where few men came and fewer survived—Umnak Island. Popov's vision clouded with darkness in the periphery as his head started to spin. He blinked it away and sipped a lungfull of arctic air. Somebody next to him mumbled something and the raft started to move. *Thank God*, he breathed to no one. Popov was a holdout to the Russian Orthodox faith in an otherwise godless country, a place where the good of the state took priority over all. He turned back to see their leader, Colonel Tolya Alexeev, focused on the growing coastline. The man looked stoic and determined. If anyone could see them through this it would be the colonel.

The eight-man rubber raft pushed through the choppy water and pointed towards a small cove just visible ahead. *America*, Tolya, thought to himself. *Doesn't look like much.*

Tolya removed his goggles for a moment to rub the stinging sensation from his blue-gray eyes. Only moments before, the goggles had protected him from pelting airborne ice crystals. Five degrees below zero with a thirty-mile-an-hour wind was no picnic, but he had seen it all before. And if the reports were correct it was only going to get worse. He absently scratched at an old scar that ran along one side of his strong cleft chin.

Their eight-man state-of-the-art raft was made of a new synthetic rubber designed to provide twice the strength of any previous model. The compartmentalized air pockets allowed it to skim across the water with ease. But it was susceptible to wind, and Tolya struggled to keep it on course. His goggles immediately started to fog.

"Clear," Tolya said, and the raft picked up speed.

Tolya squinted through drifting clouds. Operation Blind Pig. Tolya smiled. It had to have been named after one of the politburo's wives. He looked over his squad. Three were well-trained men, all Alpha group, OBSP, formed by Minister Zhukov himself. Each had arctic training from the 379th special purpose detachment.

Corporal Misha Ivanov, a six-foot-one battle-hardened commando, had been under Tolya's command during the messy Hungarian Revolution a short while back. Misha's kind brown eyes belied the true fighter inside. He was a man Tolya could trust, an extremely rare trait in Moscow's current political landscape.

Sergeant Kazimir Yegor, or Kaz, as he was called, was the pessimist of the bunch. The man never smiled, but he made up for it by anticipating anything to go wrong at any moment. He was wound as tight as a longbow with a short string. His no-nonsense attitude kept everyone in line. Kaz was probably the most loyal comrade soldier Tolya had ever known. And one day, over several shots of vodka, he just might see the man smile.

Private Andrei Tatter was a promising cadet from the Suvorov Military School in Leningrad. He even spoke some English. The boy was from solid Russian stock, sinewy, fast like a cheetah, with a perfect smile and biting sarcasm. Something very few Russians seemed to have. He watched as the boy took a nervous swig of water from his canteen to wash the dried salt from his lips.

These were the best the Soviets had to offer. Tolya could have no better company on any mission, even to an island that time had forgotten.

The rest of Colonel Tolya Alexeev's team was a mixed bag of unknowns. He looked across the unit. Each wore snow camouflage outerwear with a large fur-rimmed parka hood, and had no identification of any kind. Identical all, except for one man.

Seated on the starboard second seat, looking more like a refugee from a comedy show than a squad member, was their guide, Chikuk, a Siberian Yupik Eskimo from Inupiaq Island off the coast of Siberia. Chikuk had refused the camouflage clothing in favor of his own winter gear of sealskin and caribou, and no amount of discussion could change his mind. The man had lived and thrived in some of the harshest winter conditions on the planet. He wore a perpetually disdainful expression, as though everyone around him was inept. But if anyone could guide them through this arctic winter operation on foot, it was he.

"Ah," a man called out.

The raft had hit a particularly large crest, and subzero-degree water breached over the gunwale. Tolya watched as the man next to Chikuk lifted his feet in the air, fearful of the cold. Zampolit Traktor Yashin was what every special forces squad going to America required—a political officer. Traktor was missing most of his hair and all of a personality. He wore a scowl he had been nursing since fifty-two. His beady black eyes seemed to take in everything around him and yet managed to see nothing. For Tolya, he was a 100-kg anchor on a 5-kg boat, and if he thought he could get away with it, he would have pushed the man over the side an hour ago. Ideology and indoctrination had no place on this mission, but the Deputy Chairman of the MPA in the Ministry of Defense had insisted. Tolya was almost positive Traktor was the man's nephew.

Good old Mother Russia, ever fearful of defectors and the bad press it carried, suffered from a terminal case of paranoia. Tolya scoffed at the thought that these men would defect. They were battle-hardened Soviet soldiers. They bled Russian red and would give their lives for the motherland.

The man who looked like he was about to vomit was Engineer Marshal Sergei Popov. A transfer from the science and engineering corps, Popov was the key to this operation, and Tolya's personal responsibility. In his arms Popov clutched a waterproof canvas package that held the latest in Russian technology. An electrical leach, he called it. No matter what lay ahead, Colonel Tolya Alexeev had one responsibility: make sure that leach was activated.

Visibility dropped to near zero as the clouds finally won their battle and filled the world with billowy cotton. It was a total whiteout with visibility mere meters. The new-generation optics was a joke. Sure, it helped block ultraviolet radiation, and the second-generation polarization cut snow glare significantly, but it was useless in these conditions. The damn thing kept fogging up. The GSS's science division was great at theory, but their lack of practical application often made men like Tolya guinea pigs. As he tried to navigate, he pictured the scientists here now giving their new equipment a try. His chapped lips cracked as he smiled.

"Click." Chikuk made a soft clicking sound as the Yupik Eskimos do. He pointed with a flat vertical palm.

Tolya adjusted his course. Almost immediately, a dark mass pushed through the low clouds, and a small black rock cove covered mostly in ice appeared. The lava-strewn beach was a battle of black versus white, truly inhospitable. Tolya readied himself. This was what he was made for, the apex of extreme, living on the razor's edge with a life-and-death mission to fulfill.

He cut the engine and coasted towards the hummock-lined shore. They must operate in total silence.

Misha leaned over the front of the raft and, using an oar, broke through the hoarfrost to carve a path.

Once they reached more substantial ice, the team disembarked. Like a well-practiced drill, all gear and personnel was unloaded and moved across the frozen sea and up to the shore. The crunching of rocks and the cracking of ice underfoot was masked by the crashing of waves against the perpetually frozen barrier. A mix of stacked ice and frozen sea foam covered the shore, eventually transitioning to polished, rime-covered rocks.

Tolya glanced over at Chikuk who knelt briefly and mumbled some sort of prayer or greeting. The Eskimo then selected a smooth pebble, scraped the ice from it, placed it in his pocket, and stood for a brief moment, unmoving. Then, just as quickly, he was back helping the others drag the gear up the beach and onto the snow-covered landscape beyond the shore.

Traktor tried to stifle a sneeze as he moved empty-handed to the high-tidemark. He bent at the waist and tried to flick off the slush that had accumulated on his boots. He then stamped his feet up and down as though the American soil had tainted his soles.

Tolya looked around at the near whiteout conditions and felt confident their actions had not been seen. Given the choice, he would have approached this mission very differently, including the team selection. But the powers-that-be had turned a deaf ear to his ideas and dictated the terms. This was a "yes, sir" assignment right from the beginning. This new-fangled "cold war" was nothing like Tolya had experienced. He would have faced his enemy rather than steal around in the shadows. But different times called for different strategies. Still, he was not about to step foot on foreign soil without something to connect him to Mother Russia. He fingered his Order of Lenin medal he kept hidden away in his breast pocket, a reminder of home and why he was here.

His mind started to drift to a past mission—death, screaming, blood—so much blood. The screams of the innocent blended with the wind fighting its way up the cove.

"*Colonel.*" Kaz was looking at him. "We're ready."

Tolya pulled himself back to the moment and gave Kaz a curt nod. Without hesitation, Kaz ran to the sea. He spun the black raft around, pointing the bow out to open ocean. He pulled out his DV-1 combat knife and made several slashes in the raft. He started the motor and released it.

The squad watched as the craft moved past the waves and finally succumbed to the impassionate sea, sinking out of sight with a gurgle and a sputter from the drowning motor.

The group stood in silence. They had reached the point of no return.

Colonel Tolya Alexeev looked at Engineer Marshal Sergei Popov. "You ready?"

His pale white face with nervous brown eyes nodded. Popov held his canvas bag close.

The squad reconfigured their gear and set off at a brisk pace with Chikuk in the lead, and Kaz, his bushy eyebrows already frosted over, taking up the rear.

Here at the top of the world, the wind and clouds were a living, breathing entity in itself. It was the ultimate hunter: cruel, unceasing, inescapable. The beast slowed the squad down, blowing and scouring the ground like a ravenous creature.

Chikuk looked back and called out, "Stay close. It's not the cold that kills, it's the wind."

The ground was relatively flat but frozen so hard it was like walking on slippery uneven concrete. The sun had risen to its pinnacle for the day, just inches above the horizon. It cast a greenish-orange anemic glow as it played peek-a-boo with the transient clouds. This time of year the sun was up for only a few hours, traveling low across the horizon and providing almost no warmth. The rock-covered tundra gave way to multiple snowdrifts that had to be skirted or climbed. After eighteen miles of dragging gear and coping with the bitter cold, the team's progress had slowed dramatically.

Tolya stopped them. He crept up behind a large volcanic boulder and took out his binoculars. He could no longer feel his fingers and wondered how the rest of his squad was coping. A large steel-gray monolith, near completion, stood in the distance. It was a testament to modern man. Here on Umnak Island, thousands of miles from anything, was the most sophisticated piece of electrical engineering in the world—the DEW Line, as the Americans called it, or, Distant Early Warning System.

Tolya was proud in his belief that it was the superior military strength of Russia that had caused the paranoid American bastards to build an 800-mile chain of radar tracking and alerting stations. With it they could detect a plane crossing the Arctic Circle out of Soviet Russia, and then scramble their jets to intercept. "All that ends today," Tolya said to himself.

He panned the binoculars and focused on the base where three men worked. He saw that a single guard was stationed nearby, his eyes glazed with boredom. Tolya turned and headed back to his huddled team.

Chikuk secured the last post on a black and white camouflaged dome tent. It was a new design that could withstand extreme weather. They had placed it in a small depression, and from fifty feet away, it was invisible. Tolya stepped through the flap and was greeted with a wall of warm air that smelled of burnt tobacco and fear, and for the first time in nine hours, no wind. It was a balmy minus five degrees Celsius inside, but it felt like summer to him.

Engineer Popov's color had returned to his face. He was hunched over, inspecting and organizing his gear: three gray boxes the size of a loaf of bread with odd connectors attached at both ends, two for the mission and one as backup. These were his charge and the entire mission depended on his unique skill set. Though not a social person by nature, Popov lived in the here-and-now of electrical science. Capacitors, resistors and circuits were his domain.

In the middle of the tent, Traktor was hunched over and scribbling in a little black notebook he kept in his breast pocket. His eyes darted from person to person, then back to his writing. The political officer's patented dour expression was relentlessly on display, a shield to keep the curious away.

Tolya moved to his second in command, Sergeant Kazimir, "How's the radio working, Kaz?"

"I'm getting a ping from our shadow."

Tolya nodded as he took off his arctic combat boots and rubbed the circulation back into his toes. The boots were made of a new kind of vulcanized rubber with an inflatable bladder to act as a weather barrier. There was little doubt of their effectiveness, but still, subarctic cold had a way of infiltrating everything, even your bones.

Chikuk was off to one side eating some kind of dried meat. He seemed unfazed by the day's activities and looked as if he could do it all again. Misha moved over and sat next to him. He held out his canteen and offered Chikuk a drink. In return, Chikuk offered him some of his mystery meat. Misha took the dark chunk in his hand and sniffed it.

Chikuk smiled at his hesitation. "Walrus mixed with crowberry. It's good."

Misha took a bite and tried to make a pleasant face. "Have you ever been to America before?" he whispered. He glanced over his shoulder, concerned that the political officer might be listening.

"I have cousins that live a couple of islands to the north from here." Chikuk gestured with his hands. "We have met for hunts in the summer. Good hunting there."

"I like to hunt," Misha said.

Chikuk reached over and squeezed his arm. "Hunting keep you strong." His cheeks spread into a smile revealing a missing front tooth and genuine care.

Misha returned it with an effervescent smile of his own.

Tolya was touched. Two men, worlds apart, finding common ground.

2

October 1957 – Umnak Island – 4:12 p.m. – That Afternoon

The wiper worked overtime against a losing battle, as a mix of airborne snow and sleet attacked the windshield. Four separate thousand-watt headlamps pierced the dusk as the last rays of the day's paltry sun dipped below the horizon.

Private Jenkins gazed out of the fogged-up side window of the Le Toureau Logistical Car VC-22 Sno-Freighter, as it moved along the ice and lava rock coast. It was a unique land train built to cross deep rivers and snow while pulling 150 tons of equipment. The cockpit of the VC-22 sat fifteen feet up in the air, and the segmented windshield angled forward, giving the vehicle the appearance of a praying mantis. But it was no insect, with eight-hundred horsepower powering twenty-four electric motors, one for each wheel including the five trail cars behind it. The VC-22 was truly a train without a track. The Sno-Freighter had high ground clearance, with eight-foot-tall tires that allowed it to clear debris up to four feet in height, and all at subarctic temperatures.

Jenkins had spent the last four hours wondering how he had gotten to this place in his life. Things used to be good for him. He was respected in certain circles of Chicago. Now he was a bottom-rung private caught up in some mad race against the Soviets.

As a flyweight fighter, Jenkins had proven himself in the ring. It was a skill brought on by desperation. He was the only provider for his family. His mother Agatha and little sister Penny depended on him for everything. Agatha had lost a leg from type-one diabetes and found work to be impossible for a one-legged black woman. And as much as she hated her son Jenkins fighting, she knew it was the street for all of them if he failed.

Jenkins had excelled for a time, eventually becoming a local favorite. He leveraged that success into a chance at the national stage. That was before a bad decision and trouble with the law left him a choice: jail or the army. Now, every penny he could spare from his private's salary went to his family. When his new orders came through to this posting, he'd been furious. But when he learned it meant a bump in pay, he was all in.

The Sno-Freighter jostled through a ravine, banging Jenkins back to the present. Up ahead he could see a massive, partially-illuminated structure. Towering sixty feet in the air, its concave surface was painted navy gray. A smaller column stood at its midpoint, pointing a receiver at the huge reflecting dish.

The tungsten work light rattled as the Sno-Freighter came to a stop next to the load-out area of DEW LRR Site 42. Jenkins climbed down the exit ladder from the cockpit and jumped the last two feet to the frozen ground. He stomped his feet and looked back up at the odd vehicle. Written in a mix of yellow cursive and block letters was the company's logo, Alaska Freightline Inc. With a practiced motion, he tapped out a single Lucky Strike from his pack and ducked behind the tall front tire to block the wind from his lighter. The sweet acrid smoke filled his lungs and calmed his frenzied nerves. He had arrived.

He watched as men and equipment unloaded the Sno-Freighter. The navy gray structure towered up into the clouds. It was constructed of individual steel plates making the surface look like a one-color jigsaw puzzle, where all the pieces were rectangles. Off to his right was an unpainted wooden building about the size of a four-car garage, and beyond that was nothing but ice and lava rock. Jenkins took another draw on his cigarette and exhaled decisively. The cold here made a bad Chicago winter look like swimsuit weather. He must have really pissed off somebody to deserve this posting.

Inside the wooden building was a common area with a small well stocked bar. The walls were unfinished plywood, and the floor was covered with thin green linoleum. There was a pool table and a reading area. The duty officer's desk was to the left. Beyond that, several doors led to sleeping quarters and a communal head. Jenkins reported to the commanding officer and was issued a cot and guard duty. Two shifts, four hours on, four hours off. Nobody stayed out in the cold longer than four hours. This was a standing order based on an incident three months back. His cot was a two-tiered affair that was shared with three other workers. Privacy was a thing of the past.

Chikuk leaned against the wind with his nose held high. He took a deliberate sniff. Then, with a curt hand gesture, pointed the squad in an arc around to the left.

The sun had long since gone down and the temperature was continuing to plummet. There were no workers on the grounds of the DEW LRR Site 42, only one guard.

Corporal Misha Ivanov stayed low in a crouch as he took

his time moving silently through the loose rock, his trusted DV-1 combat blade in one hand and a grapefruit-size rock in the other.

The silhouetted figure next to a burning drum was facing away. Tolya watched, longing for the man to stay just like that. The fifty-five-gallon steel drum popped and hissed as the fire devoured the wood inside. The wind had died to a constant thirty kilometers per hour.

The plan was simple. Misha was to take out the guard, making it look like an accident, and get Popov and his gizmo in and out of the facility as quickly as possible.

But plans have a way of falling apart the moment you make contact with the enemy. Whatever the reason, no one would ever know, maybe the man's back was cold, but the soldier turned from the fire and stared right at Misha.

Misha froze. At first the soldier seemed not to notice him in the dark. He continued to puff on his cigarette, staring out into the night, right in his direction.

Colonel Tolya Alexeev tensed as the squad helplessly watched the machinations play out from a distance. Kaz pulled his Makarov MP-71 and put the bead on the soldier's heart. Tolya raised his hand to stop him. The meaning was clear: no unnecessary gunplay or noise.

Private Jenkins paused to brush at a bit of tobacco stuck on his tongue, the cold nearly freezing his open mouth. The roaring fire did little to abate the encroaching chill. He imagined himself a rotisserie chicken roasting as it slowly turned in the flames. Only in this case it was to keep from freezing.

Jenkins leaned back, looking up at a spectacle of colored flames slowly dancing across the black sky. The collage flowed and wavered in an incandescent aura of azures and deep reds.

The local Inuit called them spirit lights, but he knew them as the aurora borealis. It was a spectacular sight.

Jenkins drew the last puff on the spent cigarette and flicked it. As he watched the glowing ember spin through the air, something caught his attention. Something was wrong.

Two human eyes with a feral look stared back at him in the span between flame and blackness. This was no fellow coworker. The man stood stock still, holding a large knife in his left hand. Jenkins quickly moved to unsling his M-1 rifle and call out an alarm, but his voice failed and only an unintelligible squawk came out that was quickly carried away by the wind.

The intruder didn't hesitate. Like a cat touching fire for the first time, he leaped headlong. But the loose rocks and ice gave way and he lost purchase. Jenkins reacted fast by pulling the rifle off his parka and taking a quick shot from the hip.

Click.

He quickly realized he hadn't chambered a round. If this was a drill, he just failed. In one practiced motion he put his mitten in his mouth, bit down and pulled it off. He racked the bolt on his rifle and chambered a round. He scarcely noticed the skin on his hand as it ripped free, sticking to the frozen metal of his weapon. But he did notice that this wasn't over.

The man hurled his rock attempting to delay the rifle's firing, but Jenkins feinted left and it flew past harmlessly. The man jabbed his blade, aiming for Jenkins' ribs, but ended up getting nothing but air.

Jenkins' mind and body instantly switched to autopilot. He dropped his stance, spread his legs and returned to his days fighting in the ring. His movements came without thinking. He used his rifle to parry the man and his knife to the side and swept the butt of the rifle around bringing it full force on the back of the intruder's head.

Gore and white matter from the back of the man's head was clearly visible. Jenkins stared down at the unmoving man. He tapped him with his boot, his stomach convulsing at the sight.

Suddenly, another man came from nowhere, followed by more men.

Jenkins spun around, still in shock. The world had gone deathly silent and seemed to slowly spin. He placed his now frostbitten hand up to his mouth to call for help. From some primitive place in his brain, there grew a crunching noise, but by the time he turned, the wind was pushed from his lungs as he took flight and landed hard.

He struggled against overwhelming odds. One of the men said something in Russian. The reality of it hit. This was no drill.

Tolya tackled the soldier at full pace, and five more of his men followed behind. The guard was immediately overwhelmed. They held him tight to the ground while one man covered his mouth and nose.

Within moments the team had suffocated the guard. They quickly moved to Misha and rolled him over. Tatter held the man's head in his arms. There was no movement.

Misha, the man who had been loyal to a tee, was no more. Strangely, he wore a slight smile on his rapidly cooling face. Corporal Misha Ivanov had died doing what he loved most.

Colonel Tolya Alexeev kicked the ground in anger and loosed a few choice words. It was an unimaginable disaster, but something they had all trained for. He would have to re-focus the squad quickly, or face losing them. Later he would grieve for his friend and one of the fiercest warriors he had ever known.

Suddenly, Chikuk ran off into the stygian night. "What is he doing?" Tolya asked.

"Taking a piss," said Tatter, ever the sarcastic wit.

"Unbelievable. Tell him to fucking hold it. We have a major problem on our hands." Tolya turned to Engineer Marshal Sergei Popov. "You have five minutes, not a second more. Understand?"

His tone left no doubt. Popov dashed off with his canvas bag in hand.

"Tatter, go with him."

Private Tatter gave a quick nod as he ran off in the engineer's footsteps.

"Colonel." Chikuk had returned and was motioning to the remaining team.

"What now?" Tolya said.

"Bring body."

The team quickly cleaned the site, grabbed the two bodies and moved off with Chikuk. There in the snow was a pool of frozen yellow. It took a second, but Tolya understood Chikuk's plan. They unzipped the soldier's parka, took off his gloves, and lowered his zipper. The next shift would find him frozen while taking a piss too far from the fire. They would claim it a rookie mistake and think nothing more of it. At least that was the hope.

Popov stopped at the bottom of the radar tower where a small pyramid-shaped structure housed and connected all the wiring before sending it to the building next door. He stooped by the metal double doors that held the wiring for the antenna's receiver.

The tall tower sprouted straight up from the roof of the metal pyramid. A highly-tuned receiving unit collected waves that reflected from the surface of the immense dish. It could pick up even the faintest of distant sounds and distinguish what they were through a collection of sophisticated vacuum-tube electronics stored in the nearby building. This information was then relayed to other stations along the chain and ultimately to a quick-response base located in Fairbanks.

Picking a simple padlock was easy, but not at minus ten in the wind. Popov finally heard the click as the hasp gave way. He quickly opened the doors and climbed inside. Tatter kept watch from just outside.

Popov pulled off his mittens and rubbed his hands together trying to bring them back to functionality. He clicked on his flashlight with the red lens to protect his night vision. Popov selected one of the gray boxes from his bag and began the process of installing it between the receiving console and the output cable. He stood on top of the radio box and unscrewed the twenty-eight-wire-pin coupling that attached the antenna to the console. He quickly inspected the pin configuration and admired the level of intel they were working from. Satisfied they were a match, he reattached each end of the connector to the electrical leach and hid the whole thing in a mass of wires that ran back to the receiver.

He climbed down to the floor and sat next to a console, and pulled out his portable battery-operated oscilloscope, a marvel of modern technology. He connected it to the wires leading to the transmitter and hit the selector knob. The signal coming into the unit showed a strong, consistent, cycling green wave, like a never-ending snake. Popov then flipped a switch on the scope and the same sine wave now had a small but definite spike on the upper arch of each wave. Satisfied that his job here was done, he packed up his equipment and left the compartment.

The squad met up back in the domed tent. Misha's body lay wrapped in a tarp off to one side, a sharp reminder of what was at stake for them all. Tolya knelt next to the body. He pulled back the tarp. A stone stared back at him. His friend was no longer human. The cold had claimed him. It would probably take them all before this job was done.

Tolya bowed his head in deep respect, thinking, "Of all the unlucky…" He stopped this train of thought, as it would do him no good. He slipped the red and gold medal with the profile of Vladimir Lenin from his pocket and held it in his hand. He whispered, "You deserve this more than I, Misha." He slipped his Order of Lenin medal into Misha's breast pocket, touched the dead soldier's face for a brief moment, and finally pulled the tarp back over his head.

"Comrade Alexeev," the political officer stepped towards Tolya, attempting to engage him.

"It's *Colonel* Alexeev." Tolya put his hand up to stop him from continuing. "And we can discuss this later."

Tolya turned to the whole team, and said, "I want everything packed up now. We must be miles from here when they find that body. We leave in ten."

Tolya looked to the now-stationary Zampolit Traktor Yashin, his face betraying the challenge he had intended for Tolya. "You best get a move on, 'Comrade,'" he said. "This is a bad place to be left behind." With that, he turned his back on Traktor and went to grab his gear.

"Colonel, what do we do with Misha?" Private Tatter asked.

"We bring him with us. No evidence of any kind gets left behind."

"Understood, sir."

The whiteout was complete. Snow, clouds, and wind mixed together against the black of night. Tolya reconfigured his parka for the third time in an attempt to block out the cold. The squad pushed against the merciless gale, their quick march doing little to maintain core temperature. And after six hours battling the harsh conditions it was taking its toll. Tolya could no longer feel his extremities.

The group had slowed, moving at about forty percent of their original pace. All except for Chikuk. He looked like he was just getting started. They had over twenty miles still to go and less than forty-eight hours to do it in. It was an impossible task. Tolya gave them a thirty percent chance of success. They were poor odds, but based on their situation and what was at stake, he would take them.

Sergeant Kazimir Yegor scooted next to Tolya and pointed a small flashlight covered with a red lens at his compass. "It says we need to go in this direction."

Tolya glanced down at the needle pointing off to his left.

"This far north the declination could be as much as seventy degrees off, Kaz. I recommend continuing up this grade." He pointed towards what looked like the beginning of a hill where, just visible through the gloom, was Chikuk.

"Just keep the wind on your left," said Tolya. "It's better than a compass up here."

Kaz nodded and returned the compass to his pocket.

Tatter abruptly appeared from out of the gloom, pulling a small sled with Misha's body, his red flashlight barely illuminating the ground around him. He bent at the waist trying to catch his breath. He wore a grim expression.

Chikuk, who carried no flashlight, suddenly returned. "We need to go around," Chikuk said. "Sludge ice ahead, very dangerous."

Traktor piped up. "What's sludge ice?"

Tolya looked to the political officer and said, "I don't know, and I don't want to know." Turning back to Tatter, he said, "Do what Chikuk says."

Tolya looked at his wristwatch and did a quick calculation in his head. "We have about two hours left before sunrise. And stay together. Do not lose sight of the man in front of you."

The team moved northwest in an attempt to skirt the problem that lay ahead, sludge ice. Each step was now labored as they moved against the heartless arctic wind.

"Comrade Alexeev."

Tolya kept marching, his eyes fixed on Tatter five meters in front of him, nothing more than a fuzzy red shape.

"Comrade Alexeev!" Zampolit Traktor Yashin ran forward, now matching his stride, huffing with desperation.

Tolya gave him the briefest of glances. "What do you need, Political Officer Yashin?"

"This is madness. We need to stop. My hands, the pain."

Tolya could tell the man was struggling, but had no sympathy for a government stooge.

"I'll decide when we stop. Let me know if the pain stops. That's when you need to worry."

"No mission is worth a man's life, comrade."

"Tell that to your uncle." Tolya glanced at the man.

Traktor fought for every breath. "He sent us here to get a leg up on the Americans, not to die on their soil and create an international incident."

Tolya trudged on mechanically. Finally, he stopped and turned to Traktor, freezing him in his steps. "Comrade, I have no plans to die here, but if you do, I'll be sure to put you on a sled and bring you back to your family."

Traktor stiffened. "You know I have orders to kill anyone who even looks at the Americans with envy."

Tolya let the comment sit for a second, continuing to move

forward. "Is that so? Well, I have orders to kill anyone who interferes with this mission, and right now that's *you*." The wind howled, emphasizing that last word.

Tolya continued on, then looked back over his shoulder and called, "Besides, what do the Americans have to envy? More money than sense if they are wasting it on this silly endeavor. They will surely lose in the end."

The colonel stopped and looked straight at Traktor. "Zampolit Traktor Yashin, please get back in line before I put a bullet in your head. Oh, and please remember to put all this in your little report."

Traktor straightened and looked at Tolya with black eyes that could kill. He slowly reached for his pocket.

"Please try it," Tolya said.

Tolya shot a furtive glance just beyond Traktor, which made Traktor look over. Walking just off to his side was Kaz, and in his hand was a large pistol pointed straight at the Political Officer's spine.

"Now get your ass back in line, 'Comrade.'"

Traktor remained defiant and unmoving as he watched Tolya turn his back and disappear into the night.

Anger flushed Traktor's frostbitten face, focusing him to a single conclusion. This mission was doomed under the command of Colonel Tolya Alexeev. The arrogant ass was going to get them all killed. What Operation Blind Pig needed was the finesse and cunning of a man like himself. Not some blunt-nosed instrument like Tolya.

It was his duty to Mother Russia to remove that swine from command. He pondered at several possibilities, each ending up with the death of Colonel Tolya Alexeev. This made him smile as he savored the feeling, slowly lowering his pulsing blood pressure.

Traktor looked up. There was no one ahead in the gloom. Nothing but the unbroken parade of clouds as they whisked past the meager glow of his red-lensed flashlight. They seemed to be in a foolish hurry to some unknown destination. He blinked the frost from his eyes and spun behind him. No one behind him. Panic began to crawl up his spine as uncontrollable shivers set in. He called out several times, but only the lonely call of a howling wind replied. It seemed to laugh and mock him with its high-pitched scream. He looked to the frozen ground, but the blowing snow had erased any footsteps. How long had he been standing there thinking of Tolya's demise?

Traktor ran forward, shouting, "Comrades!"

Again, his words were grabbed and pulled away by the gale. He continued blindly forward as he pulled out his hand compass. It pointed off to his right. He adjusted accordingly and quickly trudged forward. As he moved he noticed a change in the ice. It had taken on a honey-like consistency. He continued through it, his rubberized boots temporarily holding the wetness at bay.

Then, for a brief moment, the blowing clouds parted and visibility jumped to nearly a thousand meters. A pool of moonlight speared what looked like the edge of a small shallow inlet in front of him. On the other side of the inlet was the red glow of his team's flashlights. The surface of the inlet was greasy in appearance, not solid. He screamed for all he was worth but the team continued on, unaware.

Traktor pulled his pistol out and raised it in the air. Then, remembering their strict orders about gunplay, he put it away. He quickly started moving through the slushy water around the shallow inlet to catch up with his team. It was only about twelve inches deep and his boots were holding up just fine. The Eskimo was an idiot. The political officer was saving significant distance by going this way. All he had to do was catch up before the whiteout returned.

Just as quickly as the team had appeared, the indifferent clouds once again swallowed them up. Traktor sloshed though the slushy conditions as fast as his legs would carry him. A surge of sudden adrenaline briefly warmed his core as he redoubled his efforts. He would not be left behind.

A sound like cracking ice came from behind him, spurring him on. Suddenly, the sound came from all around him. The slush began freezing at an alarming rate. Zampolit Traktor Yashin felt bile and fear stab at his guts. He panicked and sprinted for the shoreline. Then, like a shadow of a bird passing overhead, the slush transitioned from a semi-liquid to a solid. In an instant, Traktor was snared mid-calf, both legs gripped solidly by the ice. He tried to move, but he was caught like a fly in amber.

He thrashed wildly but his lower legs held firm in the grasp of the freeze. The cold fought through the layers of his clothing seeking warm skin. He screamed and pulled his Tokarev TT-30 from its holster with swollen, numb fingers. He emptied the magazine in the direction he had last seen the squad, secrecy be damned.

Tolya put his hand to his mouth and gave a quick whistle. The action caused a blast of pain across his cracked lips. The squad came to a stop and gathered together.

"Do you hear that?" he asked.

In the distance a faint clap of thunder popped. Kaz lifted his head. "Is that gunfire?" he said.

"Colonel!" Engineer Marshal Sergei Popov stepped over to

the group looking around. "Political Leader Traktor Yashin is missing."

"How is that possible?" Tolya asked Popov.

"I was just following the man in front of me and…"

Before he could finish, Tolya backhanded him across the face, dropping the man like a sack of rotted meat. Being new to Tolya's team, Engineer Popov didn't know his commander's dislike for excuses. In his squad you owned up to your mistakes.

"Form a search grid from right here, two by two," Tolya said. "Tatter, Chikuk, grid one." Tolya pointed in the direction they should search.

"Kaz, Popov, grid two. Be back here in ten minutes. Then we'll move to the next sections."

The men ran off, side by side, searching their quadrant. Tolya, as the anchor person could only pace and wait, muttering to himself, "Damn it, we don't have time for this." He looked down at the tarp that held Misha's body. The cost of this mission was already too high.

Traktor sat down on the now hard surface of the inlet. He processed his predicament. Luckily, he was actually feeling warm so he didn't have to worry about the cold anymore. He took out his knife and started chipping away at the ice that held his feet. As he worked, he felt his body get hot. He took off his parka so he could move more freely.

One leg was almost free; he could see the top of his shoe through the ice. He stifled a yawn; he was tired. This had been an arduous journey. After a short rest, he would start back up. He lay back on the ice and rested his eyes for just a moment. His hands felt too warm so he took off his gloves. *Ah, better.*

He thought of his summers back in Dzhubga, along the

Black Sea. It was a small town formed by Cossacks in the 1860's, and it was his family's favorite getaway. They had a small birch cabin on a hill that had the most incredible sunset views. He could picture the orange glow across the dark water as his mother and father sat side by side on a carved bench sharing tea as black as the ocean at midnight. He would run through the woods and pick wildflowers for the table. His mother was always so proud of him.

Traktor had an odd thought… *sludge ice very dangerous,* before drifting off.

After the second grid search, Chikuk and Tatter returned with the news. They had found their political officer.

Tolya looked down at their missing team member, lying on his back frozen solid. His feet were still trapped in the ice; his parka, gloves, and hat were off to the side.

Kaz mumbled, "Paradoxical undressing, one of the last signs of hypothermia."

Tatter looked confused, but he couldn't take his eyes off of the frozen man on the ice.

Kaz looked up at the boy and continued. "You think you're warm so you take off your clothes."

An awkward silence hung in the mourning wind. Tolya broke it. "Get him out of there."

Kaz looked at the Traktor's trapped legs. "What about his feet?"

"Cut 'em off. We've wasted enough time here." Tolya turned and walked away. He should have pushed the man overboard when he had the chance. Now they would have to drag two bodies with them.

Chikuk took out an ice saw and started on Traktor's left leg.

Two frozen corpses now rested outside the domed tent. They spoke volumes of the morale inside. Tolya sat with his hands to his head trying to relieve a headache that started back in fifty-six. The flap on the tent popped open and Chikuk and Popov entered. They had made camp just before dawn and managed to navigate within a mile of the next installation. All they had left to do was to insert the second electrical leach and evacuate off the island. The never-ending storm had taken its toll on the team, but had also made them invisible to the enemy. Every member was suffering from frostbite and exposure. The black skin on their appendages told of a future without those body parts, but going in they all knew what was at stake.

Tolya massaged his temples as his mind drifted back to Hungary where a T-55 battle tank rolled over bodies lying in the street like stacked cordwood. Sergeant Tolya Alexeev kept his men in tight cover behind the metal beast as it crunched along, pressing its advantage against the poorly armed resistance. His boots made a sucking noise as they slogged through the masticated gore left in the tank's tracks.

Moscow had changed its mind, and in an onslaught of overwhelming superiority had invaded Budapest to crush the Hungarian revolution. Nearly twenty thousand people had been killed so far and the number was rising.

Soviet soldiers were killing wounded civilians, and the atrocities were growing as many commanders turned a blind eye to their soldiers' actions. Some tanks were dragging the dead behind them as warnings to those still protesting. But Tolya had other thoughts on his mind. His OBSP team had been tasked with a very specific mission. Get to Prime Minister Imre Nagy and capture him alive if at all possible. Tolya knew that the powers back in Moscow wanted to make the Prime Minister's demise a very public event.

He tapped three times on the back of the tank's heavy armor plating with the hilt of his dagger. The tank turret spun to the command as bullets hopelessly pinged off its steel shell. The eighty-millimeter canon fired a shell at the heavily fortified entrance to the capital building. In an instant, the twelve armed men and mountain of sand bags blocking the entrance were gone. Tolya and his men dashed through the blood-spattered doors hanging loosely on shattered hinges. Bodies and parts were everywhere as poorly armed civilians had tried to protect the building. Inside, it was worse. Secretaries and paper pushers were willing to die, oftentimes with nothing but a coat rack or file drawer as a weapon.

Tolya's men made quick work of the hurdle as they moved room to room on their way to the top office. The lopsided battle finally ended with a very brave but stupid charge of eight men in suits wielding pistols. Tolya could take no more. He paused as his men and their Rexim-Favor submachine guns quickly shredded the small force, leaving nothing but carnage and moans.

Tolya sat up in a sweat, his eyes blinking the sight away. Breathing heavily, he remembered the moment he was forced to stand proud as he received his medal, The Order of Lenin, from Defense Minister Marshal Zhukov for delivering the Hungarian Prime Minister. That was nearly a year ago. It had launched his career like a three-stage rocket. Now he was here on American soil expected to do the impossible. And so far, he had.

He glanced at his Smersh watch, the radium hands ticking with a carefree precision. It was time.

The next infiltration into the American's station went much smoother. Popov had installed the electrical leach with the same exacting results—a specific spike in an otherwise perfect sine wave. They re-gathered at the dome tent, mission complete. All that was left now was to make one last push to the coast and evac. On the backside of Umnak Island, basalt rock gave way to large sections of snow-covered tundra and a small glacier that calved into the sea beyond. The plan was to exfil across the glacier and rendezvous with an old steel trawler that had been busy fishing and shadowing their movements from beyond five miles out to sea.

Kaz had tried to reach their shadow over the radio, but so far no reply. It made little difference to Tolya as their options were limited, to say the least.

All evidence was to be taken along, leaving only footprints behind to dissolve away in the snow flurries.

The wind subsided and the temperature rose to just below freezing as the beleaguered squad reached the coast five miles southeast of station DEW LRR Site 41. They had trekked a remarkable seventy-eight miles over the course of three days in some of the most brutal conditions on the planet. Truly a remarkable feat. Now, if they could just finish.

Kaz, while holding his headphones close to his ears, reached up with his other hand and waved it in the air. The radio had made contact. The remaining team leaned over to hear the one-sided conversation.

"Roger that, rendezvous oh fourteen hundred Walrus Bay," Kaz said. "That's a little tight for us..." And finally, "Understood."

Kaz put down the transmitter. "Another storm is coming. It's now or never."

Tolya glanced at his watch and calculated the remaining time: three hours. The arctic dash to the rendezvous site was taking too long. With the gear and the two bodies it was a struggle, and there was no way to bury the bodies and some of the gear, as the ground was rock hard. They were out of time.

Chikuk guided them at a brisk pace while pulling Misha's corpse. The man seemed impervious to the conditions and the weight of his load. Across the glacier was the most direct route to make their connection, but it was fraught with danger.

Tolya placed his hands on his knees as he huffed to catch his breath. The men were spent. The quick march to the coast had cost them all their remaining energy. The team would have to dig deep if any of them were to escape.

Chikuk gestured for them to go around the five-mile-long glacier, but that option died with the ticking clock.

"There's no time left, we go straight through," Tolya said.

Everyone knew the risks of crossing a glacier, but doing it in a hurry was madness. It was the Arctic's version of Russian roulette. Glaciers were constantly-moving creatures that had a way of cracking open into deep chasms hundreds of feet deep and then closing back up just as fast. And when the surface was covered with snow, there was no way of spotting the dangers below without using extreme caution, which meant taking extra time.

Tolya didn't wait. After catching his breath, he jogged with his heavy load out onto the moving ice field. The rest of the team hesitated but then followed behind. Tolya called behind him, "Follow my tracks!" He figured that if something happened, at least they could learn from his error. The cove, just six hundred yards on the other side, was their destination.

A scream died in the wind as a crack and rumble shook the ground. Tolya looked back and did a quick head count. Kaz was missing. He ran back to investigate.

One hundred feet below in a narrow ice chasm lay the crushed body of Kaz. His folded remains were illuminated by impossibly blue ice that lived at the heart of the glacier.

Kaz had followed Tolya's footsteps but the snow that had covered the chasm had given way under his load.

With no possibility of getting down to him, Tolya made the only choice he could to save the rest. "Everything over the side."

The men stared numbly.

"Move it!"

They pushed all that they were carrying over the ledge and down into the ice crevasse. Tolya moved to Tatter and put his gloved hand on his shoulder.

"Even them." He gestured to the corpses. "Hurry now, private."

The men, as reverently as possible dropped the two wrapped bodies into the crack. The wind sang a sad hymn as they stared down at the jumble of bodies and gear lying in the bottom of the gap.

"Now run!"

Chikuk watched as the small group of men ran recklessly across the uneven surface. He removed his glove and reached into his pocket. He pulled out the small pebble he had collected when they first came ashore. "Thank you for keeping us all safe," he said. He bent to the ground and carefully placed it down on the ice. "It is finished."

Three desperate men sprinted across the rest of the glacier without incident. Once on the other side Tolya paused to take in his crew. They were a mess. Tatter's nose was black with frostbite, and Popov was running stiff legged. He was probably going to lose his feet to the cold.

He waited, but there was no Chikuk.

Tolya called to Tatter, "Where's Chikuk?"

"He left."

Tolya looked confused. "What do you mean?"

"I mean, he waved at me, turned, and disappeared into the

storm." To himself, he muttered, "I guess he decided to move to America after all."

Tolya stared off into the distance, a view that included every possible shade of white. "We're done with him anyway," he said. "Come on."

The three men climbed down the embankment towards the cove. From out of the gray gloom came a black rubber raft puttering to shore. Tolya took a shallow breath of the arctic air. This mission, though critical to his superiors, had been costly. In the end, he could only hope that the evidence they had left behind would never come to light. Three of them, against all odds, had made it. Honestly, he was surprised.

3

CHERSKY, SIBERIA — 7:31 P.M. — TWO WEEKS LATER

The Tupolev TU-16 Badger accelerated down the unmarked runway outside Chersky, Siberia. It was a cold but clear night with nothing but good news for the weather that lay ahead.

Radioman First Class Vaughn Pankiv, who everyone called Panky, warmed his hands with the heat generated by the vacuum tube radio in the aft cabin. He was a scruffy man in appearance and attitude, with large ears and a squared chin. The tiny room buzzed with an electrical hum competing in volume with the two large Mikulin AM-3 turbojets' roar.

Sitting in the forward cabin in nylon-mesh seats were Doctor Grigory Nepein and his demure, nervous male assistant, Shura Mosin.

Grigory was the genius behind Operation Blind Pig. He had spent the last three years developing a counter to the Americans' defensive string of early warning radar stations across the Arctic. And the result was the GN01, a transmitter capable of sending out a very specific signal. He was one of the Soviet's best and most guarded secrets. His heavy brows and obsidian eyes were so intense that the average person often found themselves looking away rather than at the man during a conversation.

With the apparent success of the ground mission, all that was left was for him to test the GN01 transmitter. Grigory had spent most of his life at his well-stocked lab, having little contact with the outside world. The lifestyle suited him well. Five years ago, he had lost his wife during childbirth, and now his work was all he had to keep him warm in the cold Russian nights.

As with most governments, the Soviets demanded progress from their science divisions. They had been patient with Grigory, but it was now time for him to prove his worth. He was personally going to show them what a true electrical intellect could do. Success would mean unlimited resources and possibly a little more freedom to pursue his other pet projects.

His assistant, Shura Mosin, was busy with three boxes of electrical equipment stacked nearly to the ceiling. Red and green lights blinked in a systematized array as he went through a precise checklist mounted to his clipboard. Shura was the son of Polish parents who, early on, found a place for their son's exceptional intellect and had used it to better their own stations in life. His round thick glasses and perfectly parted hair contributed to his intellectual look. The flight suit they had assigned to him hung loosely on his small frame, as though he had borrowed it from a big brother. But the man was so task oriented he didn't even notice. He leaned to his left trying for a more comfortable position that would work with the Makarov in his back pocket. It was loaded with specialty ammunition deemed safe for use aboard airplanes. The minister had personally given it to him with explicit instructions to shoot Grigory in the head should anything go wrong. There was no way they could risk him being captured, should the plane go down on American soil. Shura had taken on the task like he did everything in his life, with a scientific coolness.

The skies remained clear, and the first taste of dusk was

still two hours away. The TU-16 was a cigar-shaped long-range bomber that could reach speeds of 990 kph with a range of 58,000 kilometers, the pride of Soviet bombers.

It had a large cockpit and three cabins, each the size of a small shed, running in parallel from front to back. The bomb bay could hold two nuclear weapons and deploy them both at once or one at a time, depending on the requirements of the mission. The cockpit sat on top of a bulbous nose that gave the plane its unique look and nickname, Badger.

Captain Yana Shchavelsky leveled off and set their course for ninety degrees due east. "Attention: radio silence from here on out. We have approximately," he looked at his watch and calculated speed, distance and headwinds in his head, "three-and-a-half hours to target."

The captain was a large man with even larger hands. He double-checked all the gauges. Yana's natural instinct to always plan for the worst had served him well on over fifty sorties of this type. To him, this mission was nothing more than business as usual. But the higher-ups had seemed unusually paranoid, calling it off twice before giving the final go-ahead.

Yana looked over at his first officer, a man named Toma Fukin. He was busy at his station and was certainly competent enough. "Toma, take the controls." As he turned the controls over to the co-pilot, he whipped out a dog-eared book that he had been working through, and picked up where he had left off. Toma smiled at his captain; this was a regular occurrence.

"So did she kill him or was she framed?" Fukin asked.

Without looking up, Yana answered, "I will happily loan you the book when I'm done."

"Who has the time to read these days?"

Yana gave his co-pilot a sideways glance and shook his head. *Oh the youth of today.*

This particular Tupolev bomber had been modified. The

standard, somewhat prominent nose cone had been replaced with a concave transmitting dish covered with a Plexiglass cone to protect the bomber's aeronautics. Attached to the dish was a thick braid of wires leading to the forward cabin.

Doctor Grigory Nepein wiped the sweat from his face and readjusted the wispy blond hairs that occupied parts of his scalp. In spite of the outside temperature of well below freezing, the electronics in the cabin radiated heat like a furnace. All systems had checked out and there was nothing left to do but wait. But this was not the doctor's way. So he did a double-check for the third time, running through every possible scenario, just to be sure. He knew failure would most likely result in his death and possibly global war. Everything had to be perfect, as well as himself and every crewman aboard.

"Shura, let's run the sequence again."

"Fifteen minutes to target," was broadcast throughout the cabin in an impassive female voice. The navigator, Natasha Zykin, was a highly decorated officer, with the most flights of anyone on the jet. The Soviet Union had many females in key positions throughout their military machine. Seldom were they given command, but many excelled beyond their male counterparts.

Natasha had proven herself extremely competent, and that information had leaked up the chain of command. It won her a place on Captain Shchavelsky's crew. The captain, though a bit protective of her, was always impressed with her dead-on navigation skills. She never faltered.

She was a short woman with a curvaceous figure and an ever-present smile. Her curly auburn hair was kept short. A smattering of freckles was the source of the nickname she had very slowly come to accept, Nushki.

Two years previously she managed to keep a mission on course in spite of a hurricane-level storm and a lightning strike that caused a complete electrical failure on the plane. The crew panicked and assumed the worst. But when the clouds parted to reveal the runway, she was declared a hero.

She scratched absently at the nape of her neck as she buried her face into the green glow of the radar screen in front of her. The scope's spinning light saber swept the grid-patterned screen with mechanical repetition. Nushki picked up the mic and spoke without looking at a small metal chessboard that was attached to the wall next to her with magnetic chess pieces strategically placed. "Bishop to queen three."

Panky looked at an identical board in the aft radio room. He moved the white bishop and pondered. He tentatively moved his black castle. "Castle to pawn three."

Captain Shchavelsky put his book away and took the stick. "Toma, I'll take her from here."

First Officer Toma Fukin relinquished control. He was starting to feel the tension in the air as they drew close to their primary target. "Yes, sir. You have control."

The captain looked out at the vast sky beyond. "American airspace… Well, this is a first."

Toma swallowed hard and squeaked out, "Yes, sir." Get ahold of yourself, he mouthed with mock bravery.

In the radio room, Panky reached over and flicked several switches. "Powering down the radio and radar," he announced.

"Roger that, radio and radar powering down," came a reply from the co-pilot.

"Resetting speed and altitude, Doc. It's all in your hands now," the captain said.

Panky looked back at the board and concentrated.

"Pawn to castle four," Nushki called from the cabin next to his.

He nodded at her play and moved the piece.

The captain pulled the throttle lever and adjusted the flaps as he spoke to the copilot directly. "I sure hope they know what the hell they're doing back there," he said to Fukin. He gestured with his head to the two scientists in the cabin behind them. "Or this is going to be a real short trip that ends in a ball of fire."

They shared a concerned look but moved past it, focusing on their duties.

The TU-16 decreased its altitude to 10,000 meters and slowed to 750 kph. There was more turbulence at this altitude, but the height and speed were critical for the success of the mission. The captain had flown this route many times, but had always turned around at the 190th parallel while still over international waters.

This operation was as black as they got and he only hoped they would live through it. The pride and brilliance of the Soviet Union was at stake and he would make damn sure to fulfill his role.

"Five minutes to American airspace," Nushki broadcast. She was feeling the tension grow with every mile.

"Disconnect transponder," said the captain.

Panky followed his orders. There was no going back now.

"Queen to bishop four. Queen takes knight," Panky called out. He smiled as he took Nushki's knight.

Nushki moved the corresponding pieces and called out over her shoulder. "You're getting reckless, Panky."

Panky rubbed his fingers together in an anxious fashion. Even the plane seemed nervous as it bucked and trembled trying to shove through the subzero air.

Grigory pushed a small green button on a metal console and glanced to his assistant for reassurance. A signal traveled at lightspeed to the dish in the nose of the jet. The dish amplified the signal and broadcast a very specific high-powered frequency to the world ahead.

Shura nodded timidly while readjusting his glasses on his sweaty face. "CCI is broadcasting," he croaked.

CCI was the Russian acronym for Focused Frequency Emitter. Grigory pushed the intercom and announced, "Captain, maintain this heading and airspeed. We are broadcasting."

The captain confirmed the information and then snapped his oxygen mask into place. Toma followed his lead.

The Tupolev bounced, then settled, as it held its new bearing. Nushki, while keeping her head buried in the optics of a slightly forward magnified view of the ground below, began the countdown. "Two minutes to target."

Toma and the captain could see the outline of an ice-covered island approaching in the distance.

Shura answered with, "Signal strong and steady."

Grigory rubbed his hands against his pants in an unconscious circle. He stared at the lights on his console—all green. Theoretically, the plane's broadcast frequency, in concert with the planted electrical leaches' specific frequency filter, would blind the two radar installations below to their approach.

Grigory had built a full-scale replica of the Americans' radar station based on plans smuggled out of General Electric, the company that had won the contract to build the DEW Line radar stations across the Arctic. The replica had been tested and retested against his CCI unit and leach, until Moscow was satisfied.

"Sir, I see the target now," Nushki announced.

Everyone held his or her collective breaths as the bomber passed overhead. Through her field of view Nushki watched as the shadowy silhouette of Umnak Island passed underneath.

She could just make out the Americans' gray radar installation set against the snow below.

"Passing target now."

The building fled from view.

"Target passed."

She looked up from her scope and tried to swallow, but her throat was dry. They were through, but had they been detected?

Doctor Grigory Nepein allowed the breath he had been holding to release. "Captain," he said, "you can return to our normal altitude and speed." He flicked off the green button and sat back in his seat, barely hearing the words the captain spoke in return.

"Copy that, Doc. Let's hope your little gadget worked. Nushki, set a course for our next target, and Panky, you can turn the radio back on. I want to know if you hear anything."

The navigator consulted her chart and worked out their next bearing. "Roger that, sir; course nine eight degrees, Seattle," Nushki said.

Panky returned the power to the units and concentrated on his headphones. "No contacts, sir."

"Let's hope it stays that way," the captain said to himself. "Panky, let me know if you see so much as a gnat coming our way."

Grigory leaned back and put his hands behind his head. If he had done everything right they should be completely unseen in the American airspace. Grigory allowed a rare smile to form; it had been a long time coming. With this successful test he would be a household name in the Kremlin. Good things were to come, perhaps even a summer cottage on the Black Sea.

"Target distance, ten miles," Navigator Nushki announced.

The captain repeated the information and squinted ahead

through the hazy atmosphere as the skyline of Seattle slowly grew. A sequence of events started to unfold as the crew went through the final preparations to drop their bomb.

"Ready for final bomb check."

"Final bomb check."

"Bomb fusing master safety on."

"Fusing master safety on."

"Target distance, seven miles."

The sequence continued like a well-choreographed dance, each playing their part in time with the other. At the same time the chess game between navigator Nushki and radio/bombardier Panky continued.

The young Shura Mosin removed his glasses and rubbed the lenses on his sleeve. He was no longer involved in the current mission. "Professor," he said to Grigory, "I was thinking we might be able to use the CCI technology for other applications."

"I see you have been reading my book, Shura." Grigory focused on his assistant. "What did you have in mind?"

Shura broke eye contact with his boss, now unsure of his idea. "If there was a way to remotely implant the filter without actually being there."

Grigory wrinkled his forehead at his assistant's idea. The voice over the speaker interrupted his thoughts.

"Target distance five miles."

"Open bomb doors."

Grigory held up his hand to pause Shura's words, his interest piqued but not above the current action. "Perhaps we can talk about it after we have a successful test here."

Shura fingered the gun in his pocket while he nodded.

"I have visual on the scope," Nushki announced as she began a countdown.

The TU-16 buffed slightly, then smoothed out. Everyone

was at the ready. This was what the months of training was all about, right now, this instant. Time seemed to slow for the crew as they neared the drop point. Even the sound of the roaring turbines seemed to fade away.

Then, in a clear and precise voice, Nushki called, "Release bomb."

Panky answered. "Bomb away."

As Captain Yana Shchavelsky heard those last words, he put the bomber into a hard 180-degree turn. "Let's get the *suka blyad* out of here."

Nushki watched on the aiming scope as a large metal-cased bomb dropped, ultimately making contact with the sea some quarter-mile from the city. And harmlessly sinking from sight. Seconds ticked by and still nothing happened.

"Well, Doc," the captain said, "looks like you have your proof of concept. Radar screen evaded and test bomb run successful."

"Thank you, Captain. Excellent crew you have here."

He had to agree. They had all done a great job—so far.

"Now get us back home safely so we can tell someone about it."

"Roger that," the captain replied.

Everyone stayed alert and at the top of their game as the TU-16 reversed its course and moved back through the radar gap they had created in the DEW Line. Once again the CCI had performed perfectly, and they left US airspace without consequence.

Once over international waters, Nushki worked her way to the cockpit and popped the cork on a bottle of champagne she had brought along. "Captain, do I have your permission to pour?"

Captain Shchavelsky glanced over his shoulder. "I don't think one bottle divided by six will hurt. Please do the honors, Nushki."

Nushki made the rounds for all to share. Even the doctor was in a celebratory mood. The morale was high and they were all feeling invincible. After all, they had duped the Americans' radar defenses and even dropped a practice nuclear bomb on their doorstep. All without the capitalist pigs even knowing. It was a good day for the Soviet Union.

Nushki made her way to the aft cabin and handed Panky the nearly empty bottle. "All yours."

He grabbed it and pointed to the chessboard on his wall. "Castle to king five."

Panky guzzled the remainder of the bottle. Nushki looked at his move and then a broad smile spread across her face. "Bishop to rook six. Checkmate."

Panky spit out the remaining champagne and stared at the board, his mouth agape. Nushki smiled and returned to her seat in the next cabin. She looked down at the simple red star with the crossed gold hammer and sickle on her uniform. Had she made the right decision? It was too late now.

Within five minutes the plane seemed to wander. She glanced in the aft cabin at Panky doubled over in his chair motionless. Nushki quickly moved past Doctor Grigory Nepein and his assistant, both unmoving in their chairs. Once in the cockpit she struggled to remove Captain Yana Shchavelsky from his seat, his dead weight making it a real chore. She ended up grabbing his hair to get a good hold and heaved. Once he was on the floor, she sat in his seat and belted herself in. The freckle-faced navigator would no longer suffer the stupidity of men. She said goodbye to her long hated nickname and said softly, "Captain Natasha Zykin."

She looked around one last time and pushed the control stick forward, dropping the bomber into a steep dive straight for the Bering Sea.

4

PRESENT DAY – Washington D.C. – 12:57 p.m. – FBI Headquarters – 5th Floor

Special Agent Collette Sanders, Codi, flowed with a sea of bodies exiting the glass doors of a large meeting room. She moved away from the stale air and bad cologne. Her insipid expression clung to her like a sloth gripping a wobbly branch. She was wearing a white blouse and matching navy pants and jacket. She glanced down at the pamphlet in her hands, *FBI Rules and Regulations—The Do's & Don'ts of Social Media*. It had been three painfully long hours that she would never get back.

For Codi, social media was easy—don't say anything about your work to others, ever.

And when it came to her personal life—don't post anything while drinking or that your mom wouldn't approve of, well, most moms, anyway. The fact that some idiot agents had recently posted a picture of themselves next to a mutilated body on an ongoing investigation had the entire FBI in panicked damage control. Now, every agent and employee was required to take this course. It was always that way, she thought. A few imbeciles ruin it for the rest of us. She deposited the pamphlet into the nearest circular file and headed for the exit.

She checked the time on her phone—perfect—just enough time to eat and change.

At five-foot-eight, Codi could hold her own with most men. She was an avid swimmer and took physical fitness seriously. She had even competed in college in both relay and as an individual.

After several career side trips, Codi accepted a position at the General Services Administration, or GSA, as a federal agent. She handled cold cases involving fraud and tax evasion, effectively a paper-pushing cop. She embraced the job with fervor and quickly got the attention of her superior, Director Ruth Anne Gables, a politically connected strong leader who took Codi under her wing. She pushed Codi when needed and supported her when there was trouble.

Codi was assigned to work with Agent Joel Strickman, a computer savvy agent with a heart of gold. His wiry frame and unkempt blond hair framed his normally positive curiosity for life. They had found success bringing to justice several individuals who had defrauded the US government. But it took a cold case from the forties to really test them. It had started benign enough but quickly escalated to international implications and ultimately global terror. It pushed Codi to her breaking point, unleashing her full potential. She fought through the impossible to stop a madman bent on global destruction.

It seemed that the harder one pushed her, the harder she pushed back. It wasn't stubbornness but determination born of a confidence her father had instilled in her at a young age. In the end, she was credited with saving hundreds of thousands of lives.

The case got her noticed at the FBI, and now she found herself about to go to work for the special projects division as a special agent. For Codi, her career was back on track, but her personal life was still a mixed bag.

She looked at her phone hoping for a text from Matt, Dr. Matt Campbell, a man whom Codi had become involved with on her last case. Twice, they had nearly died at the hands of that madman, but the resulting stress had formed a bond that was stronger than either was willing to admit.

After the case, they had spent nearly a month together convalescing. During that time Codi and Matt had time to heal their physical wounds and discover a love neither was expecting. Eventually, work pulled them in different directions, becoming the norm that stunted the growth of the relationship and left little time for maintenance.

Matt was away in some remote lab up near Boston. At first, the work limited his ability to reach out. Later, his compulsion to finish what he had started became all-consuming, taking over his life. Ultimately, they had a hard time connecting, with voicemails and texts often slow to return. With each passing week the fire between them dimmed. Codi bit back on her emotions as she pushed her phone back in its hip holder. She knew Matt loved her, but careers and relationships always seemed to be at odds, and this was no different.

She took one last look at her old office at the GSA as she turned out the lights for the last time. The General Services Administration had been the place where Codi found her moxie again. After a bout with depression and a downward spiral in her life, she had rediscovered her strength right here on the second floor.

She would never forget her boss, Ruth Anne Gables, the woman who had pushed her and encouraged her to be her best.

She flicked her shoulder-length brown hair and turned her trim figure out of the office door. She moved down the narrow hallway with a languid stride, just in time to see her partner, Agent Joel Strickman, come out of his former office.

He was holding three cardboard boxes precariously. He had his phone in his mouth and was trying to close the door with his foot.

"Need some help?" she asked.

"Codi. Hi. Sure," he mumbled through lips pressed against his cell.

She reached up and took the phone from his mouth and continued down the hallway. Joel looked over his stack of boxes, at her receding form. She wore black patterned fitness leggings and a casual white tee shirt that read, *Bloody Difficult Woman*. But her movement is what he noticed most—athletic, like a cat on the prowl. A beautiful cat. One that intimidated the hell out of him.

"Thanks, I guess," he said.

She glanced back with a smirk. "Hey, somebody's gotta hold the door open. Come on."

Joel hurried to catch up to her, his black wingtips tapping loudly on the marble floor. He used a corner of the top box to push his black-framed glasses back in place. Joel was computer savvy but his social skills were another thing. It was all topped off with a healthy dash of germaphobia. None of that mattered to Codi because Joel was one-hundred-percent trustworthy and loyal. That was a rare commodity in this world that made for an unbreakable bond.

Joel's expertise fell more to the technological side of their partnership. He had proven a solid performer, even in the field where germs always seemed to seek him out, or so he believed.

Codi held the trunk lid as Joel loaded his boxes into his Prius. She plopped into the passenger seat and, as Joel clicked his seatbelt in place, looked over his new Dunhill suit and tie combo. "It's moving day," she said. "What's with the getup?"

He smoothed the seatbelt across his suit. "Just wanted to make a good impression."

Codi's lips turned up. Though Joel would never win Man of the Year, he was still the perfect partner. Seventy-percent brains, twenty-percent brawn, and ten-percent social skills. He was also a completely-by-the-book agent, but Codi was working on that.

Their last mission had put them both in mortal danger. Both had been shot and, in Codi's case, also nearly drowned. They had been at odds with an FBI task force and ultimately one-upped them. Since that case, she had been offered a chance to join the special projects team as a full-fledged FBI special agent. Codi had jumped at the opportunity. But Joel needed some convincing. His overactive sense of low self-worth was not ready for the big time. But, as usual, Codi had gotten her way.

Some may have said that Codi and Joel's rise in the FBI had been meteoric, but she claimed it was more of a wrong place at the wrong time sort of thing.

The Prius pulled away from the loading zone, and Codi's phone started to buzz. She glanced at the text screen: "My office in 10 please." Codi showed the screen to Joel. "Better step on it," she said.

Joel tightened. "But this is a thirty-five zone."

Codi's eyes narrowed. "Seriously? We're FBI special agents now."

Joel looked a bit flummoxed. "But that means setting an example."

"Right, by kicking the bad guys' asses!"

Codi flicked her eyes forward and Joel reluctantly stomped on the accelerator. "I was hoping to stop for a coffee," he said.

"I know a good drive-through on the way."

Joel made a face at the thought of drive-through coffee, but held his tongue.

Twelve minutes later, Supervising Special Agent (SSA) Brian Fescue stepped around his desk to greet Codi and Joel. "Sorry to interrupt your moving day, but cases rarely take time off. Nice suit, by the way, Joel."

Joel's face beamed. He shot Codi an I-told-you-so look.

"So spill, Brian. What is it?" Codi blurted out in an attempt to change the subject.

Brian was their boss and head of the special projects task force. Officially, he was Supervising Special Agent Brian Fescue, but to his team he was just Brian. The casualness was born of too many times in the trenches together. He was a highly decorated agent with a long list of convictions to his record. He had said goodbye to field work when his wife Leila became pregnant with their second child and subsequently gave birth to a beautiful little girl named Abigail. Brian spent as much time as possible trying to be an active parent while still taking his time at the office very seriously.

Brian's island roots were only evident in his slight Jamaican accent. His piecing dark amber eyes were set against cappuccino-colored skin, making him stand out in a crowd. He was about an inch shorter than Joel but he was built like a tank. His no nonsense approach to management had made him a rising star at the FBI. The rumor mill had him in line for an assistant directorship.

Brian scratched at his close-cropped hair as he sat back at his desk. "What do you two know about the Aleutian Islands?"

Joel, a wealth of knowledge, piped up. "It's a chain of islands extending from mainland Alaska, separating the Bering Sea from the Pacific Ocean. Oh, and it's bitter cold there."

"Thanks to global warming we have a curiosity that's been pushed in our direction."

Codi and Joel shared a glance.

"I need the two of you to pop up there and do your thing." He opened his drawer and removed a flash drive. "Everything we know is on this file. I'm sorry. It's not much." He handed it to Joel. "See Mindy for your travel arrangements. And before you ask, the family's fine."

Codi and Joel snickered and Brian unleashed a smile that covered his entire face. It was a running joke that the three shared.

"Wasn't gonna ask," Codi said as she started to leave his office.

"Sure," Brian said. "Tristan scored a goal on Saturday."

Codi stopped in the doorway. "Tell him good job, from me."

The main room for the special projects division was small by FBI standards. It was a square bullpen-style room with nine desks set within tall office cubicles forming a rectangle. There was a hallway down the middle, and Codi's office was straight across from Joel's. Daylight glowed from windows on one wall where a small glass conference room was housed.

Joel dumped his boxes on the frosted glass surface of his desk just in time to answer a call from Mindy in transportation.

"Now boarding group D."

Joel listened as the airport speaker called his group, but he was in no hurry. The last-minute arrangements had gotten them tickets in the very back row of Alaska Airlines Flight 1 out of DC's Reagan International Airport. Gate C18 was a zoo. As he and Codi made their way through a sea of bodies to access the jet way, Joel kept his hand on his wallet pocket, always careful in a crowd.

Codi had been right to check as much luggage as possible because, by the time they got to their seats, there was no more overhead space available. Joel had the window seat and Codi the middle. They sat and tried to get comfortable for the long flight with multiple layovers.

Once the jet took off and reached the required ten thousand feet, Joel opened his computer. "What do you know about the DEW Line?" he asked Codi.

"As in 'I do,' the words spoken in a marriage ceremony?" Codi had her eyes closed and peeked over to see that Joel had opened up his laptop.

"No, D. E. W., Distant Early Warning System. It was an integrated chain of early warning radar and communication stations constructed across northern Canada and Alaska from 1953 into the early sixties."

Codi looked bored. The man sitting on the other side of her was just big enough that he was hanging over the invisible line separating the two seats. He was wearing oversized headphones and a red hibiscus-print Hawaiian shirt. The headphones were blasting Latin jazz that could be heard three seats away. Codi was trying her best to ignore him, and, to be honest, Joel too.

Joel continued. "It was specifically designed to detect Soviet bombers coming out of Russia in time for us to scramble fighters to intercept. During the cold war, it was a huge deal and probably saved us on some level from getting a nuclear bomb dropped on our heads." Joel read on. "General Electric won the bid to build it and the Air Force ran it."

"What's that got to do with our John Doe?"

"Doe's, as in three bodies."

This got Codi's attention. She sat up and leaned towards his screen. The plane bucked slightly as it passed through a cloud.

"Nothing," he said. "It's just the only thing that has ever

happened on this forgotten island we're heading towards, except for seasonal muskox herding."

Codi scrunched her face at the thought of a wild goose chase so far from home. She took a slow calming breath. Only fifteen more hours to go.

Joel added, "Here's something interesting. There's a small town at the bottom of the island, Nikolski. Its population swelled in the fifties when the DEW Line was being constructed, but now it's down to only eighteen."

Codi laid back in her seat thinking, "Joel you lost me at… What was the name of that town? I can't even remember where you lost me." She closed her eyes.

"Nikolski is reputed to be the oldest continuously-occupied community in the world."

"What? How is that possible? The Aleutian Islands off Alaska?"

Joel read on. "They have found archeological evidence dating back eighty-five-hundred years."

Codi processed the information. "That's before the pyramids."

"Right."

"And only eighteen people live there now? Crazy."

Joel cleared his throat, "Well, whatever it is, it must be important enough to call the FBI."

Codi tried to recline her seat, then remembered the last row sat against the back bulkhead and didn't recline. "Or we're just getting jerked around."

She tried to ignore the man's flesh pressed against her arm from the neighboring seat. Then the man let out an enormous sneeze. She closed her eyes again, thinking, "This is gonna be a long-ass flight."

"Can I get you anything?"

Codi stabbed a look to the aisle where a flight attendant was waiting, cart in hand.

"I'll take three of those." She pointed to the Jack Daniels mini bottles on the attendant's cart.

Salvation.

5

Umnak Island, Alaska — 10:06 a.m. — The Next Day

"Thanks for coming, and welcome to Umnak Island, by the way. We tried to keep the bodies untouched as soon as we realized we had something…uh…" The man searched for the right word. "Unusual." Lieutenant Silla Dobkins of the Alaska State Police seemed almost giddy to be talking to FBI agents all the way from DC. He shook their hands vigorously as Codi and Joel exited the boat, and pointed them towards a hill.

The trip to Umnak Island had been agonizing. Once they got to Anchorage, Joel and Codi had flown in a puddle jumper to Driftwood Bay, then in a floatplane to Nikolski Bay on the island's southern end. From there they took a trawler around the leeward side of the island to a small inlet. The total travel stint was over sixteen hours, and the two bleary eyed special agents were living off caffeine and borrowed time. For Joel, the exit from the boat was timely, as he'd started to turn a shade of green during the crossing.

The frail sun did little to fight the chill as it moved parallel to the horizon. Codi checked her phone to find no signal as she moved up from the shore. Her head seemed to pound in time with her footsteps. She was wearing jeans and several layers topped by a dull green parka.

Lieutenant Dobkins was a short round man with Eskimo blood and a fast pace. He led them up a small game trail alongside a dying glacier. Joel was glad to be on land, but puffed at the sudden exertion. The air was crisp and smelled like rain. His boots struggled for purchase on the loose lava rock. In his panic about the arctic cold, he had layered up until he looked more like the Michelin Man rather than an FBI agent. His movements were forced and clunky.

"One of our part-time residents found them, Bert Yazzie. He runs muskox up here in the warmer months. Says he was looking for a lost calf when he found the first body. Called us up and we got busy. Turned out there were three, all buried together. At first it looked as if a lost hunting party fell in one of the glacier's crevasses. No biggie, right? But then a few strange things popped up."

"Strange like what?" Codi asked.

"Let me show you."

As they came over the rise, Codi could see men and equipment gathered around a large blue pop-up standing at the dirty edge of the glacier, its blue heart exposed to the elements. Joel pulled up his parka hood against the sudden icy wind that assaulted them.

Dobkins made the introductions and took them to the bodies. Under the pop-up three bodies were laid out on the ice. Surrounding the bodies was an organized and tagged pile of old and mostly smashed gear. Codi could see where they had chipped some of the ice away to free the bodies. The corpses were in varying conditions. Two of them looked like they'd been ground up, frozen, and then pulverized again for good measure.

The other was in remarkable condition as though he had just died.

Lieutenant Dobkins looked down and spoke reverently. "A

glacier is a funny thing. It can grind you up, or keep you just as you were. There's no love in the ice, only cold."

Codi stepped over to the corpses and knelt for a closer look. "And all three of these…" she looked closer at the two masticated bodies "…men, were found in the same place?"

Dobkins broke out of his reverie. "Yes mam, they all went into the ice at once, and I'm guessing by the age of this gear… mid-fifties?"

Codi stood back up. "I still don't see why we were requested."

Dobkins paused; he kicked at the ground with his boot. He looked hesitant but continued. Well, it's really more of what you don't see. Looky here."

He moved to the body that was still intact, bent over, and pointed to the man's boots. "These here vulcanized boots were developed by the Russians. We get a lot of their surplus stuff here nowadays, but not in the fifties. This was state-of-the-art equipment back then."

He moved over to the tagged and piled gear. "And this radio, what's left of it, definitely looks Russian."

Dobkins pulled something shiny out of his pocket. "And the *piece de resistance.*" He held up a red and gold medal with the silhouette of a man in the middle. It was about the size of Post-it note. "This, definitely is Russian."

He handed it to Joel for a look. Joel looked it over. "The Order of Lenin, their country's greatest award."

Dobkins nodded. "Right. And if you look at the date it was issued…"

Joel looked closer. "1957."

The date hit him like a gunshot. "That's when the DEW Line was built."

Dobkins nodded, and pointed away from the glacier, "There's an old abandoned station just across on the wind-ward side from here."

Lieutenant Dobkins moved over to stand between Codi and Joel. "So the question is?"

Codi answered. "What were Russian soldiers doing on a US island during the cold war right in the middle of the DEW Line."

Dobkins held his index finger in the air. "Bingo!"

"It has fifty-six reviews on Yelp." Joel was struggling to keep up with Codi while looking at his phone and stumbling across the uneven ground. "Even a few four-stars. That's a lot for up here."

The mile-long spit extending northeast made the town of Dutch Harbor, Alaska, a natural port. Now famous for its crabbing, it was once the location of the Battle of Dutch Harbor where a Japanese carrier strike force unleashed a forty-eight-hour battle against the US Army and Navy stationed there. It included several air battles and a loss of over twenty-three US soldiers killed and ten MIA. The highlight was the recovery of the first intact Japanese Zero. The plane was shipped to US Intelligence where it was later dissected and analyzed.

After they had finished up on Umnak Island, Codi and Joel took a floatplane back to Unalaska Island to the town of Dutch Harbor for the night. There they checked in to their hotel and changed for dinner. Joel wore a pressed, new plaid flannel with jeans and boots, while Codi kept it simple, jeans and a faded purple Henley with the sleeves pushed up. They both carried their weapons, but that seemed to be the norm for the islanders.

"I'm sure it will be fine," she said to Joel.

She glanced up at the sun, which was not due to set until after one a.m. and then rise by 4 a.m. This was a strange part of the world. She would hate to have to spend the winter here where sunlight was weak and very brief, if at all. As a Southern California girl, she was all about sunshine.

Joel continued to read from his phone. "There used to be a saloon here that was rated the roughest bar in the US."

Codi looked a bit forlorn. "Too bad it's gone."

Joel looked like he'd bitten a lemon. "You wouldn't seriously go into a place like that."

Codi gave him a *heck yeah* look, to which Joel had no response.

He pushed open the swinging doors of the restaurant to reveal a pitted wooden floor. It was interrupted with white vinyl tables and chairs. Plastic red gingham tablecloths were decorated with paper plates and plastic utensils. But the real attention grabber was the rustic room's patrons. Craggy, blue-collar workers all covered in job-of-the-day, each hopped up on testosterone and alcohol.

"You really know how to show a girl a good time," Codi said out of the corner of her mouth as eyes from everywhere undressed her. Joel looked worried at his choice of eateries. He found an empty table and quickly sat down.

As he stared nervously around the room, he noticed they had entered a literal hole-in-the-wall restaurant. The south-facing wall of the room had a hole clear through it with a view to the outside. He lifted his hands from the sticky surface and used some paper napkins to try to clean the tablecloth. "We have arrived," he whispered to Codi pointing at the feature with his eyes.

The humor wasn't lost on Codi. "It was probably made by someone's head," she said.

An older stout woman with an elongated face and a wrinkle for every pore, approached their table. She wore a stained brown apron that had once been white. "Whatilitbe," she said as one word.

"Can we see a menu?" Joel croaked as he looked up to meet the waitresses' mostly toothless smile.

"Fish or crab. Name's May. Welcome to The Borealis. Fish or crab?"

She gave Joel a look that dared him to test her. Joel withered from her glare and turned helplessly to Codi for reinforcements.

"One of each, please, and two beers," Codi responded without hesitation.

Joel tried to repeat the order to May, but it squeaked out all wrong.

May gave him a concerned look and lumbered off to another table, shaking her head.

A buzz from Codi's phone pulled her attention. She read the incoming text to Joel: "The autopsy is complete. The bodies will be ready tomorrow a.m."

"Good. Then we can finish up and get the hell out of this town." Joel said the last part with a little too much enthusiasm.

That brought a sudden silence to the room, and a very unwelcome focus on Joel. As he looked around, he saw a virtual Who's Who of the mangy and rugged. He tried to swallow but his throat was unexpectedly dry.

"What's wrong with our town?" said a particularly large man with a beard that nearly touched his belly. He stood up and eclipsed half the room. Greasy black spots decorated his XXXL flannel shirt.

Joel seemed to shrink three sizes.

Codi burst out laughing. This was more to her liking, but Joel couldn't decide if he should cry or run to the bathroom. Her laughter, however, was contagious, and soon others started to join in. This made the big man turn a little more red. He zeroed in on Joel. After an uncomfortable moment, he gesticulated with his arms to quiet the room. "Quiet down, all."

He looked Joel over and shifted to Codi. A slight twinkle formed in his eyes. "You seem like good people. I will let you buy me a beer."

Just then May returned with their food and beers. "Corky, stop clowning around or I'll throw your ass outa here."

The behemoth of a man looked properly chastised as he sat back down. "Yes, May," he mumbled.

May turned and plopped the food on their table. "Don't mind him," she said. "He's always looking for a way to get free beer. And you're lucky."

"How's that?" Codi asked.

"We'd all love to get the hell out of this town if we could. Enjoy." With that, May spun on a heel and left.

The seafood was probably the best they had ever eaten, and the patrons, compliments of a few rounds of Moscow Stout, soon found a comradeship in the two FBI agents. Codi had threatened to shoot the big oaf a couple of times but she was pretty sure the bullet would never penetrate deep enough to do any good. By midnight they were all singing, laughing, and telling stories.

Codi looked up at the old gray-painted metal hangar. It was the size of a flat-roofed four-car garage. It had one rollup door wide enough for a small plane that was closed and looked rusted shut. Large chunks of gray paint were peeling off the walls and littered the ground around it. As the two agents entered a side door the hinges protested, announcing their arrival with a squeaky wail. The rotary Pratt Whitney engine of a Beaver De Haviland rushed down the nearby runway drowning out the sound of the door closing.

Joel quickly covered his ears as the noise cut through his hangover. The smell of formaldehyde and carrion hit him like a monologue from a B rated movie. He almost turned around and left. He tried to breathe through his mouth, but the stench made its way into everything. He held his sleeve against his nose as a filter and tried to focus through teary eyes.

Sitting on three steel tables in the middle of the open space were the partially covered bodies from the glacier. On a long metal table off to the side was the collected gear, tagged and organized. As Codi approached, the smell intensified. She noticed that the two corpses that had been ground up had been carefully put back together. They looked like bad Frankenstein jigsaw puzzles. The other had the traditional Y-cut from an autopsy.

Lieutenant Silla Dobkins turned and called out. "Great. You're here. We can get started. I was just starting to get used to the smell, and that's never good." He shook their hands just as vigorously as he had before.

"Lieutenant Dobkins, good to see you," Joel said.

"Please. We're past all that. Call me Sil."

"Okay, great. That's Codi and I'm Joel."

"Here, this will help with the smell."

Sil handed them a jar of Vicks Vaporub. Joel watched Codi expertly put a dab under her nose. He did the same and his eyes immediately started watering again. He blinked rapidly and suddenly a ridiculously loud sneeze took over his entire body. The glob of Vicks shot from his nose onto the floor. Codi handed him a small rag from the corner of the table. "Here"

He put it over his mouth and breathed through the cloth instead of using the burning ointment. Sil introduced them to the M.E. and his assistant. Codi shook their hands and stepped over to get a better look at the bodies. The medical examiner filled Sil in on his findings.

"I did a DNA test to determine origin. It's pretty simple really, they're all Russian."

"See, told you." Sil looked proud, like he'd just won a bet.

Joel spoke up. "Have you determined cause of death?"

The M.E. walked over like he was about to deliver a lecture. "John Doe number one was impaled by what was most likely an icicle at the bottom of the crevasse he fell into. Number two died from a blunt force trauma to the back of his head, and number three froze to death."

"Where's the rest of him?" Joel was referring to the third cadaver that was missing his calves and feet.

Codi was carefully inspecting the stumps. "It looks like they were cut off, no, sawed off."

"Yes, post mortem," the ME added.

Joel made a face.

"Okay, why?" she asked.

Sil moved around the table to Joel's side. "We can only speculate at this point."

Joel nodded thoughtfully. "Do you have an approximate year or day when this all happened?" he asked.

"The best I can give you is Fall 1957."

"How did you come up with that?" Joel asked.

"The USGS has been measuring glacier migration and melt in this area since the first satellites went up. Glaciers are like tree trunks in that they keep track of their environment at the time within the ice. And then there's this." The doctor lifted a boot from the nearby collection. "They were new and dated."

The boot clearly showed its manufacture date of August 12, 1957, in Cyrillic.

Codi paced between the bodies as she processed the information. "So Russians, most likely Special Forces based on their gear, were here in 1957 to do what?"

"That's why we called you folks," Sil said.

Joel took a picture of the three men's faces, as he spoke.

"I'll see what I can dig up, but I'm betting it's related to the DEW Line. They were undoubtedly spying on one of the installations to see what they could learn."

He checked his camera to make sure the pictures turned out okay.

"A long forgotten operation," Sil said, "and therefore, I'm betting, of no real consequence today."

"I'm sure you're right," Codi said hopefully.

6

Washington D.C. – 10:08 a.m. – FBI Field Office – 3rd Floor

"The Dew Line?" SSA Brian Fescue looked up from his desk, confused.

"US fifties technology used to track incoming bombers over the Arctic Circle." Joel had this part down cold.

Codi massaged the bridge of her nose. Last week had been a grind. As far as she was concerned the incident was old news and a waste of their time.

"As in *nineteen* fifties?" Brian asked.

"Exactly, sir."

"You can just call me Brian, Joel."

Joel nodded nervously at the familiarity.

Brian looked at the puffy bags under his agent's eyes. He stood up and walked around to the front of his desk. It was clean and organized just like his mind. A place for everything, and everything in its place.

"Okay. I don't see a reason to spend any more resources on this case," Brian said. "Whatever happened out there is long forgotten and has no implications to national security or anything else. See if you two can identify the dead. We'll notify the state department and see what they want us to do next. Hopefully we can then close it out or shelve it."

Codi was the first to stand.

As they left the office, Brian called out to them, "Good job out there."

The week had been a total bust. First, Codi lost half-a-day in some worthless CYA seminar, and then she was sent on a wild goose chase in the Arctic. If bad things happen in threes, she couldn't wait to see what was next.

The text alert on her phone announced an incoming message. Codi scrolled to read: "Codi, been buried trying to re-configure the output signature on my 'Project.' Won't be able to make it this weekend—SO SORRY—XOXO Matt."

She lowered the phone in slow motion. It had taken two months for them to block out the upcoming three-day week-end, and now, the day before it was supposed to start, it was over. Maybe, so was their relationship. She turned in the hall-way and headed for the exit thinking, "There we go, number three—*damn*."

She heard a muffled voice call after her, but ignored the instinct to answer. For her, this was the worst news yet.

Joel called her name one more time, but she continued to walk away. He let her go and shuffled back to his office. He took his phone and transferred the pictures he'd taken of the three dead Russian commandos to his computer. He then went to work tracking down their identity. He knew the chance of them being on a US database was slim, but every in-depth search had to start somewhere. He lifted his cup and sipped the freshly brewed dark Ethiopian Hambela roast coffee with its fruit and chocolate undercurrents. It was good to be back home. He looked around his cubicle and imagined ways he might personalize it. Perhaps a plant.

Park Je Kwan had effectively trained his whole adult life for the next forty minutes. He lowered the sun visor in his blue Hyundai Kona and looked himself over. He flicked a few stray hairs from his forehead and licked his dry lips. The forgettable twenty-seven-year-old South Korean was ready. He took a deep breath as his eyes defocused briefly, then flipped up the visor and left his car. He followed a coworker across the sunny parking lot to a waiting conveyance, his crisp steps in tune with the fresh alpine air. He wore khaki Dockers, a blue tee shirt, and a lightweight black coat.

Kwan took the stairs to the blue-gray military bus two at a time and headed to an empty bench seat near the back. It was important to make today look like any other. He pulled out his phone and pretended to check his Instagram. He needed to blend in, and over the last year, Kwan had collected 112 followers.

The diesel pusher lurched forward and trundled up a narrow switchback road, leaving Colorado Springs in the distance. He glanced up as the bus entered the manmade domed tunnel with the words Cheyenne Mountain Complex stamped into the steel rim opening. He watched as his phone's signal dropped from three bars to zero, the ambient daylight quickly replaced by the harsh glare of sodium vapor bouncing off the carved granite walls.

Inside the mountain the bus pulled to a stop and the passengers shuffled out. Kwan stowed his phone into his worn backpack and set it in a nearby locker along with the other workers' personal belongings. He then walked over and joined the queue to the advanced security checkpoint, just like he did every Monday through Friday.

Only today was different. Today Kwan had an organic memory chip imbedded in his right palm. The technology was new. It used his body like a battery to keep the stored information active. Once removed, it almost immediately started to lose data. But the organic material made it non-magnetic and completely undetectable, something that was most important today.

No electronics were allowed in the facility. In fact, every thing and every person had to go through a very sophisticated scan that not only detected metal but also degaussed electronics that passed through, leaving them blank and useless. If you forgot to leave your cellphone in the locker it would be dead the moment you entered.

The same was true for exiting. That's because the entire facility ran on a sealed operating system with no outside connections to the Internet or computers of any kind so that no hackers or spies could get in or out of the system. The old movie *War Games* was the genesis for the sealed and specialized operating system. It was critical for America's security and safety. But organic data was something new, experimental, and impervious to magnetism.

Kwan stared listlessly ahead at the open blast door entrance to the facility. It was three feet thick and over twenty feet tall with giant hydraulic pins that could lock it in place when shut. It was a sight he never tired of—a truly incredible feat of engineering born of fear.

One by one, the workers filed through the scanning process.

"Morning, Kwan. What happened to your hand?" The guard scrutinized Kwan's hand.

Kwan was shaken from his thoughts. He instantly became self-conscious and tried to downplay it. "Just a stress fracture, no big deal. Got it playing baseball on Saturday."

Kwan made a halfhearted fake swing with his arms.

"I didn't know you were a baller."

Kwan held his hand up, showing the metal splint that surrounded his thumb. "Apparently, I'm not much of one."

The guard nodded subtly. "Well, you know the drill. I'll have to personally search you or that splint will set off every damn alarm in the system."

Kwan stepped through the side gate and over to the guard who moved his wand over Kwan's entire body, slowly and carefully. Kwan fought to remain calm and pretended to scratch an imagined itch in an attempt to wipe away a bead of sweat that had formed along his hairline. The wand squawked loudly as it passed over the metal splint in Kwan's hand, causing him to repress the desire to run. But the guard didn't linger and instead he simply waved Kwan through.

"You're good. Next!"

Kwan walked briskly through the huge degausser and over to the changing room, where he took a few calming breaths. His legs felt leaden. He needed a second to compose himself before donning his maintenance uniform and heading out to work.

The simple blue coveralls were well worn and hung loosely on his thin frame. He glanced down at the embroidered badge on his left chest—twin eagle wings wrapped around a globe showing North America. They were split with a sword and two lightning bolts, all displayed against a blue shield. A ribbon below identified it as North American Aerospace Defense Command, commonly referred to as NORAD.

It was a large complex built in the center of a granite mountain in Colorado during the late 1950's, a joint operation between the US and Canada, tasked with detecting any airborne or space-borne threats to the two countries. The five-acre facility was completely self-contained and could be locked down against a conventional nuclear attack. Once locked, it became one of the most hardened command centers on the planet.

But since the advent of smart nukes, the facility was no longer as safe as it once was. Now, less than a hundred people worked in the mountain. Most of NORAD's essential functions were relocated to Peterson Air Force Base in Colorado Springs. But not all of them.

Once beyond the blast doors, Kwan stopped to get his electric maintenance cart. The high ceiling and walls wept with water that had seeped through the many layers of rock above. Rusty bolts and pipes snaked in all directions like a jungle with no blueprint. Kwan drove his cart past the mostly abandoned town that sat in the heart of the mountain. The paint- and steel-sided buildings showed their age. The entire city was built on a foundation of hundreds of thousand-pound springs that allowed it to move in order to withstand even the most extreme earthquake or bombing.

Kwan glanced over at the cement-encapsulated command center as he drove past. This was the heart of the NORAD system, and this was his mission. Day after day for the past twenty-eight months, he bided his time until they were ready.

Inside the open floor plan was a bevy of terminal stations that faced a wall covered with large monitors. They displayed maps and technical information, all used to pick up and track anything, from a small plane flying low out of Mexico to an ICBM traveling in the stratosphere out of North Korea. Their main purpose was to detect and give enough advance warning to dispatch the appropriate response to the threat.

Kwan unlocked the door to the storage room and stepped inside. Fluorescent tubes winked on, casting a greenish glow in the room. Because the Navy built the facility, everything had a battleship style to its architecture: steel beams, exposed pipe, and hatch-style doors.

Kwan's workbench was immaculate with everything in its place. He placed his hands on the worn steel bench and paused for a moment. It had been a long process to get here, requiring a lot of patience and even enduring some racism along the way, but his chance to prove himself had finally arrived. He had trained with a friend named Jin before coming here and he was looking forward to sharing a beer with him in celebration if all things went well today.

Kwan was born in the south section of Seoul known as Suwon. He had enjoyed a normal childhood with dreams of college and a promising career that he had a passion for. But an unexpected train accident took both his parents. The accident was blamed on poor maintenance by the Ministry of Land, Infrastructure and Transport, an unwieldy bureaucracy that swept the incident under the rug.

He was left with nothing but a life on the street, his dreams of being a civil engineer gone forever. He joined the military to escape his predicament and endured the cruelty the armed services dealt. As an orphan with no pedigree, he was given the worst of everything. When his enlistment was up, he left vowing to never look back. He traveled around the country looking for what was next.

On a cold rainy night in a small bar in the port city of Pohang, he reconnected with his estranged Uncle Hanja, or, as Kwan soon began to call him, his Funcle. The man made light of any situation. It was so contrary to the way Kwan had been raised where every step was planned, and discipline was the word of the day. Uncle Hanja enjoyed life. It was a breath of fresh air for Kwan, and it wasn't long before a smile returned to his face and he found himself feeling normal again. Things were looking up.

Until his uncle died in a shoot-out with the KCS, Korea

Customs Service. It was then that Kwan realized the life his uncle had led was not at all what it seemed to be.

Shortly after Hanja's death, Kwan found himself starting to flounder again when he was approached by a very tall, lean man who introduced himself simply as Lee. The man had worked with Kwan's uncle a few times. He opened a new door of possibilities to the disillusioned young Korean, one that set Kwan on his current path. It was a path that would give him purpose, and allow for a small measure of revenge against a status quo that had taken away everything important to him.

Kwan slid the top of his workbench back, revealing a hidden compartment below. He pulled out a small module that he had smuggled in piece by piece and then reassembled. It looked like a metal pack of cigarettes. One end contained a multi-pin connector and there was a small sliding door on the top. Kwan pressed his thumb and forefinger against its sides and the box powered up. A subtle green LED glowed on the top and the door slid open. Kwan then quickly removed the splint on his right hand and took a penknife from his bench. He gently pushed the subdural organic chip out of his hand with the point of the knife.

Blood followed but Kwan didn't seem to notice. He placed the organic chip in the box and quickly closed the door. The green light started blinking as ones and zeros flowed from the organic chip into the unit, converting organic ones and zeros to magnetic files.

Kwan let out a sigh of relief. The experimental technology had maintained its data. It had used his body to keep the chip alive until the transfer could be made. The organic chip first uploaded its own operating system onto the module, enabling the device to download specific files required for his mission. The green light stopped blinking and remained solid. It wasn't a huge file, but the information it contained was some of the most important for the cause that had ever been written.

Kwan pulled the multi-pin from the box. It looked like a small USB thumb drive with an oversized connection. He slipped it into his pocket and returned the small box back into its hidden home in the workbench. His last step was to rewrap his bleeding hand. It was time.

He exited the storage room, nearly running into Carl.

"Whoa there, K-boy, what's the rush? Afraid those toilets are gonna clean themselves?" Carl was a perfect example of everything that was wrong with America. And the redneck oaf was his immediate superior.

"You said it," he replied. "Gotta get there quick."

Kwan grabbed his cleaning cart and tried to push it away. Carl held onto it, looking like he didn't trust letting Kwan go. They shared a brief struggle before Kwan glanced up at the security camera to remind Carl it was there. Carl immediately let go, pushing the cart in Kwan's direction. The cart nearly ran him over, with the diminutive Kwan barely staying on his feet. Carl stifled a snicker as he watched the retreating form of the small Korean, and shook his head. A few derogatory words flowed silently past Carl's lips.

Kwan pushed his metal cart down the side tunnel towards the famous blast doors of the command center. Each weighed over twenty-three tons and used twenty-two hydraulic pins to lock it down. The doors had remained open since 1992, except for a brief period during 9/11. Kwan nodded to the guard posted outside the first portal as he wheeled his cart past the massive door. He swiped his ID card through the slot reader next to a recently installed electronic entry door. It opened to reveal two heavily-armed men staring him down. He used his cart like a battering ram to push past the two men, just like he did every Wednesday at this time.

The room smelled of ozone and body odor, awaiting a third smell provided by Kwan—bleach. He efficiently made his rounds cleaning, wiping, and dumping, slowly working his way to the server room. As he approached the entrance, a third guard stood near the door. He smiled at Kwan, and seeing his bandaged hand, opened the door for him.

"Thanks, Marv."

"Sure thing, Kwan. Looks like you're a bit hobbled today."

Kwan told him the same story he gave to the main-gate guard and entered the room. The hum of the electronics was mind-numbing as Kwan went about his regular duties. Marv watched his every move, but after months of uniformity the sharpness fades from even the most attentive of guards.

Kwan turned his body to temporarily block the guard's view as he stealthily slipped the thumb drive onto the multi-pin diagnostics port. The drive took over from there, uploading its contents into the sealed system.

"Hey, what are you doing!"

Kwan almost jumped out of his skin as Marv approached with purpose.

"What?" he managed to squeak out.

"You're going to ruin the electronics."

Kwan pupils instantly dilated with fear. Then he noticed Marv was pointing to his hand.

"You're dripping."

Kwan quickly realized his hand was bleeding through the bandage. "Damn it. Stupid thing won't stop."

He used a cleaning rag to wrap his hand, keeping his body between Marv and his device. He made a big show of cleaning up the mess. Marv chuckled to himself as he turned and headed back to his station. Kwan glanced at the thumb drive. The LED was no longer flashing. He yanked it out it and headed for the door.

Marv re-secured the door to the servers as he watched Kwan leave the area. "You should get that looked at," he said.

Kwan gave him a bloody thumbs-up.

Carl sat at his usual chair of stacked shipping crates. He carved on a small piece of wood while he enjoyed a large chaw of tobacco, spitting the residual with deadly accuracy into an old no. 10 can. The storage room was his domain, and he let everyone who worked for him know it. As he whittled away, he glanced over at Kwan's workbench and his mind started to drift. What would be a good prank he could pull on the little gook. He stood up and saw that there was blood on the bench surface. He moved to investigate. It was not like Kwan to leave a messy workspace. The blood looked rather fresh. He noticed that it seemed to disappear through a seam he had never noticed before.

Carl jimmied the top of Kwan's workbench. Suddenly it slipped open, revealing a hidden compartment.

"Well, looky here."

Kwan burst into the storage room holding the rag on his bleeding hand. He looked up to see Carl with a sneer on his face and with Kwan's electronic box in his hands. *Shit.*

Kwan's mind spun, trying desperately to figure out what to do.

Carl's head tilted and his eyes narrowed. "Looks like I found us a spy, K-boy."

"E-cigarette, dipshit."

"What?"

"It's an E-cigarette. I've been trying to quit and this helps."

"Bullshit. You think I'm an idiot? What's with the secret

compartment?" He motioned to the hidden space in Kwan's workbench.

"It's not mine. I found it by accident. Somebody before you or me put it there."

"And you just happen to keep this little gizmo hidden in there?"

"I didn't want it to walk away on its own, what with the people who work around here." Kwan gave Carl a hard look. "But seriously, go ahead and take it to the base commander. You'll be the laughing stock, not me."

Carl re-inspected the small metal box. Now he wasn't so sure.

"Here, let me show you how it works." Kwan stepped over and held out his hand. "It holds almost any flavor of tobacco you could think of—razzleberry, cardamom."

Carl scrunched his nose at the mention of a razzleberry-flavored cigarette. He hesitated a beat longer, then gave it to Kwan. Kwan set the device on his workbench and waited for Carl to focus on the box.

"You turn it on by pressing here."

He squeezed his fingers on the box and it powered up. The little door slid open. Carl dropped his head to get a better look inside. There were traces of blood and a round device inside. This was no E-cigarette.

With his free hand Kwan fingered a crescent wrench hanging on the pegboard. He brought it down with all his strength across the back of Carl's head. The big man dropped to the floor with a muted thud.

Mindful of the security cameras outside the room, Kwan pulled his cart into the storage room and stuffed Carl inside.

The lower section of Cheyenne Mountain City holds a crawl space that is unlike anything on the planet. The entire city's foundation is made of thick steel plates that are supported by a forest of thirteen-hundred giant springs anchored into the granite base. Each building is free-standing, all connected by hallways and ramps. Kwan rolled his cart holding the unconscious Carl along the stone floor. He found a spot to dump him deep under the mostly abandoned city. He positioned the man who had been a brutal boss just so. Then he lifted Carl's head up and slammed the back of it against one of the thousand-pound steel springs that attached to the subfloor, disguising his previous blow from the wrench with the steel of the spring. The tyrant's head made a cracking noise, ending him with a twitch.

The rest of the day was uneventful for Kwan, and he actually smiled as the transport bus exited the tunnel into the waning daylight. He watched his phone as the signal returned to three bars and then four. He selected a happy face emoji and texted it to a prearranged number. Kwan leaned back and stared at the ceiling of the bus. What was next for him, he didn't know, but after today he was ready for anything. Destined for greatness, if you will. His mind drifted to his very close friend Jin, back in China. Maybe now he could refocus on something he hoped would bring joy to his lonely life—a true friend.

Kwan pulled his blue Hyundai Kona into the narrow lane heading out of the parking lot and down the rest of the mountain. His finger drifted to the volume on his radio. He turned it up. It was celebration time, and tonight he was going to make the most of it. K-Pop blasted from the speakers as his lips curled up and his head bopped to the beat.

As he came around the first switchback he noticed his brakes seemed mushy. He pumped the pedal several times with little result. By the next hairpin turn, his brakes were nonexistent. He quickly pulled the emergency brake to slow his increasing speed. Nothing. He tried down-shifting but the transmission was locked in place. He grabbed for the key and turned it off. Again, nothing. The key turned back and forth with no effect on the engine. This was first-rate sabotage. He considered bailing out, but his speed was now too great.

Kwan held onto the steering wheel tightly as his speed and panic surged. He tried to track the dangerous curvy road to the best of his ability, anticipating the corners and using both lanes to stay on the road. The car wobbled, having trouble tracking the bends as his speedometer passed sixty. He prayed for no oncoming traffic and perhaps a miracle. Tires squealed and smoked as he fought for a semblance of control.

In a last desperate move Kwan slammed the passenger side of his vehicle into the mountainside to slow his speed. The Hyundai bucked crazily but finally started to slow. As sheet metal met the granite mountain all Kwan heard was grinding metal and popping tires. He took a small breath as a modicum of hope built. But the road suddenly turned sharply back to the right leaving him no mountain to rub against.

The blue Hyundai Kona, its steering now damaged by the mountainside tussle, headed straight for the road's edge. Kwan sailed off the road and through the meager guardrail. He took a sudden breath with the weightlessness and gripped the steering wheel as if it might provide some salvation. His car's nose tilted downward into a three-hundred-foot nosedive to the rocks below. Kwan knew who had set this up. But the memory was fleeting. His last thought was of his friend Jin and what might have been.

Lee watched through his binoculars as the Blue Hyundai accordioned on the rocks below. The impact was so violent that the engine ended up in the trunk. He felt a brief pang of regret for having to end young Kwan's life. He had been a good recruit and soldier, but there could be no loose ends on a mission as critical as this one. He lowered the glasses and looked once more at the smiley face emoji texted to his phone. Lee smiled as he flicked away a toothpick he'd been nursing and deleted the text—no lose ends.

"Watch out, driving can kill you," Lee mumbled to himself as he headed back down the trail that overlooked the road, his memory of Kwan quickly fading.

Time to head back home. His work here was done.

7

Washington D.C. – 10:08 a.m. – FBI Field Office – Special Projects – 3rd Floor

Joel lifted his spectacles and massaged his eyes with his thumb and index finger. He'd been staring at the screen in front of him for too long. Maybe a short break was in order. He stood to leave, and his computer gave a short tone. New email. Like Pavlov's dogs, Joel turned back around reflexively and clicked to open the file.

"Finally," he said to himself, as a long-awaited response popped up. The email was short but it promised to close out the last case: "Hope this helps," GeneralVladstoff@MinisryFA.Ru.

He sat back down and pounded out a message to the man at the Russian Ministry, double-checked it, and blind-copied both Codi and Brian. He leaned back for a second and then hit send.

Joel had grown up in the suburbs of Chicago. He had excelled in both the piano and his love of computers. He spent most of his youth on one keyboard or another. It had earned him a full ride to MIT at the age of seventeen. But Joel struggled to fit in with the social side of the college experience. He often would find a corner of the library to hide out in on

Friday nights, doing homework or gaming. His parents were both professionals that were happy to see their only son leave home and go off on his own. They had a once-a-year perfunctory Christmas get-together and they rarely talked or chatted with their son in between.

Joel had what it takes to be liked, with his quirky, uptight humor. He just wasn't comfortable around strangers. It was something he couldn't quite get past. So he ended up spending more time alone than not.

His career and naive view of the world changed dramatically when he was hired on at the GSA. He was assigned to a desk in the technology division where he chased fraud leads electronically. He excelled at his job, but his coworkers seemed to not even know he was alive. It took a bold move from his boss, pairing him with a newly-minted agent, Codi Sanders, to change that. The chemistry worked, and like Yin meeting Yang, they formed a solid partnership.

Joel and Codi had been thrown into a case that forced them to fight for their very lives. Joel, surprisingly, stepped out of his comfort zone and became a solid team member, integral in helping solve and stop a terrorist threat. Along the way he found the first love of his life. But sadly, he had to watch as she died in his arms. That moment changed him in a way that could not be quantified, but he was now a man driven by purpose. Even if he was still a giant nerd at heart.

Cody's fingers absently toyed with the zipper on her gym bag. She stared out across the pool as swimmers worked through their laps, each in their own lane. The one exception was lane three. It was empty and calling her name. She refused to listen. She just sat on the blue fiberglass bench by the side of the pool and watched.

The Art Deco-style pool was cocooned within gold and blue tile columns surrounded on three sides by large arched windows. The ambient light squiggled off the rippling liquid as swimmers mechanically pressed through the water following their daily routine.

Codi had taken to the water at an early age, both swimming and surfing along the coast north of San Diego where she grew up. After losing her father, she gave surfing, but swimming became an obsession. It was a fading connection to her father that she fought to keep. She had excelled at the crawl and the butterfly in high school, and had leveraged that into a way to help pay for college and to escape a home life that was cracked and flawed. She represented UCSD in the nationals three of her four years there.

Now, starting her day doing laps in the pool was ingrained into her routine as much as eating or sleeping. Every morning at 6:30 a.m. she would push herself through the water with the determination and stamina that defined her.

But after her last case where she had drowned and been resuscitated she no longer had that desire. She knew the traumatic event was controlling her actions and she knew it was just psychological, but right now it was okay with her to just let it go. Maybe today was the day. She could go into the locker room, put on her suit and hit the water. She breathed in the humid, chlorinated air, a smell that signaled comfort to her.

She reflected on the moment right before she had regained her life. She had literally been plucked from the depths of the Thames River. A white light had welcomed her. She felt joy. It was followed by a great shot of pain as it was all taken away. Theologians and scientists disagree on what causes people who are technically dead and then brought back to life to experience this. But for Codi, the memory of seeing blue sky and the man she loved, Matt Campbell, kneeling over her was better that any white light.

She believed in a higher power, but her experience with organized religion and how it often treated others had left her tepid on the subject. But to each his own. If only the rest of the world felt that way.

Codi released a breath she didn't even realize she'd been holding, picked up her bag, and left the building. Maybe tomorrow.

As Codi cleared the security gauntlet at her building, she looked up to see her partner Joel waiting for her. He was wearing his usual perfectly pressed suit, and was carrying an anxious smile along with two cups of gourmet coffee.

"Kenyan Roast. Undoubtedly the best of the African coffees," he said, as he passed a cup to Codi. "Medium roast with a sharp tang, good body, and yet a smooth winy finish."

Codi looked up with indifference, *seriously?* "Is it hot and black?" she asked.

"I waste my coffee talents on you."

She took a long sip. "Hmm, tastes great. Thanks."

Joel looked at her skeptically.

Codi turned up the corners of her mouth. "See, not wasted."

"Boss wants to see us right away."

"Good, we're probably fired. *Finally,* some good news."

Joel went rigid at the thought, as Codi turned and walked away. He was still getting used to her sarcasm. He took a calming breath and hurried to catch up to her. "Hey, that's not funny."

SSA of Special Projects Brian Fescue set his reading glasses on his paper-strewn desktop as Codi and Joel knocked and entered. "Please sit," he said.

He quickly tidied up his desktop without looking up. He

then fingered through a stack of file folders that were neatly stacked behind him, rejecting the first three, until he found what he was looking for and pulled it out. He handed over a thick faded file with tattered edges. "Your next case," he said. "Hopefully you'll have more luck with it than the last one."

He said that last comment with a straight face. Codi and Joel shared a look, not sure if that was meant as a jab or not. But the smile that grew on his face, told them the truth.

"Hey, a little boss humor for you," he said. "What do you expect? Special Projects Division means we get all the oddball and cold cases. We expect your close rate to be dismal."

Brian's smile never wavered as he changed the subject back to the file Joel was now holding. "That file," he said, pointing, "is just the overview of the case. There are twelve boxes that I had sent to your office, Joel. Sign here for them while I got you." Brian pushed a chain of custody form over along with a pen.

"But I haven't verified the contents."

"Just sign it," Brian said as he leaned back in his chair and stared at his two agents.

Joel looked like it was the hardest thing he'd ever done, signing for documents he hadn't double-checked first.

"What do you know about a man named Dan Cooper?" Brian asked them.

Codi had a blank look on her face. Joel perked at the mention, finishing off his slow-moving signature with a flourish.

"You mean D. B. Cooper, the most famous skyjacker of all time?"

"That's the one," Brian said, as he pointed to the file.

"That case was never solved as far as I know."

"Right, and it's been a stain on the bureau's record since the seventies."

Codi felt useless in the conversation, so she took the file from Joel and started to peruse it.

"Some kid found a wad of bills that match the missing se-rial numbers," Brian said. "I want you two to check it out and see if you can shed some light on a case that's been a total dead end and a black eye for the FBI for more than…" he looked up as he did a quick calculation. "Forty years."

Codi sat at her desk and checked her email. She pulled at the elastic that held her hair up. A familiar address caught her eye and she opened it with a click. An image of a large bouquet of red roses appeared with a note that read: "I am an idiot! But at least I realized it. Please accept my apologies and this symbol of my love (roses) and if you scroll down, a first class ticket to come and see me this weekend. Please accept! Love, Matt."

Codi's heart skipped a beat. She couldn't contain a smile that filled her face. She clicked reply and started to type: "I would love to spend the weekend with a known idiot," when a cry from Joel's desk got her attention.

"Hey, Codi, got a second?"

She paused mid-typing and left without finishing.

One side of Joel's office was packed to the ceiling with twelve very old cardboard evidence boxes. He'd done a quick count when he first entered, worried it wouldn't jibe with the count on the chain of custody form he'd just signed.

Codi plopped into his extra chair and then began to slowly spin as she looked through the folder Joel gave her. "So D.B. Cooper's a skyjacker?" she asked.

Joel referred to a large stack of old files he'd been going through on his desk. "1971. A man boards a flight to Seattle."

"D. B. Cooper?"

"Right. Well it was most likely an alias but that's what we know. He boards a 727 Boeing, Flight 305 from Portland to Seattle. Shortly after takeoff he tells the stewardess…" Joel shuffled through some papers. "…Florence Schaffner, that he has a bomb. He shows it to her. It's in his briefcase. He then makes her write a note to the pilot. They force-land in Seattle and trade the hostage passengers for $200,000 and four parachutes. At some unknown point after takeoff, he jumps out of the plane with the money and vanishes."

Codi looked up from her reading. "Nice, but only $200,000?"

"1971." Joel ticked off his fingers while he did a rough calculation. "That's like 1.3 million today."

"Okay, so this guy is a genius," Codi said.

Joel countered, "Or just really lucky."

"Or dead. Says here, he's suspected not to have survived the jump."

Joel leaned over Codi's shoulder to see what she was looking at. "Sounds like a hopeful agent trying to close a case," he said.

Codi held up the file. "I say we just show Brian this section: Case Closed, and we don't have to fly to Oregon. Besides, I have very important plans this weekend."

Joel's phone buzzed and he grabbed it. "Agent Strickman."

He listened to the brief message and hung up. He looked at Codi. "Our tickets are booked. We're on the next flight to Portland."

Codi slapped the file she was holding down on Joel's desk with obvious frustration. "They couldn't wait till after the weekend? This case is like forty years old. It isn't going anywhere."

Joel sympathized as he watched her leave his cubicle.

An unexpected crushing sensation took hold of Codi as she sat back down at her desk. She looked at her unfinished reply to Matt. After a moment she hit delete. Her second-chance weekend with Matt had just evaporated like a drop of water on a hot skillet. She grabbed her things and left the office.

8

Hong Kong – 3:12 p.m. – The Abattoir – 3rd Subfloor

Jin was a member of a hacking team—F1-Firefly. It had originally been formed as part of the technology and science division directly under the office of General Wang Sun, one of the leading up-and-comers within the party. The team was responsible for gathering intelligence and classified data, all under China's cyber-espionage program, and they were very good at their job.

Over the last five years, however, the politicians had been dealing with serious blowback over their diverse government-backed hacking and cyber divisions. In an effort to calm competitive fears and increase their deniability, a change was needed. Finally, eleven months ago, a breach of their internal systems had shut down part of the government's computers for three days. That was the final straw. It pushed the powers within the party to discontinue all cyber-espionage divisions. What the public didn't know was that the Chinese government simply moved the hacking teams out of their organization and into private hands.

The set-up was simple. Just like in America, the Chinese government contracted with independent companies to provide information and access to the same classified data they were getting before. Contracts were handed to loyal party members, only now with an arm's length between them. Information still flowed just like it always had, but without the bad press. The difference was that an enterprising contractor could use this same information for himself as well.

General Chow Phun was just such a person. He had taken the elite F1-Firefly team and completely rebranded and re-located them. Chow was an old-school red communist and had been in charge of many different divisions and programs over his years with the party. After the onset of Guillain-Barre Syndrome left him with numb hands and feet as well as a par-tially paralyzed face, Chow left his position in the government and continued on in the private sector. Through his many contacts, he had taken several of his pet projects along with him. He ran a host of off-the-book operations for both him-self and the Chinese government, making a bigger name for himself now than what he had before. And with it, a seemingly unending flow of currency.

Chow operated everything from a seemingly abandoned building right in the heart of Hong Kong—The Abattoir, a five-story Plain Jane, faded, white-walled concrete structure. Chow had purchased it for a song from the government, and left the visible parts in its original abandoned state. It was surrounded by a high stone wall and concertina wire. Modern stainless-and-glass high-rises looked down on the dreary, often-considered-haunted derelict. Chow used the people's natural superstitions as well as a few heavily armed guards to protect it.

A close inspection would reveal weathered, peeling walls and old rusted machinery once used to butcher livestock. Part of the roof had collapsed and the rest was unstable. It stank of mold, rat feces, and long-dried blood with standing water in several rooms.

What the public could not see was that below the crumbling façade was an underground three-story high-tech complex called the Red Baks (box). It was Chow's pride and joy. And since losing his wife and daughter to a bird flu epidemic, it had become his life. Each level was given its own personality. A Thai beach theme for the first floor held his personal offices and operations for his more legitimate businesses. A bamboo forest theme for the second floor below held his pet projects, some held over from when he was working for the party, and some more recent, each with enormous promise. And an urban jungle theme for the third and lowest level was where the once-known F1-Firefly team operated, now rebranded the Cathay Dragons. They kept as low-profile as possible. Each employee was well cared for, and Chow was proud of his team. Though they were often scrutinized by ever-present security, each had a sense of pride that they were part of something special—the elite.

Chow paid handsomely because he wanted the best. Anything less was dealt with harshly. He had no time for incompetence, and everyone who worked for him knew it.

Jin watched as his personally written program bombarded the Safran Group with a uniquely devised scrolling password. The French aerospace company had recently announced a new design for a prototype turbo-shaft engine that could produce more horsepower on less fuel. It would be worth a fortune to both the helicopter and jet industries. Chow wanted that design. Jin sipped his tea as the first firewall dropped. *Finally,* progress, he thought to himself.

The third floor was a large open oval with thick concrete beams that supported the two floors above. The walls were decorated in modern graffiti complete with neon signs and streetlights. The flooring looked like street pavement, complete with painted street lines. The cubicles were made of aged steel and smoked glass. The room's ambient glow changed with the passage of time, getting darker at night and brightening with the new day.

The only entrance to the room slid open mechanically with a slight *whoosh*. Chow stepped inside and scanned the perimeter like an owl hunting prey. He was a short man with round features, pushing sixty. Due to his illness the right half of his face drooped like a partially melted wax sculpture. There were times when drool would weep out of the downturned corner of his mouth. It was something Chow could neither feel nor control. He carried a handkerchief in his right hand and had become obsessive about patting his right chin to keep it dry. Over time, a harsh red rash had formed along the dribble line.

He walked past the cubicles of hard-working hackers bending the world to suit his and his beloved China's needs. "Jin," he said.

Jin looked up as Chow approached his cubicle. He quickly stood to greet his boss, trying not to look at the man's damaged face. "Sir."

"Lee contacted me and said the worm has been loaded. He also told me that there was a terrible accident. I'm sorry, son, Park is dead."

Jin sank back into his chair, the disappointment clear on his face.

Chow put a fatherly hand on his shoulder. "He was a good comrade and we were lucky to have been part of his life. They sure could use your help up in 212."

Jin blinked his eyes several times against rapidly forming tears. He had trained Park for this operation and they had become close. "An accident?"

"Car crash. Drunk driver ran him off the road."

Jin nodded absently. Park was never coming back.

"It's tragic," Chow said with forced remorse.

Jin tried to keep his emotions in check. He gripped his hands tightly, letting the pain focus his mind on the information while he nodded absently. After a pause, he said, "That's great news, sir, about the worm." He looked up to his boss. "212? Right away. I'll take care of it."

He left without looking back as he headed to the second floor.

Room 212 held a project Chow had inherited from a former party member. It had been an on-again, off-again operation depending on the powers and desires in charge. After a sensationally successful double-cross with the Russians back in the late fifties, the division had acquired and developed a system to make approaching aircraft completely invisible to the enemy. It wasn't stealth technology where you were still vaguely visible, just hard to see and track, but completely invisible. With the help of a female agent, a Russian airline navigator, whom they had recruited, the Chinese managed to collect the two main scientists behind a daring Soviet Union project known as Operation Blind Pig. With a little coercion, they had convinced one of the Russian scientists to work for the Red Army of China.

The result was a technology that could blind the enemy's early warning systems against a Chinese attack. It had been very popular with the higher-ups early on. Throughout the course of its development they had experienced many test successes and only a few failures. But the people in charge had never followed through and used it. Eventually time and new technologies had made the project outdated. Chow initially had planned to scrap it until an unexpected breakthrough was brought to his attention.

Jin slumped into a vacant seat next to the electronic hub. He quickly logged on and opened the program he had personally written. Doctor Shura Mosin, a sixty-eight-year-old Russian scientist-defector-turned-Chinese-asset looked over his shoulder. There was pallor to his saggy round face. Thick round glasses and a short bowl-cut hairstyle had become his trademark.

"This shit doesn't go faster with you lookin', Doc," Jin said to the man.

Startled, Shura stepped back. "Sorry, it's just that we are so close to success. I cannot begin to tell you the path I have traveled to be here right now."

"Let's not get carried away. Success is what you get when it works, Doc."

Shura nodded as he shuffled away to check on another project.

Doctor of Electrical Engineering Shura Mosin, had inherited this project after waking up in a Chinese prison in 1957. He had been welcomed to his new home and offered many things if he would cooperate. It was something he considered, but his boss, Doctor Grigory Nepein refused. After weeks of torture without success they killed his unyielding mentor right in front of him. The psychological blow made Shura jump to accept their offer.

His first assignment was to oversee the reverse engineering of the captured Tupolev TU-16. They took it apart piece by piece and then made molds and copies of every part. That design was then merged with the current Chinese Hong T5. China had just pushed their aerospace program forward by ten years. Next, Mosin was put back into a lab to refine the GN01 Transmitter that Doctor Grigory Nepein had developed. Over the years the technology had improved and had been successfully tested on many other countries, like Japan and Russia. As the computer age advanced, Mosin became one of China's bright stars for a time. But technology is an evil mistress, and ultimately Shura was left behind.

It took the creativity of General Chow Phun to put a modern day hacker like Jin together with the mind of Doctor Shura Mosin and come up with an outside-the-box solution. A way to get the same results in the modern world of satellites and computers.

The familiar blue shield of NORAD popped up on the screen as Jin opened the benign public access web page. He slid his cursor over to the far right where he selected the French tab, *Francias*. He then followed the dropdown menu to: Contactez Le NORAD. He searched the bottom links with his curser. As it moved across the empty bottom section to the right, a hidden icon popped up, Plus. Jin couldn't believe his eyes. He leaned back to take it all in. *Park had done it.* He had uploaded the worm. It wouldn't allow them access to the closed system, but it would now be blind to a very specific frequency. After all their training and practice...

They had built a mockup of the server room to practice on, piggybacked onto the latest organic storage technology hacked from a lab in Des Moines, Iowa, and deeply planted their man inside NORAD. It was years in the making, and it had worked.

"Hey, Doc!" Jin called.

9

Vancouver, Washington – 11:48 a.m. – Washington State

Codi trudged up the berm that led to the wide river's shoreline. A liquid border divided Washington State from Oregon. Here, the Colombia River flowed north along Caterpillar Island.

Jimmy Paulson was a talker. The thirteen-year-old redhead kept his lips in what seemed constant motion. Two weeks ago he'd been fishing along the gap between Caterpillar Island and Kadow's Marina. He noticed something half-buried along the shore and dug up a wad of old twenty-dollar-bills totaling $6,800. It wasn't until his mom found them stashed under his bed, along with a huge hoard of candy bars, that the discovery was reported.

The serial numbers matched the ransom paid to skyjacker D. B. Cooper. This set off a whirlwind of action as local authorities and then state police got involved. The FBI was next on the list and special projects was given the nod. Soon, news stations got wind of the story, and by the time Codi and Joel landed in Portland the story was everywhere.

"They can't keep the money," Jimmy said to Codi and Joel. "I found it. It's mine. I know the law. Statue of limits is up and I want it back."

Joel tried to get a word in to correct him. "It's evidence now and it's called statute of…"

Jimmy popped right back in. "Plus, I ain't tol' no one about where I found it. Fact is, I should be chargin' you to take you there at all."

He suddenly stopped. Joel almost ran into the back of him.

"Yeah, I should be chargin' you." Jimmy turned around. "What's the goin' rate for information nowadays? Times two." He moved an accusing finger to both Codi and Joel.

Codi pushed past him. She was at her limit. She followed the small game trail to the top of the berm, her boots digging into the soft loam. At the top, she froze.

"Hey, I'm talkin' to you, lady fed. What's the goin' rate?"

"Zero," she said.

"Wait. What?"

Joel and Jimmy ran to the top of the berm to join Codi. The Columbia River was a stunning blue-green as it moved along a deeply forested background. But as far as the eye could see, holes had been dug into the ground all along the shore, even up the bank and into the forest. There were literally *thousands* of holes. "Didn't tell anyone about where you found the stash, huh?" she said to the kid.

Codi knew that any trace evidence was long gone. Jimmy looked crestfallen and was thankfully, finally silent.

"We should charge you for wasting our time," she said.

She turned and left. It was a bitter pill, especially considering what this trip had cost her. Would Matt ever forgive her or could she even forgive herself. Codi had never responded to his email, partly because of her situation here, and partly because deep down she was still mad at him for cancelling on her before. It was petty, she knew, but the right man for her was one who was willing to do the hard stuff and make a friggin' effort.

Now that time had passed, it may be too late. Honestly, she was a little embarrassed to reach out now. She could just play it off like she'd never opened the stupid email. But that left them at an impasse, one she couldn't see around at the moment. A myriad of thoughts coursed through her head, swinging back and forth like a pendulum as she stormed back to their car at the trailhead.

After a check-in with the boss as to their dead end on a cold case that was still unsolved, Codi and Joel had a somber dinner at a fish house back in Portland. The beautiful city sparkled against the slow-moving Willamette River. Codi was wearing a slimming black dress with a slight scoop neck and three-quarter sleeves. Joel was dressed in his patented two-piece suit with a blue collared shirt.

Joel spent a good portion of the dinner talking about the D. B. Cooper case and how he was excited to be part of its history. Codi stared at her phone trying to figure out what to text to Matt, if anything. She had started several times but each time had deleted her words. Finally she put her phone away. A gentle rain followed the sun's dip to oblivion behind the mountains. It seemed to wash away the events of the day, and after a cold local beer, Whole in the Head, Codi was feeling herself again.

A chime sounded on Joel's phone and he looked at the message.

"What gives?" Codi asked.

"Finally heard back from the Russian Defense Ministry."

That piqued her attention. "And?"

"They are neither confirming nor denying knowledge of the bodies found on that island."

"Sounds about right. What about the medal, the Order of Lenin?"

"They say the recipient…" Joel looked down at his screen,

"Colonel Tolya Alexeev is buried in Saint Petersburg, so the medal must be a fake."

"You and I both know that was no fake," Codi said.

Joel nodded. A moment of silence lapsed.

"So what now, Codi?"

"I say we ship the bodies and the medal back to Moscow and say goodbye to this area." She wiped her hands together as she said, "Both cases unsolved but closed for now."

"I'm for just shipping them as well," Joel added.

Codi nodded.

"Unfortunately," he said, "it's not up to us."

She ordered another round.

The Finnair jumbo jet leveled off at forty-two-thousand-feet. Codi glanced at the state department slacker who had been assigned to them. After a short flight and two days waiting in Seattle, the bodies and the assistant-to-the secretary of something-or-other (she had stopped listening) had arrived. Nolan Pierce, a blue blood butt-sniffer for sure Codi thought, was immaculately dressed in a Brooks Brothers custom tailored suit and had his hair coiffed to perfection. A resolute expression crossed his face as he met Codi and Joel for the first time. Immediately, he tried to take control and Codi was torn between letting him hang himself and squeezing the life out of him with a single hand. The thought made her smile. Joel had picked up a nervous twitch since the arrival of the politically charged assistant.

Nolan seemed to be in everyone's business at all times. Codi thought he would make an excellent helicopter mom.

At one point, Joel leaned over and whispered in her ear, "Nothing good will come of this."

He was probably right. But there was nothing they could

do about it for now. Maybe some sleep would help. Codi reclined her seat and closed her eyes, trying to tune out the events of the last week.

Diplomacy was never Codi's strong point. She would rather bull her way to a solution than talk about it. She'd always been driven to cut to the heart of a situation and felt like she had something to prove. Her father had been one of the Navy's elite divers and had specialized in deep water recovery. It allowed time at home in between missions and training. And when home, he'd been a solid father figure in her life. During a routine deep-water dive, unexploded ordnance triggered unexpectedly leaving three families without fathers.

Afterwards, Codi became a latchkey kid. Her mother, Carolyn, struggled with the loss and dipped in and out of depression. Twice she disappeared for days at a time, and Codi was sure she wasn't coming back. They moved every year or so, her mom in search of a new job, a new boyfriend, or greener grass.

In time, Codi found that the only person she could really count on was herself. She used that as a motivator to find her independence. She would not follow her mother's path, and instead blaze a new one she could call her own.

After graduating college with top honors, Codi received several promising opportunities. But she left them all behind and joined the Marines as an enlisted soldier. She had something to prove to herself and to her father. After three arduous years she was one of the very few females ever admitted to BUDs training. Becoming a SEAL was something she had set as a do-or-die goal. Nothing would stop her from achieving it. Nothing except an all-male "boys club" that conspired against her. She was forced to tap out after a tragic injury left her ankle shattered, along with her dream.

Codi had spiraled down into a dark place that put her out

of the military and practically on the street. But she found herself, once again, after accepting a job as a GSA Agent where she was responsible for tax and fraud cases, essentially a paper cop. Though feeling like she had let herself down, Codi put her best foot forward.

Ultimately, she was teamed up with Joel, and after following up on a cold case from the forties the two had been swept into a tidal wave of espionage, international crime, kidnapping, even a bioweapon, all part of the case. The two had been integral in bringing it all to a close and stopping a madman willing to massacre for his agenda. Their success had put them on display and the FBI had recruited both to work in their special projects division.

Along the way, she met and saved Doctor Matt Campbell. They forged a special relationship that was full of promise. But lately it seemed to be dwindling with every day they spent apart.

Codi felt vindicated from her past and even proud of the things she had accomplished. All that was left now was to close their current case and then figure out what was happening in her personal life.

After an unusually long taxi on the macadam, the Finnair Airbus A300, came to a stop and powered down. Joel looked at his phone through bloodshot eyes.

"We are here. Only eighteen hours and thirty-eight minutes. We're early. I sure hope I get to see some real Russian countryside. But first I need a good cup of coffee."

Had Codi possessed the energy to roll her eyes she would have. Instead she tried to extricate herself from her seat and come to a standing position.

"Follow my lead," Nolan commanded, as he started down the aisle. "There will probably be dignitaries, news coverage, and maybe even a parade."

Nolan stepped outside and started to wave from the top of the jet stairs. He quickly realized there was no one there and put his hand down. He just stood staring blankly as Codi passed him and headed down the stairs.

"The parade must be running late," she said to Nolan as she passed.

"It's because we're early," Joel added, as he passed by.

The air was cool, and a light mist danced in the air before finding the ground. As Codi got to the bottom, a black Mercedes G wagon pulled up in front of her. A man in a gray suit that matched his hair stepped out of the back. "Pierce?" he said with a thick Russian accent.

Codi thumbed behind her to the man at the top of the stairs. "He's up there."

Pierce suddenly hurried down the stairs almost tripping and falling the last three steps. He quickly recomposed himself and shook the man's hand. "Assistant Deputy to the Secretary of State Nolan Pierce at your service," he said in flawless Russian.

The man said something in Russian back and then said, "Fedot Sokolov, Administrator to the Head of State," in equally good English.

This elicited a mutual nod.

Codi thought to herself, perfect, these two were meant for each other.

"I have car service for you, Assistant Secretary. Colonel Galkin will take possession of the bodies." He gestured as a green canvas-backed Kam AZ, a heavy-duty military transport vehicle, pulled to the rear of the plane. Several soldiers exited out the back.

Nolan got into the rear of the G wagon with Fedot and they sped off, leaving Codi and Joel behind.

"I guess we're with the truck," she said.

Joel followed her as she marched to the back of the jet.

The room smelled of old cigarettes and cheap furniture polish. It was done in heavy wood and had a definitive masculine touch. Codi sat next to Joel in the overly firm leather chairs that faced an empty desk bathed in slotted sun lines from the shutters on the window. The rain had traded places with an intense sun. Two military guards with Kalashnikovs slung over their shoulders watched from either side of the entrance door. Joel jumped as the doors burst open revealing a large bear of a man in full military dress. The guards tensed and gave a quick salute, which the man ignored.

Codi and Joel stood to greet the man.

"Thank you for coming," he said in nearly perfect English.

As if we had a choice, Codi thought to herself.

"I'm General Vasily Sokolov."

The introductions went around and they all sat down.

"It was good of you to escort the bodies of our comrades. I thank you."

An awkward moment hung in the air.

"So, what now? Why are we here?" He said, raising his hands for emphasis.

Joel cleared his throat trying to bolster his courage. "We, General, as you may know…"

"Please call me Vasily."

"Yes, well, your comrades were found on US soil, and so, just like with every government, we have to close the file on this situation. So anything you can add, we'd be grateful for."

The man looked on, unmoved.

Codi leaned in and put on an air of earnestness. "Honestly, Vasily, we are talking about a case that is more than sixty years old. No one cares who was spying on whom. We just want to close the file," Codi pantomimed a file closing action, "and go back home."

Vasily leaned back in his chair and stroked his chin. He appraised the two agents with care.

"I have read your files, and I was impressed. Your military gave you a raw deal."

Codi had a flash of panic nearly overtake her.

"But you are right to not get caught up in the current politics that are going on over at the Kremlin right now. I'm sure your associate is getting the Russian circle."

Codi and Joel looked confused.

Vasily leaned forward. "Where you talk in circles." Now it was his turn to pantomime and he did so with a rotating downturned index finger. "Nothing gets done."

Codi always believed honesty was the best policy. "Yes, we have that in the US, as well," she said.

"The American circle?"

Joel covertly kicked Codi in the shin, but she continued unfazed. "We call it shoveling bullshit."

The general paused for a moment. The corners of his mouth suddenly sprang up. "That is good. I like it!"

He paused one more time, then let it all out as one continuous thought. "So here's the deal. Yes they were spying on your early warning system looking for a weakness and, yes they must have been caught in a storm, as they were never heard from again. We apologize for doing it and we thank you for delivering the bodies back to their homeland."

He paused again. "But, as you say, those were different times. Drink?" He reached into his credenza and pulled out a bottle of Krupnik vodka, along with three glasses.

Joel mumbled, "Actually, we're still on duty and not allowed to..."

Codi elbowed him mid-sentence. "That would be great, Vasily," she said.

They finished up mostly listening to the general talk about his passion for fly fishing. Then suddenly he stood and spoke to the two guards. "See that they get safely to their hotel."

Codi reached in her pocket and pulled out the Order of Lenin Medal and handed it to Vasily. "I'm sure you'll know what to do with this."

He inspected the piece with reverence, finally looking Codi square in the eyes. He gave her a slight nod, turned on a dime and left the office just as abrupt as he had entered.

As Codi and Joel clamored out of the drab green military sedan, she said, "What was your deal back there?"

Joel looked over. "What?"

"The shin kick."

"Oh, I was sure you were going to say, circle jerk."

"To a Russian general? Give me some credit, Joel."

Joel nodded almost imperceptivity. "Sorry." He turned and looked up at their hotel. "Whoa, this place looks really nice."

He double-checked his paperwork. "This is not the hotel I have in our itinerary. To their escort, he said, "Sir, I think you brought us to the wrong hotel."

Now it was Codi's turn to kick Joel in the shin.

Before he could complain, their guard escort motioned with his arm. "Compliments of General Sokolov." He led them up to the entrance.

The Hotel National is a grand building set against flowing park-like grounds. It is the best of old and modern Russia combined. And it has a reputation for only the best.

The guard walked them through the marble and polished wood lobby and made sure they got checked in. Then, in broken English, he said, "For dinner, from General." He handed Joel a business card with a restaurant logo on it.

Joel and Codi each had a room on the top floor with private balconies and a spectacular view of the city. After all the horrible places this job had sent him, finally, Joel felt he had arrived. He lay out in his bed and took it all in. He did a quick almost reflexive clean of his glasses with his tie. As he put them back on, his view opened to fine linens, gilded moldings, a domed ceiling. This was the life. He let his mind wander, hoping Assistant Deputy to the Secretary of State Nolan Pierce was staying in a hostel. With a shared bathroom down the hall. This thought sparked a smirk on his face so big it almost hurt.

Chun Lee entered the restaurant. It was a small room with ten tables, like many along the busy Hong Kong street. He nodded to the owner and then headed to the rear of the building. A small door marked storage opened to a larger than expected space. It was filled with boxes and supplies stacked to the ceiling. There was an old rusty rollup door on the back wall that leaked light around the edges. Lee pressed a hidden button by an old sink above a crusted floor drain. A stained panel slid to reveal a freight elevator. He punched in a six-digit code and the doors opened. The elevator took him down to the first subfloor where a long stone arched hallway led him under the street to the offices hidden below the abandoned building next door. He passed through the security checkpoint where two heavily armed guards behind an armored door processed him. Once inside, Lee moved to an office at the end of the hall.

He tapped on a teak carved door and proceeded, following an "enter" from the other side.

The unusually tall, bald-headed Lee entered a

warm, cream-colored room with carved beams and an intricately-patterned bamboo floor. He ran his fingers across the belly of a golden Buddha sitting on a pedestal by the front door. Lee noted that his boss was looking worse since the last time he had seen him. His face showed signs of a complete loss of control.

General Chow Phun popped to his feet and stepped over to congratulate Lee. He shook his hand and patted him on the back. "Chun Lee, good to see you again. Nice work in Colorado. Please sit," he said as he returned to his desk, dabbing at a small rivulet of drool on his chin.

Lee sat in one of the overstuffed chairs next to Chow's massive desk. The chair was designed purposefully to be lower than the desk, but Lee's height, at just over six-three, countered the boss's ploy.

"The Dragons have picked up some chatter," Chow said, "from one of their Russian partners on an old mission that connects directly to one of our current operations. It may be nothing, but I didn't get to this position in life by taking chances."

Lee looked on with concern. "Which operation? Do you know what kind of leak? Tell me and I'll plug it."

One corner of the old general's mouth upturned. "There is something you might not know, and it could be relevant." Chow said this last part looking off into space.

A moment of silence ticked by.

Chow stood and started to pace, his numb fingers fighting to find each other and interlock behind his back. It was the simple things that Chow missed by losing his sense of touch, and it seemed to affect everything he did. Muscle memory was great, but without continuous feedback that memory fades, and with it, coordination.

"Many years ago," Chow said, "during the cold war, I

was involved in a very bold operation. The Soviets called it Operation Blind Pig. We called it... well, it was all very classified and ultra-top-secret.

"I was just a young up-and-coming officer then. But our division had managed to snatch some very cutting-edge assets and technology from the Soviets. This led us to major advancements and, for a time, we actually had the ability to cross the sovereign airspace of any country without their knowledge, the US and Soviet Russia included."

Chow continued to pace as he thought back to those times. He ran his fingers numbly across his golden Buddha, hoping for some miracle that would return his sense of touch.

"And?" Lee prodded.

Chow looked back to the man who had been like a son to him ever since the death of his wife and child. "Unfortunately, the powers at the time were too spineless to act. Imagine a competitive advantage like that and not using it. Such a waste."

"What's that got to do with our current op? The cold war, that was a long time ago. The technology has got to be archaic."

"Well, it just so happens that our little trip to NORAD is a modernized reincarnation of that same technology. Soon I will have the ability to give our comrades the power of invisibility when breaching enemy airspace."

"But we are not at war."

The comment elicited a focused stare-down from Chow. "That is a short-sighted view, Lee. There is always a war, even if it is economic."

Lee nodded to his boss, as he watched him return to his chair.

"I can't have anyone putting the pieces together before we are ready to act." Chow leaned forward with his fingers splayed flat on the desk. "Right now, there's a situation happening in Moscow and I need you to take care of it."

10

KALUZHKOE SHOPPING CENTER – 8:45 P.M. – MOSCOW, RUSSIA

"Should be right around the next corner." Joel led Codi with his smart phone along the sidewalk. They were headed to the address indicated on the card given them by General Vasily Sokolov's guard. Joel had been using his translating app to decipher the Cyrillic names on the street signs. Codi was wearing a light blue sleeveless dress with a slight shimmer and fringed bottom. Joel had changed up his usual outfit with a peach collared shirt.

Codi was smiling to herself as they strolled along.

Joel looked over at her as they passed stoic Muscovites out for an evening amble. "What?" he asked.

"Oh nothing, just thinking."

"Come on, I know that look. What gives?"

After a beat, Codi opened up. "I was just thinking that I can now cross it off my list."

"Cross what off?"

"Drinking vodka with a Russian general."

Joel stopped mid-step. The old woman behind him barely avoided a collision. "Wait," he said to Codi, "how is that even on a list. I mean, who has a list like that?"

Codi regarded Joel for a moment, and continued walking. "You'd be surprised what's on my list, Joel."

Joel hurried to catch up. "Like swimming with sharks, or bungee jumping from a helicopter?"

"Been there, done that," Codi deadpanned.

"Seriously?"

Codi flashed back to a dark time in her life. She had left the military and had healed enough to walk without a limp. Her dream of becoming a Navy SEAL was gone and she became reckless. In hindsight, it was most likely her need to prove that she could still do anything. Her outlet was almost always dangerous and life threatening, extreme versions of extreme sports. She had even tried sky surfing. That ended when she was forced to use her emergency parachute seconds before taking the big bounce. After three months of essentially failing to kill herself, Codi found an even more destructive state, a deep dark depression that threatened to consume her.

"We're here," Joel said.

The words snapped her from her thoughts.

The LavkaLavka was a farm-to-table restaurant located in a bright yellow neoclassic building on Petrovka Street. Codi and Joel passed through the gated wrought-iron archway that led eight stone steps down to the entrance. Once inside, Codi did a quick look around. The old brick walls, red painted milk-can lights, and kitschy Russian memorabilia plastered everywhere screamed bad Applebee's. The *maître d'* had their names on his list and led them past a small bar and a large family-style seating area. The smell of fresh seafood and fragrant spices filled the air. He turned left and opened two maroon doors that led down into a small cellar seating area.

He gestured, and in very broken English with an over-the-top smile said, "You sit here." He then turned and left.

Joel stepped down into the small domed room. There were

three four-person tables but only one had been set up. "I'm guessing here," Joel said, as he took a seat.

The room was decorated with large stylized food icons, comfy upholstered chairs and a modern lighting grid. The floor was polished stained concrete and even the slightest whisper echoed around the room.

"This must be where they keep the foreigners," Codi said as she checked out the empty space.

The sommelier came a few moments later and took their order. Cody and Joel sat uncomfortably alone once again. They could hear the muffled sounds of happy patrons on the other side of the wall. "This is weird," Joel said, "let's see if we can get moved to the main dining area. I feel like I'm being watched."

"Relax Joel, we are here for a reason. Give it time. Besides, we undoubtedly are being watched. If nothing comes of to-night, you can tell everyone you had a romantic dinner with me in a Russian cellar."

Joel tried to smile but it came out more like a grimace. "I should probably make a list so I can put that on it."

"The point of a list is to remind you to do things you want to do but haven't done yet. Not to fill it in *after* you do something."

"Hey, you do your list your way and I'll do mine."

The sound of high heels on tile caught their attention as a tall model-like blond flowed into the room. She wore a skin-tight red cocktail dress, cut in all the right places, and moved with a purpose. She walked up to the table and before Joel could stand, took a seat.

"Good evening, I'm Sasha, and I am pleased to make your acquaintance Agent Sanders and Agent Strickman." Her accent was just the right amount of charming.

"Hi," was all that Joel could manage, as he gawked at the buxom beauty in awe.

"Pleasure," Codi voiced while reaching out her hand.

The two women took stock of each other and shook hands. Codi smacked Joel on the shoulder to get him to snap out of it and follow suit.

They ordered dinner and made small talk, most of which seemed forced and meaningless. Codi got the white fish and Joel the Kamchatka crab salad. Both were delicious. When the meal was about halfway through, Sasha leaned forward and said, "I am here at the bequest of General Vasily Sokolov."

Finally, Codi thought to herself.

"He has instructed me to give you a message."

Joel anxiously glanced around the otherwise empty room.

"There is a person you must see before you go."

She reached inside her purse. Both Codi and Joel tensed. Then, palming her hand across the table, she pulled it back revealing the Medal of Lenin that Codi had given the general. Codi placed her hand on top of it.

"Why are you… is the general doing this?" Joel asked.

Sasha paused before saying, "Men who die in honor for their country should have their story told."

"I agree," Codi said as she turned the medal over and glimpsed a name and address taped to the back. She slid the medal into her purse.

Sasha suddenly stood up. "I must go."

Joel finally found his voice and squawked out, "Please stay. And have a drink and maybe some dessert."

Sasha's lips parted into a dazzling smile. She walked over to Joel who suddenly looked a bit shell-shocked. She ran her fingers through his hair and whispered into his ear. His skin prickled as he turned the color of the Russian flag. "Maybe next time *Lyubimiy,"* she said. "You are very cute, but I prefer a man in uniform."

With that, Sasha spun and left, clicking her way out of the room.

Joel's glowing face practically lit the whole table. "I have a uniform," he said to himself.

Codi tried to keep a straight face for her partner's sake. "Easy there, Don Juan."

"It means, 'my love.'" Joel read the definition of *Lyubimiy* from Google Translate on his smart phone.

"You're supposed to be navigating, lover boy."

"Oh, ah, turn left in five-hundred meters."

Codi turned the rental car, avoiding a bicyclist and a roving street vender. Moscow traffic had been painful but the E115 North had opened up to some beautiful countryside.

The town of Pestovo located on the Moscow Canal was a modern looking city with none of the trappings of classic Russian architecture. Even the Soviet-era block housing had a modern spin.

Codi turned down a tree-lined gravel road that led south away from town. It paralleled the famous canal that was built in the late thirties, connecting the Volga river to the Moscow river, and was used as a major thoroughfare for goods coming to and from the great city. A mixed forest grew along this side of the waterway providing breathtaking glimpses of the slate blue water between the trees.

The road continued to deteriorate, finally ending in a small parking lot where Codi pulled to a stop and killed the engine. There were several older vehicles parked haphazardly in the lot, including an old Russian Gaz-51 pickup. A faded wooden footbridge crossed a small stream leading to a mostly-white steel building that was connected to a battered dock that floated in the channel. The words on the building were in unreadable Cyrillic but the hellish potpourri of gasoline and rotting fish said Bait Shop.

Codi and Joel stepped into the small shop and looked around. The walls and the shelves were filled with a kaleidoscope of colors and shapes, everything geared towards fishing. There were mounted trophy fish everywhere and faded pictures with grizzled men holding record catches.

Codi walked up to the counter and spied the old man behind it. He seemed to pay no attention to the visitors. He had his back to them, focused on some task.

He asked a question in Russian that neither Codi nor Joel understood.

"Are you Andrei Tatter?" Codi asked.

The man paused what he was doing and turned slowly towards Codi and Joel.

Codi could now see that he had been tying a fly to a hook that was mounted on a small vise. He was wearing a ridiculous looking magnifier on his head and one eye looked enormous through the convex glass. The man took off the headset and looked at his two customers with neutral curiosity.

Codi could see that the man was very old and had spent a good part of his life in the outdoors. His skin was mottled and saggy. He had large ears, but the most defining feature was the end of his nose. It was missing. You could see right into his nicotine-stained membranes.

He narrowed his eyes and took a guess. "English?"

"No, American," Joel said.

He looked them over one more time.

"Da, Americanski. You want fish?"

"Ah, no."

Codi and Joel glanced at each other and then back to the

man. She was beginning to regret coming all the way out here. This guy was going to be a waste of their time.

"We were hoping to speak with you about this." Joel said the last part slowly, over-enunciating every syllable. He gestured for Codi to show him the medal. Codi passed the Order of Lenin medal over to Tatter. He picked it up and eyed it suspiciously. Flipping it over to read the name on the back.

Joel played a prerecorded message translated into Russian on his phone:

> Can you tell us something about this. It was found thawed out, along with three Russian Special Forces members from the nineteen-fifties on a glacier on Umnak Island, Alaska.

Tatter slumped noticeably. He used the counter to hold himself up. He whispered three names in reverence.

"Misha, Kaz, Traktor."

"You knew them?" Joel tried to write their names down on his phone.

Tatter looked up. "Come. I make tea," he said in broken English.

Tatter led them to a small room in the back. It looked as though he'd been living as well as working at the bait shop. Joel and Codi sat hip-to-hip on a small couch covered with an old blanket, waiting patiently as the proprietor made tea in silence. Joel didn't know where to put his hands as he was afraid to touch anything in the room. Ultimately he decided on his lap.

Finally Tatter brought a chipped and worn tea set over and passed cups around. He sat in a dog-eared chair across from them and took a cautious sip. The afternoon sun filtered through a small window providing the room's only illumination. Nicotine stains covered the once-white walls. Dust motes danced in the air as Andrei lit up a filter-less cigarette and breathed in the pungent smoke. He held it in his lungs as though his life depended on it, before releasing a puff through his missing nose. The smoke shot out and up in an uncontrolled spiral. A short coughing spell followed.

Andrei Tatter then began to tell them the story of a top-secret mission he had been a part of over sixty years ago, Operation Blind Pig, from the moment they landed on Umnak Island to the installation of two electrical leaches on the island's resident radar towers. He spoke of the dead in a reverent way including the gruesome task of cutting the legs off of Political Officer Zampolit Traktor. Finally, he told them about the dash over the glacier and their trip back to Russia. Only three men had survived, and all were left with a reminder of the trip.

Andrei gestured as he spoke. "Popov lost left foot and three toes on other. Colonel Alexeev lost two fingers and half an ear. And I, as you see, lost nose. Not good for army or woman."

Tatter stared at the floor for a moment, as he picked a loose bit of tobacco from the tip of his tongue.

"So I am here." He shrugged at the way his life had turned out. "How you say, frost tip?"

"Frostbite."

"Yes, terrible word."

"What was the purpose of the electrical leach?" Codi asked.

Tatter took another puff on his cigarette. "We were never told."

A long pause followed, which made Joel antsy.

"But I might have means to help," Tatter said. "Before I leave service I take papers of mission. I put in bank box."

"What do these papers say?" Joel queried.

"I never read. Too much pain." Tatter spoke the last part more to himself. He took another slow breath drawing on his half-burnt cigarette. "It has been…hard to relive."

He dropped his head, his eyes tearing up with emotion. His hand shook as he tried to put the tip of his cigarette back in his mouth.

"I'm so sorry," Codi said.

Tatter regarded her briefly and nodded in thanks. "Come tomorrow, noon, I get you... papers."

Codi and Joel said their goodbyes and left Tatter to his memories and despair.

They bounced along the gravel road north, back to Pestovo. "Come back tomorrow? Are you kidding me? I say, come back *never.*" Joel said aloud their common thought.

"Exactly," Codi said. "It's a hell of story, but who gives a crap. I mean it happened so long ago. It's just a piece of history now."

They drove in silence for a bit. The sunlight through the trees created a moving dappled pattern on the windshield.

"Do our clothes smell like dead fish?" Joel asked, as he wrinkled his nose.

"I thought that was your cologne." Codi hit a pothole as she said it and they both jarred in their seats. She lowered the windows to a much-needed breath of fresh air.

Codi's hunger got the best of her. "I bet the vodka and caviar are good in Pestovo," she said.

"The caviar here is probably radioactive."

"That's what gives it that extra bite that I love. Joel, live a little." Codi's grin was infectious and growing.

Joel slowly nodded in agreement, trying to psych himself up for what he was sure to be a disappointment. This just made Codi laugh.

"Hey," she said, "you wanted to see the Russian countryside."

11

Moscow Canal Bait Shop – 11:28 p.m. – Pestovo, Russia

Lee watched as the last light blinked out in the small bait shop. The location and target had come from one of their connections higher up in the Russian military. It was the way of the world. Countries spying on countries, each with its own agenda, each trying to one-up the other. It was a vicious loop, but it kept Lee busy. He moved cautiously across the footbridge, staying near the edge to keep the planks from squeaking. The tall and lanky assassin was like a wraith in the night, as he quickly slipped up to the front door. He kept his back to the wall, reached out with his right hand and tested the handle. He was surprised to find it unlocked. His sixth sense alarm went off.

Was this guy careless or was it a set-up? Caution had served him well over the years and tonight would be no different. Lee pulled out his silenced Russian SR-1, a gift left waiting for him at his hotel. He slowly turned the handle and let himself in, staying low as he entered. He was assaulted by the aroma of stale cigarettes and day-old fish. There was a slight blue glow from moonlight peeking through murky windows. It cast an assortment of shadow and light patterns across the stocked shelves and wall-mounted fish. He pressed forward, pistol leading the way as he began to clear the room. Each step slow and purposeful, his eyes and ears tuned to the slightest anomaly.

After a short stint in the PLA, People's Liberation Army, Special Forces, Lee had found himself at the wrong end of Chinese politics. After a bar fight with a privileged officer that had left the man blind in one eye, Lee became a guest at the Qincheng Maximum Security Prison. It was a modern prison with old world practices. Torture and threats of execution were on the daily menu, and food and water were often neglected.

But Lee held firm and never let them see weakness. Once, after two days without food or water he had been dragged into one of the various rooms used to taunt the prisoners. He acted hollow and pretended to be desperate for water. He used the ploy to draw the guard closer to him, one who had been particularly mean. Lee used the opportunity to break the man's nose with a head-butt. He was beaten severely as a punishment but the satisfaction it gave him put a smile on his face as he was pummeled and dumped back into his cell.

This information made its way to a General Chow Phun, a man always on the lookout for special men for his black operations.

Over time and many missions, Lee and Chow formed a unique bond. Chow used Lee as his personal wrecking crew, which resulted in many untraceable deaths—key deaths that moved Chow up and up the ladder of success. Soon, he had a solid reputation and a fear built around him—don't mess with General Chow Phun and, more importantly, don't fail him. Even after Chow left the military, the two continued in their prosperous association. And after Chow's family died, they developed an even stronger relationship.

Lee took his time as he stepped through the shop. He was in no hurry. A swooshing sound briefly filled the air as Lee moved next to the checkout counter. Before he could react, a huge fishhook impaled his gun hand and yanked. His gun skittered across the weathered floor and disappeared. Lee instinctively grabbed the monofilament attached to the hook and pulled with all his might as he jumped over the counter to safety.

Tatter knew every sound and squeak in his world. As he had put down his last cigarette for the night and closed his eyes, he knew immediately something was wrong. Not by any noise that he heard but from a lack thereof. Crickets were singing their nightly song and then they were not. Tatter worked his way to a dark corner of his shop, grateful that he had on his dark blue pajamas.

He quickly cobbled together a weapon. A nine-aught treble hook tied to 100-lb. test line. The hook was roughly the size of a man's hand, with three very sharp barbs. He silently watched as a tall slightly hunched stranger moved like a cat through his shop, a silenced gun in his right hand. This was no ordinary burglar. This man was here for one purpose, to kill him. Tatter flung the hook with deadly accuracy, catching the man's gun hand and setting two of the three barbs deep into his flesh. With a snap of the line, he disarmed the assassin. But the man's reflexes had surprised Tatter. The assassin jumped over the counter and pulled so hard on the line that Tatter crashed to the floor, the rod and reel yanked from his hands.

Lee gritted his teeth and jerked the large hook free of his hand. Meat and blood flew from the back of his palm and wrist. He ignored the pain and peered over the countertop in time to see an old man scramble back up to his feet. Lee pulled his Kukri, with its unique curved blade, from his belt. In one fluid movement, he moved back around the counter and took an aggressive stance.

His target tensed, like the last lamb to notice a wolf. Lee let loose a sneer as he closed the distance, eager to exact a measure of payback for his damaged hand.

Tatter backed up, looking around for something to fight with. In the pile of products that had spilled when he was pulled to the ground was a gaff hook used to hook large fish and pull them into the boat. He grabbed the large stainless hook mounted on a three-foot pole. He then grabbed a long black fishing rod that was still clamped to a display next to him. He squared his body and prepared to defend himself, one in each hand. Using the fishing pole in his right hand he was able to keep the killer at bay. He flicked it like a whip with the precision of a lifelong fisherman.

The tip of the black pole smacked Lee's face and arms repeatedly, leaving welts, and forcing him to defend himself rather than attack. It was impossible to see in the darkness. Lee tried to protect his eyes and bull-rush the man but the wizened man maintained his distance and matched Lee's moves with surprising skill. Lee feigned to the right, then pulled back left just in time to feel the whack of the pole's tip on his arm.

He tried throwing several cans of oil that were stacked on an end-cap at the old man, but they were parried away by the gaff pole.

The battle continued for several minutes like that, cat versus old mouse.

Finally Tatter stumbled and fell backwards over a metal hand net while trying to back-pedal. Lee jumped at the opportunity and moved inside the effective range of the pole. He sliced down, severing the fishing pole at an angle, then swung the blade, clanging off the steel hook from the gaff pole. He pressed his advantage on the fallen man who was unable to find an opening to get back on his feet and had to fight from his back. Lee used the blade expertly to keep the man pinned, the poor visibility on the floor finally declaring a winner as Lee's blade found its mark.

He parried the gaff hook and countered, plunging his knife towards the old man's larynx, while at the same time pinning the gaff hook to the floor with his knee. But the old fisherman was surprisingly strong and stopped the blade right at the skin.

In a desperate move Tatter removed one hand and reached for the severed fishing pole that lay next to him. He shoved it at the assassin's ribs for all he was worth. But the man barely seemed to flinch. Instead, he used the moment to finally plunge the tip of his Kukri deep into Tatter's throat.

Lee held the pressure on the knife until there was no struggle left. He rolled over onto the debris-littered floor to catch his breath while the body next to him twitched and gurgled. He felt a sharp pain in his side and looked down to see the handle of the severed fishing pole sticking out of him.

Lee lay there trying to catch his breath, waiting for the pain to subside. He moved to a seated position with a bit of a struggle. He pulled the pole from his side with a gasp, nearly passing out from the pain. He tried to breathe through the agony as he took a rag and put pressure on the wound. A wheezing sound was heard as air escaped through the wound with each breath. Gradually Lee stood on shaky legs and stared down at the old fisherman who had been so hard to kill. He spied his gun and collected it. Then, with much pain and effort, Lee spread gasoline on the corpse and room. He flicked a lighter he had taken from Tatter's pocket and stumbled out of the burning building.

"Eventually, smoking will kill you," he said with a rasp and a pained smile.

After much debate, Codi and Joel decided to stay the night in Pestovo. Even their boss Brian was good with the idea. But to Codi, it seemed like more trouble than it was going to be worth. They should undoubtedly turn the whole thing over to a military historian.

The rainy evening had been uneventful. They found a nice bed and breakfast just outside of town and the quiet evening had been a good calming influence. But after a breakfast of fried eggs with Russian *kolbasa* and dill, Codi and Joel were Jones-ing to get going, finish with Tatter, and head back home.

An intense sun had scattered the clouds from the night before creating a clear, beautiful Russian day. They rode in silence, each waiting for the coffee to kick in. Joel drove, tapping his hands unconsciously on the steering wheel to the beat of an unknown song. Time on the road allowed for a closeness you didn't get with your average coworker. Joel and Codi had been through a lot together, including being shot, kidnapped, and the subjects of a massive manhunt in England. It had formed a bond few share. They were starting to think alike, and moments of silence were no longer awkward.

"So what's with you and Matt?" Joel said. "I haven't heard you talk about him like you used to."

Codi took the words in and let them brew for a moment. Recent events seemed to be going against her. "I don't know, we're both so busy. We've tried to get together and make it work but we keep failing. Maybe it's not meant to be."

Matt had been the closest thing to real love she had ever

found. An unexpected case had thrust them together and pushed their limits. They found each other capable partners. The relationship had excelled under the immense pressure of life and death, but the real world seemed to lead them down different paths. No longer needing each other to survive, they had drifted apart. Maybe the effort it took to keep it going was more than they were willing to expend.

"Work."

Codi glanced sideways at Joel and his comment.

"You have to work for love," Joel added.

"Sounds like a bad eighties song."

Joel smirked but continued. "Maybe it is but it's still true today, maybe more so. What with all the social media, no one talks anymore. And sharing emotion through a text? It seems shallow, without feeling."

Joel selected an emoji on his phone and showed it to her. "A heart emoji is nice but doesn't cut it. It takes work."

Codi let the comment simmer.

"Heads up," she interrupted.

As they came around the corner to the Bait Shop's parking lot, they were met with fire and police vehicles. They could see the blackened, smoldering remains of the bait shop. A charred body was being carried to a stretcher, and a policeman was walking their way. He signaled for them to turn around and yelled something in Russian.

Joel hit the brakes and flipped a U-turn, following the officer's instructions. The policeman watched them return to the tree-lined gravel road before turning back to his job.

Codi and Joel drove back in silence as they processed what they had just seen.

"Damn, what a waste," Joel said. "I guess we'll never know the purpose of Operation Blind Pig."

"Yeah, breaks my heart. Now let's get the hell out of this country and go ho–"

Before Codi could finish her words an old tow truck T-boned them from a side trail. The impact was so sudden, Joel had no time to react. His head hit the side window smashing his glasses and skull. Codi was slammed towards Joel and recovered just as the vehicle's passenger side tires caught on a small berm along the canal, forcing the car to flip through the air and into the water.

Almost immediately, the car began to sink, first on its side, and then it righted itself, the curved roofline of the Russian rental disappearing last under the water.

Lee stepped slowly out of the tow truck, still holding his wounded side that was now leaking again after the impact of the crash. He was covered in sweat and struggled to remove his silenced pistol. Everything hurt. His right hand was bandaged, so he used his left to hold the pistol. He watched the water with the focus of a blue heron searching for fish.

Codi rolled down her window and grabbed at Joel to follow her. Water quickly filled the vehicle. She fought a rising panic that had gripped her ever since she'd drowned on her last mission. For her, the water now held only terror. She briefly flashed back to the incident and felt panic's cold fingers take hold of her body. The experience of drowning a second time was too much. She fought to gain some control, as water filled the car around her.

Certain death sometimes has a way of jumpstarting the antidote for fear—adrenaline. Codi fed off it like a hungry infant with a fresh bottle. She pinpointed her focus to her days competing on the college swim team. She needed to deal with the first problem at hand, get out of the car.

She started to swim for the surface, feeling her confidence in the water return. Just before surfacing she looked up. The silhouette of a man with a gun standing at the shore rippled above her. She grabbed Joel and shoved him back down. Joel fought the panic at being pulled away from the air that he needed so desperately. Codi pointed to the man with the gun on the shore. Joel, who was just about to exhale reflexively, nodded with bulging cheeks and eyes as big as saucers. They were trapped.

Lee looked on, as the water's current erased all evidence of the incident. He felt a slight disappointment at not being able to finish them off when they came to the surface, but the results would be the same.

Cody pulled Joel back inside the car and up to the ceiling. The curved roof of the Russian rental car held about four inches of trapped air. Codi and Joel arched their necks and gasped what little oxygen they could glean from the small reservoir.

They wouldn't last long.

"Stay here," Codi motioned with both hands, before dropping back into the water.

Joel raked his eyes over to the side to see what on earth Codi was doing, afraid to leave the security of the air pocket.

Lee lowered his weapon as a slow-moving boat came into view. He could smell it almost before he saw it. A garbage barge. He backed away from the shore but never took his eyes from the water.

A moment later, Codi returned. She could tell that the air had begun to stale. They had but a few viable breaths of oxygen left. "We've got a bit of a swim. Follow me." She pulled as much air as she could into her lungs and dropped back into the water. Joel sucked in several gulps and followed.

She stroked for the other side of the river, staying deep as she went. A dark shadow came over them and she started for the surface. The air she had taken into her lungs was already depleted of much of its life-giving oxygen and she was struggling much sooner than she expected. Her body fought and spasmed to breathe in but sheer force of will kept her going.

Lee watched the barge carefully as it moved up river. No human could still be underwater and live. But a few more minutes wouldn't make a difference. He considered swimming down to the car and checking it for bodies, but the wound on his side was getting worse. The wheezing intensified with every breath. He needed medical attention, and soon.

Codi surfaced on the far side of the barge with a desperate gasp, and heaved air in and out of her exhausted lungs. Joel popped up right behind her and looked like he might not be able to continue. She quickly stroked to the passing hull and clung to a line buoy that was dangling. She grabbed Joel as he tried and failed to do the same, and pulled him to her.

Lee watched the barge pass and, finally, after nearly ten minutes of waiting turned back to the tow truck. Smiling to himself, he murmured, "Careful, water can kill you."

Codi and Joel clung to the buoy on the far side of the garbage scow. They waited for their strength to return and then climbed up onto the deck. Both collapsed and just lay still for several minutes, until the surrounding smell reached their consciousness.

Joel made a face. "We're laying in garbage, aren't we?"

"Yep, and there's a sun-ripened, poop-filled diaper awfully close to my face. But, hey, you wanted to see the real Russia. This is pretty real."

Joel started to laugh at the ridiculousness of it all and Codi couldn't help but follow. Somehow, they were still alive.

"Privet!" A voice yelled from behind them.

They turned to see a man yelling at them in Russian from the raised bridge of the barge. Another man was climbing down a ladder and moving their way.

"I guess this is our stop," Codi said, as the two agents stood on slightly wobbly legs and jumped off the barge back into the water. They swam to shore amid Russian swear words coming from the moving vessel.

Joel crawled up next to Codi on the shore.

"Just another day in paradise." She huffed between words.

Joel looked over skeptically. "We need to get to a phone."

"Ya think?"

Lee checked in with Chow, giving him an update. The loose ends had been tied up and there was no possibility any blowback would come their way. Chow loved how efficient Lee worked and made a mental note to congratulate him upon his return.

Chow arranged for him to meet a doctor they knew who worked off the books. "But first," he said, "get well, my friend."

Chow looked down at the only picture he kept on his desk. A gold-framed moment with his wife and child. They were all smiling, a task he now found difficult. It would be a dishonor to them to not leave a legacy, something to keep their memory alive, a place of honor for him and his family's name. Chow didn't think of himself as a psychopath, more a determined man with a plan. And he was a firm believer in the end justifying the means. And finally, the end was in sight; he was close. After many years, Chow would leave his China a better place. A place of power and strength. Where foreigners would no longer subvert their culture and traditions. His China would have the world powers trembling in fear.

The two drowned rats finally stood and walked along the shore, following the now distant barge. The beautiful Russian countryside of white birch and Olgan larch eventually gave way to a small town. They were able to find some local clothes, a disposable cellphone, and a rental car to get them back on their way. Joel navigated while Codi drove.

"How you doing without your glasses?" Codi asked.

"Fine. Just don't ask me to read any street signs."

"Noted."

Joel was wearing a black tracksuit with gold tennis shoes. Codi wore a yellow collarless summer dress with a muted floral print, and a white sweater.

"All you need is a gold chain," she said to him.

"What do you mean?"

"You look like a Russian mobster in that outfit."

"I'll take that as a compliment, coming from Maria Von Trapp," he said, citing Julie Andrews' character from *The Sound of Music*.

They headed south back to Moscow. The traffic was light and they were making good time, as Joel dialed up their boss.

"Fescue." His voice was thin and distant.

"Hey, it's Joel and Codi."

They brought him up to speed and both parties came to the same conclusion—someone doesn't want this story getting out.

Was there a connection? If so, what was it? There were too many unanswered questions. But something about this case was still active and someone didn't want it made known.

"Look, I need you both to get back here to DC," Brian said. "I can't have you creating another international incident."

Codi couldn't imagine how an international incident could be her fault, but she let it go.

"I have a few friends in our counterintelligence division. I'll see if they can take it over. We'll close our side of the case from here and set up a meet so you can turn over everything you know."

Codi hated the idea of unfinished business, but the FBI had its own way of doing things. As an agent, you followed procedure or found another line of work.

"Besides, I have something a little more current I need you on," Brian added.

Joel couldn't agree more. He gladly redirected Codi to the airport. The thought of a case that was more current helped Codi accept that she would be letting go of this one.

Once in the terminal, the two agents purchased enough personal items to get them home, all on the company credit card. They used the bathroom to freshen up and rendezvoused back at their gate. Codi settled next to Joel for the hour-and-a-half wait before takeoff. She had ditched her dress for slacks and a blouse. Her hair was up in a ponytail and she had found some more comfortable Nike's, most likely Chinese knock-offs, to wear for the long flight home.

Joel leaned back in his chair and crossed his arms over his chest. He let his eyes close and tried to tune out his surroundings.

"You're right."

Joel's eyes cracked opened, waiting for what came next. Codi repositioned herself in her chair, pulled her legs up, and turned to face Joel. "Love does take work. And lately, I've been doing too much regular work to put the time into making what matters most work."

This made Joel think briefly about the love of his life, Agent Annie Waters, and how she had died on a recent mission in spite of his best efforts. It had left him hollow for some time. He had yet to even consider dating again.

He looked over at Codi. "It would be terrible to lose something so precious without trying your hardest."

Codi nodded almost imperceptibly. "That's why when we get back, I'm going to take a week off and make the trip to Boston. Matt and I are either going to work things out, or move on."

"Good for you," Joel said.

He handed her their recently purchased cell phone and Codi started in on a carefully worded text to both Matt and her boss. After several moments of personal debate, she hit send on only one text. She needed a clear head for Matt and now was not the time. She would find the right words on the flight back home.

The flight out of Moscow Domodedovo Airport finally boarded. Codi and Joel had been late to book the flight and had their usual back section of the plane, each in middle seats, separated by three rows. But the thought of coming home seemed to make up for the lack of leg and arm room. Joel seemed to have finally perfected sleeping in an upright position. Codi was seated in between a husband and wife that refused to sit next to each other but continually chatted across her in a language she couldn't understand. Her best guess, Mongolian. It took some doing, but finally she tuned them out and got some sleep.

They dropped out of the clouds into Shanghai's Pudong Airport eight-and-a-half hours later. Codi could make out the distinct glass and steel wave-like roofline of the terminal as a light rain fell. She rubbed a kink from her neck and managed to look back over her shoulder to a sleeping Joel. A three-hour layover was to be followed by business-class seats for the rest of the journey. She watched as he jolted awake to the double impact and squeal of tires hitting the tarmac. It gave Codi her first reason to smile in many hours.

They waited interminably for their chance to exit the jet way, all so they could stand in another line at customs. In an attempt to get through the wait faster, Codi and Joel chose different queues but gave that up when a new line opened up.

Codi slid her passport to the officer in the booth. He swiped it with bored efficiency. A slight negative tone sounded and he re-swiped it. Again, a negative beep. Without emotion he pressed a button on his desk and handed her passport to the responding agent.

"You go with him."

"Is there something wrong?"

"No wrong. Go with him."

"Next."

The customs agent looked to Joel who was next in line and saw the concern on his face as Codi was escorted to a nearby room.

"No problem, random search. Passport, please."

Joel fumbled for his passport.

Codi stepped into a small side room. There was a high countertop separating part of the room and a door that exited out behind it. Bare LED strip lights illuminated beige carpet and walls. It was the polar opposite of the grandiose terminal she had come from.

The agent, in very good English, said, "Sorry, this should only take a minute."

Codi visibly relaxed until the door behind her opened and Joel stepped in followed by another agent. Something was amiss; Codi could feel it. The new agent moved around behind the countertop to join the other one and they had a two minute conversation that neither Joel nor Codi could understand. The first agent finally dismissed the other agent and looked up at Codi and Joel.

"Again, I apologize for the delay." He stamped their

passports and turned to exit the back room. "Give me a couple of seconds and you should be on your way."

As he closed the door behind him, Codi started to feel woozy. "Something's not right. We need to get out of here."

She turned to kick down the door, only to feel her body fail. It was a weird sensation, as she watched her point of view fall sideways to the carpet, just before everything went dark.

The agent reentered two minutes later to the sound of an exhaust fan clearing the room. He was followed by a couple that was remarkably similar in look and stature to Codi and Joel. The couple stripped the two comatose bodies of their clothes and redressed themselves in their outfits. They took Codi's and Joel's passports and exited back into the terminal as if nothing had occurred. After a long wait, the two imposters boarded the plane for DC, reclining comfortably in their business-class seats.

Lee leaned on the doorjamb of the address he had been given. He had staggered down a dark narrow alleyway to a green door marked by a single bare bulb. His soft knock was followed by a door opening to a small one-room clinic. The surprisingly young woman gestured for Lee to come in. She had pale skin and raven, shoulder length hair with eyes that matched almost perfectly. A medical white smock was tied around her waist. A spider web tattoo peeked above her collar along one side of her neck. She pointed to the table in the middle of the room, lit by a strong overhead lamp. Lee used his last remaining strength to scale it. The wound was only oozing now but a bright reddish color radiated on the skin around it. His breathing came in rasps. She immediately went to work cleaning his skin and listening with her stethoscope. "You have a punctured lung." She spoke in Russian, a language Lee was not fluent in.

He answered in French and the woman switched over without a missing a beat.

She finished cleaning and closing the chest wound and stitching up Lee's hand. She gave him plasma for the blood loss and a few pills for the pain. At some point along the way Lee mercifully lost consciousness.

Blackness parted as Lee cracked open his eyes. His mouth felt dry and sluggish. He was expecting a bright light in his eyes, but the room was lit with ambient lighting. He turned his head, to find a smiling face.

"I see you're back," the doctor said with a smile. She inspected Lee's pupils with a small flashlight. "You should be okay, but take it easy for a couple of weeks and finish all your medication. You don't want that infection to spread."

Lee thanked her and, with much effort, exited the premises, his tall frame stooped over with pain as he moved back down the narrow alley.

12

RED BAKS — 10:14 A.M. — SUBBASEMENT, HONG KONG

Lee entered his boss's office on the first floor of the Red Baks. He was not quite himself. The surgery had gone well but the infection was slow to depart. One lung had been punctured by the fishing pole and he was still having trouble taking a full breath. General Chow Phun looked up as Lee entered his office. He let out a slow breath, resigned to the fact that his perfect weapon was no longer perfect. "I see you are healing."

"Yes," Lee rasped. His breathing was labored and a rattling sound accompanied every breath he took.

"So now the two of us are not so…" Chow searched for the right word.

"Yes, but I will heal from what ails me," said Lee, wheezing as he spoke.

Chow let the comment hang for a moment. "Perhaps." He decided to press on. "I assume there were no further leaks from Russia?"

"All evidence is up in smoke." The corners of Lee's mouth turned up at the Americanism. After spending so much time there lately, it was becoming second nature.

"And the Americans?"

"Drowned. I shoved their car into the river and waited at the water's edge more than ten minutes. Nothing."

Lee pulled a pack of cigarettes from his pocket and tapped the bottom. Remembering his condition, he put them back. "I think you can stop worrying about your leak. I have plugged it."

Chow stood from behind his desk and moved around the massive polished surface to the front. "The Americans are here."

A brief look of panic flashed across Lee's face. *"Impossible. There's no way they could have survived."*

"And yet they did."

"How?" Lee leaned forward in his chair.

Chow lowered himself into the chair next to him. "I have no heart to remove you, Lee. You have been like a son to me."

Lee's head was spinning. How could this be happening? To him, of all people.

"And you a father to me, sir," Lee replied without emotion.

Chow nodded at the truth of Lee's statement. "You have been instrumental in many of our successes. But I have a reputation that is more valuable to me than any one person. And failure, as you know…"

Lee finished his words. "Is never tolerated." Lee looked down at his feet. "I am the one who carried that message to the world for you, sir."

"Yes, I know," whispered Chow.

"And the Americans, they are truly here?"

"Yes," Chow whispered.

Lee nodded slowly, knowing he had no moves left, none he was willing to make. "Sir, if you will permit me one small kindness."

Chow looked at him, despondent.

"I would like to finish what I started. Please let me finish off the Americans. I'll find out what they know, and once that is done, let me be the one to carry out my own punishment."

Chow watched as a single tear wormed its way down Lee's cheek. He could see the truth in his enforcer's words. "So be it," he said, as he slowly stood.

He put his hand on Lee's shoulder for a moment. Then, as in a symbolic emotional severing, wiped his hands clean on his own shirt. From his pocket he handed Lee a small vial of brown liquid. Lee accepted this final gift as tears flowed uncontrollably. Chow turned and walked away, never looking back.

Codi cracked open an eye. Nothing. Darkness, no light whatsoever. She listened for a moment and then sat up, blinking her eyes into focus. She tried calling out in a hoarse whisper. "Joel?"

She listened for a response.

"Hey, Joel?"

She tried to see her environs, but the stygian darkness was void of all light. She used her fingers as probes to tell her the story. There was a small cot with a foam pad about two feet up from a smooth concrete floor. The walls were also made of concrete, as was the ceiling. There was a small sink/toilet combo thingy in the corner that she regretted touching with her hands. A locked steel door set into one wall was the only way out. No light or switch of any kind. She was in some kind of prison and the fact that there were no lights meant it probably wasn't government sponsored. She slumped back on her cot letting her mind drift.

Codi hadn't experienced this kind of darkness since a special forces team building exercise she'd been a part of two years ago. She and three other soldiers had repelled into a reverse funnel-shaped cavern. The instructor cut the ropes they had just come down on and tossed them a half-charged flashlight. He then leaned over the rim and shouted, "You have twenty-four hours to find a way out." He looked down at his watch. "Starting now."

They were a squad of four soldiers: Conrad, Suarez, Codi, and Grimes. Conrad picked up the flashlight and inspected it. It was an old school bulb-style with two D batteries inside. The way back up was impossible, as the cave walls funneled and narrowed towards the top.

Codi began coiling up the two rope ends that had been cut. It looked like they had about ninety feet in total. She threw the coiled rope onto the floor. "Okay," she said. "Everything in a pile. Let's appraise our assets."

Suarez bristled at the thought of taking orders from a woman.

A small pile formed as they emptied pockets. Half-a-pack of Camel unfiltered cigarettes, a lighter, four knives, the flash-light, eighty-six cents, and a pack of Wrigley's gum. All that was left were the clothes on their backs.

"Well, we ain't getting' out that way," Grimes said, looking back up at the afternoon daylight that streamed down from the entrance forty feet up.

Codi looked around the chamber. They were in a lime-stone room about the size of a round convenience store. There were three tunnels that shot off in different directions but no obvious clue as to which one to take.

"*Shh*. Listen," Conrad said.

The squad got quiet and watched as Conrad, a twenty-three-year-old African American, moved from one tunnel entrance to the next, listening. "Nothing," he said.

They huddled back up and made a plan. Conrad, Codi and Suarez would each take a tunnel and go as far as they could, based on the ambient light of the cavern. Grimes would stay put with all the gear and be ready to assist should anyone need it. They would all meet back in ten minutes.

Codi moved down her tunnel slowly, waiting for her eyes to adjust to the near total darkness. She used her hands like sensors, running them along the cave's surface to detect other openings or problems ahead. As long as she kept in touch with the wall she could find her way back. She couldn't help but think she was going to put her hand on a bat or a snake at any second, but fought hard to push that thought from her mind. She slid her feet along the floor, to prevent stepping into a sudden drop-off. Each step thrust her further into the darkening void, heading towards a blackness so dark you couldn't see your hand right in front of your face.

The further she went, the less detail she could see. Finally she reached total darkness. She pushed herself to go just a few more yards before heading back. She relied on her only remaining viable sense, touch. As she pressed around a bend in the ever-shrinking tunnel, she smelled it.

Codi stopped immediately. Her hands had hit something mushy. She held back a horrorstricken expression as she took a quick sniff of the substance on her hands—bat shit, her second-worst nightmare.

"Oh, God," she murmured. It clung to her skin like cement, but worst of all, she could hear the dry rustle of wings and faint sound of echolocation sonar from hundreds of now fully-awake bats.

Codi had no ill feelings towards most creatures, but there were a few that pushed her to the limit of her comfort zone and a few more she had an abject hatred for. Bats were right at the top of that list. She tensed in panic, as hundreds of the furry critters mobilized and took flight, right in her direction.

Their sonar bouncing around the tunnel in a jumble of chaos, like Christmas weekend in Times Square.

Waves of leather wings and claws swooped past her, some hitting her, some getting stuck in her hair. It was a nightmare of epic proportions. She lost contact with the wall and slipped and fell into what could only be described as mushy hell.

The floor was a layer cake of guano, built over time. The cake was topped off with a surface of dripping water, cockroaches, and other bugs feeding on the potent slurry. Before she could find the strength to even panic or scream, the bats had fled. Flapping out the tunnel leaving nothing behind but the stink of fresh excrement. Codi took a slow breath to calm herself, but the ammonia burned her lungs. She waited until her hands stopped shaking and then, with all her will, pushed herself out of the muck and into a sitting position. She could see nothing in any direction. And she was so turned around she had no idea which way was back. This is how people get lost and die in caves, she thought. At least she had a fifty-fifty chance of going in the right direction.

She tried to think, rather than react.

Grimes sucked on a half-finished Camel as one by one the scouts returned. He spit out a bit of tobacco as Suarez settled on the boulder next to him. "Well?" he asked Suarez.

"Nothing but blackness. Let me have a puff."

Grimes flicked the loose ash from his cigarette and passed it to Suarez. He took a deep drag and passed it back.

"Dead end."

Suarez and Grimes looked up as Conrad returned from his exploration.

Conrad looked up at the entrance hole and saw the fading

afternoon light. "Once the sun goes down, we'll never see an exit hole unless we stumble right through it."

Codi stepped into the room. Her odor preceded her. Her face and clothes were smeared with dirt and excrement. Her hair looked like an abandoned birds nest. But the overwhelming odor of ammonia in the room was almost debilitating. "I'm pretty sure I found the way out," she said, "but you're not gonna like it."

The three men shared a disgusted look.

"Lucky for you, I chased off all the bats. Now we just have to wade through a shitload of guano."

Suarez in a slightly panicked look, blurted out, "You're shittin' me, right?"

He realized what he just said and slowly but surely each man started to laugh. Even Codi found the humor in it; her white teeth shining through mud and crap-covered lips.

She led the team back down the tunnel she had explored. They pushed through the guano as best they could, using the dim flashlight to avoid a repeat of her experience. They pressed themselves through several very tight gaps. It only took an hour more before the blackness of their world began to brighten. The squad found a small exit hole about eight feet up on the side of the tunnel. With a little teamwork, they managed to escape their stone prison.

Their instructor was quite surprised at the quickness of their escape. The normal evac time was almost double theirs. He tried to hold an AAR, (After Action Report), but the smell of crap coming off the squad was so strong, his eyes burned. He finally dismissed them to the showers, and he wasn't far behind.

Joel felt like he was drifting in a lifeboat at sea. He had a burning desire to drink ocean water. He thought he must be lost at sea, and found himself saying, "Don't drink the salt water!" His eyes slowly fluttered open, and the reality of his situation began to be clear. A very different story unfolded. He remembered being gassed in the little room at the airport. Drugs explained the rocking sensation he was experiencing. He tried to move his mouth, but he was so dehydrated he had difficulty opening it. *I've been drugged!* It was a thought he shouted without words. That would explain the weird dream, he thought as his mind slowly cleared.

He was in a small industrial space. There was a glow of artificial light through the bottom of a rusty metal door. The floor was cement with a drain in the center. When he sat up his head swirled and his body rocked like a punching balloon clown. The aroma of chemicals and a recently emptied mop rack told him where he was. There was an old metal cabinet on one wall. He used the handles to help himself stand. The world spun again. He held tight to the cabinet for stability. Finally he spread his legs so he could stand on his own. The cabinet was locked, as was the exit door. He was a prisoner in a broom closet.

Chow and Jin exited the armored door to the Red Baks facility. Chow looked back at his two security guards, and said, "Make sure no one comes or leaves before I get back." He looked at the gold Audemars Piguet Royal Oak on his wrist. "I'm guessing by three tomorrow afternoon. Until then, we are on lockdown."

"Yes, sir." The guards responded.

Chow and Jin left. The guards closed the heavy exit door behind them. It clanged shut with an ominous thud. Chow led the way up to the street through the secret entrance and into a powder blue Bentley waiting curbside. They made good time to the private terminal of the airport. From there it was a three-and-a-half-hour flight to Beijing, followed by one of the most important meetings of General Chow's life.

It seemed like morning, though Codi couldn't be sure. What she was sure of was that something very bright was literally burning out her retinas through eyelids that were slammed shut. Hands grabbed her and quickly subdued her with handcuffs and ankle chains. She was dragged along a straight hallway and then deposited into a room with two metal chairs and an even brighter light. She was cuffed, both hands and legs, to a chair and left smoldering in the powerful spotlight. After what seemed like an eternity her eyes adjusted to the glare. Two days without light, food, or water had left her a little off her game. She glanced down and saw that her chair was bolted to the floor. She tried to focus her mind, but a raging headache fought back. All she could think about was how thirsty she was. Definitely off her game.

Joel lay on the floor peeking through the rusted gap on the bottom of his exit door. He had a weird bugs-eye view of a hallway on the other side. He could see beige carpet. Two steel doors were across the hallway, and a large dust bunny sat right in front of him. Joel suddenly heard a familiar voice with a few choice words coming from his emotionally-charged partner from down the hall. He shoved his left eye up close to see what he could.

Two men carried a struggling Codi past his door. He was pretty sure calling out would get them nowhere. Instead, he watched to see where they were taking her. Three doors down on the left. He sat up. He had to do something.

He stood back up and approached the locked steel cabinet. Had they emptied it or just locked it before he was stashed here. Joel found it hard to think as his brain struggled with severe dehydration. He tried the handles again. Nothing. He tried kicking at the handles. Again, nothing.

13

Washington D.C. – 9:24 a.m. – FBI Field Office – Special Projects – 3rd Floor

Brian called both Codi and Joel's cell for the fifth time and still got no answer. He hung up and drummed his fingers on his desk as he stared off into space, thinking. Was their burner phone not able to take incoming international calls? That seemed unlikely. And in light of what had happened in Russia, something was off. The FBI had protocol in place for a missing agent, but he wasn't sure they were actually missing. He had received a text from Codi before they left Russia, requesting time off when she got back to tie up some personal issues. He was glad to give it to her, but he thought she would at least check in before leaving. What was most troublesome however, was Joel. He was supposed to meet with counter intelligence and download everything.

Brian was hoping he could close out this last case so he could get started on the next one. Codi could be read in on the case once she got back. Joel was so punctual he'd be on time for his own funeral. Something was wrong. He could feel it.

By Tuesday, Brian had taken action. He engaged a task

force to find them—two agents from the regular FBI and one of his special projects agents. He set them up in a bullpen across from his office, requesting frequent updates on their progress. He made sure they were briefed on everything he knew. Something had happened to his two agents and he wanted the team scouring every lead, including searching their apartments for clues.

After at least an hour of waiting while tied to a chair, Codi slumped to the side. Her hair hung in a messy tangle and her eyes looked sunken. She had been dressed in a gray jumpsuit with a zipper down the front. A slight clicking sound signaled the opening of the door. She tilted her head up. There was a wheezing sound as the other metal chair was dragged slowly across the concrete floor and placed just behind the light, out of Codi's sight. Someone sat in the chair and continued with his noisy breathing, each breath making that wheezing sound. No words or actions, just that sound, in and out—the breathing of the damned.

Finally the man spoke. "Collette Sanders, you have been found guilty of espionage and murder. Both of these are executable offenses."

He had a slight Chinese accent. Codi gave him her best devil-may-care glare. She knew there was nothing to be gained by speaking. This was a classic lose/lose situation and she was the loser.

Lee sat there staring at the impossible sight. The woman was still alive. He had seen her go down with the car and never come up. Quite incredible, he thought.

He played with his yepian, rolling it in his fingers. It was a weapon that he had personally created and named; it meant leaf blade. It was a small, four-foot bamboo rod not much bigger in diameter than a pencil. Attached to the end was a small but very sharp perpendicular two-inch blade. The thin bamboo could be flicked like a whip, and he had become very accurate in its use. Cutting and slicing with the precision of a surgeon. He had once kept a man alive for two days as he slowly whittled him away piece by piece. He remembered how much pleasure it had given him.

"My name is Lee. You are mine to do with as I please, but I will know a few things before I am finished with you."

This just got friggn' real, Codi thought.

"But first let's have some fun."

Lee reached with the Yepian and slowly moved the blade along Codi's arm, touching it just enough to scratch a thin line of blood and nothing more. Codi watched helplessly as the curious weapon dug a small groove in her arm. She was bound tight and no matter how hard she fought she was unable to move any more than a slight lean. Lee moved the blade up to her eye and closed the distance to less than a millimeter, the point so close her eyes could not focus on the blade's edge.

She stiffened in fear as her assailant moved the sharpened blade surprisingly fast right next to her right eye. She dared not move for fear of losing her eye. Sweat started to drip from her already dehydrated cells.

The man spoke again. "How did you escape the car crash in the river?"

Codi remained unmoved.

With a whip-like motion, Lee flicked the yepian in an arc and down.

Faster than Codi's eye could register, the blade imbedded itself into her right forearm. It flicked away just as fast, leaving behind a hole and a growing trail of blood.

"You dick!" she yelled at him.

"Tell me what I want to know!"

"Screw you!" This psycho would get nothing from her.

Lee's lips danced with a smile. This would be his final chapter, but he could see this woman was going to make it very worthwhile. Perhaps he would take her up on her of-fer— screw you. The two of them could go out with a bang. Surely Chow wouldn't care if he had his way with her before completing the mission. She was not ugly, quite the contrary. This woman was lean, athletic, with strong cheekbones and a seductive figure. She had brown eyes with flecks of gold in the irises if he was not mistaken. Yes, this would be a pleasure for both of them.

He flipped out the yepian again and it snapped the zipper on the front of her overalls. Then another, and another, until the front of the jumpsuit was shredded, revealing a flat stom-ach and a pink bra.

Codi wriggled in the chair but the restraints held firm. Panic started to lay claim. She tried to force her mind to calm against the rising surge.

Beijing, which means northern capital, is one of China's most modern cities. It is home to twenty-one million people, mak-ing it the third most populous city in the world.

General Chow Phun and his top hacker, a young man who went only by the man of Jin, crossed Tiananmen Square. It was filled with a mix of working professionals and tourists as the early sunlight glinted off the morning frost. The sky was transitioning from orange to blue as they passed the guards that protected Chairman Mao's tomb. Chow gave the tomb a furtive glance. It was a layered building with multiple columns across its entrance. China, Mao's China and true communism, were in the past. Chow knew that for a fact. But there was no reason that they couldn't rebuild a better, stronger, and more feared China. A China that could take her growing capitalism and strong nationalism, along with Chow's superior technology, and grow it into the one-and-only world superpower. And that is why Chow and Jin were there today. To help start China down a path that would soon have every other nation in the world living in fear.

But that could only happen if everything went perfect. Chow had finally achieved the success he had been striving for and he was eager to share it. He was sure he had politically lubricated the right men. But politicians were a fickle lot. They could only be trusted to serve their own self-interests.

Jin almost stopped as they passed the location where Mao's tanks had infamously stopped for a single protester, a single citizen who thought he might hold back the power of the state. He had been a fool. Nothing marked the man's act. No one knew whom he was or if he was even still living. It was a moment that lived only in memories.

At the far end of the square stood a gigantic building. Chow and Jin climbed the wide band of triple-tiered steps that passed through looming marble pillars. This was the Great Hall of the People. It was over a thousand feet in width and six-hundred feet from front to back, making it larger than any capital building the west had to offer. Chow was dressed in a fine hand-tailored suit made by a friend in Hong Kong. Jin wore a white turtleneck under a two-piece tweed suit. Their polished shoes clicked in unison on the marble floor as they entered the lobby. Once through security, they would take one of the many red carpet runners that led to the executive elevators.

"Let me do most of the talking," Chow said. "If they have any technical questions, you handle that."

Jin nodded. It was show time.

Agent Tony Kwuo and Chelsea Keener of the recently formed FBI task force had made themselves comfortable in the bull-pen. Each had established a work area and was busy on their phones and computers finding and following leads. Special Agent Gordon Reyas had moved all of his equipment down from his cubicle to join them. The room had a small round table in the middle surrounded by metal chairs and a row of tables with office chairs along two walls. The front was all glass and the people who worked there had nicknamed it The Fishbowl. It was bare bones and there was no place to hide, but as a work environment it was functional.

Gordon had acquired the last known footage of Codi and Joel as they were processed through customs on their return trip from China at the Ronald Reagan Airport in DC. He brought it up on the big screen mounted on the wall. The image angle was dodgy, as it was slightly from behind, but you could see a tall and lanky man in a tracksuit and a lithe brunette in black slacks and a white blouse.

"There they are." Tony pointed them out.

"What is he wearing?" Chelsea leaned in to take a closer look.

"Russian gangster chic," Tony said.

"Are his tennis shoes *gold?*" she asked.

"That's the fashion of a case gone bad, or a lot of drinking on the job," Brian said. "Okay, so they landed here in DC, and then what?"

"Customs said they cleared at 3:27 p.m.," Tony said.

"That matches the time stamp on the video as well," Chelsea said.

"See if you can get any hits on a camera outside the air-port," Brian said. "Maybe we can piece a trail together."

Tony started hammering on his keyboard. "Ok, give me some time."

The three agents worked to piece together a clearer picture of where Joel and Codi went after arriving in DC. Delivery pizza arrived and went cold; most of it lay forgotten on the table.

Joel mechanically kicked at the steel cabinet with his left foot. His right foot had gone numb about twenty minutes ago. He was making little progress, but knew they were in a desperate situation. His mind seemed to go in and out of focus as his body fought the lack of fluids in his system. He stopped briefly and leaned his head against the cabinet staring down at his beleaguered feet. He had reached the end, and there was no going forward. His vision was blurring in and out and he was sure he now had three feet, no, make that four. As he looked closer, he realized it wasn't a foot but one of the cabinet handles. He had succeeded in knocking one off. He dropped to his knees and held the chrome piece of metal in his hands. It took a full minute for him to realize its significance. He shook his head and reached up and pulled at the other twisted handle. The doors popped opened.

He stood motionless in shock. A distant scream, muffled through the door, penetrated his brain fog. *Codi!* She was in danger.

Joel stood back and surveyed his smorgasbord. Every shelf was full. The top shelf had medical supplies, including a six-pack of 200 ml Nongfu spring water. He immediately guzzled two bottles and felt as if the world just might continue to rotate. The second shelf had cleaning supplies, like bleach and soap. There were a few odds and ends like aluminum foil and clothespins, and in the back corner was a butter knife. The bottom shelf had paper products like toilet paper and paper towels. Joel mentally dug through his newfound inventory and came up blank.

He sat back on the floor and tried to noodle a solution as he sipped on his third water bottle. He could start a fire possibly but that would just bring the bad guys to him. A chemical concoction of some sort, again, would just affect him unless he could get it out into the hallway somehow. But the effects would be limited at best. He forced himself to focus.

"Come on Joel, you got this," he told himself.

Then, all those nights of watching random YouTube videos clicked. *Thermite.* You could make thermite out of aluminum foil and iron oxide—rust. He'd seen it done. It melted right through steel plate.

He grabbed the roll of aluminum foil and the butter knife. He then began to scrape the rust from the bottom of the door and from a spot just inside the cabinet. He wasn't sure of the proportions needed but felt reasonably sure it was something like three-to-one. His confidence grew as a small pile of rust amassed on the foil. He laid the foil flat on the floor and spread the rust evenly across it. He began folding the foil on top of itself in one-inch-wide strips. He then smashed it and folded it until he had a band about the size of a school ruler. He used the butter knife to cut it in two and then proceeded to wrap the exit door's two steel hinges with the combo. Now he just needed to find an igniter. Joel searched through the cabinet again.

"Seriously?" He came up short and collapsed back down in bitter disappointment.

Codi did her best to stay defiant, but the reality of her situation was bleak. Her clothes were shredded and her underwear clung in place by a thread. Both her arms were bleeding as was a spot on her left cheek. But the cut that worried her most was the side of her neck. She could feel the warm blood running down her neck and with it, the last of her energy. She prayed that her jugular had not been pierced.

She decided to take another tack. "I'm sure you're aware that I am not a spy but a duly appointed federal agent for the United States government."

The words came slowly to her, as severe dehydration, blood loss and intense stress combined together. She concentrated with all her capacity. "I am in the act of closing out a cold case and there is no information I have that I can't share."

The silence after her speech made Codi think he had not heard her. She decided to call it out louder, but before she could, the man spoke.

"But how did you escape the car crash?" he asked.

"That's the bug up your ass?"

She told her torturer how she and Joel had escaped, how they had used the trapped air in the rental car's curved roof and then swam underwater to the far side of the passing barge. The man seemed to hesitate as silence filled the room.

"What do you know of Operation Blind Pig," he asked, "and who else knows of it?"

Codi looked up slowly and deliberately. "Everything. It is being declassified as we speak. Check the Internet and see for yourself. The conspiracy nuts are having a field day with it already."

"Liar!"

A sudden excruciating pain followed as the Yepian tore a chunk out of her thigh.

Codi had played her last hand and it had been for naught.

Her head dropped in despair. Now all she had left was hope. A thin chance, at best.

The carved rosewood walls were just visible through the smoke-filled haze in the room. General Chow Phun and Jin took their appointed seats, and the meeting began. The round conference room was purposefully set in the center of the capital, and was shielded by a barrier wall that prevented eavesdropping. There was a series of high-tech screens along one wall with a control station attached to it. Sitting at the large circular table in the middle of the room were eight of China's junior elite assistants. Not quite the power brokers Chow had hoped for. But they were all looking for a path up the ladder. Maybe Chow could provide them one, or at the very least, get them to pass his message up the chain of command.

After brief introductions, Chow began. He told them of a Russian operation from the fifties that had developed a technology they called CCI that could blind the enemy to approaching bombers. Jin explained that they had used an electrical leach planted in the enemy's radar installations. The leach would filter out a very specific frequency from all others. The radar system would appear to work as normal and any regular incoming aircraft would be identified and tracked. But if a bomber were adapted with hardware to transmit this specific frequency, it would be invisible to their radar.

Chow then told them how they had stolen the Russian technology and the scientists behind it in a clever twist that the Russians never thought possible. For a while, China had the ability to breach any major government's airspace.

Chow looked around the room as he spoke. The men seemed interested in his story, but like any good up-and-coming politician or poker player, they looked unfazed.

The man from the Central Secretariat said, "Chow, who cares? This was so many years ago. Why do you waste our time with a history lesson?"

The man from the State Council agreed and soon others

joined in. Chow motioned with his arms for patience. "Please, just hear us out. It will all make sense momentarily, I promise."

Chow continued. "We have modernized this technology."

This statement seemed to dull the murmur. "I now have..." He let that statement hang in the air for just a moment. "We now have the ability to send a missile right into Washington DC without them being able to see it, or detect it. In fact, the first they will know of it is when they hear it screeching down on their heads."

The room went silent. Even the hanging cigarette fog seamed to clear.

"Jin." Chow prodded him to take them through the basics.

"That's right," Jin said. "We have implanted a transparent code within NORAD that will make everything seem to work as usual, except it will be blind to one very specific frequency. And if we broadcast this frequency from, say, a missile as it cruises, that missile will effectively be invisible to their detection equipment."

Jin interlocked his fingers and sat back down, satisfied with his simple and direct explanation.

That started a choir of voices, all clambering to be heard, some very excited, some very fearful.

"China is not at war with the US."

"We depend on them for a large part of our GNP."

Chow had expected this. He adjusted his suit and stood for emphasis. "That kind of thinking has made us weak." Some spittle flew from his rubbery lips as he spoke. "We used to be powerful and feared. Now we make toys and TV's, and we panic when sales drop."

The room quieted, as no one knew what to say.

"Perhaps if you would authorize a test," Chow said. "Say, a medium-sized rocket, no bomb, just a rocket, launched into America's heartland and left for them to see our ability. They would know that they couldn't stop us from doing it for real. Now, imagine the next time you go the bargaining table. What would the war-fearing Americans do? They would think twice before taking Japan's or South Korea's side in a trade dispute, that's for sure. We would call the shots for a change. We would dominate the east *and* the west, as others lived in fear, fear of the great red dragon. I implore you to talk with your superiors to help them understand. We would be happy to give them a test of the technology."

An argument flared between members of his audience again. With that, Chow gave a slight bow and said, "I await your decision."

He and Jin exited the room amid a parade of petty arguments, each underling opinionated but essentially powerless.

14

Washington D.C. – 4:32 p.m. – FBI Field Office – Special Projects – Fish Bowl

"Cab!" Gordon called out.

The other two agents turned.

"Got Joel entering a cab." Gordon cast the image up to the big screen.

Tony stepped closer for a better look at the man entering a cab. "Weird," he said. "It's like he's aware of the cameras. We keep getting these glancing views from him."

Chelsea asked, "Where's that cab off to?"

"I'll contact the company and see if they have a record."

Throughout what was left of the day, they followed the trail, slowly piecing it together.

"Got him!" Gordon pointed to an image of Joel exiting the cab and, finally, it was a straight-on view that he'd acquired from an ATM camera just ten feet away. "He's coming out of the cab on Dalworth Street."

"Who the hell is that?"

The three agents turned to see Special Agent in Charge Brian Fescue standing behind them. They looked back to the screen.

"Increase the resolution, Gordon," Tony requested.

They all moved closer to the screen as Gordon fulfilled the demand.

A better quality picture appeared. It was not Joel. It was someone who looked like him, but it was not him. Four mouths sagged in unison.

Joel looked at the slice on his thumb. It was still seeping blood. He had sliced it open on the rusty bottom of the door while scrapping it. Initially, the cut had been a minor nuisance, but now it was beginning to throb. Maybe tetanus from the rusty edge, he thought, worried. He grabbed a first aid kit from the cabinet. He popped it open. Inside was an impressive collection. He found a Band-Aid and some antiseptic. Luckily, most items were labeled in both English and Chinese. He picked through the kit and lifted a small jar of glycerin. Its high viscosity made it move like syrup in the glass container. It was an emollient used to treat skin irritations.

Gaping at the slow moving fluid, a memory kicked in. He dug through the kit until he found what he was looking for—Potassium Permanganate, used as an antifungal. He had his igniter. He had seen an exothermic reaction take place when it was mixed with glycerin. *Thank you, YouTube!*

Joel placed the dark purple crystals in a bowl shape he formed from the foil, on top of each hinge. He then retrieved the glycerin bottle. He held his breath as he poured about one teaspoon of the viscous liquid over each pile of the Potassium Permanganate. Almost immediately there was a reaction. First smoke, then flames. The exothermic reaction was hot enough to ignite the homemade thermite. The thermite, once ignited, burned at just over four-thousand degrees, melting the hinges like they were butter.

Smoke filled the small space, and shards of liquid metal fountained out from the conflagration.

Joel took cover in the corner until the thermite completed its mission. He then kicked at the melted hinges and the door gave way. He was free.

Smoke started to fill the hallway. Time was limited. Someone would soon notice.

Chow and Jin had been quiet for most of the trip back to Hong Kong. As the G550 flared and lowered its flaps on approach to Shek Kong Airfield, Jin could feel his boss's gears turning. The man was a genius and never suffered fools.

Chow was disgusted by how the meeting had gone. Friends that had been loyal to him during his stint in the military seemed to shun him lately. Was it his age or the disease that left him looking like a severe stroke victim? He might never know. But as of today he needed to take the reins. It was time for his plans to be unleashed, and he knew exactly what to do.

"Our country's youth." He shook his head with antipathy.

Jin looked over as his boss dabbed at his chin.

"They speak boldly but have no spine when it comes to action. I fear that smart phones and memory-foam mattresses have made them soft and lazy."

Jin slid his smart phone out of sight.

Chow sighed softly as he put on his seatbelt for landing. He looked over at Jin with a fire burning in his eyes. "This was unfortunate, but not entirely unexpected. It is time to take matters into our own hands, Jin."

Jin nodded. He feared for those whom his boss's wrath was now focused on. The jet bobbled in the air and the wheels locked in place. Jin turned and looked out the window at the fast approaching runway, unsure what would come next.

Joel ran down to the door he'd seen them drag Codi through. He carefully turned the knob. He slipped in and, completely silent, closed the door behind him. He gripped the butter knife so hard he was losing feeling in his trembling fingers.

A few feet in front of him was a tall lanky bald man sitting in a chair facing Codi. There was a large bright spotlight illuminating her bloody and battered condition. The man was whipping a bamboo-looking pole at Codi, while he degraded her verbally, telling her what he was about to do to her and how she was powerless to stop him. The jumpsuit she was wearing had been shredded, and her bra was held together by a thread.

For probably the first time in his life, Joel didn't hesitate. He moved silently towards the man and jabbed the dull knife into the side of his neck with all his might. The man spun on Joel faster than Joel could have imagined with a look of surprise and anger. But somehow, Joel brought down both his fists in a sweeping tomahawk motion and dropped the man to the floor. He was out cold.

He dug through the man's pockets and fished out a set of keys to the handcuffs, a cellphone, and a handgun that was holstered in the back of the man's pants. He quickly released Codi and helped her to stand.

"We've got to get out of here now."

A confused Codi looked up to the man standing next to her. "Joel?"

Joel could see she was in a bad way. He sat her back in the chair and ran, calling over his shoulder, "Wait here."

He dashed to the storage room and grabbed the first aid kit and the remaining waters. He dashed back down the hall, as the fire alarm initiated a soft beeping. Codi had staggered out of the room and was leaning against the doorjamb, holding a bamboo rod. On closer inspection, he could see a blade was attached to the end of the pole. *WTF?*

He grabbed Codi's arm and the two moved along the hallway to a door down the hall. He pointed the confiscated pistol and pushed the door open.

It was a server room. A small console was manned by a young man with heavy black-framed glasses. He had started to go bald prematurely and had embraced the comb-over. Joel pointed his gun at the man and gestured for him to get on the floor. The timid man obeyed with a wild look of fear, not fully understanding the words coming from Joel's mouth. Joel grabbed Codi and pulled her inside. He kept an eye on the man while he had Codi drink as much water as she could. He quickly wrapped her neck wound and all of the deeper cuts. She had lost some blood and was going into shock, but otherwise she was in fair condition.

It was amazing what water can do under the right conditions. After finishing her second bottle, Codi looked right in Joel's eyes and said, "Thanks."

He nodded in his classic self-deprecating way but he was so glad to see her.

"So, how did you escape?" Codi asked in a raspy voice.

"Never lock a YouTuber in a supply closet—too many possibilities."

Codi raised one eyebrow at Joel, who tried to be tough and stoic, but the corners of his mouth betrayed him.

"You okay?" Codi asked.

"Yeah, I just sliced my thumb, trying to..." He realized the stupidity of his statement and stopped mid-sentence. "I'm good."

"So what's next?"

He checked the clip of his stolen pistol. Full. "We reach out and try to touch someone."

Codi pointed her bamboo weapon to the man on the ground and pantomimed taking off his pants. He looked more scared of Codi's weapon than he was of Joel's gun. He tossed his pants to Codi. She put them on and quickly tied what was left of her coveralls into a fashion-statement blouse only a Parisian could love.

The Fishbowl was silent as the four agents tried to process their failure. Codi and Joel had simply disappeared, and in this modern world of surveillance, that was nearly impossible.

"Okay let's try this again," Brian said. Something was not right and things were now getting very serious. Where and what had happened to his two agents?

"Go back to the beginning," he said. "Recheck everything, starting with them leaving Moscow. I want to know if this is the man who cleared customs as Special Agent Joel Strickman or did we screw the pooch trying to track him."

Three heads nodded.

"For all we know, they could be in serious harm's way. So let's get to it now, people."

Gordon turned back to his console, typing furiously.

Brian left The Fishbowl, his mind swirling.

Lee opened his eyes to a throbbing at the back of his skull. He sat up, and a shooting pain in his neck added to that pain. He reached up and found the handle of some sort of table knife protruding from his neck. He yanked it out without a second thought. Blood poured from the wound, but he could tell nothing vital had been severed. His fingers moved over his front pocket and found that the poison vial given to him by Chow had broken with his fall. He processed this fact for a moment and then came to a conclusion. He no longer had the luxury of an honorable death. Chow would have to wait.

It was time to clean up a mess, time for vengeance. He would sweep the world of these two Americans, but not before they groveled and pleaded for death.

He stood with effort and staggered out the door. Smoke and a fire alarm filled the hall. He reached for his gun, gone; his cell phone, also missing. He turned and moved quickly towards security, blood leaking down his neck onto his shirt. Time to take control of the Red Baks.

Joel, hoping to get a message out, looked at the keyboard covered with Chinese characters. It was an impossible task. He closed his eyes and typed regularly as if he had an English keyboard. The words on the screen were gibberish. He looked over to Codi with a shake of his head.

Codi held up the stolen phone to make her point. "No cell service here either."

"Yeah, wherever *here* is."

"I guess it's time for Plan C," she said.

"I didn't know we had a plan A."

"Trust me, there's always a plan A."

"So what's plan C?"

"I say we burn this place to the ground."

Codi held up a lighter she had taken from their prisoner. Joel couldn't agree more. He worked quickly to take down the server. He yanked wires and pulled and smashed equipment. Codi collected as much flammable material as possible and put it in a pile. She took a moment to break the bamboo weapon she had been tortured with and laid it on top. She removed the blade and put it in her pocket. The water she drank was starting to work through her system; even her brain was firing again.

She kept an eye on the IT man they were guarding and

noticed that he had peed himself out of fear. She was happy to have copped his pants before that happened. She almost found herself feeling sorry for him, but after her last forty-eight hours, her compassion was on empty.

Codi did a quick check of the room for any possible assets but found nothing useful. She opened a small closet door and noticed, thanks to a bilingual sign, the fire control shut-off valve. She quickly spun the valve closed. They started a fire and escorted the IT man out of the room in front of them.

Using the IT man as a human shield, the two agents moved down the hallway at a brisk pace. The smoke from Joel's earlier experiment had mostly dissipated, but a black, tar-like, toxic cloud from the fire Codi had started billowed out from behind them.

Codi suddenly stopped. The door next to her had a lightning bolt symbol on it along with some unreadable Chinese characters. She tried the handle but it was locked. It took Joel two bullets to change that. She wasted no time pulling all the breaker levers down and shutting off all power to the building. The fire alarm turned off and the battery backup lights flickered to life through the sudden darkness, doing a poor job of illuminating a small area every twenty feet with a pale red glow.

The security station was at the end of the first floor hallway. It led into the only exit tunnel. The sealed armored door could only be unlocked from the inside and was secured with both electronic and manual dead bolts. There was a small station for the guards to work from and an airport-style screener to process employees, both coming and going. The two security guards looked spooked. They had been tasked with keeping the place locked down, but the fire alarm and faint smell of smoke had them on edge. Then a complete power outage killed the electronic locks on the door and left the area in partial darkness.

They were ready to shoot at shadows when Lee ran up to them and assuaged their fears. No one had come or gone since the boss had left—good.

"Sir, you are bleeding," one of the guards said.

"Get me a bandage," Lee snapped with a wheeze.

The guard attended to Lee's neck wound, while Lee armed himself.

"Come with me," Lee told one of the guards, and they started back into the heart of the facility. They would clear it one room at a time until he had his prisoners back.

A sudden flow of humanity heading towards the exit forced them back to the security station. Lee held his AK-74 into the air and shouted, "The next person to take a step forward will be shot."

The mob stopped in their tracks.

Codi was hoping that between the fire and the power outage the workers would evacuate the building so she and Joel could slip out unnoticed in the confusion. As employees started to head for the exits, it looked like her plan might be working. They had released their captive and he had scampered off with the escaping hoard, like panicked rats before flames. Codi and Joel followed. The hallway split into four directions like an intersection. The two agents watched as the evacuees turned down one direction—the exit. They discreetly followed a group up two flights of stairs and down a short hallway that split to the right.

Codi stopped dead in her tracks at the sight ahead.

A mob of about thirty employees was yelling at three

heavily armed men that were preventing them from leaving. Codi and Joel moved back and peeked around the corner. There was shouting and yelling. But the image was clear to Codi. The place was locked down and no one was getting out. She could just glimpse the man who had nearly gotten the best of her. He was armed, standing with the guards and shouting something at the employees. She fought back the urge to charge directly at him and take her revenge. Another place, another time, but soon.

She spun back to Joel and whispered, "The guards look a little busy. Time to take things up a notch. Come on."

Codi pulled Joel with her as they set about igniting more fires throughout the facility. The area was filling with toxic fumes and smoke. She improvised two wet towels she'd found into rudimentary gas masks. They stayed low as they moved, just to be safe. Smoke inhalation was no joke, it killed long before flames did.

With hurried caution, she popped open a door that led into a large room filled with cubicle offices. The room was empty save a larger glass-enclosed room on the left. Inside, an old man with a short bowl cut looked up from a desk. He pushed up his thick black glasses on his nose as he took in the new arrivals. He hurriedly kept typing on his computer. The man was not Chinese, but rather had more of an Eastern European look to him, and he looked to be well into his eighties. Codi moved quickly through his open office door. He looked down at the gun in Joel's hand and dropped to his knees, almost crying, and blubbering in Russian.

Codi and Joel did not respond.

He tried again in rough English. "Please help me." That, they understood.

"I am Doctor Shura Mosin from the Russian science and

technical division," he said. "I have been kept here many years against my will. Please take me with you. I beg you."

Joel held the gun on him while Codi did a quick frisk.

"He's clean."

She grabbed him by the arm and helped him to his feet.

"How do we get out of here and where is here?"

"There is only one exit. You are in China." He looked perplexed. "How is it you do not know this?"

"Up until ten minutes ago we were prisoners as well," Codi said. "Come on, Doc, let's get out of this dump." She gestured for the man to follow.

Shura looked back at his screen. He seemed pleased that whatever he was doing on his computer was completed. He followed Joel and Codi as they continued lighting fires. They led the doctor out of the room as flames billowed behind them. The hallway was empty, but a layer of smoke was growing by the second.

Lee had the crowd starting to calm down. The fire alarm had stopped and the emergency lights were doing their job. The problem was the smoke. It was getting worse. They had no choice but to evacuate. The question was how Lee was going to do it so that he could get the employees out, lock the place back up, and hunt them down. He took the exit key and moved towards the heavy door, instructing the frightened employees on how he would allow them to leave—one by one.

Shura looked over Codi's shoulder at the heavily compacted crowd gathered at the exit door and spilling into the hallway.

"Joel, gun," she hissed.

He tossed it to her, and she handed him her knife.

"Find something to get this crowd moving faster. Doc, see if you can help him."

Joel and Shura Mosin ran off, while Codi kept watch on the exit hallway.

In the bathroom down the hall, Joel found a steel soap canister and yanked it off the wall. He handed it to the doctor and told him to empty it out.

The doctor poured the powdered soap on the floor and then held the canister while Joel refilled it with his remaining Potassium Permanganate and a wad of paper towels.

"Here hold this." Joel handed the canister to Shura and fished the glycerin bottle from his pocket. He set it on the sink. He took the small blade from the stick weapon Codi had given him and poked a few small slits in the canister. He handed Shura his knife as he grabbed the canister and turned to reach for the glycerin on the sink.

"Hold it right there, doctor!"

Joel looked back in shock to see Shura frozen, ready to stab him in the back. Codi was standing in the doorway pointing the pistol at him.

"Thought you might try something," she said to the doctor. "Now put the knife down very slowly."

Shura lowered his hands and started to place the knife on the floor.

"You will never get out of here alive," Shura said with a sudden new-found strength. He spun, unexpectedly flinging the blade at Codi while diving to the left. She never took her eyes off him. She didn't hesitate, and pulled the trigger while feinting to the left to avoid the flying blade. The bullet punched through Shura's C5 cervical vertebra, knocking him to the ground. His black glasses skittered across the floor. Codi stood over her him, gun raised.

Joel had frozen at the sudden noise of gunshot in the bathroom. The cordite stung his eyes and his ears were ringing. He blinked the abrupt tears away and tried to take in what had just happened. Codi bent down to Shura and inspected his wound. He was paralyzed from the neck down.

"Looks like you were only half right doctor. *You* are the one never getting out of here alive."

Shura's eyes bulged. He desperately tried to speak, but only his mind, heart, and lungs were functioning. He could hear and see, but nothing more.

"What, no witty reply? Shame."

Joel finally found his voice. "How…how did you know?"

"Didn't. Just wasn't taking any chances. Now, are you ready with your little toy there?"

Joel looked at the canister in his hands. "I think I can cause enough of a panic to get us out of here. Come on."

Codi knelt down next to Shura. She placed the glasses back on his face. "Wouldn't want you to miss the end."

Doctor Shura Mosin watched with tilted strained eyes as the two left him behind.

Once back at the corner, Joel poured the glycerin into the container and quickly replaced the lid. The exothermic reaction spewed flames and smoke at a high velocity out the slits and seams of the canister making a loud fizzing sound. He rolled it down the hallway to the now partially subdued group that was starting to exit one at a time under Lee's watchful eyes.

Fearing it was a bomb, the panic level spiked to an instant ten. The fear of being blown up quickly overcame the fear of being shot. Like frightened lemmings, the hoard pushed for the doorway, shouting. Shots were fired but there was no stopping them now. Codi and Joel pressed into the crowd, flowing with them. There were shrieks from the wounded and then screams from the guards as the tables turned. Bodies flowed like a raging river out the exit door, chased by smoke and heat as the Red Baks slowly died behind them.

Codi and Joel shoved through and over a pile of bodies as they pressed through the passage. She could see a tunnel ahead. A thin veil of hope began to surge.

15

Washington D.C. – 4:32 p.m. – FBI Field Office – Special Projects – 3rd Floor

The phone on SSA Brian Fescue's desk rang. He grabbed it without looking. "Fescue."

Brian's eyes practically popped out of his head when he recognized the voice on the other end. "Codi, Joel? Where the hell are you two?"

"Our best guess is somewhere in Hong Kong." Joel's voice sounded flat and digital.

"China? How are you in China?"

They started to debrief him on everything that had happened, when he said, "Hang on a sec."

Brian dashed over to The Fishbowl and put the call on speaker. "Okay, go ahead."

Codi and Joel went through their harrowing last few days. As Brian listened to the unbelievable story, a giant weight was lifted from his shoulders. His agents were okay. Battered and bruised, but okay.

Once finished, Codi and Joel signed off with the promise to check back in after they ditched their stolen cellphone for fear of being tracked, and got another one.

It was time to bring his people back and work this case from the safety of the USA. Brian punched for a new line and dialed up his friend at counter intelligence by memory. He had his friend's team arrange for the American embassy to send a man with a valid government credit card and new phones to meet Codi and Joel. He was to stay by their side until they were delivered to safety.

For Codi and Joel, it was time to do some shopping—food, clothes, and a shower, all on the FBI's dime.

Brian hung up and turned to look at his team. They had been searching the D.C. area without much luck and he'd been worried sick. But worst of all, they hadn't even been close to the truth. Something much bigger than they could have imagined was in play, and he was going to get to the bottom of it. He turned to the two temporarily assigned agents.

"Looks like you can pack up now that our agents are found. I want to thank you for your assistance."

Special Agent Tony Kwuo and Chelsea Keener nodded as they shook his hand.

"Glad things worked out," they said. They turned and started packing up their things.

"Gordon," Brian said, "I want to see you in my office when you have a sec."

The last thing Lee remembered was a mass of humanity mashing its way past him. He had opened the exit door to allow an orderly evac of the premises, but the crowd had suddenly rabbited. He remembered shooting a couple of runners, and then there was a blinding flash as something shoved him into the metal doorframe. He untangled himself from two corpses and stood.

With his head already compromised from being

cold-cocked earlier, he felt groggier than he should. Plus, his neck was throbbing. First his side, now his neck. The smoke was thick and caustic. Lee knew he would not last long in these conditions. He closed the large metal door behind him and stayed low as he staggered down the exit tunnel. There was a rumbling sound. The infrastructure of the facility started to compromise. He had escaped just in time.

Inside the bathroom on the first floor, Shura Mosin was right where he'd been left. An old, wounded man who could do no more than watch, as tons of concrete and rebar gave way making a direct path for his skull. He thought of his homeland, the one he had betrayed, and then he thought of nothing ever again.

Lee gasped at the fresh air of the city as he stepped into the street. A giant dust cloud followed the collapse of Red Baks, sending pedestrians running and screaming. He was now a man without home or country. It was time to access his old underground contacts and call in a few markers. He had but one desire in his blackened heart—to find and execute the two American agents.

The nine-story glass and steel police station was laid out like any other. An entrance that controlled the flow in and out, restricted access to the main offices, with holding cells and interrogation rooms in the back. After an incredible meal and a change of clothes, Codi and Joel had been taken to the Yau Ma Tei Police Station by their babysitter. The embassy man seemed more than happy to be rid of his delivered charges as he sped away. From DC, Brian had pushed his hardest to get things moving along, but red tape and political negotiations forced him to work a deal with the Chinese police. Codi and Joel would tell the police everything they knew about their kidnapping and ultimate escape. In exchange, the Chinese would safely escort them to the airport and facilitate their return. It was a political win, a win for both sides, but Brian just wanted to get his agent's asses back on US soil ASAP.

The FBI had no jurisdiction in China, and he didn't want things to get blown into a public and political fiasco. He knew that politics would trump expediency and even life if things went south, so he would just have to be patient.

Brian had arranged for Codi and Joel to meet with Inspector Ang, a man who had come very highly recommended from their assets at the US embassy. As with most political hot potatoes, a representative of the US embassy and the Chinese politburo would be joining the meeting. Brian prayed it would grow no further and that, in a few hours, his agents would be on a plane home.

Inspector Ang seemed like a level-headed down-to-earth policeman. Codi could tell right away that the man had earned his position, not been given it. There was none of the pretentiousness that goes along with that. Ang was dressed in a nice silk suit that fit his five-foot-ten frame perfectly. His jet-black hair was short and well groomed. Codi and Joel had taken time to purchase practical clothes for the trip home. She wore a plum-colored pair of Lululemon studio pants and a gray loose-fitting long-sleeve tee. They were probably knock-offs, but they were comfortable. She had her hair up in a ponytail and had purchased a small black backpack to hold a few personal items. Her neck had been properly bandaged, and the other cuts were covered as well. Joel had charcoal checked slacks and a white collared shirt. He had rolled up the sleeves and had found a replacement pair of glasses that worked well enough. His thumb had a Band-Aid on it. A small duffle held his phone, hand sanitizer, and a toothbrush.

Codi and Joel had been advised to share everything with the Chinese police, so they did, starting with handing over the gun they had taken from the tall unknown suspect.

They then proceeded to spend four hours cooped up in a small overheated interrogation room where question after question was asked and answered. Codi had initially given a direct and honest statement. But the Chinese political officer dismissed her story. He told her that if they hadn't been FBI agents, he would assume they were making the whole thing up. There was no evidence and no suspects other than a tall, mean Chinese guy. This did little to pacify Codi's rising anger against the man.

"What do you call this?" she said, pointing to her many bandages.

After another thirty minutes of essentially calling them liars, Codi was done. "Look," she said, "if you don't want to believe the truth, I'm done trying to explain it to you."

The officer bristled at the woman's bold words. An intense silence followed as the two gave each other the stare-down.

Joel cleared his throat in an attempt to cut the tension. "Maybe you could check the hospitals," he said. "He had a butter knife imbedded in his neck." Joel demonstrated with his finger on his neck. "Or, run the gun we brought in, or go to the building and see for yourself." Even Joel was getting frustrated.

"It's called *police work,*" Codi added in disgust.

In the end, the political officer from the politburo simply said thank you for your time in broken English and left. Inspector Ang apologized for the man's behavior and then closed out the meeting.

Once outside the building, the political officer took out his phone and texted a brief message. He re-pocketed his phone, got in the back of a black sedan, and it sped off.

Inspector Ang had Joel and Codi sign multiple layers of paperwork and then walked them to the exit. The US representative shook hands with Codi and Joel. He then hurried back to his office to make his report.

Paperwork was the backbone of every government.

As the three left the building, dusk had settled over the city. The change in light hit Joel like a kick to the skull, reminding him just how exhausted he was. A uniformed police officer stood next to his vehicle, lights on the roof bar flashing. He saluted Inspector Ang. The Inspector introduced his officer as the man who would be taking them to the airport. He said his goodbyes to Codi and Joel and they got in the back of the vehicle.

Inspector Ang closed the door and watched as it drove away.

Chow and Jin turned left on Fuk Wa Street. They could see smoke in the distance. A fire truck thrust past them in a hurry to its destination. Chow seemed lost in thought, oblivious to the blare of the siren. "When we get back," he said, "I want to meet with you and Shura. I have a little something I need you to get started on."

"Sure."

"This is going to be an eventful week," Chow said, rubbing his unfeeling hands together.

As they approached the abandoned abattoir where his beloved Red Baks was housed, Chow paused, looking at the smoke and flames rising from below. Part of the old building had collapsed into the offices below ground, and the fire brigade was doing their best to stop it from spreading. It was a total loss.

Chow found himself unable to speak for the first time in years. His love and passion was gone. He had built it, he had grown it, and he had ruled it. What could have happened? He had no idea, but someone would pay.

Jin leaned to their driver and said, "Don't stop. Take us back to the airport."

Special Agent Gordon Reyas tapped on his boss's door as he entered Brian's office. Special Agent Tom Calloway, also with the special projects division, was sitting in one of the seats across from his boss. At forty-eight, Tom was the oldest agent in the office. His hair was long since gone, along with a sense of humor. He gave Reyas a simple nod and then folded his arms across his chest.

Reyas took the empty seat. Brian was on the phone, and it sounded serious, but hearing only half the conversation made it difficult to piece together. Finally, Brian hung up. He drummed his fingers on his organized desktop.

"You wanted to see me, sir?" Reyas asked.

"Yes. Something's going on in China and I want to get ahead of this thing before it bites us in the ass." He paused to stare off for a moment, thinking. Reyas and Calloway shared an awkward glance.

Then Brian outlined what he wanted from them. "I want you two to stop what you're doing and put all your efforts on this and this alone. Understand?"

"Yes, sir," Reyas said.

"I'm having you interface with Agent Callan over in Counterterrorism. And I need you all up to speed *yesterday*."

The police vehicle pulled up behind a white van stopped at a red light a few blocks from the police station.

Codi and Joel were spent. They had suffered a complete overload during the last three days. Joel allowed himself a half-smile. It was finally over. They were going home. He stared out the passenger side window, numb to the sights and sounds of the electric city.

Hong Kong at night was a sight to behold. It made the lights of Vegas look like amateur hour in comparison. Locals and tourists roamed the sidewalks as neon and backlit signs vied for their attention promising a good deal, a good meal, or a good time.

An old black sedan pulled up and stopped along their passenger side. It was unusually close, but hey, this was China. Joel thought nothing of it. Codi was still pissed from a wasteful interrogation that she was powerless to do anything about. She was having trouble letting go and wanted to let loose a string of expletives. It didn't help that the political officer was a sexist pig who'd kept eyeballing her during the briefing. She'd been close to calling him on it, but held back in an effort to just make it all go away. Besides, it would change nothing. But maybe she would be feeling better right now. She noticed the driver in the black sedan next to them climb over and exit through the passenger side of the vehicle.

"Something's wrong," she said, reaching for her door handle.

Before Joel could react, the police officer driving them killed the engine and turned with a gun pointed at Joel and Codi.

"This is my stop," he said.

He exited the vehicle holding his gun level and true. He kicked his door closed and backed away. A propane truck with a single tank on the back pulled up close along the driver's side, blocking them inside the police car. Their driver turned and ran.

Lee exited the truck and pulled the pin on an incendiary grenade he was carrying. He set it next to the tank in full view of Codi and Joel. He gave them a smile meant only for the damned, and sprinted away.

"Shit!" Joel cried. He did his best not to crap his pants as reality hit.

Codi jarred him out of his panic. "We got about ten seconds before that incendiary device burns through the steel of that tank and we go up like a roman candle."

Inspector Ang was happy to be done with the two FBI Agents. His job was hard enough without dealing with international and political ramifications. He turned and headed back towards his office, taking the entry steps two at a time. As he opened the glass door that led to the lobby, a sonic boom assaulted him. Three blocks away he saw a large flame-ringed mushroom cloud moving skyward.

Without hesitation Ang spun and ran towards the source.

As he came around the corner, he stopped, frozen with disbelief. It was a mess—flames, car parts, and pieces of bodies filled the intersection. He recognized a few pieces that were left of the squad car that was holding three police officers, two of them American. He mourned the dead, but mostly mourned for himself. This was just the first explosion. This whole mess was off and he feared it would all land in his lap.

16

Chung Kong Road – 5:18 p.m. – Hong Kong

Joel quickly tried to open his door but it was a police car and the back doors could only be opened from the outside. Plus, the two vehicles on either side were so close it would be impossible to exit even if they could open them.

"We're trapped," he said, glancing at the fuse still burning on the grenade.

Codi didn't hesitate. She removed the headrest from the seat in front of her. It had two ten-inch metal rods that allowed for height adjustments. She gripped and swung it towards Joel's side window with all her might. Even hopped up on adrenaline, it took three hits for the window to crack and a fourth for it to shatter.

The incendiary grenade was housed in a soda can-like container, much like a smoke grenade the police use. It has a five-second fuse, and once pulled, starts a chemical reaction that lasts over thirty seconds. During that time, it burns through even the most heavily armored of steel, creating a small ball of extreme heat. Incendiary grenades are typically used to destroy unused or unexploded ordinance but can be effective against tanks as well, as they will melt right through the heavy armor and cook everyone inside.

The grenade ignited in a small unimpressive flash. It quickly grew into a cauldron of burning magma as the phosphorous and benzene reacted. It burned at over five thousand degrees, melting through the steel propane tank.

Joel was first out the window, and Cody didn't wait. Her shoulder shoved his butt and legs out of the car as if he'd been shot from a canon. She quickly followed, and they rolled across the black sedan's roof. Codi dropped to the gutter next to Joel, as the propane tank ignited, initially shooting flames out of the burned hole like a flame thrower. People all around screamed and ran for their lives. The gutter at the intersection had a steel grate cover that accessed the sewer below. Codi used the rod from the headrest she was still holding and lifted and yanked the cover aside. As the flames reached the inside of the tank, it could no longer maintain its integrity. The tank blew. A giant fireball expanded out and up. Steel and rubber vaporized.

Codi followed Joel as they dove into the flowing sludge ten feet below. The massive explosion sent flames and a concussive force after them, slamming them to the bottom.

Lee watched from a safe vantage point three blocks away. He saw the grenade burn through the steel tank and ignite the gas inside, creating a giant flamethrower. He watched as, remarkably, Codi and Joel escaped the police car and rolled over the roof of the car next to them. He almost started chasing after them, until he realized the danger. Lee watched them drop down to the gutter and never get back up, as the ignited gas moved into the tank, changing the flamethrower into a powerful bomb. The explosion was so intense that Lee was knocked on his ass with his ears ringing. The fifty-foot area around the truck held nothing but a few vehicle parts and scorched earth. No one could have survived.

Inspector Ang surveyed the burning mess. He was at a loss for an answer. Accident or deliberate, it was unclear. But as a cop, he found it too convenient. Maybe Codi and Joel's story had merit and someone really did want them dead. His training kicked in and he searched for a bystander that seemed out of place. Most bombers stick around to watch the fallout they had caused. Perhaps he could, at least, spot the culprit.

Nothing.

Too many unanswered questions and not enough evidence to go on.

Codi was the first to push from the sticky murk. The sewer was lit by burning rubble a few feet from her. Joel still laid face-down in the brown soupy flow. She pulled him from the sludge, put her arms around his chest, clasped her fingers together, and yanked. Brown goop shot from his mouth and he started coughing. He followed it up with several retches and finally blinked his way back into cognizance. It took him a few moments to realize he was sitting in a river of flowing crap.

"God, it stinks in here," he yelled over his ringing ears.

He turned and vomited once more. Codi looked like she'd been dipped and coated, but the whites of her eyes still shined in the dim light. Joel looked puzzled at her slight smile.

"What?" he said.

"I'm glad that worked."

"What?"

Codi shouted louder to be heard. "I'm glad that worked.

For a minute there, I thought I might have to give you mouth-to-mouth."

"Oh, yeah."

"Well your mouth was full of…" She pointed to the brown sludge that flowed past them.

"So, what, you would've just let me die rather than get a little poop in your mouth?"

"No," she lied. "I'm just glad it worked."

Joel nodded slowly, then turned and vomited again.

They made their way downstream, looking for the next exit ladder. The experience was overwhelming beyond their ability to handle, their intellects mercifully shutting off some of the details and dulling their senses.

Inspector Ang had moved closer to the flames as they subsided. Emergency response was on the way and other police officers had joined the disaster, everyone trying to get a handle on the situation and help as many people as possible. As he stepped onto the curb, Ang noticed that the sewer grate had been removed. It didn't seem all that out of place, given the situation, but it did deserve checking out.

Cody pulled her way up the ladder of the next exit grate. She used her back as leverage to dislodge and move it aside. A glow of neon and traffic noise filled the sewer pipe. She reached for the lip to pull herself up, but a hand reached down and grabbed her. She resisted instinctively. But then a familiar voice cut through.

"Agent Sanders, let me help you."

It was Inspector Ang. He helped them out of the sewer, and quickly moved them off the street into a back warehouse of a small shop next to the street.

He managed to borrow two blankets from the proprietor after flashing his badge. Ang asked them to wait while he got his car. Cody wasted no time dropping her soiled clothes. She ripped a chunk off the blanket to use to wipe her face, and wrapped the remainder around her body. Joel followed suit.

"Damn it," she said. "This is the second time something like this has happened to me."

"You've landed in crap before?" Joel asked.

"Guano, and I'm not sure which is worse."

"At least you can check that off your list," Joel said without mirth.

"Funny."

Joel looked around. There were stacks of boxes and other inventory surrounding them. A half-coconut shell full of old cigarette butts was on a small shelf. Codi sat next to it on a tree stump that had blackened with time and dirt. Joel sat on a large wooden crate with smudged red Chinese writing on the side. He looked forlorn as he awkwardly tried to place his hands somewhere without touching anything.

"Joel, you gotta just go with it," Codi said.

"I'm sure I have yellow fever, typhoid, and several other deadly diseases. Maybe even the H1N1 virus was down there."

"I know of one you got for sure," Codi said.

He looked up at his partner's words, still uncomfortable in his skin. "What one?"

"Shibreth."

Joel looked baffled. "Shibreth? Is that a Chinese virus, a waterborne pathogen? What is it?"

"Your breath smells like shit—Shibreth." Codi's lips parted in an uncontrollable smile as a slow chuckle escaped.

Joel started to snicker at the absurdity of it all, which made Codi laugh even more. Soon they were both giggling like school kids.

Inspector Ang entered the warehouse in time to hear two adults cackling like children. He was puzzled, but hey, they were Americans.

Lee watched as the police and rescue vehicles began to swarm the area. His work was done. He turned and began the ten-block walk back to a parking lot where he had left his car when he picked up the propane truck. *Finally,* he thought with a rare smile. Now to plan for what came next. His future with Chow was over, but fate had dealt him another chance. Lee needed to disappear or end Chow if he was to go forward from here. Much to consider.

He pulled out in his white coupe Shuanghuan Noble, heading for a well-deserved drink and perhaps some female companionship. The car was a three-door hatchback made by Shuanghuan Motors for China and Canada, as innocuous as any car in Hong Kong. And for the moment, it fit his needs perfectly.

Lee had never been good at relationships with the opposite sex, and the current male to female ratio in China did him no favors. It wasn't because he was unusually tall or that he looked like a feral cat hunting a trapped mouse. It was his job. He was a solitary hunter/killer, not a team player, and not especially nice by nature. But luckily for Lee, money could get you almost anything you desired.

As he turned left at the intersection of Heung Yip Road, he just about drove off the street. Sitting in the car in the opposite lane was one very much alive female American agent.

Impossible.

Lee waited for them to pass by and then spun around to follow them at a discreet distance.

They rode in Ang's car, a white four-door Citroen Fukang, back to his place. Joel was laying down in the back seat moaning

181

like he'd been poisoned. Codi took the time to brief Ang on the recent attempt on their lives. He was furious at the betrayal of his officer. It was a problem in modern China, a government rife with corruption doled out at the highest level. The officer was no doubt one of the many plants that the Tong and other groups use as information conduits.

Inspector Ang found himself breathing out of his mouth as the smell that clung to the two agents became overpowering. He opened the car windows and finally pulled his shirt over his nose as he drove, seeing through tear-filled eyes and suppressing his gag reflex. Ang finally pulled to a red curb along Kwun Tong Harbor. He placed a police placard in the windshield and walked Codi and Joel towards the water. They crossed several floating walkways made of old wooden planks and crowded with tethered boats of every size and condition. Most were made from leftover materials, seeming to defy the laws of physics by staying above water. The air was ripe with burned cooking oil, old fish, and diesel. Families lived and died here. The sounds of children laughing reminded Codi that perception often dictates one's happiness. Ang stopped at a fifty-foot Chinese junk floating along a section of dock.

The junk evolved during the Song dynasty in 960 AD. This one was a teak, two-mast boat with full red sails and a back-up diesel engine. It had the classic high stern and projected bow. A wooden plank ramp angled up eight feet to the deck above.

He invited Joel and Codi to board with a wave of his hand. "Welcome to my home. All aboard."

Lee parked dockside just in time to see Ang close the cabin door of a junk. He turned off the engine of his vehicle and settled in to wait. He considered the extreme possibilities that could have allowed the female to survive the explosion.

Codi and Joel wasted no time hitting the showers. After buffing every cell of skin on his body, Joel exited the bathroom in borrowed clothes.

He tapped discretely on Codi's bathroom door. She opened it to see Joel's face twisted up and moving side to side. He was trying to follow his nose to a source of odor only he could smell. Codi was wrapped in a towel with glistening wet hair flowing over her shoulders, the gold flecks in her brown eyes sparkling.

"Something still smells," Joel said.

"You know, it's possible your sense of smell is just off."

"I don't think so."

"And that's my problem, how?"

Turning and sniffing in every direction, he looked pathetic as he tried in vain to source the smell on his person.

Codi took pity on him. "Fine, come in."

She pulled Joel inside and inspected him with a sniff. "Oh, God."

"You found it already. What is it?" Joel asked.

"It's your aftershave."

Joel lifted his hands in defeat. "I didn't have a choice, so I tried to drown the smell with some brand of Chinese cologne I found in the medicine cabinet."

"You should have chosen differently. This is twice as bad. It has my eyes burning."

She grabbed a couple of cotton swabs and took his jaw with one hand to cock his head to the side. "Hold still." She inspected his head, hair, and ears.

"Ah."

"Ah, what?"

"Stop moving," she commanded. Codi started to clean

his left ear. "This must be the first time you've had to clean excrement off your person."

Joel could only mumble an answer with Codi's vice-grip on his jaw.

"There." She let go and came away with two very brown-tipped swabs.

"Thank you. That was driving me crazy. I couldn't figure out where the smell was coming from."

"You're welcome. Here, these are yours. Now scoot."

Joel carefully took the soiled swabs and slowly headed back to his own bathroom, but not before glancing over his shoulder at the beautiful towel-clad woman who'd just saved his ears.

Ang served a round of Baijiu, a rice-based liquor. Codi held her shot into the air. *"Ganbei,"* she exclaimed as the others repeated the toast and followed her lead. As a warm sensation spread through her body she began to feel human again. Joel swished his mouth before swallowing, just in case there was remaining bacteria.

They sat in the teak-walled salon in silence. Codi took in her surroundings. The room was warm and inviting with an intricately-patterned wood floor, leather seating, and a white-paneled ceiling. The salon flowed into a spacious galley accented by a large through-hull mast beam and three port-holes on the starboard side.

"Your boat is lovely," she said. "Thank you for your aid."

"It was my father's pride and joy," Ang said. "And now, with houses going for over a hundred million dollars here in Hong Kong, it is my home."

Ang nodded towards a prominent picture of a gray-haired gentleman with a look of confidence. "Living here keeps me close to him, even though he is no longer with us."

"I'm sorry."

Ang just nodded. The casual banter eventually turned to the events of the last forty-eight hours. The mood went somber.

"So what next?" Ang asked. "I assume you will head back to the states."

"Yes. I'm sure we're past due at the office and there's most likely a task force being put together to find us," Codi said, *"again."*

Joel stood up. "I'd really like to get this guy who, three times now, has tried to kill us,"

"And, thank goodness, failed," Codi said with little emotion.

Joel's anger was elevating. He started pacing. "Nobody blasts me into a river of shit and gets away with it. Plus, he tried to rape and kill you. And who knows how many people died in that explosion? This man is still out there. He doesn't get a pass, and I want him *bad."*

He looked almost deranged as he said these words. It was a side of him Codi hadn't seen before. Honestly, she felt the same way. It was time to change from defense to offense. No more being a target.

"As far as anyone knows, the two of you are dead," said Ang. "Blown to bits in that explosion. This is a rare chance to make a play for the people who are behind this without them seeing it coming. For all you know, there could be a leak coming from your side of things."

Joel and Codi contemplated his words. If they were honest with themselves, he was right, they didn't know.

"Maybe it is better if we stay dead for now," Codi said thoughtfully.

Ang looked down in contemplation, clasping his hands together. The room grew suddenly quiet.

He raised an eyebrow and followed with, "Perhaps we can

help each other." He looked up and made eye contact with the two Americans. "As I see it, we can get you false papers that will get you on a plane tomorrow morning and out of China. Or, I could use a couple of rogue American agents bent on revenge and completely disregarding their authority and orders, to help crack this whole thing open." He smiled at the thought.

Codi and Joel shared a glace, well aware what going forward might mean—forced leave, fired, even jail. But they were not going back home without their pound of flesh. It just wasn't going to happen.

Joel looked away thoughtfully. "It's time to burn the boats," he said.

"What?" Codi asked.

He turned back, more sure of himself. "1519. Capitan Hernan Cortez. When he arrived in Veracruz, he burned all his boats in a desperate move to motivate his soldiers. They ultimately conquered Mexico."

Codi nodded. "No going back."

"Exactly."

Ang interrupted their thought. "We might not need to be so desperate. The British were very good at monitoring and collecting information while in control of Hong Kong. My father worked with them as part of a division of MI6. And…" Ang contemplated his next words. "I do a little something for them now and then."

Codi and Joel perked at this revelation.

"Obviously, it would not go well for my current employer to know this."

"Obviously," Joel said.

Codi and Joel followed Ang over to a built-in mahogany desk set against the back bulkhead. Ang pressed a hidden button and a wood panel slid open to reveal an advanced electronic display. "Action will be required to put an end to this," Ang mumbled as he waited for the system to boot up.

Codi had always been a woman defined by her actions, but perhaps she had just irreversibly overstretched. Still, going back without some satisfaction was not going to happen.

Ang pressed several keys and the large screen came to life with a login. He entered his password, and a blank page popped up with a single search bar. "Okay," he said to them, "tell me everything you can remember about this man."

"His name is Lee," Joel said. "I heard a guard call him that."

Ang cocked his chin and narrowed his eyes at Joel. "Lee?"

"Yes."

He took an incredulous breath and entered it into the search bar. "That narrows it down to half-a-billion people. What else?"

Codi and Joel gave Ang a detailed description of the man. With each detail, the list of suspects narrowed.

Ang said, "The fact that he was able to get inside information and put together the ambush in the street, tells me he's probably connected to a triad or black market group. These men share information and favors when it suits their needs. But it must have taken some serious horsepower to burn a mole at the station just to get to you."

Ang entered some additional data and a list of about two hundred names, complete with pictures popped up. "Looks like there are less Chinese assassins over six-feet-tall then I thought. This list is quite manageable." Ang looked pleased.

Joel and Codi scrolled through the pictures until they came to number 157. The picture was grainy and old, but there was no mistaking the predatory expression of their assailant. Joel leaned in and read the English words next to the Chinese characters below the photo.

"Chun Lee, alias Kwai Chang Caine, Kwi Gon Jinn, and Kato. That's funny."

"What is?" Ang asked.

Joel pointed to the names. "The alias names, they're all TV and movie character names."

"I guess he has a sense of humor."

"Not that I've seen," Codi said.

Ang leaned closer. "Looks like he's ex-military special forces. Hmm, he was on death row for a while and was then recruited for a special mission."

"By whom?"

Ang clicked his tongue absently as he searched for the information. "Just a sec."

He drilled deeper into the E-file. "Doesn't say. It also doesn't say why he was on death row. Looks like some high level redaction has taken place."

Ang read on. "He is suspected of ties to the Green Dragon Triad and the Chu Lon Fue, a nasty black market group that operates mostly in southern mainland China."

Ang continued to glean all he could from the file, but most of the rest was his physical description, something they already had. Codi stifled a yawn. Her eyes were bloodshot and she was feeling the effects of the drink.

"Red Baks," Ang said.

"What's that?" Joel asked.

"It's just a notation here at the bottom."

"Sounds like hemorrhoid cream," Codi said.

Joel tried not to smile by biting down hard on his lips. His body jerked several times suppressing a laugh until he found some control.

The late hour, lack of sleep, and crazy recent events were making them punchy. Ang looked up at Joel who was now beet red and trying to control himself.

"If you got a case of Red Baks," Joel said, "you'll wanna shut that down."

He and Codi both started laughing.

"Maybe we should get some rest and pick this up in the morning," Ang said.

"Perhaps," Codi said with a giggle.

Ang hid a smile of his own and showed the two laughing agents to their rooms.

Americans, he said to himself. He would never understand them.

Lee watched from his car as the lights on the junk winked out. The five Advil he had taken were doing their job on his pain, and he still felt alert. He checked the time on his phone and started his car. He had gone through every possible scenario in his head, but for the life of him, could not figure out how Codi had survived. Seeing her drive off with that man from the police station nearly made Lee drive his car right into theirs, but that was not how he operated. This would be done on his terms and tonight. He marveled at the ridiculousness of it all. First the river, then the Red Baks, and now an explosion that had obliterated most of a city block. It was unimaginable to him. He let the anger in his body grow and flow. His thoughts turned to the task ahead and his own mortality. It had become a mission he must complete.

He briefly reviewed the kaleidoscope of his life's memories. He had been a good soldier and a great assassin. These were the things he could take with him when he was gone, things he could be proud of.

He put his car into drive and pulled away.

Soon, he thought.

17

Washington D.C. – 4:32 p.m. – FBI Field Office – Special Projects – 3rd Floor

The message left little doubt. Agent Sanders and Strickman were dead. They had been involved in an unfortunate gas explosion that decimated an entire block on the east side of Hong Kong. The investigation was still underway, but a detailed report would be filed through the proper channels. An FBI representative had been assigned from the Hong Kong office, and he would keep Brian updated on his findings. Brian hated politics but he knew that there was no way around them. Learning how to play the game was critical to one's success, especially in DC.

His superiors were compassionate but unyielding to Brian's plea to be part of the investigation. They had even denied his request to send agents from his office to China to support the effort. They wanted no part of this Hong Kong hot potato. Brian informed Agents Calloway and Reyas to stand down for the moment. He paced his office, feeling helpless. The space had never seemed smaller. It was time for him to change his perspective. He grabbed his coat and left the office before five o'clock for the first time in over a year.

Agent Fescue opened the front door to his beautiful wife Leila and their youngest child Abigale sitting at the kitchen island. It was a white kitchen with a dark granite-topped island with seating for four. They were surprised to see Brian home so early.

"Hi, guys." He gave his wife and child a kiss. "Where's Tristan?"

Tristan was their energetic five-year-old son, a wavy-haired boy with the same mocha colored eyes as his dad.

"Backyard playing, why?" said Leila. "What's wrong? Is everything okay at the office?"

Brian let loose a smile that filled the room. "Tristan come on in here," he called out the back door.

To Leila, he said, "I just needed to realign some priorities, and there is nothing more important than this." He gestured to his family.

Tristan ran into the room yelling, "Daddy, Daddy!"

He hugged his dad.

"Come on, go get cleaned up," Brian said. "We're going to Chuck E. Cheese's for dinner."

Tristan did his celebration dance. They were going to his favorite restaurant.

Leila stepped close to her husband, gave him another kiss, and whispered, "You hate that place."

"I know."

Ang leaned back from the computer screen and checked his watch. It was 3:07 a.m. He stretched and decided he was done for the night. He felt and heard a creak from someone moving on his boat. Ang reached stealthily under his desk and came away with a Glock 23, a present from his part-time employer.

He spun to the source of the movement, gun leveled and ready to fire.

"Easy, Ang."

Ang recognized Codi's voice, as she stepped into the salon and the glow of his monitor.

"Sorry."

She yawned between words. "I crashed like the dead, but I just couldn't quite keep it all turned off."

"Same here," Ang said, as he put his gun down on the desk. He reached over and flicked a small light on next to him. "While I was up, I did more digging, even reached out to a couple of contacts about Red Baks. Turns out it's not hemorrhoid medicine but a think tank run by an old-school red communist general named Chow Phun."

Codi moved next to Ang and looked at the face on the screen. It was a very unique face captured as he was exiting a limo. She guessed the man was in his late sixties. He had black intelligent eyes that seemed to pierce right through you. The right side of his face hung like a wet tee shirt while the left side seemed normal.

"He stepped down from his position to head several off-book projects for the politburo," Ang said. "I'm sorry to say he is very connected."

"Looks like he has some kind of ailment, maybe a stroke," Codi said.

"Yes. That might be why he stepped down when he did. The thing is, the Red Baks is the complex you and Joel destroyed."

This information galvanized Codi almost instantly. "So he's the one behind all this. But to what end?"

"With the Red Baks gone, we no longer have a lead as to his plans or whereabouts."

Codi sat in the chair next to Ang. "So what, we don't know where he is and we can't go after him?"

Ang spun his chair to face her. "No. We just have to be very careful how we do it. Luckily for me, I have you two to blame if anything goes wrong."

"I was thinking the same about you, Inspector." Codi held the inspector's stare with equal intensity.

"Perfect." Ang smiled. "Let me show you something."

He pulled up what he had found.

It had taken Lee fifteen minutes to silently move the gas cans into position on the bow of the docked junk. He attached a remote igniter to the closest can and then checked the matching remote in his hand. The green micro LED on the roll-of-dimes-sized device meant it was primed and ready. He pressed his left thumb down and held it there.

He headed for the nearest hatch, pulling a pistol from his waist as he moved. The chrome door handle was well maintained and turned without a sound as Lee slipped inside. Muted voices came from the salon ahead. He moved like a wraith, following the voices.

He waited for the perfect moment before stepping into the room. "Good evening."

Codi and Ang spun with equal speed and disbelief. Lee's pistol remained leveled at them, ready to fire.

"Drop it on the floor, carefully," Lee commanded. He pointed to the gun resting next to Ang's keyboard.

Codi raised her hands and turned slowly. Ang judiciously picked up his Glock by the barrel and dropped it to the floor.

"Now kick it away."

Ang kicked his pistol hard in the direction of Lee. Lee stepped over the sliding gun as it skittered across the polished wood floor beyond, his aim never faltering. "Foolish man. Now both of you put your hands on your heads."

Ang and Codi complied.

"Slowly." Lee cautioned.

Lee moved closer to his seated victims, trying to process the perfectly healthy woman in front of him. "I have tried to kill you and your partner three times, but apparently the cosmos are not in favor of this happening. This is difficult for me to accept. But I feel as though it is no longer in my hands."

Codi and Ang shared a brief glance in confusion.

While keeping the gun on Codi and Ang, Lee moved to sit on the small couch across from them. "Two days ago," he said, "I failed my protector when you survived the river. I have therefore forfeited my life. He allowed me a second chance. This was a most generous act, as it has never been allowed before, and I was not going to spurn it."

Codi stared daggers at the man who had tortured her and planned to rape her.

"But after the two of you escaped, I took another approach and dedicated myself to your demise at all costs, no longer under the protection of my boss. It was personal."

Codi practically rolled her eyes trying to will the man to get to the point. It was bad enough to be killed by him, but she was in no mood to be forced to listen to his life story first. Please just shoot me now, she thought.

"I now find myself at odds. Three times you have proven yourself incapable of being killed—*three times.*" He stopped, looked at his gun, and then back up.

"I have faced my own mortality. That changes you. The things I've done, the people I've hurt. And looking at you now…"

A moment of silence followed before he continued. "I had planned to go out in a blaze of glory, taking you all with me as a final grand performance. But now, as I sit here, I am moved in a different direction, a change of heart, if you will."

Codi decided it would be worth the risk to dive at the man's gun. She'd take a bullet, but maybe Ang would overpower the assassin and have a chance to live. She leaned forward ever so slightly onto the balls of her feet, ready to spring.

"In fact, I find myself unable to continue as planned. There could still be more for me, even a second chance to do things I have never allowed myself. So maybe you are not supposed to die quite yet and there will be some type of redemption for me."

What? Codi was sure she misheard.

"Therefore, I have decided to help you."

Lee lowered his head and weapon in complete submission. He sat in the love seat across from them and slumped. Codi and Ang both tried to process the information, but nothing was adding up. It was so far out of their box at the moment.

Lee looked as though, perhaps for the first time in his life, he didn't know what to do next. He wanted to just be a regular person but had no clue how to get there.

Codi finally leaped at the opportunity. "You say you want to help us?"

Lee looked up, distraught, and slowly nodded his head.

"Then who ordered you to kill us?"

"General Chow Phun."

"And that's who had us taken at the airport?"

"Correct."

"Do you know where is he right now?"

The assassin hesitated.

"Lee, redemption comes at a cost," she said.

"Probably at his second base of operations in Fenghuang. He has a house there."

Ang caught on to Codi's plan, quickly realizing this moment might not last. "Maybe we should hold the gun." He gestured.

Lee looked to the gun now lying by his side and nodded.

"Why does he want us dead?" Codi asked.

Lee stood and held his pistol out for Ang to take.

"You were getting too close to a technology they were preparing to test on–"

Two quick shots deafened the room as blood spouted from Lee's torso. The once-assassin-turned-ally crumpled to the floor. He wheezed as he turned to see his executioner. "You? You are supposed to be dead."

Lee's life poured out onto the floor and his head dropped, along with a final statement: "Use caution when trusting your enemy."

Joel stepped through the cordite smoke holding the Glock.

He had awakened to voices and carefully moved to investigate. Seeing a Glock 23 on the floor, he picked it up just in time to see Lee point his weapon in the direction of his colleagues. Joel wasted no time in ending the man who had plagued him since Russia.

Joel was ecstatic. He had saved the day.

Codi was pissed. Joel had killed their best chance of getting to the bottom of things.

Ang was confused about the small device with a black button and a small flashing red light that had just rolled out of Lee's other hand.

"What did he mean by 'use caution when trusting your enemy?'" Joel asked, confused.

A sudden beeping sound coming from the small device on the floor was followed by an explosion. It rocked the bow of the junk so violently that it nearly broke in half. Flames grabbed at the wooden vessel, quickly engulfing the bow and forward cabins. The bulkhead turned into a spray of wooden daggers as the entire ship bucked with the concussion. Codi was the first to dive for cover. Joel, who was standing closest, was knocked across the room. Ang caught a large sliver of teak in his abdomen and was spun to the floor.

Codi crawled to Ang and helped him to his feet. She pushed him to the exit hatch and ran back for Joel, calling his name through blown-out eardrums. With the hull of the ship breached, black sea water rushed to find equilibrium. Codi had been on a sinking boat before and it had nearly cost her her life. There was no chance that was going to happen again. She shook Joel awake and helped him to the exit. By the time they reached the top of the floundering junk, they had to step up to reach the dock.

Ang collapsed on the dock, and Codi stepped over to investigate. A wood spike the size of a dagger was imbedded in his side. She wasted no time and pulled it out before he could brace for the pain. A low moan escaped him.

"You'll be okay," she said. "It looks like it just punctured muscle."

"She hates hospitals," Joel added needlessly.

They wrapped his wound with part of Joel's shirt and plodded off for Ang's car.

The last of the flames sizzled out as the junk slipped below the water.

General Chow Phun abruptly stood, slamming his hand down on the solid wood table. He felt no sting or pain in his numb hands, only heard the sound they made. He had been irritable and angry ever since seeing his precious Red Baks destroyed. And his incessant pacing had continued to wind up his black mood. He had gone through two handkerchiefs dabbing the constant drool from the corner of his mouth, and the persistent rash was bright red.

Jin had been living on pins and needles, not sure when or

if the general's angst would be turned his way. They had flown the jet to a small strip where a four-door olive green Beijing BJ212, a cheap knock-off of the old Jeep Wrangler, was waiting. The thirty-minute drive through the countryside was breathtaking. Lush forest, streams, and hills made way for a narrow winding road. There were a few terraced rice fields among the hills, and an earthy smell filled the journey. The people who lived here were the real heart of China, Jin thought to himself. A quaint town came into view as they rounded a verdant hill. Fenghuang was an incredible sight. A slow moving river cut through a town that seemed time had forgotten. Chow had taken them to his home there, a place he called Chongde Hall.

It was a four-story structure built by the wealthiest man in town over three-hundred years ago. Chow purchased it from his estate eleven months back. The design was classic box-style Chinese architecture with a front portico and a tier shape. It was made of teak covered in many layers of finish that had gone dark with the passing years. The wood was set off by two stone lions guarding either side of the entrance. Inside, polished wood floors supported beams that curved up, meeting in the center of a domed ceiling in a spoke pattern, and supported by a large central stone column. The rounded design continued throughout the home giving it a hobbit-like feel, but for grown-ups. A wide, curved staircase granted entry to the upper levels. It was made of carved rosewood with two dragons intricately wound through the banisters. Carved wood lintels and a collection of antiques adorned every room.

Chow finally sat down and took a calming breath.

"Jin, I want to thank you for your loyalty. It is the most important thing to me."

Jin simply nodded.

"I am a man with a finite expiration. It is not far off. But before then, there is much good we can do for our country. If you will help me finish my mission, I will make it worth your while."

Jin leaned in towards his boss. "Boss, I am humbled by your offer and I will give my best to your needs."

Jin kept his real feelings to himself. He said the words his boss needed to hear, but in truth, he was trying to find an exit strategy that didn't involve his demise.

"How was I supposed to know he was on our side? The man was a killer. Or that he was holding a dead-man's switch? I thought I saved your life. He killed nineteen people and injured dozens of others, just to get to us. Surely, I did the right thing."

Codi was driving Ang's Citroen Fukang with Joel yammering in the copilot's seat. She absently scratched at one of her wounds that was actually starting to heal. Ang was resting in the backseat, his abdomen throbbing in pain. Truthfully, Codi was glad that Joel had killed Lee, although she wished he had done it after they had gotten what they needed from him. Of course, she would never tell him that. It was way more fun listening to him postulate.

Joel continued. "I mean, what kind of FBI agent kills a man, then leaves the scene of the crime to do God knows what next, probably more crime? This is going to come back on me big time."

The road trip to Fenghuang was nine hours and required two pit stops and a refueling. Joel had talked non-stop for the first three hours. Finally his adrenaline wore off, along with the emotions that followed the killing of another human, and he lapsed into slumber.

Fenghuang, or Phoenix Ancient Town, is one of the most idyllic well-preserved ancient settlements in all of China. Once a frontier town built in 1704 and a center for trade and cultural exchange, Fenghuang was now a breathtaking riverside town with narrow winding alleys, temples, and rickety stilt houses built along the Tuo River. The town borders the lazy river that ran through a spectacular mountainous tree-filled region. It was exceptionally tranquil and a full step back in time.

Codi pulled their vehicle to a stop in an outlying parking lot. "Looks like we walk from here," she said.

Matt Campbell sat back in his wheeled office chair and rubbed his eyes. It was late. Selecting the herd had taken much longer than expected. They had placed thirty bovines in a pen erected in the back warehouse, each carefully selected for its condition. BRDC, or Bovine Respiratory Disease Complex, had been diagnosed in each cow. Most had clear mucus running from their nostrils and some coughed incessantly. They were a veterinarian's nightmare.

Matt stood and went to the viewing window as technicians prepped the FCBT (Focusable Cellular Beam Technology). It was the acronym given to his invention that was once called SkyStorm by the man who had stolen it and caused an international incident. It was an invention that had nearly infected half of London with a deadly illness, and nearly killed Matt in the process. Since getting it back, the military had taken charge. They had given the device the odd acronym. Matt suspected they'd done so without consulting anyone from marketing.

The lab where he now worked was on heavy lockdown with what Matt thought to be ridiculously over-the-top security. He was monitored and second-guessed at every step. But things were still developing, and Matt found himself just happy enough to keep moving forward one foot in front of the other.

"Sequence nominal, all systems operational," someone said from behind Matt.

"Initiate sequence and fire on my mark," Matt's boss called out.

They watched as the FCBT was pointed at the herd. There was a brief hum and then a small snapping noise. That was followed by a winding-down sound as the system transitioned back to its standby mode.

"We have a successful firing," someone yelled.

Matt watched as the cows continued to move around the pen as if nothing had taken place. But he knew differently. In an instant, all thirty cows had been vaccinated by the FCBT. It had sent the vaccine through the air at a cellular level, penetrating and inoculating their every single cell at once. The improvement in the bovines' health would be remarkable by morning.

With the test completed, Matt's mind started to wonder. He found himself thinking about Codi. He had sent her an apology email and a first class ticket to Boston in an attempt to make up for his inability to host her the previous weekend. So far, he'd heard nothing since then. Was she mad? Did she even get the email? When it came to women, he was no expert, but other than his love for his work, she was it for him.

Maybe he should try calling Brian or Joel to get the real story. He looked at the time and picked up his phone.

18

CHONGDE HALL – 5:02 P.M. – FENGHUANG, CHINA

The sound of a door bursting open broke Jin from his thoughts.

"Finally," Chow shouted.

Jin looked up to see eight very serious looking men enter the home. *Mercenaries,* he thought. Each carried a large duffle and seemed to follow the command of one, a salt-and-pepper shoulder-length-haired man with a ridiculous Fu Manchu and the eyes of a predator—Poh. He looked like he had seen and done horrible things. The squad was followed by two studious looking men who clearly were struggling to fit in.

Chow greeted the man, Poh, and welcomed him to his home with a traditional slight bow. He made no other introductions and asked them all to join him for a cup of tea. The group sat around the large table that could seat twelve and made small talk. An old gray-haired woman with a stoop entered the room carrying a tray of tea and rice cakes for all. She had a wizened no-nonsense look and a slight tremor that caused the pot to shake, nearly spilling the tea. Each time she poured, the men watched in rapt attention. Would she spill the tea or not? It was a strange ritual and Jin almost laughed out loud at the absurdity of it. He studied her for a moment, thinking she looked more Malaysian or Nepalese, but they were in the south of China, so who could really tell.

After tea, Chow took the time to introduce everyone and personally thank them for being part of the new China they would all help create. "Each one of you is an integral part of our success or failure. And I ask that you give me your best during the next twenty-four hours." Chow looked around. Each and every person nodded or replied to his request.

They were ready.

From the parking lot, Codi and her team crossed the Hong Bridge. Its three arches and pagoda-topped pass-through spanned the slow moving river, providing wind and rain protection for residents and tourists alike.

Codi looked slack-jawed at her surroundings. The town was a study in duality. Most residents preferred to live their lives the old way, including their dress. But because Fenghuang was a must-see tourist destination, there were people from all over the world mingling with the locals, each with their smart phones and modern ways. It was only a matter of time before the local holdouts gave way to the crushing advance of modernization. But in the meantime, it was truly magical.

Using Ang's contacts, they checked into a private guesthouse across the river. It was a funky place with a central courtyard decorated in a hodgepodge of modern and time-worn. Codi crossed the garden's stone steps that led to her room where a white birdcage chair hung from the ceiling. The room was lit by an ornate stained glass window, and next to it was a small bed with a green lotus-patterned comforter. She sat with a plop, trying hard not to just lie back and give in to sleep after the long drive.

Ten minutes later, the three met back in a small common

area just off the kitchen. With a detailed map spread out on the table, they started to make a plan. The first step was to locate Chow's historic home and survey the area.

The team mingled with the scores of tourists as they slowly made their way to Chongde Hall. Codi dipped her feet in the river as she scoped out the historic building, pretending to take pictures of the area. There were two heavily armed guards that were alert and patrolling. Joel and Ang chatted as they worked their way down the alley behind it. Ang was still hurting from his stab wound but did his best not to show it. He glimpsed to the security cameras and the locked steel gate covering the back door. This was the place.

The group met back at the Miss Yang Restaurant for a local dish called River Fish. It was surprisingly tasty even though Joel was sure it was full of heavy metals.

"So here is the situation." Ang proceeded between bites. "We can only assume that Chow Phun is there. Without hard evidence, there is no way I can make a raid on Chongde Hall. It would be the end of my career, and whatever the general is up to would still transpire. Thoughts?"

Codi didn't wait for Joel to answer. "I didn't come all this way to start playing by the rules."

"I didn't think you had, Agent Sanders," Ang replied.

"Good. Please call me Codi. As I see it, one of us could slip in over the rooftops at night, find whatever hard evidence is needed, and then slip back out." She used her fingers to make quote marks around the term *hard evidence*.

Joel added, "You call in the authorities, and *bam,* the whole stinking thing is behind us. Most of it legal and by the book."

Codi's lips arched upward. "Or we could just go in with guns blazing."

Ang said, "Since the only guns we have are two back-up pistols from the trunk of my car, I suggest Plan A."

He had shown them his trunk before leaving Hong Kong. It was meticulously organized and well stocked, with lift-out drawers and a host of supplies, including climbing gear, emergency water jugs, extra clothing, and even tactical gear.

He must have been a boy scout in a previous life, Joel thought at the time.

"The problem is," Ang said, "I'm the only one who speaks Chinese, but I am not in any condition to do much climbing." Ang pointed to the wound on his side. "So you will have to see, not hear or read, something worthy of hard evidence."

Codi briefly focused on a distant point with a half-nod. The task had just gotten that much harder.

"Fescue." Brian said as he picked up his phone.

"Brian."

It took a moment for Brian to recognize the voice. "Matt. What's going on?"

Brian put down the file he was perusing and focused on the call. The two friends covered the small talk territory quickly and got to the heart of the matter—Codi. Brian was not about to tell Matt the official version so he watered it down. He hadn't heard from her and was worried.

"That makes two of us," Matt said.

Since her mission to Russia was not covert, Brian had no qualms about giving Matt some particulars. The hard part was how she had gone missing in China, resurfaced, and was now presumed dead. All very strange and troubling. But until he had absolute proof, he would keep that information to himself.

"Look, Matt, I can't tell you everything, but you know Codi as well as I do. She's probably kicking butt and taking names."

Brian lied, knowing that the prognosis was bleak. "I promise I'll call the minute I know anything."

This seemed to appease Matt and the two hung up.

Matt turned hopeful. Maybe Codi had been too busy to reply, or maybe she didn't see his email. She might not be mad at him after all.

But then again, how hard was it to send a text.

The arrival of the men had completely changed Chow's disposition. He was now actively engaged, and Jin could feel the darkness lift from the room.

"Ok, down to business."

Everyone at the table stopped talking and looked to Chow.

"I am afraid our leaders have grown soft suckling on the wealth of the west. It is now up to us to bring about the change our people and our country needs. A path is now open to return to our true communist roots, more important now than ever. Soon, others will fear not just our billion-man army but our technology as well. Soon, we will show them what is possible, and it will leave the rest of the world in dread. They will know we can strike at them anywhere, anytime, and they are powerless to stop us."

This started a small wave of excitement among the men.

Chow laid out his plan, and the squad got to work. Poh interjected a few times with concerns and ideas. Ultimately all agreed, and each went their own way, setting the plan in motion. Jin found a quiet corner to set up his computers as the squad busied themselves preparing a cache of weapons, grenades, and other paraphernalia. The two studious men moved to the third floor where an open work area was established. They worked on a prototype that was nearly complete. It looked like a small radar dish attached with cables to a toaster-sized box. They double-checked everything, including Chow's plan. It was only a matter of time before all would be ready

Codi pulled herself up onto the roof of a clothing store three buildings over from her target. Joel and Ang watched from the alley below. The town had gone to sleep, save for a few wandering tourists. The moon had peeked over the mountain and was casting a cold distorted reflection on the river's surface. She was dressed all in black, some from Ang's trunk and some from a local shop. The tiled roof made for treacherous going, but she kept three points of contact at all times, looking like a giant spider moving across the skyline.

As with most cities in China the space between buildings is often very narrow or nonexistent. She scaled up to the edge of Chongde Hall, where she jumped and pulled herself onto its roof. She moved slowly and carefully. This was not a race. The top of Chow's home allowed for a spectacular view of the river, as lit homes and shops along its bank reflected a myriad of colors across the water. The peak of the portico held two small windows. Codi lowered herself down and checked the lock on one. It was old and flimsy. She used her knife to quietly force it open, and lowered herself inside.

The room was dark and smelled of dust and mold. The glow from the small window illuminated several bodies standing in the room. Codi drew her pistol instinctively and dropped behind a wooden chest. She peeked out to see that the bodies were made of stone. She felt stupid. On closer inspection she realized they were not stone but terracotta warriors. In the dim glow they looked very realistic.

She had always wanted to see the display in north-western China. More than eight-thousand warriors, one-hundred-and-thirty chariots, and over five-hundred horses were built to protect the first emperor of China in the afterlife. She ran her fingers along the plated armor. The detail was incredible. Too bad she didn't have time for a selfie.

Codi turned the door handle and moved down an empty hallway. It appeared that this section of the house had seen little use lately. She peeked down from the top of worn stairs that led to the floors below. She could hear voices in the distance. If only she had the gear to plant a bug. She could be on her way back out the window right now. Instead, she moved down the stairs one step at a time staying close to the edge to prevent any creaking as she moved.

The room below opened into a large open space. There were two fifteen-foot rows of tables, approximately six feet apart. They were covered with equipment, testing electronics, even a satellite dish that looked like it was for receiving cable TV. Codi had had some experience with rogue technology in the past, but everything here looked innocuous. And without knowing its purpose she had no real evidence to initiate a raid on the general. She pulled out the phone Ang had given her and started recording. Using the digital zoom, she captured tight shots of the gear littering the worktables. She hoped the audio would come through and that Ang could make something of the conversation that was taking place.

A door to the room suddenly opened. Two men struggled to carry in a crate and place it at the head of the table to the right. Codi leaned down to get a better view. There were Chinese characters on the box, but nothing that would help her ID the contents. Luckily, one of the men in a lab coat, picked up a crowbar and started to crack open the crate. The wood panels fell away to reveal a black cone-shaped object. She snapped two quick pictures. She recognized it right away—a guidance nosecone for an intercontinental ballistic missile. *Shit.*

Joel and Ang waited in the darkness of the alley. Ang was on his third cigarette, his mind filled with worry, the wound in his side throbbing. Suddenly, he smashed his cigarette out and pulled Joel back further into the shadows. A pair of guards appeared moving along the alleyway. They had not expected security to make such a wide sweep. Ang held their one remaining pistol in his hand, as he and Joel crouched behind a wooden trough used to catch rainwater. They held their breaths as the two guards surveyed their surroundings, being careful not to miss anything suspicious.

The cool evening air had little effect on Joel. He started to perspire. He could hear the guards speaking softly to each other but had no clue what they were saying. Ang hunkered lower as the two guards moved in their direction. The glow from a hand rolled cigarette illuminated the face of the man on the left as he drew in a restricted breath. He placed his hand on his partner's arm to stop their walk.

They both pulled AKS-74U machine pistols from their shoulders and readied themselves for action. The AKS-74U, a slightly more modern and compact version of the AK-47, fired a slightly smaller bullet but at a faster rate.

The man on the left flicked his cigarette away. He was all business now. Something had their attention and they were looking right at the trough that hid Joel and Ang. The guards started to investigate. Ang quietly cocked his gun, using the palm of his hand to hide the noise. He was coiled like a tight spring ready to leap. As the two men stepped up to the trough, a laugh caught their attention.

They turned to its origin, a group of three German tourists laughing and staggering down the alley. They started singing a bit too loudly, obviously drunk. The two guards put their guns down and watched as the group moved past. The guards then followed behind them at a respectable distance, but not before the guard on the left retrieved his tossed cigarette and sucked it back to life.

Joel and Ang let out a collective sigh as a distant sneeze caught their attention. It was followed by a rattling noise, a muffled cry, and then a giant splash that doused them with the trough's water.

Codi breeched the surface, sputtering and flicking the soaked hair out of her face. She coughed up some of the water from her lungs. Joel and Ang looked like matching drowned rats. They stared in shock at their partner as she climbed out of the trough.

"Sorry," Codi said in a forced whisper. "I was holding onto a roof tile while you two were playing hide the weenie with those two guards. There's a bird nest up there and I must be allergic to something in it. That sneeze came out of nowhere, the tile broke off and, *voila,* swan dive."

"Well I give you a ten on your entry," Ang said, with a slight smile as he brushed the water off of his clothes.

"It might be bird flu," Joel added, in obvious concern.

"No bird flu here," Ang said, unaware of Joel's tendency towards germaphobia. "It started several hundred miles to the north."

"Did you see Chow?" Joel asked Codi.

"No. Come on let's get out of here." She was already leaving as she spoke.

Joel hurried after her calling in a loud whisper, "What did you find out?"

Codi held up the smart phone. "I found out that this phone is not waterproof."

"Intercontinental ballistic missile guidance nosecone? Are you sure?" Ang asked Codi.

"Ninety-five percent. I was stationed at Kaneohe Bay in Hawaii for a time and there was a missile display with several Chinese and Russian mock-ups."

Ang nodded his head in understanding. "Okay. I can't think of anything good you could use one for. I'll make some calls on the landline, since our only cell phone is dead."

Ang stood from the yellow Formica table at their guesthouse and moved to the old rotary phone in the living area.

Joel placed their soggy smart phone in a bag full of rice, saying, "At least it's easy to find rice around here."

Codi moved to the refrigerator to see what she could manage for a snack after her high-calorie-burning adventure.

Ang walked back in a moment later. "I contacted a friend of mine in the Ministry of State Security. We have to assume that the local police are in Chow's pocket and unable to handle this anyway."

"Good call," Joel said.

"They're sending a squad of two trucks and twelve men."

"That's great news. When will they get here?" Joel asked.

Ang hesitated. "Tomorrow noon."

Codi let out a short breath. She should have known. Bureaucracy moved slowly in every government.

Joel looked at his watch. "Twelve more hours."

"It could be all over by then." Codi looked like a lioness in a cage as she paced, knowing there was nothing she could do but wait. She tried the power on the drying cell phone. Still dead. "We should at least stake the place out and make sure no one leaves Chow's home. I'll take the first watch."

It was a sound idea and Joel volunteered for the second watch, with Ang taking the last.

Chow watched as his men loaded the canvas-backed truck under the glare of several work lights. They had converted the vehicle to look like a military FAW MV3 4X4, complete with a red star on both doors. He was wearing his old PAL general's uniform adorned with his many medals. Two of his men were dressed like military aides to match. Chow looked down at his phone expectantly. No new messages. The one working corner of his mouth dropped mechanically.

"Trouble sir?" Jin had seen the general's reaction and was feeling the tension of pre-mission jitters himself.

"No. Just waiting on an important text." He pocketed his phone and gestured to Jin with a swish of his hand. "Get on board, son."

Once the truck was loaded they pulled out through the cover of a heavy mist that buried the town in mystery. The trip to the silo would take twenty minutes, giving them another two hours before sunrise.

19

Guest House – 5:48 a.m. – Fenghuang, China

After a fitful sleep, Codi breathed in the aroma of freshly brewed coffee. It drew her from her bed to the small kitchen.

"Where did you find this?"

"There's a hotel down the street that caters to tourists." Joel beamed, as his coffee ritual was finally back.

Ang entered the room. "Something's up. About fifteen minutes ago the two guards went back inside and then the lights in the whole house went out. I crept up to a window and saw no activity. They were very focused during their shift and now they're gone."

"Anyone enter or exit since?"

"Not a soul," Ang replied.

"Could they be sleeping?"

"Maybe, but they were definitely on a schedule last night. Things were very busy. It seems improbable that they would work through the night, allow the guards to take a break, and what, they just all go to sleep? I double-checked the back door, and nothing. It's like they disappeared into the fog."

Joel set his beloved coffee down and stood holding the phone in the rice bag. "It's working."

The cellphone powered up. The text message was unreadable to him. He handed it to Ang.

"Problems," Ang said. "The road from Wuhan has been washed out. They are having to reroute and the new ETA is more like three p.m."

"Damn," Joel said.

"This just keeps getting better and better," Codi muttered.

"We should check out the house," said Joel.

The morning mist clung to the town like a mud facial, leaving visibility at less than ten feet. Codi and Ang moved through the Hong Bridge across the Tuo River. The sleepy fog-enshrouded town was awe inspiring, but they had no time for sightseeing.

Joel was assigned a different path, approaching the house from the other side. Two-hundred yards up was a stepping-stone path across the river. Each step was a stone column two feet in diameter and placed two feet apart. They spanned the river but were not recommended for anyone who'd been drinking, as you had to stride or jump from stone to stone. The mist was so thick that Joel couldn't see even halfway across the river. He took a deep breath and started to make his way across, half-hopping and half-stepping as he went, keeping his arms out at his side for balance. About halfway, he came to a sudden stop. A young woman materialized out of the fog, coming the other way. She was holding a baby, and there was no way to pass. Joel forced a smile and started back.

After she reached the bank, Joel started over again, hopping and stepping his way across. This time Joel ran into a man carrying a small bundle of firewood. Joel had made it more than three-quarters of the way and was not willing to go back again. He gestured for the man to back up, but the man refused and stepped on the stone directly in front of Joel. Joel gestured again, but the man gave him the universal sign for not a chance; you back up. This was getting old fast and Codi and Ang were counting on him. Joel did the only thing he could think of at the time. He shoved the man into the water. "Sorry," he said, "but I got a thing."

Joel continued moving to the other side, glancing over his shoulder to make sure the poor soul could swim. Just the opposite was true. The man had lost his firewood and was struggling to keep his head above water.

Joel stopped.

"You gotta be kidding me."

Once they reached Chongde Hall, Codi and Ang dropped low and surveyed the building. All was quiet, just as Ang had said. There were no guards stationed at the front door.

"Thoughts?" Codi asked Ang.

"I have been instructed to wait for our reinforcements," he said.

"Right. How long are you planning to hide behind us?"

"My hands are tied. But if you were to storm the front door, I would have to follow and try to intercede."

Codi slunk over to the entrance. The argument had been short. Codi and Joel would take the blame if anything went wrong, and Ang could live with that.

The front door was an ancient affair with bronze rivets and thick wooden beams. In place of the old lock was a modern deadbolt. Ang quickly worked to unlock it.

Once inside, the beauty of the large domed ceiling set in dark wood was lost on Codi. She and Ang moved to clear the home one room at a time. The problem was, they had only one gun between them. Codi had a mostly sharp kitchen knife, hoping to pick up a weapon along the way.

They worked in tandem, professionally clearing each

room. Soon the first floor was done—empty. The second floor was mostly bedrooms. They crept carefully from room to room, and the message was becoming clear. The home was empty. At the top of the stairs was the third floor, the open room Codi had seen the night before. But other than a few parts, the room and tables were empty. No hard evidence, no intercontinental ballistic missile nosecone. With practiced efficiency they finished their search but both knew the answer: they were too late.

As Codi and Ang returned down the carved wooden staircase to the first floor, they each processed the trouble that was coming their way, both political and legal.

They were discussing quickly exiting the building and denying ever having set foot in it, when Joel burst through the back door.

"FBI, nobody move!" His gun was drawn, ready to shoot. His clothes were soaked and he dripped all over the wood floor.

"You're late. And wet." Codi said.

Joel sheepishly put his gun away. "Sorry, got hung up."

He hooked a thumb over his shoulder. "Back door was open so I popped in. There's no sign of anyone out there."

"Same in here. It looks like they left sometime early this morning," Ang said.

"The question is how."

A grating sound from the back wall caught their attention. A large wall panel was rising upward, revealing a passageway illuminated with bare bulbs strung along the ceiling. Two armed guards were chatting as they made their way back into the home.

Ang yelled out, "Police! Freeze or I'll fire."

This caught the two men by surprise and they panicked, diving in opposite directions. Ang fired a shot into the space where the man on the right had just been standing. A quick reply of 5.45 mm full-auto lead sprayed back in Ang's direction, shredding the staircase. Codi, who didn't have a gun, wasted no time diving for cover behind the banister. Ang ducked and fired blindly, as bullets chewed up the space surrounding him.

Joel, who had not been detected by the two hostiles, dropped to the floor and emptied his clip in their direction. The man on the right twitched and died, his finger falling from the trigger harmlessly. The other man dove behind a large jade dragon. He reset his sites on the man who had just killed his partner. The temporary reprieve of bullets aimed in Ang's direction allowed him to jump over the railing and seek cover behind the stairs.

Joel rolled for a yellow upholstered sofa, leaving a snail trail of water behind him. He hid behind it as a full assault of gunfire dissected the couch and the wall behind it. Joel continued to scramble, and dove out from behind the far side of the couch, followed closely by hot lead. The only amnesty was when the assailant's clip ran dry. Joel had nowhere left to hide. It was a good fifteen feet to a warrior statue in the corner.

The guard quickly reloaded another clip and leaned out to reacquire the soggy man across the room. Joel had no more ammunition. He was now nothing more than a moving target.

Ang had anticipated the guard's move and had wormed his way into position for a shot. As soon as the man leaned out to reacquire Joel, Ang fired two quick bursts. The first one hit the man in the neck and the second in his temple. It ended the man's life but not before reflexes caused his finger to clamp onto the trigger. A wild spray of bullets flew everywhere, like a loose garden hose turned on full. It ended with a giant chandelier crashing to the floor, sending crystal shards everywhere.

The room was a mess, but Codi, Ang and Joel had somehow survived. The three moved to the center of the room to survey the damage. Codi took the occasion to arm herself with the dead man's weapon. Joel bent over to examine a bullet hole in his heel of his shoe. "That was close," he said.

Codi looked over to Ang who was brushing the dust out of his hair. "You got a little something on your shirt," she said.

Ang looked down to see three bullet holes stitched under his right armpit. "Whoa."

Abruptly, the back door opened and an older, hunched-over woman shuffled in, carrying groceries. She stiffened at the sight of the carnage. She looked over to see three strangers aiming weapons at her. A sudden scream escaped her, followed by groceries crashing to the floor.

The glow of two pole-mounted lights revealed Sheng Luo PLA missile silo 089. It was disguised as a fermentation house in the middle of an orchard. From a distance, it blended into the agriculture of the area and would be right at home in Napa Valley. It had a red-tiled roof and beige stucco walls with arched windows and a fermentation tank rising from the ground next to it.

The military-looking truck came to a brief stop, and half of Chow's team jumped out and moved off on foot. One of them started climbing a nearby telephone pole. Another, carrying a sniper rifle, jogged into the nearby orchard.

The driver let out the brake and continued on to the silo a half-mile ahead.

Jin triggered the jammer that would prevent any communications in the area. The truck pulled to a stop next to the building. A large wooden door opened to reveal two heavily armed guards who took the unexpected arrival seriously. They squinted through the headlights' glare of the truck. General Chow stepped down from the passenger's side and walked slowly and deliberately over to them. The two guards stiffened even more at the sight of the backlit general.

Chow called out, "At ease, gentlemen."

They disregarded the order.

"General Chow Phun of the People's Liberation Army southern division under the direct orders of the Vice Chairman." Chow pulled out an official looking document that had all the needed details, as far as a lowly guard would know.

"I am making surprise inspections to twelve PLA Missile Silos today."

"I will have to check this out sir," said one of the guards. "We don't get generals just stopping by, especially at night."

"Of course, but please hurry. I have a full day ahead of me."

The driver of the truck stepped down casually and lit a cigarette. One guard eyed him suspiciously, while the other went back inside to confirm the general's orders. Chow paced around, looking put out. He went over to his driver to join him for a smoke.

The operations room for the silo was a large rectangle. It was state-of-the art electronic sophistication with human and analog redundancy for everything. There were two matching control consoles that looked like a cockpit for a computer geek. On the desk-like surface was a sophisticated terminal with an extended keyboard. The rest of the room held various electronics and communication devices. The floor panels had the ability to lift up so you could access the electronics and wiring running throughout. On the back wall was a set of elevator doors. On the opposite wall was an armored exit door leading to the security room and then the outside.

In one of the cockpits, technician Wei flicked his lighter

for the tenth time and swore. The fluid was empty. "Got a light?" he asked his co-worker.

Zhang stepped over and pulled his Bik lighter out. He watched as the flame ignited the tip of Wei's smoke.

Wei inhaled to complete the action and nodded his thanks. The twelve-hour shift they worked was far from over, but nicotine helped him stay calm in a room with no windows. His claustrophobia was just strong enough to be a constant reminder that he worked in a space that was more dungeon than office. Luckily, the military had never discovered his secret and his career as a military tech was showing promise. Just last week he had interviewed with his superiors to potentially oversee the technical operations on the entire southern missile defense network, a job that would get him outside from time to time and put a few more Yuan in his pocket every month. He drew another puff into his lungs and let the tension go, as he contemplated his future.

Ang turned to Joel and Codi.

"She says her name is Tenzin. She works and lives here but she speaks a southern dialect of Mandarin that is really hard to understand, so I could be completely wrong."

They were gathered at the kitchen table. Codi had given her a glass of water and Ang was trying to kindly interrogate her. They went back and forth speaking rapid fire Chinese. Ang did his best to keep things calm and level-headed. Joel had followed the secret passage to an empty street exit three buildings over. He returned, carrying the fallen groceries.

"They definitely left through the passage, and there is no sign of anyone, just the two dead guards," Joel said as he entered the room.

"Nice shooting, by the way," Codi said to him.

Joel just nodded. He never liked to take a man's life and the weight of it was often unbearable. In fact, had he given it some thought, he'd realize that he'd never even shot at another human being before he met Codi.

Ang summed up their situation. "We got nothing here but two stiffs, an old woman, and no evidence."

"Looks like Chow is in the wind and able to finish whatever it is he has planned," Joel said.

The utter failure was hard to take, especially after all they'd been through. His body language screamed defeat as Joel sat next to his partners.

"Okay, let me sum things up." Joel ticked off his fingers as he went through the past several days. "Something we discovered from a Russian special ops mission in the Arctic during the fifties called Operation Blind Pig, is making a retired General Chow Phun very nervous. So nervous, in fact, that he arranged to have us killed, kidnapped–"

"At an international airport, which is no small feat," Codi added. "Oh, and replaced with lookalikes to throw off our office."

"Right." Joel continued his summary of the last few days. When he got to his third finger on his second hand, he stopped. "Electrical leach."

"What?" Codi asked.

"Electrical leach. That was the term Andrei Tatter used, the fishing guy. What if Chow has a modern day equivalent?"

"But we don't know what it does or if it even exists," Codi said.

Joel took on a faraway stare, as his fingers absently tapped on the table. "Maybe, but back in the fifties it was attached to the DEW Line system, an early warning radar-based structure. What if they used the leach to bypass the system somehow?"

Joel looked around the room. "Now we have a missile

guidance nosecone and possibly a way to make it untrack able."

"An intercontinental ballistic missile that is untrack able. That can't be good," Codi said. She rubbed the back of her skull trying to thwart an oncoming headache. "We gotta find and stop Chow."

"Easier said than done," Ang said, with a look of defeat.

They sat in silence, no one suggesting their next move.

"You want to stop Mr. Chow Phun?" All three agents looked at the old woman who had just spoken English. Each looked like they had just bit into a lemon.

"You speak English?" Joel could scarcely say the words.

"Who are you?" Codi dared to ask.

The old woman stood, no longer hunched over. She looked at the group with sharp appraising eyes. This was not the frail housekeeper they had thought she was.

"My name is Tenzin. I work for a group called The People for Tibetan Freedom. We monitor various people and facilities throughout southern China with many such as I. In Tibet, we have no military to push China from our borders, but information can be a different type of weapon, and we wield it with all our might. What little autonomy we now enjoy as a people was hard fought, using blackmail and information leaks."

Joel's mouth dropped open in disbelief. "Incredible."

"Yes, but I'm afraid you might be too late to stop Mr. Chow Phun."

"What do you mean?" Ang asked.

"Yes, tell us everything you know," Codi said.

"One moment, please," Tenzin said.

The very short woman with thick gray hair moved like a cat out of the room. Codi peeked out the door just to make sure she didn't run off.

Tenzin returned and set an old leather-bound book on the

table. She flipped it opened. Inside was a carved out section filled with handwritten notes and drawings.

"I do what I can to spy, and copy anything that happens in this house. Mr. Chow Phun has been busy building some kind of radar or satellite blocking system for ground-based missiles."

She pulled out a piece of paper showing a very detailed drawing of a rocket nosecone with a satellite dish built into the front. It was covered over by a clear dome to maintain its aerodynamics.

"I saw something like this last night," Codi said.

Tenzin pointed with two fingers to the document. "Here. This is what they took to Sheng Luo."

"Sheng Luo?" Joel asked.

"A rocket silo."

The three agents were trying to catch up but her words were processing too slowly in their brains.

"Don't tell me you don't know what he's up to?" Tenzin said. "How were you planning to stop the unknown?"

Codi was the first to respond. "We may not totally know everything but we are determined to stop him. Where is this silo?"

Tenzin told them everything she knew about Chow Phun's plans, which turned out to be nothing more than a location and a plan to attack and take over the silo. As far as his designs and use of the nosecone, nobody knew for sure. But it seemed very clear to all that Chow and a mystcry rocket nosecone, along with access to a working ICBM, was really bad news for both their countries.

20

PLA Missile Silo 089 – 4:58 a.m. – Sheng Luo, China

The console buzzed in the operations room. Zhang grabbed the headset. Wei listened to his partner's one-sided conversation.

"Hang on a sec."

Zhang told Wei about the issues outside.

There was nothing worse than a pissed-off general looking for payback. Wei quickly dialed his superior—nothing. He tried the hard line—dead. Then the radio, then the keyboard. Nothing was getting out. Wei had been through communication failures in the past, but never all four backups failing at once.

"Protocol six," he told his partner.

This signaled a complete lockdown of the facility.

"Tell the general we are sorry," Wei said. "Protocol six is in effect and we are locked down."

Wei hung up the receiver and started flipping switches that were part of the lockdown procedure. Wei pulled out the operations manual and severed the chain that anchored it to the desk. He noticed his hands were starting to shake.

The first guard came back out of the building looking a little concerned. "Communications are down, sir," he said to Chow. "Even the hard line is not working. That means we are going on lockdown. I'm afraid I can't let you in."

"I understand your orders, but I have mine as well," Chow said. "And I'll be dammed if a rice-slurping private is going to turn me away. Do you know the hurt I can lay on you and your family for this?" Chow said the last part with real venom in his voice.

"Yes sir, but my superior can do the same, so no matter what I choose, I'm screwed. Therefore, I'm following protocol as dictated by my direct superior. Sorry, sir."

The two guards backed towards the entrance watching the truck and the general carefully. Just before they got to the door, a shot from the nearby grove rang out.

One of the guards dropped face-first to the ground, a piece of his skull missing. The general and his aides quickly overpowered the other guard before he could react. They held him face-down in the dirt while they zip-tied his hands and feet.

"It's about time. Come on," Chow said.

The driver gave a whistle and bodies quickly swarmed, emptying all of the truck's contents. They efficiently hauled everything into the security room.

"Five minutes before the next satellite passes," Jin called as he watched the proceedings. "Get that truck out of here, I want everything to look normal for the next flyover."

The last of the gear and men hustled inside the building, as the truck moved away.

The security room was small, and with all the men and gear they were literally crammed inside like sardines. There was a guard desk with two chairs and a steel blast door that was secured on the back wall. The desk had a half-completed

Mahjong game and a small terminal with a keyboard. A large monitor showed a view of six cameras covering a 360-degree view of the surroundings. A shelf on the sidewall held a hot plate with a kettle and tea supplies.

Poh grabbed the guard that was still alive and shoved him against a wall. "What is the code for entering the armored door?" he asked the man.

The guard shook his head in fear, not uttering a word. He had seen his friend shot right beside him and had no doubt the same awaited him, even if he talked. Poh pulled his knife and placed it next to the man's right eye. The guard forced his eyes shut not wanting to see the danger.

Poh asked him again, and when the guard continued to refuse to answer, he flicked the blade, puncturing the man's eye. A gelatinous ooze spilled out to the sound of a mournful cry. The pain was intense but short lived as the guard's right vision dimmed and his eye died.

"What is the code!"

The guard whimpered through tears and blood. "Protocol six, the door can't be opened."

"We know there is an override code. What is it?" Poh countered.

He moved the knife to the guard's genitals.

"Last chance. How about one ball to go with one eyeball." He chuckled at his joke. "Or I could just make a clean sweep of everything down there. Wouldn't take much. What is the override code!"

The guard was so traumatized that he was blubbering incomprehensibly. The knife pressed higher and the words suddenly became more panicked but now understandable.

Jin wasted no time imputing the code into the terminal on the guard's desk. He glanced over at the game of mahjong that was spread across the desk. Several red tong and green dragons in evidence on the discard pile. A loud click followed, turning every head in the room. The steel blast door started to open.

Inside the operations room, Wei heard the click that signified the opening of the blast door. He grabbed the operations manual and hit the alarm button. A claxon and red flashing lights filled the room. He ran for the elevator, screaming to his subordinate, "Hold them off!"

Wei punched a code in the keypad next to it. The elevator doors started to open and he dashed through, hitting the down button repeatedly. As the doors slowly closed he could just make out Zhang all alone, armed with his pistol, standing his ground. He was ready to stop the intruders.

Two of the general's armed men crashed low through the large door's opening gap, their silenced guns drawn and ready. From inside the elevator, Wei heard two quick muffled pops followed by a thud. As the car slowly descended, ridiculous music played a happy folk tune.

The general's team moved quickly into the operations area. It was nearly three times the size of the security room. There were two large control consoles touting a collection of indicator lights, switches, and keyboards. Crumpled on the floor with an unused pistol was a blood-soaked operator, Zhang.

"The room is secure sir, but there is no sign of the lead tech."

Jin held up the severed chain attached to the console. "Operations manual is missing."

"Get me that tech before he destroys the manual," Poh ordered. "He couldn't have gone far. Go."

Poh ran to the elevator doors and listened. A decreasing whir told him what he needed to know. With a couple of hand gestures, his men used steel bars to pry the elevator doors apart. They hurriedly attached two rappelling ropes, and two of his men dropped into the shaft chasing the receding car to its final destination.

Wei knew he was out of time and opened the operations manual. He grabbed his lighter and flicked it. He prayed for a flame so he could burn the book to ash and with it the ability to operate the missile silo. A small flame burst on the wick but it died as quickly as it was born. He tried again—nothing. Wei flicked and flicked until his thumb was raw. It was no use.

Finally, the car came to a stop at the bottom. Wei started to shred the first page by hand as a pair of combat boots crashed through the access panel on the car's roof. Wei reached for his pistol but was struck in the face as his assailant dropped to the floor. Wei spun with the impact, just as the elevator doors opened to the subbasement level. He reacquired his aim before the soldier could drop his rappelling rope and bring his gun to bear.

Four shots echoed in the tight space. Wei watched as his combatant slumped to the floor, dead. He then looked up at a second man holding his smoking weapon through the access panel. It was pointed in his direction. The man was struggling to get through hole. Wei looked down to see two red dots on his chest bloom with color. The gun in his hand dropped to the floor as his legs started to wobble. He grabbed the book and exited the elevator.

The room was a large tube-shaped area with a ninety-eight-foot-tall ICBM standing in the middle. It was painted olive green and had its model name, DF-5B, stamped on the side. Black metal scaffolding held it aloft and gave technicians access to the rocket. In the middle of the floor was a black hole that allowed for exhaust.

Wei wobbled like a raging drunk for the rocket, his plan desperate and poorly thought out. He hoped to throw the manual into the abyss of the missile's exhaust tube. His vision was dimming as he staggered forward. The railing to the exhaust exit was just ahead. But his feet failed him and Wei dropped to the floor, scattering the book out of reach. He tried to crawl to it. Just a little further...

The assailant in the elevator's access panel had fired two shots down into the lead tech almost at the same time as the tech had fired at his partner. He then had to re-holster his weapon and untangle his rappelling rope to get down into the car. But the rope caught on an attachment bolt to the elevator. He saw the tech stumble out of the elevator with the operations manual. He flicked out a knife, cut himself free, and dropped into the car. He ran after the tech.

Inside the main silo, the soldier paused. There was a dead man, the tech, his fingers touching the operations manual. It was just inches from a deep exit tube built directly below the rocket to vent the flames.

The soldier dropped to the floor and picked up the book. He looked up at the giant ICBM, one of man's greatest military powers. He stood and started back to the elevator.

Jin placed the blood-spattered manual on the console and opened it up. He pieced the torn first page back together and began the startup process. The first thing on his list was to get the silo out of lockdown and turn off that obnoxious alarm.

The Southern Great Wall is a shorter version of its famous brother to the north. It is often overlooked, but was at one point 150 kilometers in length. Though most of it is now destroyed, there are several sections that stretch across the lush southern landscape, a reminder of a long forgotten hatred between the Mio and Chinese people. Codi looked out the passenger window of their car as it paralleled the Southern

Great Wall for several hundred meters. It was a marvel of engineering, housing over five-thousand soldiers at its apex.

Ang finally had some good news. Their back-up had re-routed and was now only fifteen minutes behind them. All that was left was to find Chow and point them in the right direction.

They pulled off the road onto a dirt trail that stopped just before the peak of a hill. Their backseat driver, Tenzin, had been a chatterbox for most of the way, pointing and gesticulating her directions. She exited the car and hustled up to the top of the hill, not waiting for the others, and lay down on the ground.

Codi followed to lay beside her, impressed with the old woman's fortitude. Ang and Joel followed. Tenzin pointed to a quaint building in the tranquil valley below. There was a red tile roof set on a rectangular building covered in flowering vines. A small domed fermenting tank was attached on the left side with a matching roof.

There were a few arched windows, a large wooden door and stone pavers encompassing the foundation. The building was surrounded on all sides by an orchard of peach trees. The smell was intoxicating with ripe peaches hanging from every tree.

"It looks like a fermentation building at a vineyard," Codi said.

"Yes, for making peach wine, but that is what they want you to think. It is Sheng Luo PLA Missile Silo 089," Tenzin replied.

Codi looked skeptical and borrowed Ang's binoculars. On closer inspection there was some seriously heavy-duty conduit piping on one wall. The roof had several small aerial antennas and a satellite dish partially hidden by the roof's peak.

Tenzin pointed to the side building that looked like a small tower. "The dome opens up for launch."

Codi panned her view to the smaller round tower. Its domed roof had visible seams, and the ground held three large exhaust vents, angled away from the building. "That is definitely *not* what it appears to be," Codi said, as she handed the binoculars back to Ang.

The group pulled back down the hill. Tenzin looked up at Ang. "Well, good then. My work here is done."

"What?" Codi said.

"Wait. We might still need you for–" Joel started.

"For what, to point my accusatory finger in another direction?"

"We don't even know if General Phun is in there," Ang countered.

"I can guarantee you, *that* is Mr. Chow Phun's target. I am but an old woman, I can be of no further use to you now."

Tenzin turned and started to walk back down the dirt road calling over her shoulder. "Just remember, Mr. Chow Phun is a very smart and clever man."

Ang stared for a moment and then turned back to Codi and Joel. "Smart woman."

Joel looked worried. "Yeah. She may be the only one who gets out alive."

Tenzin called out from a distance. "Try not to get yourselves killed."

"And she's a mind reader too," Joel added.

21

PLA Missile Silo 089 – 8:22 a.m. – Sheng Luo, China

The dead were dumped unceremoniously in a stack on the silo's concrete floor. The two scientists, with the help of one soldier, moved the replacement nosecone down to the sub-basement. From there the scientists took their tools and began to climb the scaffolding to the missile's top. The soldier used a gantry crane to attach and lift the new nosecone up for installation.

The alarm stopped. It was as if a great weight had been lifted from Jin's chest. *"Finally,"* he mumbled.

Chow stepped over next to him and looked at the screen.

"I'm into the system," Jin said, "and there are a lot of things I can do, including launching the rocket. But without an authorization code, the nuclear portion will be inert."

"Start by filling the rocket," Chow ordered.

Jin's fingers flew over the extended keyboard, and with a flick of the enter key, hydrazine along with liquid hydrogen and oxygen began to fill the individual tanks in the lower stages of the rocket.

It took time to remove the original nosecone and replace it with their prototype. That was followed by several electronic dry runs to confirm everything was operational. Chow spent most of the time pacing and watching Poh double-check security on the perimeter.

Ang pulled out their cellphone to check on their reinforcements' progress. He pushed send several times without luck. "I got no signal."

"Is it still wet?" Codi asked.

"No, it's working. It just won't go through."

"They're probably jamming the area," Joel said, while looking around for a source.

Codi felt useless just waiting there for backup to arrive. In principle she was not really a backup kind of girl, preferring instead to forge ahead no matter the cost, pulling the troops along with her. But they were not in Kansas anymore and the last thing she needed to be was the focus of an international incident. She would wait a bit longer.

"That means the general is most likely already in there," Joel added.

"And doing God knows what while we all sit around talking about it," Codi said.

A rumble punctuated Codi's comment, as two smaller troop transports came to a stop next to Ang's car. A small but sturdy colonel stepped from the passenger's seat of the lead vehicle and approached. He shook Ang's hand, as Ang introduced Codi and Joel. The colonel eyed them with disdain and refocused on Ang almost immediately.

"This better not be a waste of my time," he said to Ang. "Getting here was a real bitch. You said there might be a breach in one of our silos?"

"Yes. Sheng Luo PLA missile silo 089. It's just over the hill."

Codi and Joel felt helpless listening to the two men speaking Chinese.

The colonel pulled out a map and located the silo. It was indeed just over the hill next to them. "I should take look. You three wait here," he said in broken English.

He climbed to the top of the hill and peered down at the lone building in the middle of a peach grove.

Codi walked over to Ang and spoke quietly to him. "This is bullshit."

"What would you have me do?"

Codi knew he was right, but the slow, uncaring quality of their new leader was driving her crazy.

The colonel stomped back down the hill. "All is quiet."

Codi could not hide her disappointment. The colonel seemed unaffected.

"I don't like it."

She turned to look back at him. Had she heard right?

He switched back to Chinese and spoke to Ang. "We'll go in and investigate. Once we have secured the facility we will come back for you."

"If the general's in there, they may be expecting trouble," Ang said.

"*If* the general's in there, I will buy the first and second rounds tonight for all, but I doubt this is the case. But don't worry, my men are highly trained and ready for anything."

The colonel switched back to English and addressed the Americans. "You focus on staying here. I don't want to throw you in jail for interfering."

Codi had to bite the bottom of her lip to stay calm.

With that said he turned and left.

"Corporal Ling!" the colonel called out.

A young man with a buzz cut and a can-do attitude hustled up to the colonel and gave him a terse salute.

"Let operations know our position."

He nodded and ran off to the truck.

Ang interrupted, holding his smart phone up as a demo. "They are jamming the signals here."

"Interesting. We use a specialized military signal, so not to worry." He said the words with a heavy patronizing measure.

Ang knew when to attack and when to retreat and now was the time for playing nice. "I'm sure you are right."

Ang moved to stand beside his two American cohorts.

"What was that all about," Joel asked, not understanding what had been said.

"A simple case of might makes right."

Codi and Joel both knew instantly what Ang meant.

"Great," Codi whispered.

The three watched as the energetic Corporal Ling ran back from his truck and saluted the corporal. "Sir, there is no signal getting in or out."

Codi leaned over to Ang, whispering through nearly closed lips. "Let me guess, they're being jammed."

Ang slowly but purposely nodded his head.

"Take the radio and go as far away from here as you need to get a signal. Let them know that we are being jammed and are going to investigate."

Ling ran off with his orders.

The colonel turned his attention back to Ang. "Inspector, do I have to leave a few of my men here to babysit?"

"No, we will do what you ask. Just be damn careful, please."

"I intend to."

The colonel called his men together to form a plan. They loaded up in the vehicles and roared off towards the silo.

The scientists scrambled out of the subbasement, their task complete. The ICBM looked just like it always had, except the green tip had been replaced with a clear Lexan tip, complete with radar dish and some very specific equipment housed inside.

"We got activity outside," one of the men called.

"What? How?" Chow hurried to Poh's side to see the security feed. "I'm counting on you to make this go away."

"Of course," Poh said. "It is what we do." The squad leader called out brisk orders and his men readied for a fight.

Codi waited until the trucks were out of sight, and ran to the hilltop to watch the fallout. Joel tried to catch up.

"*Codi*. We were supposed to wait here. I gave them my word."

Ang, exasperated flung his arms in the air and ran after them.

From their vantage point they watched as the two vehicles approached the silo. They paused for a second and several soldiers exited the back of the truck. They followed behind the truck, using the sheet metal as cover.

Codi watched. Sitting on the sidelines was hard, but if they could watch the man who'd caused them so much strife go down, it would have to suffice.

As the truck and the men neared the building the arched front door opened slightly.

"Get out of there," Codi mouthed to herself.

Poh hinged open the door and stood to the side as two of his men aimed their Type-98 recoilless rifles at the two troop transports. Nicknamed the Queen Bee, they shot a 120 mm projectile from a handheld fiberglass tube. The multipurpose warhead rocketed to its target in less than ten seconds from the pull of the trigger. It was capable of penetrating up to 800 mm of armor-piercing steel and then fragmenting the pieces throughout the vehicle, killing all of its occupants.

Target acquired," the two men said.

"Fire on my mark," Poh said. "Three, two, one, *mark.*"

Two rocket-aided projectiles shot from the building. The drivers of the trucks instinctually parted company in different directions at the sight of the streaming fireballs. But the guided explosives tracked their movements. Before they could get ten feet, both vehicles exploded in balls of flame and flying steel.

Several of the soldiers who were on the ground returned fire and a brief but intense firefight ensued. As the last bullet flew, the picture was clear—two down on the general's team and none left on the assault team.

Chow's remaining men pulled back into the silo, and Poh reported, "All of the attacking force has been put down, General. They appear to be regular PLA army."

"I am at a loss as to how regular army could have gotten wind of our plan and acted on it so quickly," Chow said, pondering.

"General, before you start pointing fingers within your own organization, let me say they were not in an attack formation."

The general looked at him with a new curiosity.

"It was more like a routine approach. They were most likely only here to check on something."

Chow paced, ready to explode at any moment. But he took the time to re-center himself and get back to the business at hand. How they got there was no longer his concern. Keeping focused on the mission was. "Get a team out there right away and clean up the evidence," Chow ordered.

"Yes, sir."

"Jin!"

Jin hammered a few strokes on his keyboard. "We have... thirteen minutes till the next pass, sir."

"We are on it." Poh said, and left, barking orders to his men.

Codi turned from the carnage, sickened by the careless waste of life. Joel and Ang watched as three soldiers moved through the battlefield dispatching anyone who was still breathing, occasionally bending over to rob the dead.

"They're playing for keeps," Joel said. "I can't imagine we have a chance at success here." He sounded despondent, half-shaking as he spoke.

Codi sat back up. "I've been thinking, Joel, it's time for you to get back in the game."

"What?"

"Back in the game," Codi repeated.

Joel looked confused.

"I know you really loved Annie. We were all lucky to have been a part of her life."

Agent Annie Waters was one of the original team members. During a case, she and Joel became very close and found love at a time and place that would normally make it impossible. They say love will find a way, and it did. But Joel had to witness Annie's death at the hands of a traitor, and was helpless to stop it. As she died in his arms the flame that the two had built winked out, leaving Joel battered, enraged, and lost.

"And now is the time to talk about this?" Joel asked.

"Why not? You get one chance to go through life. Every day is a gift, and you, my friend, have a lot to give. If I don't make it past today I would never forgive myself for not bringing it up."

"Please tell me you're not going to do what I think you are," Joel said.

"Well, first of all, I'm not telling, I'm doing."

Codi stood. "You two stay here. I'm going to make this whack job go away."

She started to move down the hill towards the building.

"Codi, wait! I think I have a better plan," Ang called.

Cody paused and turned back to Ang.

"Look," he said.

Codi turned to see several men exiting the building into the cleared area around the building. She ducked down and moved quickly back to the cover of the hill.

"And for the record," Ang said to Joel, "Codi's right. You should get back in the game."

"Seriously, you too?" Joel felt surrounded.

"Inaction leaves a regret you can't forget," Ang said.

"Sounds like a fortune cookie, but I agree," Codi said.

"Believe me, I have made that mistake, but never again," said Ang.

Ang and Codi shared a knowing look.

They watched as six men, two in regular clothes and four in uniform, quickly spread out and went to work. Two men put out the fires that were once troop transports filled with men, and the rest moved the bodies and debris over to the ruined vehicles and began stacking them in a pile.

"What the hell?"

After all the flame and smoke was gone they tugged two large bags out of the building.

"Camo netting," Joel said.

"They're hiding the evidence of the battle," Ang added.

"But why?" Joel asked.

Codi pointed up with her finger, as a smile grew on her face. "Satellite."

"Of course, Chow's hiding it from the satellites," Ang said.

"And they're running low on soldiers," Joel said.

"What makes you say that?" asked Ang.

Joel pointed for emphasis. "Two of those guys are not in uniform. I'm betting they got pulled off the tech side of the operation to help out."

"They're working really fast," Ang said while looking up in the sky. "The next pass must be coming soon."

Codi stood and motioned with her hand. "Come on, I have an idea."

Ang and Joel followed her back down the hill to Ang's car. They grabbed the three 3.5 liter jugs of water that Ang kept in his trunk kit and emptied them out. Ang went through his kit and pulled a few things together: a first aid kit, climbing gear, and a bulletproof vest size Small. It would fit only him.

Codi grabbed her kitchen knife and went to the hood.

She cut the heater hose from the engine, and Joel used it to syphon gas from the car's tank into the empty water jugs.

"Hey."

Joel jumped a mile at the sudden comment from an unknown source, spilling gas on his shoes. Corporal Ling, holding his radio, stood nearby watching.

"Jeez, you scared the crap outa me," Joel stammered.

"Hey." Ling smiled showing crooked tea-stained teeth. He wiped his free hand through his disheveled hair.

Ang popped his head up from the trunk and Codi from the hood at the surprise visitor. It was clear that Corporal Ling spoke only one word of English, *hey*.

Ang filled him in on what happened and all were surprised how well he took the complete elimination of all his comrades. He fell to the ground for a few moments, letting the information course through him. After a brief moment he looked up and asked Ang what he should do next.

"Did you get a signal through?"

"Yes," he said proudly."

"What did they say?"

"They said they'd make a note of it and run it by his commander once he returned."

Ang translated.

"Typical," Codi said, familiar with the standing military policy around the world of do nothing until you see the enemy with your own eyes.

"Ang, translate this for me, would you?" Codi said. "We are not waiting for backup that may or may not arrive. We are going in there and we are going to stop Chow. You can either come with us, or you can hike back to where you had a signal and try to convince someone to send immediate help. But if you come with us you'll be taking orders from us, understand?"

Ang translated and the two went back and forth a few times.

"He says he wants to come with us."

"Okay, so, where's his gun?" Codi asked.

Ang asked the question.

"He left it in the truck when he ran off to use the radio."

"Perfect, four against the world, one unarmed. I have…" she opened the curved banana clip on the AKS-74U she'd taken from the dead soldier at Chow's house, "half a clip. Joel?"

Joel opened his pistol's clip and looked. "Three bullets."

"Ang?"

"One mostly-full clip."

"Well, there you have it, that and some climbing gear. How can we lose?"

Codi grabbed a jug and started for the hill.

Joel handed his jug to Ling and pantomimed for him to carry it. Ling grabbed the jug happily and somehow his crooked yellow smile got even bigger. "Hey!"

"Yeah, hey,' Joel deadpanned as he turned to follow Codi.

They carried the jugs up the hill and waited. There was no

sign of any movement outside the silo. The four moved stealthily through the peach trees towards the edge of the clearing where the silo sat. Codi had laid out her plans in advance so no talking was required.

They kept the camo netting between them and the silo, as they crept low carrying their improvised gas containers. Joel collected his jug back from Ling.

"Hey!"

"Hey." Joel smiled at the blithesome Ling. He held his hand up to signal *wait here*. But as he started to leave, Ling followed anyway.

Each used their jug to make as big of a letter as possible. Three jugs, three letters. Ang had assured Codi that the Chinese would recognize the international call for help—SOS.

They strategically placed their gas letters next to the camo netting hoping to get a two for one. Ang used his lighter to ignite the letters and the four ran back to the cover of the peach grove.

Joel spoke with excitement. "That should get their satellite's attention."

"An SOS in flames next to a nuclear missile silo? You would think," Codi added.

From the cover of the trees, they split into two groups. Ang and Ling went counterclockwise and Codi and Joel went clockwise, working their way to the backside of the building. Ang's wound was bothering him and he had a slightly stooped style to his run. Codi and Joel moved as quickly as possible without making any noise. It was going to be close.

22

PLA Missile Silo 089 – 9:13 a.m. – Sheng Luo, China

"Looks like the fire didn't stay out," said one of the guards in the outer guardroom, while looking at the security monitors.

The screen clearly showed a view of smoke and flames building up just beyond their camouflaged netting.

The other guard went to the exit door and looked back at his partner before opening. "You see any movement?"

"Nothing out there is still alive. But we better get those flames out before the general has a coronary."

"Hey, we get the same pay whether he lives or dies." He laughed at his perceived joke as he opened the main door and moved out into the courtyard with a fire extinguisher. The second guard left the monitor and pushed to the doorway to watch the proceedings. He kept his rifle pointed in the direction of the reborn flames.

Codi and Joel had sprinted through the groves and dashed for the back of the building at a dead run. They stayed under cover of the trees and waited. As soon as Codi saw the guard with the fire extinguisher, she ran to the side of the building. Joel kept at her heels as they moved to the front of the building, with their backs against the wall. Codi held her gun ready for battle.

They had hoped that the fire would provide the needed distraction for them to cross the clearing from the orchard to the back of the building without being noticed. They were ten feet from the door on the hinge side, unable to see if it was clear or not.

After reassuring himself that there were no threats, the guard relaxed and decided it was safe to have a smoke.

Codi heard the telltale sound of a lighter click and used the distraction to her advantage. She used her left arm to pin Joel to the wall out of the way. With gun raised, she pulled the kitchen knife she'd taken from the guesthouse out of her belt. She swapped guns with Joel taking his pistol for close quarters combat. Joel tried to look less awkward than normal, holding the assault rifle. She stepped carefully to the open door, which provided a small modicum of protection. She could feel the soldier on the other side of the door breathing, as he watched his partner disappear behind the netting to put out the flames. A puff of smoke cleared the door as he exhaled. Codi took a slow breath and pounced. She held the knife low to her torso and thrust it up and away as she twisted around the door towards the man.

The guard caught movement from the corner of his eye and reacted by moving away from the source. Codi extended her elbow to the limit catching the man mid rib. The blade scraped across protective bone and found the soft tissue between. It pushed through his lung tissue and just clipped his left ventricle before all forward thrust was lost. Codi pulled the blade from the man, causing a sucking sound, and cocked her arm for another thrust. But it wasn't needed. The soldier slumped to the floor, his left foot twitching to the beat of an unheard song. She quickly looked in the room for more targets and was relieved to find it empty.

As he rounded the camo netting, the guard noticed that

the fire was in the shape of three large letters. Immediately, he knew something was wrong. He turned and ran for the cover of the building, calling out a warning to his comrade.

Codi heard the man yelling in Chinese. She turned in time to see the other soldier running back to the silo waving and yelling. When he realized Codi was not his partner, he dropped the fire extinguisher. He drew a bead on this new threat. Codi quickly took aim as the running man lifted his weapon to fire in her direction, but before she could pull the trigger, two quick bursts from beside the building ended the man's progression. Joel walked out from behind the door, the barrel of his gun smoking.

Codi pulled the dead man out of the entrance and relieved him of all weapons and ammunition.

"He must have realized that someone was still out here when he saw the fires," Joel said, practically hyperventilating as he spoke.

"Well, don't just stand there, Joel. Go get his gun and ammo."

Codi almost rolled her eyes as the admonished Joel ran off to the man he'd just shot. The fire had spread to the netting and the whole battlefield would soon be exposed again.

Hopefully, the satellite would catch it.

Ang and Ling came running around the other corner of the building, out of breath.

"I heard shooting, are you two okay?"

A quick nod and the toss of the dead man's gun to Ling was his answer.

Things were looking up. They had a way inside the silo and were significantly better armed. Codi moved into the doorway and stepped into the room. Her first instinct was to shoot out the security camera mounted on the sidewall. A rattling caught her attention. She looked over as two grenades rolled across the floor. She saw a large steel blast door at the far end of the room closing behind them.

"Grenade!" Codi screeched as she dove out of the room between the standing forms of Ang and Ling.

She hit the ground and immediately rolled right. Ang and Ling followed quickly behind as a percussive wave from the blast killed everything within a thirty-foot radius.

Poh waited on the other side of the now closed blast door with two of his men. He counted down the grenade's fuse and then hit the button to open the automated door, once the two muffled blasts sounded. With guns blazing his men surged through the opening, sending bullets around the now blackened security room. As they reloaded, Poh covered his men from the doorway. A dust-covered shape from outside the room rolled into view and fired, cutting one of the guards nearly in half. The other guard was forced to dive behind what was left of the security desk.

Codi inched to the edge of the doorjamb using it for cover as bullets pinged just above her head. Joel ran back from his kill and crouched on the other side of the doorpost, splitting the shooter's attention. Codi glanced back in time to see Ang and Ling. They had taken the worst of the blast. Ang was dazed and trying to sit up.

"Stay down!" Codi called to him. She turned back and exchanged shots with the soldier inside.

"Seal this door now!" General Chow Phun screamed, sputum flying from his drooping lips. He was waving his hands in the air, his face flushed and angered.

"Hold! I still have a man out there." Poh fired off a burst to keep the two intruders at the front door from entering.

"Move it," Poh called to his man as he laid down cover fire again.

But the general didn't wait. He pushed the button on the wall that activated the armored door.

Codi saw the man behind the desk make a dash for the steel door. She held her barrel around the corner and fired blindly at the man. A bullet to the thigh spun him to the floor. He crawled as fast as he could to the closing door, reaching for his leader to pull him through. Poh was forced to pull back with the closing door. The man willed himself to move, half crawling, half stumbling. He finally leapt forward the last few feet. But his leg gave out and he fell half-in, half-out of the jamb.

The steel blast door hardly noticed the screams and cracking bones as it reset itself to the closed position.

Codi turned, unwilling to allow the visual to enter her memory. Joel walked into the room just as the man was bisected. His eyes grew large as saucers as steel severed flesh and spine right down the middle. He froze momentarily and ran outside to puke.

Poh turned in disgust as the top half of his men died right in front of him. He wanted to scream and shoot Chow for closing the door too soon, but knew it would change nothing. Instead, he ordered the door welded shut. He would not have this sacrifice wasted.

Jin watched as a stick welder fired to life, binding door to jamb, sealing him inside the operations room. A note of finality suddenly struck him as he now knew for certain he was on a one-way journey. This was not in accordance with his plans.

An internal struggle of epic proportions ensued. As he saw it, his options were now extremely limited, and only one hundred percent success would give him any hope of getting out of this place alive.

So be it. Luckily, this was one of his specialties. He had always been a one-hundred-percenter.

Codi and her team entered the decimated security room. They looked at the sealed blast door at the end of the space. There was no getting through it. Every control panel was blown or shot to bits. They now controlled the outside and one room inside the silo, but had no way to get inside.

She inspected the blast door that led into the rest of the facility. She could feel the warmth generated by the stick welder on the other side.

"We need about a hundred pounds of Semtex to get past this door," she said.

Joel tried to lighten their situation. "Sorry, left it in my other trousers."

He had a pale glow about him as he looked through the burned and melted computers on the bullet-ridden security desk. He poked around, hoping to revive one. "Total bust here too," he finally said.

Ang returned with Ling from their inspection of the outside. They were shaken but still going. "No other entrances," Ang said. "The windows are for show only. It's solid concrete behind them. We did manage to take down the rest of the cameras so at least they are blind."

"Desperate men locked inside a missile silo. That's a recipe for fun and games," Codi said.

Ling was making some strange gestures across his face.

"What's he doing?" Joel asked.

"Oh, he walked right through a huge spider web out there," Ang said.

Joel checked the floor to make sure the spider hadn't made its way inside as well.

Ling noticed they were talking about him and stopped wiping to look up. "Hey," he said with a grin.

Joel, was starting to like this guy. "Hey, back," he said.

Ang, turned their attention back to the matter at hand. "Okay, so no entrances means they can't get out either."

"Yes, but the fact that they welded this door shut might be significant," Codi said.

"What, like a one-way mission?" Ang asked her.

"That's what I'm thinking."

"Damn."

Codi turned to Joel. "Looks like the only way in is through the sewer."

"I'd rather die."

"Careful, you might get your wish."

Joel nodded, suddenly more wary of their situation.

Inside the control room, Jin wiped a bead of sweat from his brow as he finished up the sequence that would launch the rocket. All that was left was to insert the code. That would activate the trigger system on the nuclear warhead, making it operational. He would feel some joy, retaliating at the country that had killed his friend Park Je Kwan. Plus, with a successful launch, he felt sure they would be allowed to leave.

He and Park had spent many nights together before Park left for his mission in America. They had grown close, and a unique friendship and bond had formed. They had talked of plans and dreams for when he would return as the conquering hero. But his unexpected death by a drunk driver had taken all of that away. America would now pay.

General Chow Phun felt a vibration in his pocket. He pulled out a small black box. It was tuned to a special frequency that allowed it to work around the jammer. There was a brief text starting with, "You're welcome." It was followed by two twenty-seven-digit passwords. His lips quivered with a small crooked smile. This was it. "Jin!"

Chow set the box down on the console and watched as his computer genius opened the nuclear activation page and entered the GO codes. A green "accepted" prompt returned and Chow knew his contact had been worth every Yuan. He dabbed at a line of drool that was headed for his uniform with numb, scarcely responsive fingers. He knew his mortality was short, but he would make sure to leave lasting prosperity and power for the country he loved. He placed a fatherly hand on Jin and waited for the young man to turn to him. He looked into his eyes and in a soft and kindly voice, said, "It's time."

Jin nodded solemnly at his boss, turned, and went to work. After a few moments of flashing keystrokes, Jin hit the last key with a flare.

He announced, "Ten minutes until ignition."

A low electronic alarm with flashing yellow lights confirmed his statement. A digital display started counting down from 09:59.

The announcement echoed in the small security room. Codi and Joel did not understand the words but the message was clear. "Times about up," Codi said.

Ang added, "Ten minutes until the rocket blasts."

"We need a way inside, and now," she said.

The four-person team churned with energy that would not focus. They needed a viable plan, and nothing was obvious.

Joel sank to the ground. His adrenaline rush had run its course.

"Wow, you four really screwed things up without me around." Four heads turned in unison to the source.

"Hey?" Ling asked, unsure if the new arrival was friend or foe.

Tenzin walked into the blown-out security room like she was strolling through a park.

"I thought you said you were too old to help out." Joel seemed genuinely confused.

"I'm also too old to sit by and watch Mr. Chow Phun play you for fools."

There was no witty retort. The journey to this ultimate failure had taken its toll.

Joel pantomimed morosely as he stared at the blackened floor in front of him.

"The only access door is welded shut," Codi said, "and we are fresh out of explosives. We don't have a way to cut through the steel mesh on the outside vents. We have a few bullets and some rope, but no way to stop the launch."

"Exactly," Tenzin said. "As I see it you have everything we need for the perfect plan."

23

PLA Missile Silo 089 – 9:41 A.M. – Sheng Luo, China

Jin was feeling the tension as a single drop of sweat ran down his cheek. He had always been a hacker, and as a hacker, or sometimes called a black hat, he had always worked remotely, several steps removed from the actual damage he caused. This was different. The moment Chow had their exit welded shut, death was looking more and more likely as his only escape. He began to doubt his decision to stay on. Ever since their operation in the Red Baks was destroyed, Chow had become reckless and desperate. And now, staring at the potential loss of thousands of lives, maybe they had gone too far. But Jin could think of no way out.

"Sir."

Chow stepped over to Jin and put a reassuring hand on his shoulder. "Yes?" he asked.

"Once the rocket crosses into America, our work is done here," he said. "How are we supposed to get out?"

"Poh!" Chow called out.

The Squad Leader stepped over to Jin holding a small canvas case. He reached inside. Jin flinched, assuming it was a gun. But Poh pulled out a battery-powered grinder.

"I have the key." Poh smiled like a shark.

Jin nodded uneasily and slowly went back to work.

Chow and Poh shared a laugh and moved away.

The two scientists fiddled with their temporary equipment. It was designed to initiate the specific signal transmission that would render the missile invisible to America's defenses. Once engaged, the electronics in the nosecone would continue to broadcast until obliterated by the nuclear detonation. "All dry runs nominal, switching to automatic," one of them said.

Chow watched as the man pressed the keys that would make the signal autonomous.

"The rocket is now in control, sir."

"Excellent work, gentlemen. Poh they are all yours!"

The two scientists both stood in a panic as the menacing and heavily-armed Poh moved in their direction. The one remaining soldier joined him. He pointed his rifle at the scientists.

"You both have had military training, am I right?" Poh asked.

They nodded fearfully.

"Good. I am a little low on men," Poh said.

He handed each man a weapon, saying, "The only way inside here is that door." Poh pointed as he spoke. "We don't know the size or capabilities of the force out there, since they took out our cameras. We think it's a few of the PLA regulars left over from our skirmish."

Poh finished with his pep talk and stationed them in positions to help thwart any attack through the door.

Jin looked back and forth over his shoulder, listening to the instructions. They were down to one soldier, Chow, himself, plus Poh and his two new recruits. It was less than optimal, in his mind. He would need to be very careful from now on if he was to survive his current predicament.

"Mr. Chow Phun is sick. His days on earth are numbered. I don't think he's planning to survive this operation," Tenzin said.

"So, you're thinking they'll stay locked up in that room, all safe and sound, till the missile hits its target?" Joel asked.

"Precisely."

"How does that help us? Joel asked.

"It gives us about five more minutes. I say we sit and relax before that missile fires off."

Codi immediately knew what Tenzin was proposing. "She's right. We've been so focused on the direct approach, that once it failed, so did we. There is nothing we can do to stop this thing from launching." She finished speaking and sat down next to Tenzin. She crossed her legs and leaned her head back.

Joel looked apoplectic. But soon, Ang and Ling followed until he was the only one pacing back and forth.

"Hey, do you mind closing the door while you're up? I don't want to get cooked when that missile goes off," Codi said.

Joel slammed the door. "Anything else?"

He stared at his four team members, all sitting on the floor relaxing. He could barely breathe.

The domed roof on the faux fermenting tower opened like the petals of a flower, allowing plenty of egress room for the ICBM. The pre-ignition sequence started, and the first vapors shot out of the two thrust chambers. It mixed with the fuel, and the booster engines enflamed, completing the ignition sequence. The center sustainer engine followed suit, and the resulting combustion forced through the thrust chamber created more than fifty-thousand pounds of lift, enough to push the missile from its perch.

"We have ignition." Jin smiled. He had always wanted to say that.

Flames shot through the vents on the side of the tower, scorching anything in its path. The flowering vines along the wall that gave the building much of its charm were atomized. The missile gradually lifted from the launch pad, its support scaffolding withdrawing as it ascended.

Chow screamed, "I can't see anything!"

"We're blind, General," Jin called out. "They shot out all our cameras. Give it time, there is one they missed on the roof."

Sure enough, the clear tip of the ICBM appeared on the rooftop camera, purposefully pointing to the sky. It was followed by the olive-green cylindrical shape of the missile, with each stage growing in size. Chow watched, rapt, as the final stage entered the screen, its distinct fins flared out for stabilization.

The half-smile that he could muster on the good side of his face nearly reached his ear. The room rattled with the immense controlled explosion of the rocket's ignition. It increased in magnitude until it finally cleared the silo and moved up into the air. Chow watched as the fearsome weapon continued upward into the morning sky. It was a glorious sight.

The burnt-out security room became very quiet. As the rumble in the room intensified, Codi and Tenzin quickly laid out their plan to the team.

Tenzin found a large steel caster that had blown off the security desk, and thought to herself, this should do nicely.

Codi ran from the room to the tower. The roof was opened like a lotus blossom. They had mere moments until it would close back up. She threw the rope, lasso style, up over one of the triangular pieces of roof, pulled the ends together, and began to climb the double rope up to the gaping hole. Soon, Ang and Joel followed.

"Hey!" Joel called and waved his hand for Ling to do likewise. The man was part monkey, and scampered to the roof in a blink.

"Hey." He smiled, looking at Joel.

Ang tested the temperature of the steel roof supports. They were still hot from the rocket. He wrapped his coat around the metal and then tied the rope around the coat. The coat started to smoke. They needed to hurry. He dropped the loose end of the rope down a hundred and twenty feet inside to the silo floor.

Ling was the first to slide down. Codi wasted no time. She sent Joel and then Ang down before Ling had exited at the bottom. As she turned to join them, the roof mechanism engaged and started to close. The sudden movement caught her off guard and she fell from the roof.

"The roof is closed and all systems are nominal," Jin said.

Chow was pleased. He stood to pace for the third time in a few minutes. If only he could make things go faster.

"We got action on the other side of this door," one of Poh's new recruits called.

Poh went over to investigate. He put his ear to the steel and listened. There was a distinct scraping sound moving across the door. Everyone in the room watched as he listened. *Bam!* A sudden rap of steel on steel rang through the room. Poh jumped back.

"I think they are preparing to blow the door," the soldier said.

The banging continued about every two seconds.

"What are they doing?" Jin asked.

"They'll knock holes in the seams, and then force a plastic explosive like C-4 in the gaps," Poh said. "The resulting explosion will open this door, welded or not,".

"Best guess?" Chow asked

"Twenty minutes, maybe thirty."

"Then we'd better use the time wisely."

The room bustled with activity as they fortified positions to combat the coming threat.

Poh was the only one left who knew how to fire the Type-98 recoilless rifle, so he would man it.

"Time to target, Jin?" Chow called.

Jin looked at the digital map that showed an icon for the ICBM and its American target of Chicago. The counter showed thirty-nine minutes, twelve seconds. He called it out.

Chow nodded his head slowly in anticipation. It would be close.

Codi grabbed blindly as she fell, hooking her left hand on a beam of the roof's infrastructure. Her hand gripped the metal piping like a vice, as her body jolted to a sudden stop. The jerk threatened to pull her hand free and drop her to a sure death. She managed to hang on, swaying by her fingertips for a beat, before she swung over and grabbed the rope. She wrapped her feet around the rope and took a second to recompose. That's when she noticed the seared flesh on her hand from the metal piping. She sucked it up and slid down to her waiting team. Once on the ground, Codi put hands to knees as she tried to catch her breath. Her hand throbbed but it could wait.

The bottom of the silo had a fresh coat of burn on everything. It was circular in design to match the ICBM's shape and devoid of any material that might burn with the rocket's launch. The scaffolding was blackened and retracted. Ling stared in wonder at the sight of the large underground space. There was a small black mound that used to be human on the floor.

Codi moved to the burn cover on the elevator control panel. It was set back away from the main blast zone. She lifted the panel to find only a single black button. "I guess no security is needed from this side. Thoughts?"

"If we push that button, they'll be waiting to blast us the moment those doors open up to a room we know nothing about," Ang said.

"And if we take the time to climb the shaft, we might be too late," Codi countered.

"What if we were to…" Joel started.

Codi pushed the button before Joel could finish his thought. He let out a short sigh. "So, shoot first and talk later?"

Codi smiled. The training of her partner was finally working.

They all took defensive positions to cover the elevator doors the moment they opened.

Ling leaned on his trigger, ready to pull, as the two doors split apart. The car was empty. Codi released a breath she didn't realize she'd been holding, and stepped out from behind a large pipe. She led the way into the car. Ling, smiling, followed next. It was all a grand adventure for him. Codi worried that he was unaware of the danger that might lie ahead.

Once loaded, she leaned over and hit the Up button.

"Going up?" Joel asked with a jumpy grin.

24

PLA Missile Silo 089 – 10:30 a.m. – Sheng Luo, China

The constant tapping on the armored door was getting to all of them. It started as a scraping sound, which then transitioned to banging. When would it stop, and did it signify a forthcoming explosion? Chow dabbed at his chin as a drop of nervous sweat trailed down his temple. The missile had launched. Now all they had to do was stay fortified here until they were past the failsafe point.

Jin felt the most vulnerable with his back to the door. Everyone else was bunkered in a defendable position, each anticipating a firefight that was ticking down with each bang on the wall. Suddenly the tapping stopped. The room tensed. Jin grabbed his keyboard and pulled it with him as he hunkered down under his console.

General Chow said, "Jin, can you lock-out the missile so it no longer takes commands?"

Jin shook the nervous tension from his hands. "We are not past the failsafe point yet, General."

"How much longer?"

Jin glanced out from his spot under the console at the screen. "Three minutes and twenty-eight seconds, sir."

"Okay. At three minutes and twenty-nine seconds I want the missile locked-out."

Jin started the process that would close out his side of the rocket's control so no one could stop it. He peeked with one eye over his desk again so he could confirm the operation as he typed. Once complete, the missile would no longer receive data, making it impossible to abort or cancel its mission. He watched as the time ticked down, his finger hovering over the return key that would send the code.

The ridiculous Chinese folk tune that played in the elevator must have been put there as a joke, Codi thought. But it continued on its happy merry way as the car slowly rose to the operations room. She looked over at Ling who was humming quietly along with the song. This day couldn't get any weirder, and if today was her day to die, weird wasn't the worst way to go. The team split into two per side of the car, one low and one high, using the door gap for cover. The car slowed to a stop. It paused for what seemed like an eternity, before a ding was followed by opening doors.

The tapping suddenly started back up again, only much faster.

"They're getting desperate," Poh called out in false hope. The prolonged tapping was even getting to him as he dried his hands on his shirt.

A soft ping from the back of the room was hardly audible over the room's tension and the now fervent knocking. Jin looked over his shoulder. The elevator doors opened to an empty car.

"Hey, what's with the eleva–"

Gun barrels, followed by bullets, answered his query.

Cody went high and Joel low as they swept the right side of the room. A mirror action followed with Ling and Ang from the other side. The room had been so focused on the blast door that they were caught off guard. The rear attack took the lives of three soldiers almost instantly, two of them recent recruits.

Poh and Chow had been bunkered further back and were able to get to safety. Jin ducked further under his console taking his keyboard with him. He then did his best impersonation of the ostrich defense and buried his head between his legs. But he kept a mental count of the time left before he could lock out the missile.

It quickly became a stalemate, with both parties pinned down, and bullets pinging back and forth without finding a target.

Poh saw the Type-98 recoilless rifle that was just out of his reach lying on the floor. He reached out a leg and started to slide it towards him. A bullet pinged off his anklebone, shattering it. He pulled his leg back without a sound and fired a few rounds back at the elevator while gritting his teeth. He reached out and grabbed the weapon and pulled it back to safety, furious at the lucky shot that had undoubtedly maimed him. He quickly loaded it and pointed it at the elevator.

Chow held his hand up to stop Poh from firing, an action that would mean the deaths of everyone in the room. He called out to the force occupying the elevator. "Come out with your hands up. You have nowhere to go."

Codi looked to Ang and held up her finger to her lips. Though she had no idea what the man had called out in Chinese she could easily interpret the message. She answered Chow in English. "What do you want?"

Chow's mind raced, as he struggled to understand the situation. "Am...Americans?"

"Not just Americans. The ones you kidnapped and tried to kill!" Codi called out.

His head started spinning. This made no sense. *"You!"*

Codi remained silent waiting for Chow to make the next move.

"You are too late to stop the missile. Your precious Chicago will be uninhabitable for the next thirty years."

Joel and Codi shared a look at this revelation—*Chicago*.

"What about all the innocent people," Joel called out. "Civilians that have done nothing to you or your country."

Codi held up both her hands to get Joel to stop. She could tell they were just spinning their wheels. The clock was ticking and a prolonged conversation with a psycho would do them no good. They needed a plan to get them out of the elevator. Maybe she could goad Chow into making a mistake.

"Too bad about your lab in Hong Kong," she said. "Red Baks, I believe it was called right before we burned it to the ground."

This solicited a string of swear words and bullets all aimed in their direction. But the general maintained his hidden position.

Joel tapped his watch. They were out of time.

"Enough stalling, General," Codi said. "It's over. Come out with your hands raised."

"No, you come out with your hands raised," Chow relied. "We have a very large weapon pointed in your direction ready to fire. If so much as one more bullet comes out of that car, I will obliterate you."

This was not what the team wanted to hear. Was he crazy enough to blow everyone up, along with himself?

"Jin," the General called out, "how much time!"

"Ten seconds," he replied.

"You have ten seconds to comply," Chow said with confidence.

Ling waved at Joel. He didn't understand the words being spoken but he knew his duty.

"Hey," Ling pointed to himself.

Joel looked perplexed at his gesture. Then it hit him. "Hey, no you don't!" he said.

But Ling gave him a short bow and ran out of the elevator, rifle blasting.

Codi used the distraction and followed behind, shooting at the muzzle flash of Ling's attackers. As they zeroed in on the moving target, Ling, there was a short but sustained engagement. And then it was over.

Codi ran to the fallen general and kicked the gun from his hand. She noticed a man with a Fu Manchu holding a rocket launcher. He was staring at the ceiling with only one eye. The other eye was now an entrance wound from a 7.62 mm bullet.

Joel ran to his friend Ling. He was lying on the floor with a few rounds stitched across his torso. He knelt down and looked at the man who had sacrificed himself for them. He placed his arm under Ling's neck and held him up.

"Hey," he said weakly, as he looked into Joel's eyes.

"Hang in there, Ling. You're gonna be okay," Joel lied.

"Hey," Ling said, even weaker, this time with a half-smile set against blood-stained teeth.

"Hey," Joel answered as tears filled his eyes. Ling's smile grew from ear to ear, and then his eyes fluttered and closed.

Ang surveyed the mess, trying to decide where to begin. He heard knocking on the other side of the door. Movement caught his eye as a man slid across the floor and snatched up a fallen pistol from one of the scientists.

Jin had felt trapped like a rat in a cage as a firefight roared all around him, bullets pinging off the various steel surfaces. He was hoping to just wait things out until he could surrender. But suddenly their attackers were speaking English. Americans—here. How was that possible? A rage built in his soul, just thinking about how they had been responsible for the death of his friend Park. It was at that moment when Jin realized Park was not a friend but something more. He had loved Park. He had loved him like no one else he had ever known, and America had taken that away. He spied a pistol lying on the floor a few feet away. He hit the enter button on the keyboard and locked out the missile. He dove for the gun. He grabbed it and pulled the trigger until it stopped firing.

The woman turned from her position next to the general and without hesitation, fired a quick three-round burst. His body bucked with the impacts and he dropped his empty gun. He staggered and fell to his knees.

He tried to make sense of his life as he gaped at the floor in front of him. His lips tried to speak but only for a brief moment, like a fish out of water. He died a confused and conflicted man who had never been able to act on his feelings. In the end, Jin had been nothing more than a pawn to a mad man.

Codi turned her attention and her weapon back to the general, not giving him any quarter. She called out, never taking her eyes off Chow. "Ang, what's the damage!" she yelled.

Ang looked around and then down. "Two down, Ling... and me."

There was a fresh hole in his shoulder. He slid down the wall leaving a red smear behind. Codi was conflicted with which path to take. Save the general or save her friend.

"If I had more time, I'd ask you a few questions or maybe take you to the authorities," she said to Chow. She could tell by the man's look he would never talk in time. And frankly, after all she'd been through, she didn't care.

Chow leaned up on one elbow, coughing up blood from his wound. "How is it you are even here? I must know." The general sneered at her with hateful eyes, blood and spittle drooling down one side of his twisted face as he spoke.

"Prepare for disappointment," Codi said. With that, she pulled the trigger and ended the man who had only taken from her.

Codi turned to see Joel sobbing over Ling's body. "Joel, snap out of it! We've got to find a way to stop that missile!"

Joel nodded though his tears and found his second wind. He quickly wiped the tears from his eyes and surveyed the room, taking in all the technology. Some was shot up with bullets, some seemed to be working just fine. A unit about the size of a toaster with an antenna was sitting on the top shelf. He powered it down. "Jammer's off," he announced.

Codi stuffed a rag in Ang's shoulder to staunch the bleeding. "You're gonna be fine," she said, "maybe even get a medal. Now help us stop this missile."

Ang nodded and stood on wobbly legs. He joined Joel at the terminal to help translate.

Codi took Ang's phone and dialed. She stared at the screen, willing it to work.

"Director Fescuc."

"Working late?"

"Codi! Where the hell–"

"Shut it. Now listen very carefully. I got about…" she looked at the phone's screen. "…one bar on my battery, and Joel, how much time?"

Joel looked at the map showing the ICBM icon and the

United States coming into view as it streaked across the northern Pacific.

"Fifteen minutes."

She said to Brian, "And you've got fifteen minutes until a nuclear-tipped ICBM hits Chicago."

"*Shit.*"

"Tell me about it."

Codi quickly filled her boss in on the last forty-eight hours, skipping everything that was not related to the next fifteen minutes.

"It's eight p.m. here, and seven p.m. in Chicago. Stay on the line. I'll be right back," Brian said.

Joel hit the abort button on the console several times. Nothing happened. With the help of Ang they tried to recall the missile through the keyboard.

"Can you stop it?" Codi asked.

Joel took a deep breath as the reality hit him. "Not from here. The missile's been locked-out. There's no way to abort it."

"No recall or self-destruct?" Codi added.

"All locked out."

"I could contact authorities here in China but it might take more than fifteen minutes just to get them on the line," Ang said.

"Fourteen minutes," Joel announced.

The tapping on the blast door was getting quieter. They all shared a solemn moment. Had they come this far just to fail?

"Wait a minute!" Joel brought up the map. "We can't stop it, but I might be able to track it." He quickly laid a grid over the missile's path and with Ang's help calculated the trajectory and coordinates that it would follow. He patched it into a webpage and sent the address to Fescue's email.

Codi watched over their shoulders, and the second it was

sent interrupted her boss. "Check your email, the one labeled 911."

Agent in Charge Brian Fescue was in a panic. The path to action in a bureaucracy was overgrown and circuitous. Two hurried calls, no answers. First to his boss and then to the director of the FBI. Time was ticking. Finally, he got through to the vice chairman of the joint chiefs of staff's assistant. The assistant gave him a number they used for emergencies like this. It had cost precious time. Their ability to scramble and intercept was almost gone.

He pulled up the site and could see the missile was just crossing over the west coast.

To say the call was challenging was a gross understatement. General Dilworth was extremely skeptical. Brian had finally gotten the general to open the webpage.

"This looks Chinese," he murmured.

"That's what I've been telling you, *Chinese* ICBM." Brian was trying to keep calm as he knew it would do no good to get angry.

"How did you get this number?" the general asked.

"Sir, we haven't much time, *please.*" Brian decided to beg.

"Just a second. Hold your horses, son."

The general made a quick call to his contact at NORAD.

Brian was a wreck with the slowness of everything. NORAD did a check and recheck, but no missile appeared to be headed for Chicago, let alone, anywhere else.

The general was not about to scramble emergency fighters without proof. Besides, if it was good enough for NORAD, it was good enough for General Dilworth. But just to be on the safe side maybe I'll…

Brian had had it with this man. He decided to push a little

harder. "General, if you don't listen to me right now, you're gonna have a five-megaton nuclear missile right up your ass!"

"General?"

Silence.

"Son of a bitch!" Brian slammed the phone down. "Codi, you still there?"

"Yes, Brian."

"I'm having trouble getting a response that will fit our timeline," he said, trying to regain some sense of calm.

"I understand." She lowered the phone trying to think.

"Seven minutes," Joel mumbled. "I have an aunt in Chicago. She's really cool too. Makes these coconut macaroons that are to die for."

"Joel!"

The worried energy was getting to him, but Codi's reprimand silenced his rambling. "I'm trying to think here."

A thought that was born out of desperation began to grow. First the seed and then the plant. Codi lifted her phone to her mouth. "Call the FAA," she told Brian.

"I see where you're going with this. Okay. It's a long shot. Hold tight." Brian grabbed his landline and started to dial.

"The Future Farmers of America?" Joel asked.

Codi glanced down at her phone. The last bar was starting to blink. Without looking up she said, "Not the FFA, the FAA—Federal Aviation Administration, dork."

"I knew that," Joel said, properly chastised.

They shared a knowing smile. Then Codi put her arm around him. They were in this together, no matter what. Sink or swim, live or die.

"Sorry about the dork thing," she said.

"It's okay, I deserved it."

25

Twelve Thousand Feet — 6:18 p.m. — Franklin Grove, Illinois

Colleen Simpson was a thirty-eight-year-old mother of three and the bread-winner for her family. She had started a small brick-and-mortar cosmetic store called CosMore in an Internet world where most retail operations were dying. She had focused on customer service and free samples, with plenty of lighted mirrors for customers to try things out. Everyone had told her she was nuts. But in spite of her critics, she had grown the business to a chain of twenty-six stores across the mid-west. Her husband worked as an electrician, and she let him spend his paycheck as he pleased. They'd had their ups and downs, as do most couples, but lately there were more ups.

Colleen had spent so much time going from store to store, that her family was suffering. An inspiration took hold of her a while back, and after several night classes and a few trial runs, she obtained a pilot's license and a near-new Cessna 210. She used it instead of a car, for her commuting, and the time back home had increased dramatically. Three years ago they bought into a community just outside the city with an airstrip shared by all thirty homes in the association. She set up her corporate offices in the space above their four-car garage and could now come and go in her plane right from her house.

Early that morning, Colleen had flown to Cedar Rapids to replace a store manager that was causing more problems than he was solving. She had carefully documented everything over the last two years, but the event was still a nightmare, with screaming and threats, all aimed in her direction. He would probably sue for wrongful termination. Oh well, the cost of doing business, she told herself. The extra drama had ruined her schedule. She was going to miss her six-year-old Chloe's piano recital. Chloe had been practicing her song for the last month, and this was going to be her big moment. Colleen watched as the sun dipped towards the horizon. It would be dark within the hour. She hated to fly at night and was hoping to make it back home before the sun plunged to dusk, just in time to help Casey with his math homework. She smiled at the thought, as mild turbulence bumped her around in her seat. Another ten minutes and she would be home.

Since 911, the US government has put in place several quick reaction programs that get agencies to work together. The goal is to place critical information in the right hands ASAP. The confusion that reigned while terrorists flew our own jets into the twin towers and the pentagon would never happen again. At least, that was the design. Special Agent in Charge, Brian Fescue was not having the success these programs were intended to give. One of them that the FAA had implemented allowed information to be relayed directly through to the air traffic control system. In a last ditch attempt, Brian called the emergency number and explained the problem. The man on the other end got it. *Finally,* Brian thought. He relayed Brian to the lead air traffic controller at Midway International Airport just southwest of downtown Chicago. They quickly brought the controller up to speed in hopes of getting their message out. They needed an actual sighting of the missile. Then they would have the proof they needed. But the problem was time—they were running out of it. The lead controller pressed the transmit button and began broadcasting on the emergency frequency. It was a message they had both agreed upon.

"Codi!"

She heard Brian's voice over the phone.

"Yeah. Hello… Brian? Hello?" She looked at her phone. It was dead. She lowered the phone.

"You did all you could," Ang said.

"*We* did all we could," she said.

Joel looked to the screen with the ICBM's icon as it approached the Midwest. "Four more minutes," he mouthed listlessly.

The tapping on the door was getting erratic.

"Ang, you got any strength left to help me with that door?" Codi asked.

Ang held up a battery-powered metal grinder he had almost tripped over earlier. "I got just the thing."

Codi cut though the welds and Ang pressed the button to open the door.

The large steel blast door slowly swung open. Tenzin stood there, arms raised holding her dented steel caster like a weapon. When she saw Codi and Ang. She lowered it along with a sign of relief.

"*Finally.* I was getting a blister."

After all Codi had been through, she was taken back by her statement. Her forehead scrunched. "A *blister?*"

"Yeah, and I think I chipped a nail too." Tenzin said light-heartedly, as she looked at her finger while stepping into the room. "So, how'd we do?"

"Not so good," Joel said.

Tenzin looked around at the carnage and nodded slowly, understanding the sacrifices that had been made. Now was no time for levity. "I'm sorry," she said.

"You've been shot," she said to Codi.

Codi looked down to see a blood trail draining from a hole in her thigh. She'd been so focused and hopped up on adrenaline that she hadn't even noticed it. She ripped a strip off the bottom of her shirt and wrapped it tight around the wound. "See if you can do anything for Ling," she said to Tenzin.

Ling lay motionless on the floor, his chest red from blood loss. The old woman knelt next to the soldier who had bravely charged the room. "And you too!" she said to Ang.

Ang gestured helplessly with his hand, as if he could have prevented it. His other hand pressed tightly to his injury.

"SOP," Joel said.

"What?" Tenzin said.

"Standard Operating Procedure with Codi. Everyone who works with her eventually gets shot."

"Not everyone," Codi countered.

"Name one."

Codi looked upward trying to think of someone.

Tenzin changed the subject. "So did we stop the bomb?"

Joel pointed to the screen. "Just one minute left and it doesn't look like we did."

They all gathered around the screen watching the final seconds of a catastrophic event they were powerless to stop. Joel reached out and held Codi's hand and she let him.

"Thirty seconds."

Colleen heard a transmission come over her headset. She switched to the emergency frequency of 243.0 MHz. She listened to the distressed voice through her headphones.

"Mayday, mayday, this is Air Traffic Control Midway International Airport. We have an emergency need for a visual confirmation. There is a possible unidentified flying object, possibly a missile coming out of forty-one degrees and seven minutes from the north/northwest. We are needing an immediate visual confirmation. I repeat, we nee…"

Colleen dismissed it as not her problem. As the voice gave the approximate coordinates, she realized she was flying almost that exact course. She tapped her finger on the yoke and thought about her situation. She double-checked her GPS location. Yes, she was right in the area.

"Damn it, I don't have time for this. It's getting dark," Colleen huffed, as she pulled her plane up and around in an arc to get a better look at her six, or rear.

She lifted her head and surveyed the sky as her Cessna made a gradual 180-degree turn. The orange glow on the horizon transitioned to a growing purple sky. She caught a glimpse of something flying at forty-one degrees and seven minutes out of the northwest. She corrected her path to get a better look. It was a small spec on the horizon but was moving incredibly fast. There appeared to be a significant jet trail growing behind it, reflecting off the setting sun. Her jaw dropped and she pressed the transmit button on her plane's yoke. "This is Cessna N2815P. I have a visual on your missile."

Her hands began to shake as the rocket quickly grew in size.

"Roger that, Cessna N2815P. Can you give us a location?"

"I'm just over…" She quickly peeked out the window. The missile was even bigger now.

"I'm just over Waterman. And it looks about ten miles away, moving incredibly fast."

"Waterman. Oh my God, we're too late." The Lead Controller went silent after his unintended exclamation. They all knew there was no time to do anything more than a quick prayer.

"Is this for real?" Colleen asked.

"I'm afraid so, mam. God speed. Attention, all aircraft, this is not a drill, redirect immediately to–"

Colleen went numb as the emergency broadcast continued on. She was looking at the beast as it grew on the horizon.

"... may the Lord have mercy on us all."

Codi and her team watched as the missile icon moved towards the city. She was done hoping for a miracle. And besides, something was shaking the building. She stepped through the open blast door into the burned-out security room. Like a moth to a flame she walked out into the light. It was another beautiful morning as though this part of the world had no idea what was about to happen. As she looked up, three military helicopters came swooping in, fully loaded and armed. One, a Mil Mi-26 heavy transport with a detachment of fourteen armed men. The other two were WZ-10 attack helicopters.

I guess they saw the SOS fire, she thought.

The heavy transport landed, sending dirt and debris flying into the air. The two attack copters patrolled the air, their guns locked and loaded.

Could this day get any better, she thought while shaking her head.

Smartly, Codi knelt down and clasped her hands behind her head, the international symbol for I give up because I just don't give a shit.

Within moments her entire team was zip-tied and thrown to the ground like a sack of potatoes. Soldiers ran back and forth trying to make heads or tails of the situation.

26

Undisclosed Location – 8:34 a.m. – Wuzhou, China

The sound of rifle fire woke Codi with a start. She squinted at the rush of light as the door to her cell screeched open. Two military guards goose-stepped in and dragged her out into the hallway. It took her a moment before she was able to stand and walk along with them. It felt like every muscle in her body was in protest. The partially dressed bullet wound in her leg throbbed with every step. Her brain screamed for relief, but her mouth was too dry to relay it. Her tongue was stuck to the roof of her mouth and felt like it was made of wood. She cracked her head to the left and recognized Joel. He was walking stiffly next to her, also held by two guards. He looked like hell, and she could only imagine how bad her reflection might appear.

They had been taken at gunpoint from the silo. There were no questions, only orders, and they were followed to the letter. All four of them had been forced to lie face-down in the bed of a metal troop truck with their hands bound behind them. The truck then proceeded to bounce over rough terrain for the next two hours. Finally they hit pavement and the ride smoothed out. The vehicle stopped with a lurch, and a hasty unloading of the prisoners commenced. With guns locked and loaded, pointed in their direction, Codi and Joel were forced to march straight to a dark cell, with a concrete bench for a bed.

Codi had managed to doze off and finally get some much-needed sleep. There'd been no sign of Ang or Tenzin since they'd been imprisoned. Codi assumed they had either been shot or had talked their way out. Perhaps they were waiting for them, wherever they were now going.

She tried to get her mind back up to speed for what might come next, but she was feeling completely hung-over. It was amazing what a lack of everything could do to one's self. Normally, she would have to do some serious hard drinking to feel like this.

The procession exited the building into a dirt courtyard, where a line of several more soldiers waited. Joel looked at his current situation and started to fight against his guards, but their iron grip was no match for a beat-down, sleep-deprived, dehydrated, all-out exhausted federal agent. His struggling stopped almost as quickly as it started.

The guards released Codi and Joel. They turned and joined the others in formation. Codi's hoarse voice squawked to Joel as she took in their surroundings. There were nine soldiers all armed standing in a line in front of them. The concrete wall behind them was covered in bullet holes and the ground was a mixture of straw, dirt and blood. "It's been real, Joel."

Joel looked at her, and back at the armed soldiers, staring at them with a crazed twitch. A forced chuckle escaped his throat. This was not the way he had hoped to die. Where was the sleep and the bed?

The soldiers just stayed in formation, rifles on their shoulders. Codi and Joel stood in front of them, each looking at the other, daring one side to make the first move. No one spoke, some didn't even blink. Joel, exhausted, bent at the waist and put his hands on his knees, too tired to stand erect any longer. Codi glanced once more at the bullet holes and blood stains on the wall behind them. There were tell-tale drag marks on the ground going off to the left. She and Joel had been through the ringer and had somehow come out the other side, but even she had a breaking point. She took a moment to run her fingers through her hair and straighten her shirt. If she was going out, it would at least be on her terms. She rubbed the top of her shoes on the back of her pants and tugged her torso to attention. She was ready.

The rocket had no fear, only ones and zeros flowing through its circuits. It was simply a mechanical organism that followed a preset list of instructions guiding it forward to its target. It followed the guidance computer's feedback, making micro adjustments to its position based on wind, elevation and GPS. It took no notice of the cobalt blue sea below it, or the verdant fields that followed. Once it reached its apex, its programming triggered a gradual path back to earth. It continued to transmit its unique frequency signature that would make it invisible to detection. At one-hundred miles out, a pre-arranged sequence of events was initiated, with tests and redundancy checks on all vital systems. At fifty miles from target, the shielding on the plutonium core would pull away and arm the core. At one-thousand feet above ground, an implosion into the core would occur. This implosion would trigger a nuclear reaction that could not be contained, creating a violent detonation that would ensure a maximum destruction radius.

Back in DC, Brian had been following the conversation and FAA broadcast. He was watching helplessly as the webpage sent to him counted down the time to impact. The emergency broadcast had finished by warning all aircraft out of the area followed by a short prayer. Brian slumped in his chair, dazed. How was this possible? How could a missile get through our defenses? The information Codi had given him before her phone died seemed impossible. But she was not known for hyperbole.

The emergency transmission stopped after a brief prayer. Colleen's brow was beaded with sweat as she considered her place in this world. She had but a second to make a decision, one that would change her life forever. She thought of her business and her family. Her family. Little Chloe, Casey, the ever-pragmatic Makenzie, and her loving husband. The years flashed before her eyes in an instant as the tears started to flow. Then uncontrollable sobs took over. With trembling, tear-stained hands she pushed her yoke forward and into the path of the fast-approaching ICBM.

The odds of making contact were stacked against her. There was no explosion as the wing of her plane clipped the fuselage of the rocket, tearing the wing off of her plane. The Cessna 210 began an out-of-control spiral to the earth. Colleen's yell grew to a scream as she plummeted to her death, not knowing if she had made any difference.

The rocket continued on, the small slice in its skin a minor inconvenience. Hydrazine began to leak out of the rip. At first it was just a mist, but soon a dribble, both quickly atomized in the speeding air. As it flowed to the burning jets, a new flame followed the source back towards the damaged skin. The slice spewed flames like a mad blowtorch, causing the rocket to wobble as oxidizer and fuel met outside of their controlled environment. They ignited with a sudden burst, sending parts and pieces of the rocket outward like a roman candle. By a mere five seconds, the atomic warhead had not reached its arming target and therefore had not been allowed to go nuclear in the premature explosion.

Nine thousand feet below, the town of Sugar Grove, just fifty-two miles from Chicago, was hit with a rainstorm of burning debris. It caused many fires and a few injuries. What was left of the warhead fell through the sky and landed in a bowling alley that had been closed for remodeling. The radioactive fallout was contained, but the former site of the 1994 PBA World Bowling Championship would be uninhabitable for many years to come.

The waiting and the silence was too much. Joel was starting to crack. His body began to shake uncontrollably. Codi stood defiantly with her head held high.

"Please, just get it over with. I'm begging you," he pleaded.

As if on cue, the soldier on the far left of the formation barked out something in Chinese. The other soldiers all in unison grabbed their rifles, and with a frill, spun and twirled their guns before coming to rest across their chest.

Joel held a hand out in front of himself. "I was kidding."

It was the weirdest firing squad maneuver Codi had ever seen. It looked more like something you would see at a parade. It just needed a marching band and some cheering fans.

"Joel, keep it together," she whispered.

Two black limos pulled up and stopped between the soldiers and the two agents. Two officers with medals adorning their chests exited the rear limo and stepped next to the prisoners. They gave a curt bow and shook hands with both Codi and Joel.

"Congratulations," one of them said. "You save many lives."

A photographer ran up and snapped a few photos. The prisoners honestly seemed confused by it all.

"Wait. What is he talking about? Did they stop the missile?" Codi asked the man who had spoken.

"Yes. Missile stopped. You did good job."

The two officers shook hands with the Americans once again.

Then the front passenger side of the limo opened, and Corporal Ling slowly exited. He was using a cane to move, and he had one arm in a sling. He was dressed in a Lieutenant's uniform and a smile. Joel was speechless as his injured friend slowly moved up to him and shook his hand. "Hey."

"I, I thought you were... Hey," Joel replied. He grabbed Ling's hand and shook it a bit too hard. It made Ling flinch in pain. But the smile on his face was electric. Ling gave him a salute, and Joel returned it.

He then shook Codi's hand, and gave a mutual bow, which caused severe pain.

After a moment, Codi and Joel were escorted into the first limo. It moved out of the courtyard, spitting dirt, straw and blood from the rear tires. Sitting across from them was Ang. He had a weary smile that seemed to match their mood, and a white sling holding his injured arm. Joel and Codi each grabbed a bottle of water that was sitting in the small bar. They drank like they hadn't been given water in three days, which was true.

"I thought they were going to shoot us," Joel said as he crushed his plastic water bottle and pointed it at Codi like a gun.

"Easy there, muscles," Codi said.

But Joel was worked up after what had just transpired. "Shoot us, right then and there. And you! 'It's been real, Joel?' That's all you had to say? After all we've been through. And

Ling, a friggin' colonel. We get thrown in the slammer and he gets promoted? I thought he was dead. Dead! I cried for him. *Shit.*"

Joel then pointed the crumpled bottle at Ang. "The things we've done for this country! I'm calling bullshit right here and now."

"Lieutenant, not colonel," Ang said.

"What??"

Codi and Ang both started to smirk. This pissed off Joel even more and his rant elevated.

"It's not that I don't like being shot at, kidnapped, arrested, and drowned, but the least they could do is say thanks or something. I mean where's my medal…"

That set off Ang and Codi even more and a giggle turned into full delirium as they drowned out Joel's monologue.

Soon all three were laughing at the ridiculousness of it all, and for the first time, Ang had become one with the crazy Americans.

After a few miles they fell into silence.

Codi found the strength to break it. "So what happened? Where's Tenzin and how the hell did we stop the missile?"

Ang sat up in his seat and scratched something behind his ear. "She could talk her way out of the Minotaur's Labyrinth, I swear. She dropped back into that southern dialect that no one can understand, all hunched over and frail. She was out and released the next day."

Codi smiled at the memory of the quirky old woman who had helped save so many lives. "Probably back in Tibet planning her next infiltration."

"Yes, she is really something," said Ang. "As for the missile…"

Ang filled them in on the events that transpired after they'd been taken prisoner.

"It took three days for me to convince the authorities that

we were not part of Chow's operation. Really, it was Ling who set them straight. They were ready to bury us and this whole thing six feet underground."

Ang paused for a moment remembering all that had transpired. "For the first time in my life I am glad to see the politicians get involved. They will spin-doctor this whole thing right under the rug."

It was always the way. Whenever things in the world got too intense for the masses they were given the vanilla version. It kept them in check and promoted that thin illusion of security the public needs to believe in, because without it markets would crash and riots would rule.

Matt ran for the entrance to the terminal. The call had just come through ten minutes ago. Codi was alive and being transported to the airport for her return to the states. He had rinsed his face and brushed his teeth while using his free hand to put on his socks and shoes. After a cab ride and an early exit due to stopped traffic, Matt had come across a florist. He dashed inside and purchased two-dozen red roses.

He held them like a baton as he sprinted the last few blocks to the airport, leaving a fragrant trail of blossoms behind him.

Supervising Special Agent Brian Fescue was on a similar mission. He had been at the embassy working with the state department to get some word of his agents' disposition. After the failed attack on Chicago, Brian had been a sudden focus and the adoration of his superiors. He had used this leverage to get back involved in the case.

He had taken the time to update Matt and they both hopped a flight to Hong Kong. SSA Brian Fescue was assigned a state department lackey. The woman had no horsepower and fewer connections, but Brian's expertise in China was nil, so he had to use what he was given to move things along. Matt, on the other hand, was stuck playing the waiting game and it was killing him.

They had finally gotten word that Codi and Joel were being held at a PLA base in Wuzhou but were refused any contact or additional information.

Brian and Matt both found a flight to the Wuzhou Changzhoudao Airport and a hotel with fast Internet. They had pushed and pleaded as much as they could, but this squeaky wheel was being ignored. It had been the culmination of extreme frustration after what Brian had been through back in the states. This was no way to run a case: agents disappearing, being pronounced dead, and then phoenix-ing back in time to help stop a nuclear strike. It was crazy. And now being held prisoner when they should be given big-ass medals.

It was an unexpected call from the embassy that had set them both in motion. Brian from the Wuzhou police station, and Matt from his hotel room.

Matt dodged cars and bicycles as he turned the corner that led to the terminal. He was suddenly struck with the thought of what he would say to Codi. He hadn't given it much attention and there was no time like the present to figure that out.

He thought about all the hiccups they had experienced recently and it all seemed so trivial. He knew in his heart that he loved her. Now all he had to do was figure out how to tell her. His distracted thoughts cost him dearly, as he did not see the vehicle pulling out of the alleyway. At full speed, Matt went over the hood and crashed to the gutter on the other side. He popped up amid honks and yells from the driver. He hobbled away with a severe limp. He grimaced in pain as the driver behind him berated his character. He had a nice gash on his shin and a knot on his cheek, but he held tight to the roses.

Brian opened the door to the limo as it pulled to the curb.

He felt a wave of relief overwhelm him as Agent Joel Strickman and Agent Codi Sanders exited the vehicle. One look told him all he needed to know—bruised, battered, but still going. They looked like they'd been run through a spinning industrial dryer filled with ball bearings.

They took a moment, and then shared a professional hug. Codi introduced Ang, and they all made ridiculous small talk.

Joel brought the conversation back on point. "So let me guess, as far as both governments are concerned, this never happened."

"Yeah, that about sums it up," Brian said. "There's a hell of a debriefing waiting for us back in DC, and then the case will be closed and sealed."

"So much for your medal, Ang," Joel said.

Ang raised his one good hand in an *oh well* gesture. "I'll always have this to remind me," he said, referring to the sling that held up his bullet-wounded shoulder.

"I know what you mean," Joel said "I told you, everyone who works with Codi gets shot. Last time it was my turn."

Codi shook her head in mock defiance. "Not!"

The conversation finally died out to a moment of awkward silence, which left an opening for a subject change.

"Ok, I have a plane waiting. Let's get you two back home," Brian said.

Those words sounded wonderful to Joel. They all shook hands and watched as Ang got back into the limo and sped off.

"I could really do with a good burger and a brew about now," said Joel. "Oh, and some quality coffee too," he added.

Brian let out, "Oh almost forgot…"

"Codi!" A hoarse shout bellowed.

They all turned. Matt ran up the sidewalk and stopped. He was heaving, completely out of breath and looked like he might throw up any second. His clothes were tattered and covered with stains and dirt. His hair was disheveled and had something brown clinging to one side. He had several cuts and scrapes on his arms and face. And he was absently holding out several smashed and shabby flowerless stems that were once twenty-four beautiful roses. He finally caught his breath enough to speak. "Codi." He huffed several more breaths. "I got these for..."

He couldn't finish without a few more breaths. He held out the flowers, unaware they were nothing but stems.

Codi was taken aback. She had no words for him. How had he gotten here? What had happened to him? And... "Matt?"

She rushed to him and held him for all she was worth. Tears mingled with dirt as emotion consumed them both.

Joel nodded his approval and then put his hand on his boss's shoulder. "I'm taking a week off."

"But the President has asked to see the both of you right away. Plus the debriefing. It's at the Joint Chiefs of Staff," Brian said.

Codi loosened her grip on Matt and called over her shoulder. "Make that two weeks,"

EPILOUGE

Gray clouds that hid a waning sun threatened to drop rain. Codi was standing next to Joel, both were dressed in their FBI formals, suit and tie. The previous two weeks were behind her and there was great promise for her future. Her bullet wound had been superficial, and with the proper care was now almost pain free. She and Matt were back in a healthy and growing relationship. They had made standing plans to get together every other weekend with the hope of something more permanent in the future.

The turnout was supposed to be moderate, with only a few invitations given out. But once word of its political importance leaked, the number doubled overnight, in spite of it being a closed, private affair.

The president knelt before the empty casket and paid his respects. He was followed by a cavalcade of the Who's Who in DC, each trying to one-up the other. Codi watched the display with a knowing disdain.

The Speaker of the House gave a short speech, some of it pertinent to the occasion. He was followed by a general, who was part of a flag-folding ceremony that ended with tears. They handed the triangle fold to the widower standing next to his three motherless children.

Codi looked over at the broken family. She could see the sorrow in their faces, but strength as well. She knew from experience that it would be a long road, but that they would be okay in time.

Colleen Simpson was a true American hero. She had sacrificed everything to save so many lives. It was an act born of desperation and love. Love for her family and love for her country.

The press continued to drone on about a satellite that had malfunctioned and spread its contents across the city of Sugar Grove, Illinois, but the reality was still safe with the few.

Once everyone had his or her moment to shine, the empty casket was ceremoniously lowered into the ground. The pastor finished with a solemn prayer, and the crowd started to dissipate just as the first few drops of rain began to fall.

"Good to see you again Agent Sanders."

Codi turned to see the President standing right behind her. "Twice in one week, sir."

They shook hands.

"I wanted to thank you again for all you have done. The country owes you a great debt." He leaned in a bit closer and lowered his voice. "And if there is ever anything I can do for you..."

He let the sentence fall off, gave her a nod, and turned to leave. One of the secret service agents stepped up and handed Codi a card. She looked down and saw the presidential seal on one side and a hand-written number on the other. Codi slipped it into her pocket.

She had met with the man just four days previously as she, along with Joel and Brian, had received unofficial commendations for their efforts. It was a small ceremony held in the oval office behind closed doors. No pictures or records were taken, but it's the thought that counts, right?

Now he owed her a favor. Her mind spun with the

possibilities. All the things a president could do for her career, for her future. It was staggering.

But Codi was a creature of habit. She liked to do things only one way, her way. She pulled the card from her pocket, turned it in her hand, and dropped it in the grave as a shovelful of dirt followed behind it.

She felt a load lift from her shoulders, as she ran to catch up with a receding Joel. "Hey."

"Hey."

After a moment of silence Joel spoke. "I've been giving this a lot of thought, even did some calculations. Do you know what the odds are of a Cessna 210 traveling at 230 mph hitting an ICBM moving towards it at 15,000 mph?"

Codi looked over at her partner as he demonstrated the collision with his hands.

"Let's just say it's an impossibility. How she managed to get her plane in front of that missile. Was it skill or dumb luck? The odds are less than–"

"Joel. You know better than to play the odds. This is *us* you're talking about. Plus, in all your calculations did you ever stop to consider a higher power?"

"You mean like God?" he asked.

"Yeah. Some things just can't be explained. I believe that and I've seen that. It takes a little...faith."

"Okay. Let's say God had a hand in it and intervened. Why didn't he do it back in China and save us a whole lot of drama?"

"Fair enough. But drama, that's what makes life interesting."

Joel just shook his head. His partner was one of a kind.

"Hey," she said, "how 'bout a slice of pie? My treat. David Mamet said, 'stress cannot exist in the presence of pie.'"

"Okay, but I get to pick the place."

"Deal."

"Somewhere with good coffee."

"You mean great coffee."

"Precisely."

The rain intensified. Codi and Joel moved off together with the confident gait of experience, and one chapter in their lives laid to rest.

IF YOU LIKED THIS BOOK

I would appreciate it if you would leave a review. An honest review helps me write better stories. Positive reviews help others find the book and ultimately increase book sales, which help generate more books in the series.

It only takes a moment, but it means everything. Thanks in advance,

Brent

AUTHOR'S NOTE

This is a work of fiction. Any resemblance to persons living or dead, or actual events, is either coincidental or is used for fictive and storytelling purposes. Some elements of this story are inspired by true events; all aspects of the story are imaginative events inspired by conjecture. *Blind Target* was a true labor of love. Like life, the writing process is a journey, one meant to be savored, and to me it's more about the pilgrimage itself than the destination. I learned a ton while writing this book, and I hope it's reflected in the story and the prose. Only you, the reader, can be the judge of the results. Drop me a line if you have feedback or just want to say hi.

Brent Ladd Loefke, 2019, Irvine CA

INTERESTING FACTS

For more facts go to my website and see as well as read these details. brentladdbooks.com

DEW Line or Distant Early Warning System
The DEW Line was a string of radar stations in the far north Arctic, from Canada to the Aleutian Islands of Alaska. It was set up to detect incoming Soviet bombers during the Cold War. It provided early detection and allowed Strategic Air Command time to scramble jets to intercept. The 63-base Line reached operational status in 1957 and was eventually decommissioned in 1988.

Nikolski Bay on Umnak Island
Umnak is one of the Fox Islands within the Aleutian chain of islands. It is mostly volcanic and there are no trees that grow there. The town of Nikolski is located on a small southern inlet. It is reputed to be the oldest continuously-occupied community in the world, with a current population of 18. Archaeological evidence from Ananiuliak Island, on the north side of Nikolski Bay, dates as far back as 8,500 years ago.

LeTourneau Sno-Freighter
Alaska Freight Lines had the contract in the early 1950's to transport supplies for the construction of DEW Line. They commissioned heavy equipment specialist Le Tourneau

Technologies to build a land train capable of fording semi frozen rivers and deep snow. Powered by two Cummins engines generating 800 HP the Sno-Freighter was able to pull 150 tons of material through temperatures as low as minus 68 degrees Fahrenheit. Much like a rail based locomotive the diesel engines powered electric motors located on each of the 24 combined wheels of the power unit and the trailing wagons.

Sludge Ice

Ice the consistancy of honey is called sludge ice. This is water that is in an early stage of freezing. It offers little resistence at first but can be a deadly trap as it will often times quickly solidify, without warning.

Tupolev TU-16 Bomber - Badger

The Soviet Union was strongly committed to matching the United States in strategic bombing capability. Their first bombers with frontal aviation entered service in 1954 with the TU-16 service designation. It had a large swept wing and two Mikulin AM-3 turbojets. It could carry 20,000 lbs. in warheads and was still in service until the early 1990's.

NORAD, or the Cheyenne Mountian Complex

Cheyenne Mountian Complex is a military installation and defensive bunker located in unincorporated El Paso County, Colorado. Formerly the center for the US Space Command and NORAD—North America Aerospace Defense Command. The Complex is built under 2,000 feet of solid granite. It boasts a full city floating on springs and a twenty-five-ton blast door. The overall facility is built to deflect a thirty-megaton nuclear strike.

D.B. Cooper

D.B. Cooper is a 70's icon that was the most successful

skyjacker in US history. He extorted $200,000 in ransom and then parachuted out of a passenger jet to an unknown fate and certain fame. The FBI's case has over 60 volumes of information, but has never been solved. Years later, a young boy did discover a wad of cash along the Columbia River with matching serial numbers.

The Abittoir
The Abittoir is an old meat processing plant that is still standing in Hong Kong. It has been long abandoned and is considered by many to be haunted. It is currently a popular destination for urban explorers.

Fenghuang China
Fenghuang is a truly magical town that time has forgotten. It has colorful buildings with stilts holding them up all along a lazy river that rolls past. There are several bridges connecting the two sides of the town and a stepping stone crossing made of stone columns. Even Chongde Hall is located in the city, built in the 1700's by the town's wealthiest resident.

The Southern Great Wall or Miaojiang Great Wall
The Southern Great Wall is a lesser known structure to the Great Wall of China. It was built in the mid 1500's to protect the Chinese against the Mio people in the south. It stretched over 190 kms. and housed over 5000 soldiers. Much of the Southern Great Wall has been lost to time.

ACKNOWLEDGEMENTS

With deep appreciation to all those who encouraged me to write, and especially those who did not. I wanted to thank the following contributors for their efforts doling out their opinions and help to keep my punctuation honest. Jeff Klem, Kristin Woodruff, Natalie Call, Brad Simmons, Carol Avellino, and Wade Lillywhite. A host of family and friends who suffered through early drafts and were kind enough to share their thoughts. My lovely wife Leesa, who is my first reader and best critic. And my editor Cathy Hull.

A special thanks to my publisher, Archway Publishing, who helped make this all possible, as writing is only half the total equation. Finally, to Patrick Fitch for the cover design.

As many concepts as possible are based on actual or historical details. Special thanks to the original action hero—my dad, Dr. Paul Loefke.

Lastly, writers live and die by their reviews, so if you liked my book, *please* review it!

More Codi Sanders coming soon! – BrentLaddBooks.com

ABOUT THE AUTHOR

Writer Director Brent Ladd has been a part of the Hollywood scene for almost three decades. His work has garnered awards and accolades all over the globe. Brent has been involved in the creation and completion of hundreds of commercials for clients large and small. He is an avid beach volleyball player and an adventurer at heart. He currently resides in Irvine, CA, with his wife and children.

Brent found his way into novel writing when his son Brady showed little interest in reading. He wrote his first book making Brady the main character—*The Adventures of Brady Ladd*. Enjoying that experience, Brent went on to concept and complete his first novel, *Terminal Pulse, A Codi Sanders Thriller*—the first in a series, and followed it up with *Blind Target*.

Brent is a fan of a plot driven story with strong intelligent characters. So if you're looking for a fast paced escape, check out the Codi Sanders series. You can also find out more about his next book, and when it will be available. Please visit his website – BrentLaddBooks.com

CPSIA information can be obtained
at www.ICGtesting.com
Printed in the USA
BVHW072206040719
552614BV00006B/56/P

9 781480 878440